SECOND EDITION

Fish WISCONSIN

WITH DAN SMALL

Dedication

To the community of Wisconsin anglers past, present and future,
who share the dream of finding the perfect place to fish.

Published by:

krause publications

700 E. State Street • Iola, WI 54990-0001
Telephone: 715/445-2214

Library of Congress Number 90-34111

ISBN: 0-87341-248-6

Printed in the United States of America

Contents

Author's Preface

Much has changed in the three short years since the publication of the first edition of *Fish Wisconsin*. On the resource front, the new size limits have already had a noticeable impact on fish populations in many waters. There are more bass and walleyes of catchable size than just a few years ago, and the average size of the fish caught by anglers has increased. On some musky waters, 40-inchers are now as common as 30-inchers were a decade ago. Trout streams are recovering from the effects of the drought years of the late-1980s, and trout populations are responding well to the protection afforded them by the new trout regulations. As receptive as they were to these modifications, Wisconsin anglers continue to resist stricter regulations on the harvest of panfish, although these, too, may come to pass in another year or so.

Water quality continues to improve in Lake Michigan, where PCB levels have declined more than 80 percent in the last decade, yet contaminant levels are still high enough in some sportfish species to constitute a health hazard for some persons. Each update of the *DNR's Health Guide For People Who Eat Sport Fish From Wisconsin Waters* also lists a few more inland waters where high levels of mercury have been found in walleyes and other fish.

On the user front, the DNR and local sportsmen's groups have improved public access on many lakes and streams, but some waters still need better landings, larger parking lots and other facilities to serve the growing throng of anglers and boaters who already stretch the capacity of existing facilities to their limit. Anglers' contributions, through state license and stamp fees and federal Dingell-Johnson excise taxes have gone a long way toward paying for some of these improvements, including the installation of barrier-free fishing piers that can accommodate wheelchair-bound anglers and others who do not have boats to take them to good fishing water, but more funding will be needed to continue this work.

What else can you do to help preserve the sport you love? For one thing, join a club. Fishing clubs keep a finger on the pulse of issues that deal with water quality on a local level, and that's where problems most always start. Clubs are often among the first to mobilize support for measures that will protect our water resources, and that is of benefit to us all.

There is one more thing you can do: take a kid fishing. We must all accept the responsibility of teaching our youth to value a clean environment and care for our natural resources, and I can't think of a better way to do it than to teach them to fish in an ethical manner. Many youngsters today, though, grow up far removed from daily contact with the outdoors and lack the guidance of a knowledgeable adult to teach them basic fishing skills. The loss of one future fisherman would create only a minor ripple, but the loss of a generation of anglers would send waves pounding long and hard on resource management here and across the nation.

For nearly 20 years I have had the privilege of exploring and writing about Wisconsin's vast and varied fishing opportunities, "from Green Bay to where the St. Croix sings," and "from Kettle Moraine to Superior's shore." My travels as host of *Outdoor Wisconsin* have boosted both the number and intensity of these explorations. Some of my trips have ended in fishless frustration, but many have produced exciting fishing and left me with lasting impressions of the people, places and events that are the real reasons we fish in the first place. I hope that this book can convey a portion of those impressions to you, the reader, and in its own small way help you create some of your own.

In preparing this second edition of *Fish Wisconsin*, I have made every effort to track and report on these and other changes of interest to fishermen in the waters covered in these pages. I have also personally checked every reference to bait and tackle shops, boat landings and other services to ensure that those listed are as up-to-date and accurate as possible.

This new edition features more maps, many of them updated and more readable than those of the first edition. Photographs have replaced the line drawings, and the book has been printed on higher-quality paper. This edition also contains eleven new chapters that cover 30 lakes and streams not featured in the first edition, including a chapter on some of Wisconsin's top trout waters.

Reader response to the first edition of *Fish Wisconsin* was gratifying. The new publisher, Krause Publications, my editor, Steve Heiting, and I have made every effort to make this edition an improvement over the first, and we trust that it, too, will meet with your approval and serve your angling needs.

Dan Small

April 1993

Acknowledgments

I thank all those who have made this book possible. The list includes, but is not limited to, the following: employees of the Wisconsin Department of Natural Resources who provided detailed data and insights on the lakes and rivers covered in this book, chamber of commerce representatives from all over Wisconsin who helped gather information on services of interest to anglers, and all the guides, bait dealers, marina operators and dockside kibitzers who have helped me keep my bow pointed in the right direction.

In the firm belief that a fisherman's greatest resource is other fishermen, I especially want to thank all those with whom I have had the pleasure of sharing a boat or stretch of stream in a lifetime of fishing. First and foremost is my father, Gene Small, who is responsible for getting me hooked on this crazy and wonderful sport at the tender age of 2-1/2. I also thank my mother, Bess Small, who tolerated the wet sneakers and muddy jeans of my early years and encouraged my exploits as I grew older. Other partners include my brothers Mike and Pete, my sister Chris, my son Jon, and many more, from kids on their first outing to some of the top guides and tournament pros in the country. I can honestly say I have never met a fisherman I couldn't learn something from, and I thank you one and all for sharing so freely your knowledge and love of fishing.

Finally, I want to thank my editor, Steve Heiting, and publisher, Pat Klug, for their guidance, patience and understanding as this second edition came to life.

5

Introduction

Spread out a Wisconsin state road map and what do you see? Rivaling the red ribbons of the major highways that tie together the yellow patches where most of us live nowadays, another color stands out. Just look at all that blue! That's water, my friend, and there's lots of it.

Bounded on the west by the St. Croix and Mississippi Rivers, on the north by Lake Superior and a slew of rivers and lakes we share with Michigan's Upper Peninsula, and on the east by Green Bay and Lake Michigan, Wisconsin is blessed with an abundance of water. Nearly 15,000 inland lakes (2,500 of them in Vilas and Oneida counties alone!) cover over a million acres of Wisconsin's surface area, and the outlying Great Lakes add another 6-1/2 million acres and 800 miles of shoreline. The state's rivers and streams, from tiny brooks to the imposing Wisconsin and Mississippi, total over 26,000 miles.

In all that water swim fish of every kind, from the tasty and prolific panfish -- perch, crappies and bluegills -- to walleyes, bass, northerns and, of course, our state fish and largest freshwater predator, the musky. White bass, saugers, catfish and sturgeon abound in some inland waters, and brook, brown and rainbow trout inhabit many of our cold water streams and deeper lakes, while the Great Lakes add lake trout, coho and chinook salmon to the list of major species that await Wisconsin anglers.

Such abundance can be overwhelming, however, especially for an angler new to the state, new to the sport or one who simply wants to explore some different waters after getting to know the local lakes and rivers. Where should you go to catch a few eating-size walleyes, a trophy bass, or a mess of jumbo perch? When is the best time of year to take these and other species on different waters? What tackle and techniques will help you land a musky or let your youngster have a ball with a school of bluegills?

The text and accompanying maps of *Fish Wisconsin* give you the information you'll need to answer those questions and more. To help you choose the lake or stream that will provide the kind of fishing you seek, this modest book details over 100 of the most productive and enjoyable fishing waters Wisconsin has to offer.

The text of each trip covered in the following pages tells you where the lake or river is located and describes its features in detail, giving specific information on fish-holding structure such as weedbeds, rock bars, dropoffs, channels, sunken islands and more. You will learn when, where and how to fish for the major species found in each of the waters, along with proven techniques and baits used by successful anglers on those waters. The author has also included personal anecdotes, many of them relating to the production of *Outdoor Wisconsin*, when they seemed relevant to the discussion.

In addition, the text provides information about public boat landings, bait shops, boat rentals and contacts for lodging and other nearby services. Hydrographic maps supplement most of the trips to help you pinpoint the features discussed in the text.

The sources used in compiling information on lake features, boat landings and other services were the latest available at the time of publication. Such things as water depths, stocking programs, phone numbers of bait shops and other factors we often count on to be immutable have a way of changing when we least expect them to, just as fish sometimes refuse a bait that has always worked on a given lake under conditions identical to today's. The author trusts that readers will be kind enough to understand that such changes are beyond anyone's control, and resourceful enough to fill in these and other gaps that might occur in the information provided.

As with any guide, the usefulness of this book will depend to a great extent on how you apply the information it contains. It won't put fish in the boat for you, but it will suggest ways you can use the angling skills you already have and offer some new ideas you may not have tried. Anglers who learn to adapt to different conditions, especially those brought about by seasonal changes or weather patterns, are the ones who will catch fish on a regular basis.

Many species of fish move about daily and some undertake seasonal migrations of many miles. This is especially true of trout and salmon in the Great Lakes and walleyes in river systems and flowages, but even bass and crappies in small inland lakes may feed along one weedline today and suspend over deep water tomorrow.

Professional walleye angler Mike McClelland says the biggest mistake most fishermen make is to fish "memories," sticking to places and techniques that worked once or twice before, even though they may no longer be productive. If you heed its advice, *Fish Wisconsin* should at the very least get you out of the rut of doing the same old thing in the same old place and get you started on the path toward becoming a knowledgeable explorer who creates new fishing adventures. The rest is up to you.

How To Use A Contour Map

Most of us wouldn't think of going out on a new lake without our depthfinder, but a surprising number of fishermen don't take the logical next step of acquiring a hydrographic, or contour, map of the lake they plan to fish. Although when compared to the cost of a modern LCD, CRT or paper graph locator, a lake map is inexpensive indeed, your copy of *Fish Wisconsin* comes complete with contour maps, saving you the trouble of purchasing separate maps for each lake.

A hydrographic map uses a series of lines that connect all points of equal depth to show the lay of a lake bottom, just as a topographic map does to show the relief, or topography, of a land area. Most maps use a five-foot contour interval, but maps of some larger, deeper lakes use a 10-foot interval and maps of very small or shallow lakes may use a one- or two-foot interval. The map legend, which interprets all the symbols used on a map, usually indicates the contour interval. In most cases, the contour lines are also labled to aid in reading them.

Holes and underwater humps are indicated by concentric circles. To help you tell one from the other, hachure marks that point inward are sometimes used to mark small holes. A map of a lake with a very uneven bottom might have a series of concentric circles or parallel lines that turn and wiggle all over the map. An area with few or no contour lines represents a flat bottom.

Contour lines that are evenly spaced and wide apart indicate a gradual dropoff, while lines close together indicate sharper drops and banks. To find areas that might hold fish, look for lines close together that show a sharp dropoff from a bar into deeper water. These may occur anywhere in a lake, but are most often found along steep shorelines, around islands and off points. Gamefish often hang out near "inside turns" in a reef, bar or other underwater structure. These inside turns are usually very small, and often the only way to find them is by checking a map. They are indicated by a tight bend in a series of parallel contour lines that are close together.

You can often get an idea of what the lake bottom looks like from the slope and composition of the nearby shore. A sandy beach that gently rises from shore is often mirrored underwater by a sand bar that slopes out gradually into the lake, and a rock cliff or steeply sloping shore often continues to plunge well below the surface. By comparing your shoreline observations with a map and the readout of your locator, you can begin to piece together a picture of the underwater structure that will help you fish more effectively.

A map's legend usually indicates the scale of the map. The map may have a simple bar scale, it may be written as "one inch equals 800 feet," or it may be expressed in a ratio such as 1:9600. In the last case, one unit on the map -- an inch, a centimeter, or a pine needle -- equals 9,600 of the same units on the lake bottom. You can calculate map inches per real feet and simplify ratios by dividing the larger number by 12. Thus, 1:9600 becomes one inch per 800 feet.

Contour maps can be used as navigational aids on unfamiliar waters and they give you a picture of the entire lake that you can't get with a depthfinder. For the fisherman, though, the biggest advantage of the better maps is that they clearly show parts of the lake you might never find without them, including out-of-the-way bays, hidden dropoffs, submerged weedbeds, inlets, outlets, old river beds, and channels that provide passage to adjoining lakes. A contour map provides an excellent overview of the lake, while your depthfinder supplies the fine detail.

The maps in this book were provided by Duramaps and the Clarkson Map Company. To obtain their catalogs, contact: Duramaps, P.O. Box 24, Ogdensburg, WI 54962, telephone (414) 244-7851; or Clarkson Map Company, 724 Desnoyer Street, P.O. Box 208, Kaukauna, WI 54130, telephone (414) 766-3000.

Buffalo Lake

Endeavor to Montello, Marquette County

Buffalo Lake is undoubtedly one of central Wisconsin's best-kept secrets. It wouldn't be a lake at all if it were not for the dam in Montello that backs up the Fox River some 13 miles to Endeavor and creates this 2,500-acre flowage. Its deepest hole might be close to 10 feet, but most of the river channel runs only five to seven feet deep, and much of the lake is shallower still. Weeds choke this long, skinny lake in summer, practically immobilizing boats, so the local lake district now harvests weeds in a ladder pattern, cutting a channel up each side of the lake with connecting cross channels to facilitate boat travel.

Buffalo Lake

So far, you're probably thinking this is a secret best left kept! But if you've been watching *Outdoor Wisconsin* faithfully from the beginning, then you've seen Buffalo Lake and you know all about its amazing northern pike fishing. On a show taped there one October, you watched Tom Newbauer and Daryl Christensen catch pike after pike, sometimes two at a time. Most of those fish were modest in size, not trophies but not "snakes" either. Then, near the end of the segment, Daryl hooked the biggest pike of the

day, but the fish shook free of the hook before he could land it. In a typical Christensen understatement, Daryl said: "I kind of released him a little quicker than I wanted to." Tom and Daryl agreed the fish easily went 15 or 20 pounds, but our cameraman said it was really closer to 10.

A month later, in November, Daryl and I tried to duplicate the great fishing he and Tom had, but on the day we picked the pike had lockjaw. All we caught were a couple small northerns on diving crankbaits fished very slowly near the dike. Daryl wanted me to feel the weight of a heavy fall northern, but I had to settle for looking at pictures of him holding big pike as we sat at his kitchen table and warmed up after fishing.

Northerns, weeds and shallow water are only part of Buffalo's secret. Bass and panfish are the rest of the story. Nice bass and very respectable panfish you can fish for without worrying about locators, thermoclines, deep structure and all the other things some lakes make you deal with before giving up their fish. Buffalo Lake is definitely user-friendly.

Buffalo Lake's primary structure consists of the river channel, fill around the culverts under the Hwy. D causeway at Packwaukee, abutments that support the railroad trestle west of Packwaukee, a few sandy shoreline areas, creek inlets on both the north and south shores, and some springs along the north shore. These areas and weedbeds hold most of the fish and produce good action at different times of year. Since Buffalo Lake is part of the Fox River system, the gamefish season is open the year round.

The average Buffalo Lake northern weighs four to six pounds, but 10- to 20-pounders are taken often enough to make pike fishing interesting. Soon after ice-out, most pike spawn along the marshy shoreline between Packwaukee and Endeavor. After spawning, they work their way back east, holding near weedbeds and creek mouths, where forage is more plentiful. Small baits worked slowly now will take fish. Minnows produce well, as do 1/4-ounce walleye jigs tipped with plastics. The Bait Rigs Slo-Poke ought to be a killer on Buffalo's pike.

The lake warms quickly and you can almost watch the weedbeds grow. Good pike action moves from west to east as spring slides into summer. In hotter weather, work the river channel along the north shore and channels cut by the weed harvester. Spinnerbaits and topwater lures will produce now, as will weedless spoons fished right in the slop.

When weeds start dying back in the fall, perch and other baitfish will move into remaining weedbeds and the pike will follow them. That was the situation when Tom and Daryl fished in October. Work big, flashy spinnerbaits with tandem blades or large willow-leaf blades just under the surface along and over weeds. Pike almost always strike from below, so keeping your bait high in the water makes it more visible to them and ensures that they will hit the skirt and hook rather than the spinner blade. Let the bait helicopter down into pockets of open water where pike often hang out.

November pike action can be fast, especially on warmer days. Now is the time to try large minnows or slow-moving artificials along the dike at the east end, creek mouths and springs along the north shore, and causeway culverts. Soon after freeze-up, ice fishermen take some nice pike on both sides of the causeway and along the river channel.

Daryl Christensen unhooks a small Buffalo Lake northern pike that nailed a crankbait. Photo by Dan Small

Bass fishing is drawing more angler attention here every year, starting early in spring when bass warm themselves in the shallows prior to spawning. Creek mouths are especially productive now, as are most of the north shore and the railroad bridge abutments. Floating crankbaits and plastics fished very slowly get the best results.

In summer, surface baits produce well in and around weedbeds, while in fall it's back to crankbaits and spoons or plastics, as bass feed heavily before shutting down for the winter. Bass grow fast here, and five- to seven-pounders are caught every year.

According to DNR fish manager Jim Congdon, Buffalo's panfish are abundant and above average in size and growth. Perch, crappies and bluegills all provide good fishing throughout the open-water months as well as in winter. Crappies school in the channel and deeper holes wherever you find them during open water, moving toward creek mouths and springs in fall and winter. Perch hang out in the extensive weedbeds and respond best to live bait. In winter, try the channel on both sides of the Packwaukee causeway. Bluegills spawn along both shorelines wherever there is sand in May, and later you'll find them around weedbeds. Like the crappies, they'll move to creek mouths in fall and winter.

While Buffalo Lake itself holds no walleyes to speak of, the Fox River from the dam in Montello downstream to Lake Puckaway is a dynamite walleye river in spring. Walleyes first, then white bass and crappies, move up to the dam where anglers take thousands right from shore, along with occasional smallmouths, catfish, and northerns. The state now owns the land between Highway 22 and the dam on the south bank and has improved access there for anglers, adding a riprapped shoreline, gravel walking trail, picnic area, large parking lot and handicapped-accessible fishing deck. This mini-park is now the Andy Krakow Memorial Fishing Area, named for a DNR warden killed in the line of duty. When reconstruction work on Highway 22 is completed in 1997, the area will be operated as a city park.

There is a paved public boat ramp with plenty of parking at the dike in Montello, one off Highway C on the north shore, and one in the village of Endeavor, along with several more at private establishments on the north shore. The Holiday True Value, on Highway 22 South in Montello, carries bait and tackle; telephone: (608) 297-7170.

For a map, brochure listing motels, resorts, campgrounds, fishing guides and other services, and a Marquette County Guide, contact: Montello Chamber of Commerce, Box 325, Montello, WI 53949, telephone (608) 297-7420.

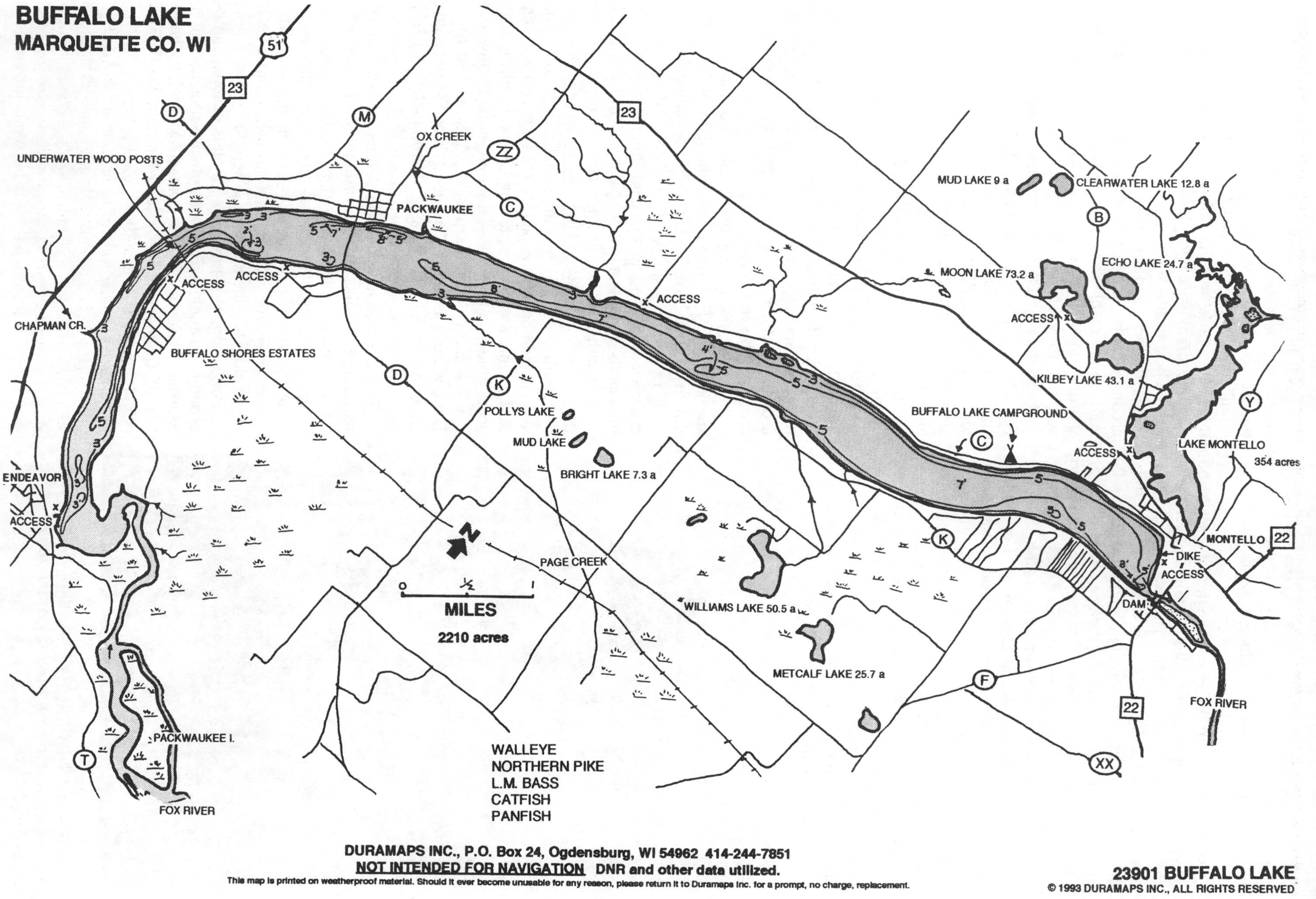

BUFFALO LAKE
MARQUETTE CO. WI

CLEARWATER LAKE 12.8 a

ECHO LAKE 24.7 a

MUD LAKE 9 a

MOON LAKE 73.2 a

KILBEY LAKE 43.1 a

LAKE MONTELLO

354 acres

MONTELLO

DIKE

ACCESS

DAM

FOX RIVER

ACCESS

BUFFALO LAKE CAMPGROUND

METCALF LAKE 25.7 a

WILLIAMS LAKE 50.5 a

BRIGHT LAKE 7.3 a

POLLYS LAKE

MUD LAKE

PAGE CREEK

ACCESS

OX CREEK

PACKWAUKEE

BUFFALO SHORES ESTATES

ACCESS

ACCESS

UNDERWATER WOOD POSTS

CHAPMAN CR.

ENDEAVOR

ACCESS

PACKWAUKEE I.

FOX RIVER

MILES

2210 acres

N

WALLEYE
NORTHERN PIKE
L.M. BASS
CATFISH
PANFISH

DURAMAPS INC., P.O. Box 24, Ogdensburg, WI 54962 414-244-7851
NOT INTENDED FOR NAVIGATION DNR and other data utilized.

This map is printed on weatherproof material. Should it ever become unuseable for any reason, please return it to Duramaps Inc. for a prompt, no charge, replacement.

10

Butternut Lake

Park Falls, Price County

Butternut Lake became something of a symbol in the intense debate over Indian treaty fishing rights during the late 1980s, as pro- and anti-treaty rights demonstrators chose to confront each other here during the brief tribal spearing season held each spring. Demonstrations at the boat landing received a lot of media attention, including some national TV coverage, and gave a lot of people the impression that Chippewa spearfishermen were killing tons of walleyes on Butternut and decimating the fishery.

The spearers still come to Butternut, but the protesters have faded away, as most northern Wisconsin residents have come to believe what DNR fisheries biologists were saying all along, that the impact of Indian spearing on the resource has been minimal. "Tribal spearers have taken a little over 100 walleyes a year," says DNR fish manager Gerry Bever, "and that's not enough to make a difference."

The most significant impact spearing has had on Butternut is to reduce the daily bag limit on walleyes. Sportfishing bag limits are set after the tribes announce what percentage of the allowable safe harvest they intend to take, and limits remain in effect for the year, regardless of the actual spear harvest. Daily bag limits of two or three walleyes draw some complaints from sport fishermen, but do not discourage most from fishing. In fact, quite the opposite is true. Bever says it is not unusual to see 100 shacks on the lake in the winter now, while a decade ago there were rarely more than 10. Open-water angling pressure has increased as well.

Butternut is long and narrow, covering just over 1,000 acres, with about 11 miles of shoreline and a maximum depth of 32 feet. Like many northern lakes, Butternut's water is stained dark, restricting visibility to just a few feet for fish and anglers alike. Five inlets feed this natural lake, and one outlet, Butternut Creek, flows southwest to the Flambeau River. Sand and muck dominate the lake bottom, but extensive areas of rock, gravel and rubble, along with dozens of man-made fish cribs, provide excellent structure and help make Butternut Lake one of the North Country's most consistent producers of walleyes and muskies.

Walleyes are the primary gamefish on Butternut. Until recently natural reproduction sustained a catchable population of five to 10 fish per acre. Bever reports that the walleye population declined dramatically over the past five years, however, due largely to overexploitation by hook-and-line anglers. Butternut is among the lakes exempted from the statewide 15-inch minimum size limit on walleyes because growth here is slow. Bever also reports that catch-and-release fishing is catching on here with many walleye anglers. He encourages fishermen to keep a couple fish in the 15- to 20-inch range and release those few they take over 20 inches, ensuring that there will continue to be an adequate supply of spawners and potential "wall"-eyes. For now, the DNR will stock 25,000 walleye fingerlings in even-numbered years until the population becomes stabilized again.

Some lakes take forever to turn on in spring, but walleye action is hot on Butternut as soon as the season opens in May. As much as 60 percent of the annual harvest occurs in this month. If spring is late in coming, walleyes will still be in shallow gravel areas when the season opens, having just completed spawning. Look for them in 10 to 15 feet of water on the north and west sides of the island at the south end of the lake and just off any of the gravel points at the north end. The shoreline just south of the public landing is a spot worth trying. The traditional jig and minnow is the favored spring walleye rig, although a minnow on a slip bobber can be deadly when fish are inactive.

In summer, concentrate on dropoffs, such as those at the narrows and the points mentioned above. Fish cribs placed strategically in 12 to 15 feet of water off nearly every natural point also hold baitfish and walleyes. Drifting with crawler harnesses or a plain gold hook baited with a leech or crawler produces well in summer, and some anglers report taking walleyes at night by casting floating crankbaits along shorelines and over shallow bars.

Ice fishermen take plenty of walleyes on tip-ups baited with minnows. Fish any of the points or near concentrations of teepees and shanties. Try working a Jig-A-Whopper or 1/4-ounce Swimmin' Ratt tipped with a chunk of cut bait on a jig rod while waiting for a tip-up flag to pop.

Butternut is one of the better musky lakes in the region, thanks to plantings of 2,000 musky fingerlings in odd-numbered years by DNR stocking crews. The average musky caught measures 35 inches, and a number of fish over 50 inches are taken each year. The practice of catch and release has boosted the musky catch rate in the last few years. Popular musky spots include most of the shallower bays and bars, especially those around the island at the southern end of the lake. At the north end, try the Butternut Creek inlet and flats along the west shore both north and south of the landing.

Musky action picks up gradually as the season progresses, but is best from late summer through fall. Bucktails and big jerk baits are popular among musky anglers, although some prefer to drift with a live sucker.

My son Jon and I taped an *Outdoor Wisconsin* musky fishing segment on Butternut a number of years ago with Leo Stecker, who at the time worked as a fish technician for the DNR. We figured catching a musky was almost guaranteed, since Leo handled so many fish there in the course of survey operations and must almost know them all by name. What we didn't figure on was a clear, blue sky and a high-pressure, post-cold-front day.

Leo showed us every inch of Butternut Lake, and we got some nice footage of duck broods and great blue herons, but nothing we did had any influence whatever with the lake's muskies. Paul Schluter, an executive with the St. Croix Rod Company in nearby Park Falls, cruised by in a sailboat and offered some encouragement, but even that didn't help.

When we broke for lunch at Bob's Northern Pines Resort on the southeast shore, owner Bob LaPorte showed us a couple mounted 30-pound-plus muskies that had come from Butternut. Jon was duly impressed with their size and went back to casting his Hi-Fin Creeper with renewed interest. I have never wanted anything as much as I longed for a 20-pounder to ka-whomp that surface bait with the camera rolling and the kid on the other end of the line, but it was not to be. We ended the segment with Jon's comment: "The only muskies we saw were on the wall in that restaurant." Maybe we should have been panfishing instead.

Bright-colored crankbaits are an effective bait for muskies in the dark waters of Butternut Lake. Photo by Dan Small

When the walleye population dropped, panfish numbers increased. Crappies are the dominant panfish and good catches are reported. Try a spot just off the landing known as Hoffman Rocks, and along any of the cribs. In June, look for them on spawning beds on some of the shallow points. Small jigs and plastic tails will take as many crappies as minnows will, and artificials are more fun to fish anyway. Stick with flu-

BUTTERNUT LAKE
PRICE CO. WI

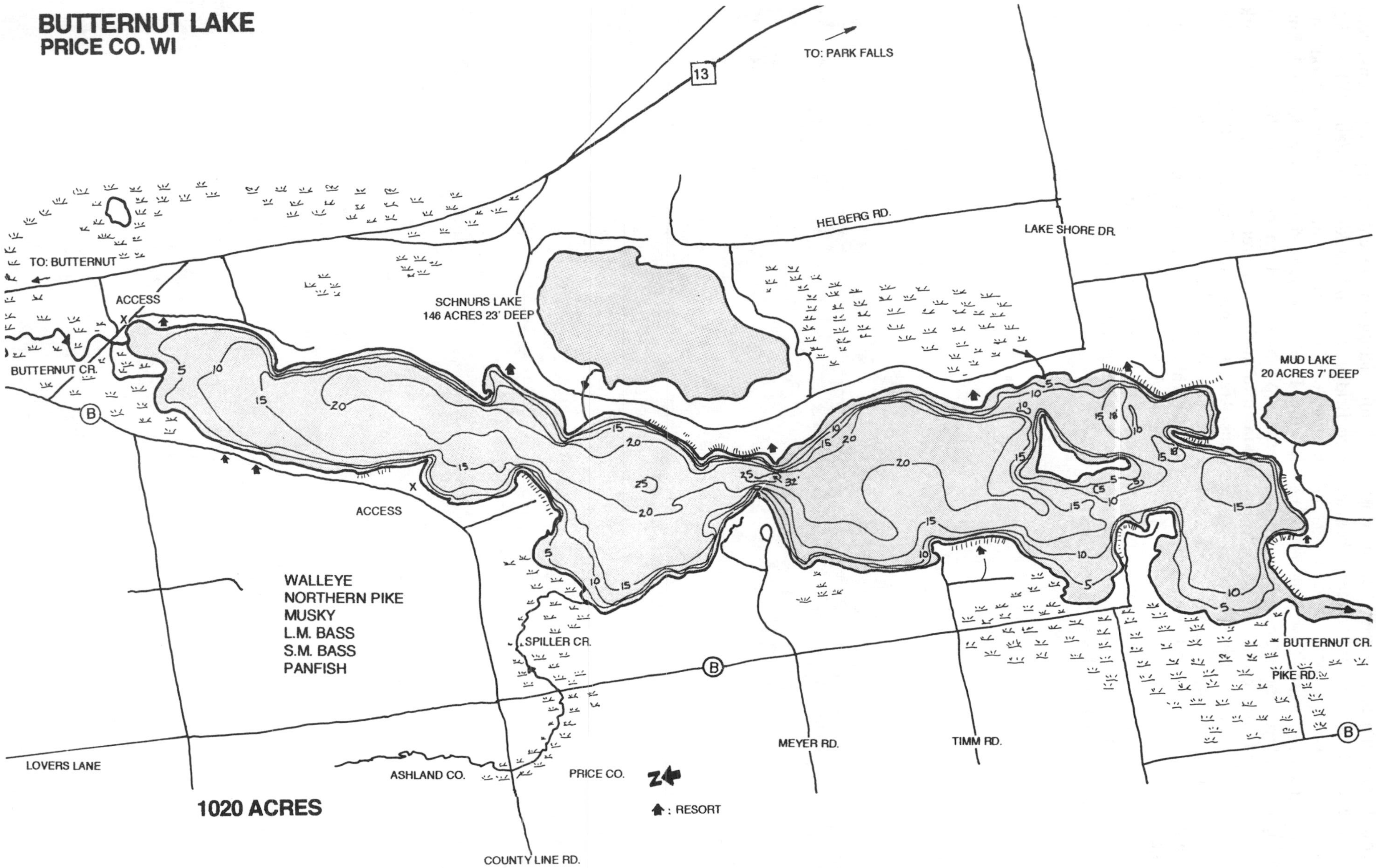

TO: PARK FALLS

13

LAKE SHORE DR.

HELBERG RD.

MUD LAKE
20 ACRES 7" DEEP

BUTTERNUT CR.

PIKE RD.

15

10

5

16

15

10

5

20

20

15

30

25

25

20

SCHNURS LAKE
146 ACRES 23" DEEP

15

10

5

20

15

10

5

ACCESS

X

ACCESS

TIMM RD.

MEYER RD.

SPILLER CR.

PRICE CO.

ASHLAND CO.

COUNTY LINE RD.

LOVERS LANE

WALLEYE
NORTHERN PIKE
MUSKY
L.M. BASS
S.M. BASS
PANFISH

1020 ACRES

TO: BUTTERNUT

BUTTERNUT CR.

ACCESS

X

B

B

B

N

↑ : RESORT

25102 BUTTERNUT LAKE
© 1993 DURAMAPS INC., ALL RIGHTS RESERVED

DURAMAPS INC., P.O. Box 24, Ogdensburg, WI 54962 414-244-7851
NOT INTENDED FOR NAVIGATION   DNR and other data utilized.

This map is printed on weatherproof material. Should it ever become unusable for any reason, please return it to Duramaps Inc. for a prompt, no charge, replacement.

13

orescent colors so crappies can see your offerings better, and use ultralight rigs and nothing heavier than four pound test line.

Anglers also take incidental bass and northerns while fishing for walleyes, but populations are too low to warrant concentrating on them. A few trophy largemouths are reported every season. If walleye or musky action is slow, try casting spoons or shallow-running crankbaits in the bays and around inlets for bass or pike.

There is an excellent public landing with a paved ramp and plenty of parking on Highway B at the northwest end of the lake. For lake maps, bait, tackle and information on current fishing conditions, contact: Bridge Bait and Tackle, Park Falls, WI 54552, telephone (715) 762-4108. For on-lake food and lodging: Bob's Northern Pines Resort, Route 2, Butternut, WI 54514, telephone (715) 762-3001. For more information on area facilities, contact: Park Falls Area Chamber of Commerce, P.O. Box 246, Park Falls, WI 54552, telephone (715) 762-2703.

And while passing through Park Falls, stop at the St. Croix Rod Company on Highway 13 on the south side of town. You can often pick up some real bargains in their outlet store.

Caldron Falls Flowage

15 Miles Northwest of Crivitz, Marinette County

The Peshtigo River begins a few miles north of Crandon in Forest County, where its West, North, Middle and South branches come together, and winds southeastward for miles through the lowland swamps and wooded uplands of the Nicolet National Forest and into Marinette County. In its upper reaches, this tea-colored river is a prime trout stream. As it gathers more water and momentum in its rush to Green Bay, it turns into the kind of river kayakers and thrill-crazy canoeists will drive halfway across the country to run. Experts rate the Roaring Rapids section of the Peshtigo the most difficult stretch of sustained white water in Wisconsin.

Then a short way below the Highway C bridge, the Peshtigo comes to a screeching halt, as a series of four hydroelectric power dams tap its energy and create four warm-water flowages. The farthest upstream and second-largest of these is 1,100-acre Caldron Falls Flowage. The river runner's loss here is the angler's gain, as Caldron Falls offers some mighty fine fishing for muskies, bass and crappies in a wilderness setting hard to match anywhere.

Caldron Falls Flowage

Wisconsin Public Service Corporation owns virtually all the land surrounding the flowage, so there is almost no development. You'll find the miles of rugged shoreline, punctuated here and there by the white wedge of an eagle's tail, a visual treat in itself worth the trip. But then add in the fishing, and you'll understand why the anglers who have discovered Caldron Falls consider this a very special place.

Caldron Falls is fairly shallow, with extensive back bays filled with stumps and abundant vegetation. Near the dam, rocky structure drops off sharply into deep water. A large bar a couple hundred yards offshore tops out at about five feet, where a good cabbage bed provides cover for game fish and forage.

Muskies draw the greatest interest among anglers here. According to DNR fish manager Tom Thuemler, muskies have been stocked here annually for over 20 years, and they are doing well indeed. Natural reproduction has improved in recent years, allowing a reduction in stocking from 2,000 to 1,000 fingerlings each year. All are true muskies, and all planted fish are fin-clipped, so if you catch one with all its parts intact, you know you've got a native. Half the muskies handled in a spring 1991 survey were naturally produced.

As an interesting part of the musky management plan, Wisconsin Public Service Corporation cooperates with the DNR to draw down Caldron Falls Flowage some time in February, which drains water from adjacent marshes and disrupts northern pike spawning. Water levels are allowed to return to normal again before muskies spawn in April. This manipulation gives muskies a competitive edge over northerns. Anglers catch and release many muskies measuring 40 to 50 inches every year.

Mike Mladenik, of Crivitz, who guides and fishes the flowage regularly, knows the habits and whereabouts of muskies here as well as anyone. Musky action is good early in the season, Mladenik says, and it continues right on into fall. Early in June, cabbage beds are already well established in the shallow bays. Mladenik and his clients have taken muskies in the 20- to 25-pound range in June over new cabbage on chartreuse and yellow bucktails. The better fish hang out along the deeper weedlines in seven or eight feet of water.

In summer, Mladenik likes to work crankbaits just outside the deeper weedlines. Six-inch Bagleys are his favorites, but others will also produce. By fall, most muskies have moved out of the bays. Now, Mladenik concentrates on deeper water in the river channel and near the dam, where he works deep crankbaits and jerk baits almost exclusively. He also works around the many fallen trees that extend out into deep water along the west shoreline and provide good cover for muskies. Mladenik's basic strategy is to fish areas other anglers overlook. Since most people pound shallow bars and weedbeds, he spends more time working fallen trees and deep structure.

There are few smallmouths in Caldron Falls, but Tom Thuemler says largemouths have made a strong showing in recent years. The weedy back bays and stump fields provide good cover, and natural reproduction is adequate to sustain them. Several clubs hold bass tournaments here every year, and these events have produced fish over seven pounds. You could spend several summers just working your way around the flowage, poking up into back bays where lily pads and drowned timber invite your buzzbaits and topwater stickbaits.

Largemouth action can be good early in the season, when you'll find them in shallow, dark-bottomed bays. Floating Rapalas and similar baits worked very slowly will draw strikes in May and June. Mladenik usually waits until July and August to fish for largemouths here, when smallmouth action slows down on High Falls Flowage, the flowage just below Caldron Falls. He likes South Bay, Crane's Bay and especially the fallen trees that line the west shore. A jig and pig or plastic worm is his bait of choice, rigged weedless so he can fish it right in the sticks.

Walleyes were stocked here for several years in the late '70s and early '80s, but they did not do well. None have been planted since then, but Thuemler says the DNR may resume stocking walleyes as early as 1994. There is some minor natural reproduction, and an occasional whopper still shows up now and then. Northerns, too, are limited, although musky anglers hook a big brute pike once in awhile.

Crappies are the mainstay of panfishermen on Caldron Falls. They don't run large, but consistent reproduction assures good numbers of them year after year, unlike the boom and bust situation common on many lakes. In May and June, you'll find them in the stump fields and weedy bays. Later, they'll tuck themselves right into the tops of downed trees where they can feed on minnows and avoid predators. Twitch a small marabou jig near this type of cover or drag a weedless swimming jig right through the trees and you'll catch crappies. They also suspend five to 10 feet below the surface over deep water near the dam and in the river channel, where slip bobbers and small minnows or Bait Rigs panfish spinner rigs will take them.

Crivitz guide Mike Mladenik with a nice largemouth bass from Caldron Falls. Summer action is hot along the west shore. Photo Courtesy Mike Mladenik

Crappie fishermen also do well through the ice here all winter long. Most fish are taken off the edges of dropoffs, near weedbeds and suspended over deep water. Some anglers jig with small minnows, while others stick to artificials.

There are six landings maintained by Wisconsin Public Service Corporation, numbered in conjunction with those on High Falls Flowage. Landing #8, just south of the Caldron Falls Dam, has a wheelchair-accessible pier and a sandy swimming beach. (Watch out for the rock outcrop about 200 yards off the landing here.) Other good landings are #12 at Roaring Rapids at the far upper end of the flowage, and #10 on North Bay on the flowage's north side. All are on roads that bear the same number as the landing. WPSC plans to improve several landings and add another wheelchair access when their hydro dam license comes up for renewal in the next year or so. Camping is not permitted on WPSC land on Caldron Falls, but there is a private campground at Fisher's

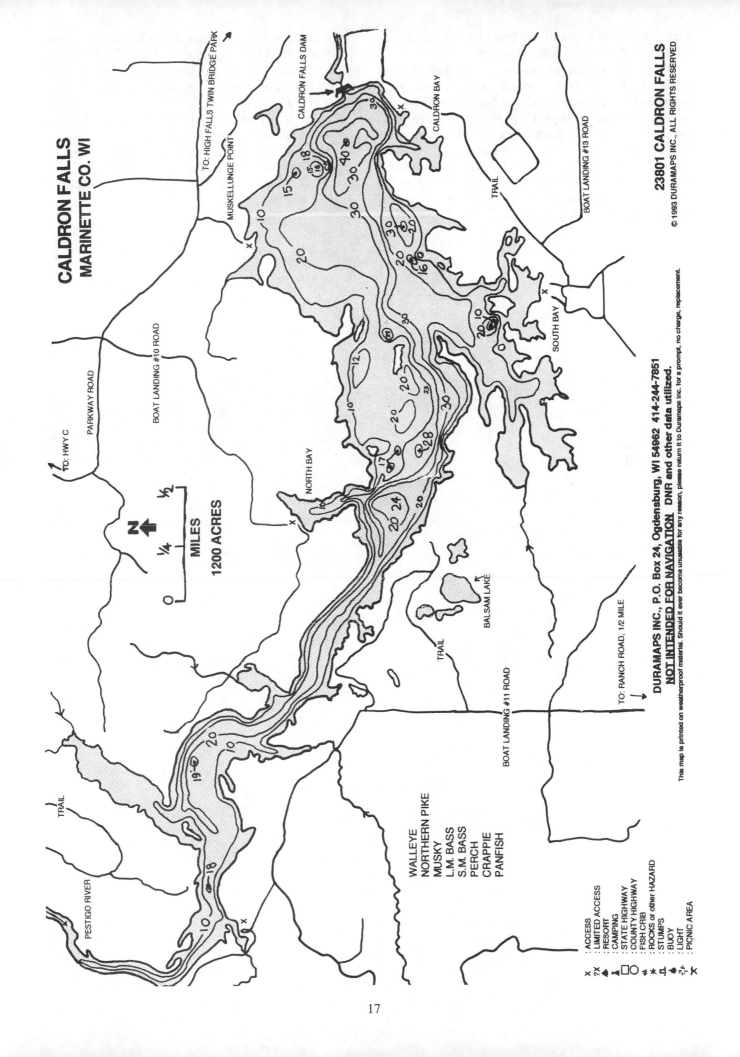

CALDRON FALLS
MARINETTE CO. WI

MILES
1200 ACRES

WALLEYE
NORTHERN PIKE
MUSKY
L.M. BASS
S.M. BASS
PERCH
CRAPPIE
PANFISH

x : ACCESS
?x : LIMITED ACCESS
▲ : RESORT
□ : CAMPING
○ : STATE HIGHWAY
○ : COUNTY HIGHWAY
✳ : FISH CRIB
✳ : ROCKS or other HAZARD
☐ : STUMPS
⚓ : BUOY
☀ : LIGHT
⅄ : PICNIC AREA

TO: HIGH FALLS TWIN BRIDGE PARK
MUSKELLUNGE POINT
CALDRON FALLS DAM
CALDRON BAY
TRAIL
BOAT LANDING #13 ROAD

TO: HWY C
PARKWAY ROAD
BOAT LANDING #10 ROAD
NORTH BAY
SOUTH BAY

TRAIL
PESTIGO RIVER

BALSAM LAKE
TRAIL
BOAT LANDING #11 ROAD
TO: RANCH ROAD, 1/2 MILE

23801 CALDRON FALLS

© 1993 DURAMAPS INC., ALL RIGHTS RESERVED

DURAMAPS INC., P.O. Box 24, Ogdensburg, WI 54962 414-244-7851
NOT INTENDED FOR NAVIGATION   DNR and other data utilized.

This map is printed on weatherproof material. Should it ever become unusable for any reason, please return it to Duramaps Inc. for a prompt, no charge, replacement.

17

Camp on North Bay and a public one at Twin Bridge County Park on High Falls Flowage.

There are bait shops, resorts, and other services along Parkway Road, which crosses the river between High Falls and Caldron Falls. Popp's Resort, on the east side of High Falls Flowage, carries bait and tackle, and is a good source of information for fishing either flowage. Address: Route 3, Crivitz, WI 54114, telephone (715) 757-3511. For bait and tackle in Crivitz, try: Tracy's Sport Shop, Box 456, Crivitz, WI 54114, telephone (715) 854-7867; or P.J. Sports, Crivitz, WI 54114, telephone (715) 757-2156.

For guide service, contact: Mike Mladenik, Route 3, Crivitz, WI 54114, telephone (715) 854-2055. For more information on area services, contact: Crivitz Recreation Association, Crivitz, WI 54114, telephone (715) 757-3651.

For a free map of Caldron Falls Flowage, showing boat launches and wheelchair-accessible piers, contact: Wild Shores Brochures, Public Affairs Department, Wisconsin Public Service Corporation, P.O. Box 19002, Green Bay, WI 54307-9002, telephone (414) 433-1116.

Castle Rock Flowage

Wisconsin River, Adams and Juneau Counties

Back in the 1940s, Aldo Leopold loved to hunt grouse along the tiny alder runs that headed in the broad swamps of Adams County and flowed west across the sandy flatlands to merge with the mighty Wisconsin River. Those headwaters are still there, many of them protected in state wildlife areas, and the little creeks still flow west as they did then, but if he could only follow one today as it meanders to the Wisconsin, Leopold would be in for quite a surprise.

The river still courses through Wisconsin's central plain, but where it flowed unfettered through Juneau and Adams counties in Leopold's day, today a series of hydroelectric power dams harness the river's force and back it up for miles, forming the sprawling Petenwell and Castle Rock flowages. Castle Rock Flowage, named for a local geological landmark on the river below the dam, covers some 16,000 acres. Its deepest holes plunge to 36 feet or so in the old river channel, but the bulk of the flowage has an average depth of 10 to 15 feet.

There are extensive areas of stump-filled backwaters that create holding cover for fish and navigational hazards for boaters. A high carp population and relentless wave action caused by strong winds keep the water quite murky and prevent the growth of rooted vegetation, although there are some areas of bulrushes along the shoreline. In some years, a fairly heavy summer algae bloom reduces visibility for both fish and anglers.

Water quality here has improved markedly since the paper mills and other industries bordering the Wisconsin River from Rhinelander to Port Edwards began cleaning up their effluents in the late 1960s. Castle Rock's fish are tested regularly for mercury, PCB and Dioxin contamination, and recommended consumption levels are published in the semi-annual health advisory available from any DNR office. New DNR regulations requiring lower phosphorus levels in industrial discharges should reduce algae blooms and further improve water quality.

The Federal Energy Regulatory Commission (FERC) relicensing process will begin soon for the hydro dams on both Castle Rock and Petenwell Flowages. In preparation for relicensing, the DNR is working with power companies, paper companies and public officials to draft a comprehensive management plan which will assess the water quality and fisheries resource of both flowages and propose measures for continued improvement.

Carp are the main concern right now, according to fish manager Scot Ironside. They are too contaminated to allow commercial fishermen to take them for human consumption, but Ironside may have found a marketable solution to this problem. A Minnesota plant uses a hydrolization process to turn carp into a low-contaminant liquid fertilizer. An oil byproduct contains most of the contaminants, while bones, scales and other residue are turned into a lightweight "ash." Ironside hopes to get a similar plant up and running to deal with Castle Rock's carp.

Ironside reports that all year classes of walleyes are present in good numbers, thanks to excellent natural reproduction. Walleye growth rates here exceed the statewide average, and the 15-inch size limit has helped boost the average size of walleyes caught by anglers. A 13-pound walleye was taken through the ice in the winter of 1993.

Castle Rock Flowage

CASTLE ROCK FLOWAGE

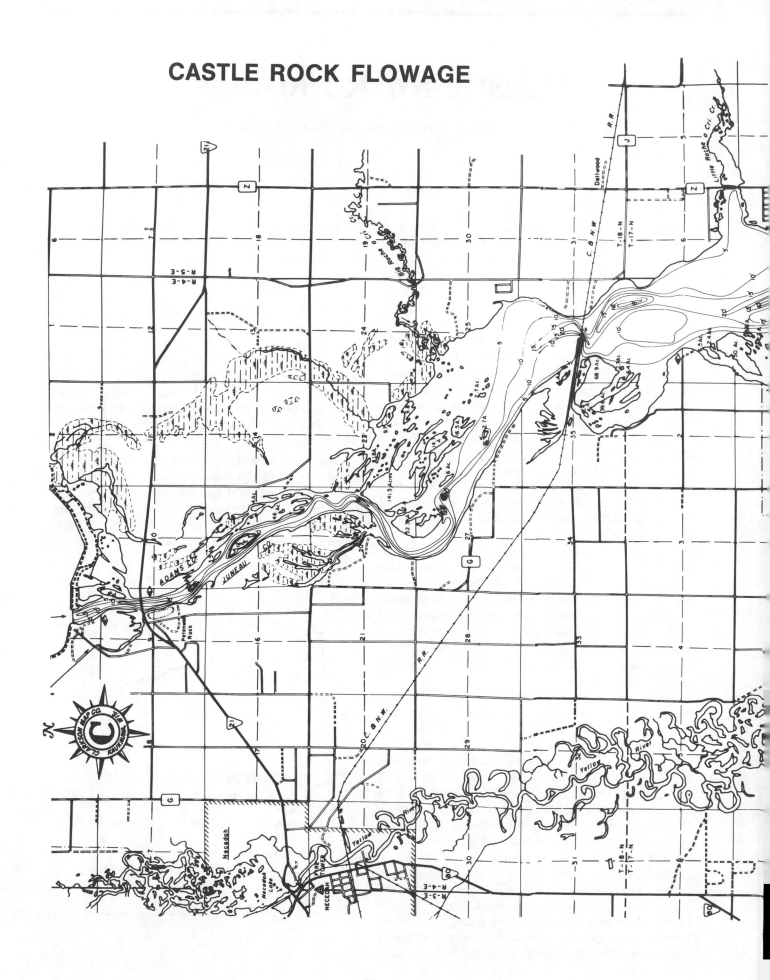

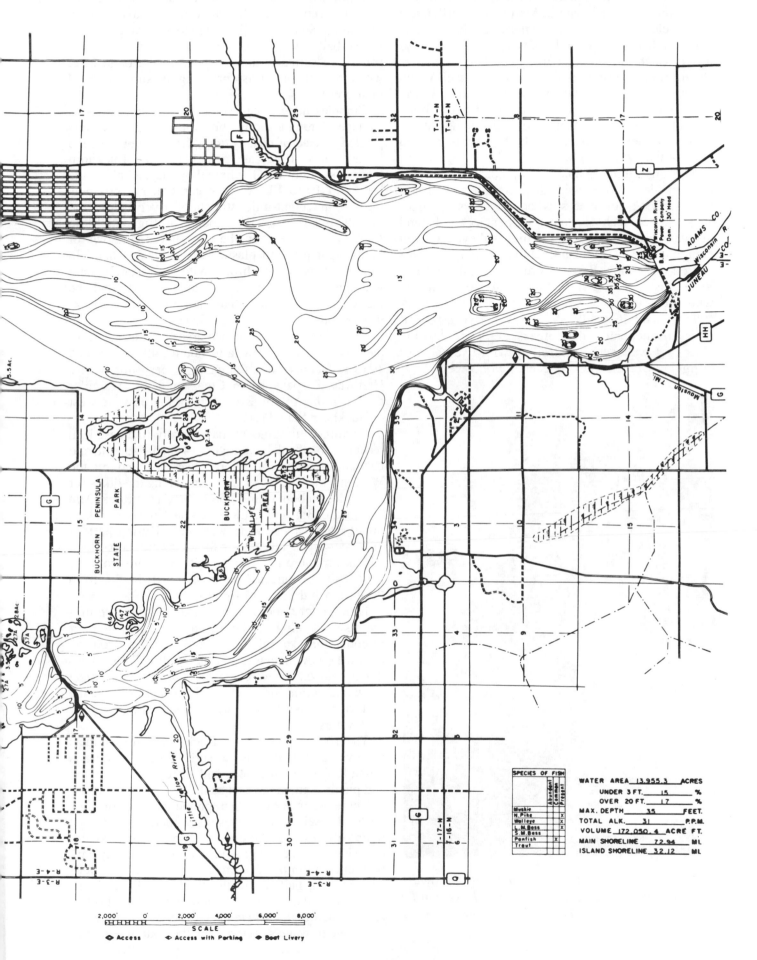

SPECIES OF FISH	Abundant	Common	Present
Muskie			X
N. Pike			X
Walleye		X	
L.M.Bass			X
S.M.Bass			X
Panfish		X	
Trout			

WATER AREA __13,955.3__ ACRES

UNDER 3 FT. __15__ %

OVER 20 FT. __17__ %

MAX. DEPTH __35__ FEET.

TOTAL ALK. __31__ P.P.M.

VOLUME __172,050.4__ ACRE FT.

MAIN SHORELINE __72.94__ ML

ISLAND SHORELINE __32.12__ ML

2,000' 0' 2,000' 4,000' 6,000' 8,000'

SCALE

◆ Access   ◆ Access with Parking   ◆ Boat Livery

21

Fishing pressure is highest a couple miles upriver, below the Petenwell Dam in March and April. Creel census clerks noted 20,000 angler-hours here in that two-month period several years ago. Ironside says that to catch the tailwater fishery just right, anglers should wait until the ice leaves the Petenwell Flowage above the dam, followed by two or three warm, sunny days and perhaps a warm rain. The combination of rising water levels and rising temperatures triggers walleyes to bite, and the first boats there in the morning will clean up.

The larger females hold in deep holes downstream from the dam, while males flock right to the tailrace waters. Look for places where fast water passes slower water, such as eddies, backwaters and behind instream obstructions. You'll find walleyes as well along the brushy river banks above the main flowage and on the Yellow River upstream toward Necedah. Work this cover slowly with a Slo-Poke jig, tipped with a chartreuse or white grub tail rigged Texas-style to make it weedless. Later in the year, the old river channel and other breaks are good holding places for walleyes. Backtrolling with live bait rigs or jigging with crawlers or leeches works well.

Tom Newbauer admires a Castle Rock white bass. Castle Rock's abundant white bass can be lots of fun when they run upriver after the walleye run. Photo by Dan Small

Castle Rock's abundant white bass can be lots of fun. They run upriver after the walleyes have finished spawning, and small jigs, minnows, crankbaits or spinnerbaits will take them in the dam tailrace waters. In summer, they suspend in the open lake, where schools of baitfish breaking the surface reveal their presence.

Crappies hang out in some of the same areas as walleyes later in spring, but you'll find them suspended instead of near bottom. Try the mouth of the Little Yellow River and just below the Buckhorn Bridge on Highway G, where they suspend along the breaks in 10 to 12 feet of water. Other good spots include the eight-mile stretch of river below the Petenwell Dam and the mouths of Big and Little Roche a Cri creeks on the east shore. Minnows or lightweight jigs and plastic tails will take them. In summer, they scatter throughout the flowage, where you can pick them up a few at a time around the many stumps in places like the Yellow River backwaters above the Buckhorn Bridge.

There are fish cribs in two areas that attract crappies, bluegills and a few largemouths: 40 were placed 10 to 12 feet deep in a slough on the east shore where Highway Z spans Klein Creek, and 25 at similar depths in the Yellow River arm of the flowage west of Buckhorn State Park.

Smallmouth numbers have really increased in recent years, thanks to both the 14-inch size limit and habitat improvement. Riprap was installed by the Wisconsin River Power Company along the dikes for two miles on both shores above the Castle Rock Dam and in the Big and Little Roche a Cri creek inlets. Small crankbaits seem to work best. During periods of heavy algae bloom, smallmouths hit best along whichever shore is cleaner, so if winds are from the west, fish the Juneau County shore; if they're from the east, fish the Adams County shore.

Late-winter flood-control drawdowns leave northern pike spawning habitat high and dry, causing poor reproduction, so pike numbers are low. Ironside hopes the new management plan will call for maintaining adequate water levels during the critical spawning period for northerns. Ice fishermen take the bulk of the pike harvest with tip-ups in the stumpy backwaters.

The river below Castle Rock Dam also attracts walleyes and white bass in spring. Shore fishing is possible from both banks, and there is a boat ramp and picnic area on the east bank.

There are many excellent public landings on Castle Rock itself. On the west arm, there are six boat ramps off Highway G: one with a picnic area, swimming beach and campground at a Juneau County park two miles north of the dam; another ramp at O'Dells Bay Marina, halfway to the Buckhorn Bridge; one just south and another 1 1/2 miles north of the bridge; and one across the bridge in Buckhorn State Park.

On the flowage's eastern arm, there are five launch

sites: one on the west bank of the river below the Petenwell Dam; one at a wayside park on Highway 21 on the east bank of the river; one at an overlook on the west bank of the river off Highway G; one two miles farther south on Highway G at the railroad trestle; and one on Highway Z at Little Roche a Cri Creek on the flowage's east shore.

Randy Kreisler, who runs Castle Rock Sport Shop just north of the Highway Z bridge over Klein Creek, rents boats and carries all the bait and tackle you'll need to fish Castle Rock. Address: 2328 Highway Z, Friendship, WI 53934, telephone (608) 339-3701. Other services on the east shore include Dell Aire Campground and Marina, 1942 Dakota Lane, Friendship, WI 53934, telephone (608) 339-4714; and Edgewater Marine, 2350 Highway Z, Friendship, WI 53934, telephone (608) 339-3707. On the west shore, Skipper Bud's operates O'Dells Bay Marina, N. 7424 17th Avenue, New Lisbon, WI 53950, telephone (608) 562-5504.

For information on area services on the west shore, such as campgrounds, motels and restaurants, contact: Juneau County Visitors Bureau, P.O. Box 282, Mauston, WI 53948, telephone (608) 847-7838. For the same information for the east shore and a list of guides, contact: Adams County Chamber of Commerce, P.O. Box 301, Friendship, WI 53934, telephone (608) 339-6997.

You can get an excellent free map of the flowage with locations of all the boat landings, marinas and other services from Wisconsin River Power Company, P.O. Box 50, Wisconsin Rapids, WI 54494, telephone (715) 422-3073. Another free map showing both flowages and listing area services is available from: Castle Rock-Petenwell Lakes Association, Rt. 2, Necedah, WI 54646, telephone (608) 565-7112.

Big Cedar Lake

West Bend, Washington County

The mention of trophy pike to most anglers conjures up images of those slick color brochures put out by Canadian fishing lodges that you and your kids bring home by the bagful from the sports shows every year. You know, the places named after loons, wolves and pine trees way up in northern Saskatchewan, Manitoba or Ontario where, for the amount you've budgeted for the next three years' family vacations, you can enjoy a week of fly-in fishing with the hope of taking a northern or two like the one the smiling lady on the front of the brochure is struggling to hold up for the camera.

Big Cedar Lake

Don't get me wrong. Canadian fishing can be lots of fun. I've been there and have caught big northerns and seen even bigger ones, like the 24-pounder a very happy Illinois angler took out of Ontario's Red Lake while I was there. In fact, that monster pike was a twin to one taken by Bob Borsh of Milwaukee several years back a heck of a lot closer to home. In Big Cedar Lake, to be exact. So, you can squirrel away your vacation money for a couple years and head for northern Canada for a week, or you can trailer your

boat up Highway 41 to the Slinger-West Bend exit and fish Big Cedar Lake any weekend you like, or every weekend, for that matter. It's your choice, and your money.

Big Cedar Lake is among the largest of those wonderful depressions gouged out by the Wisconsin glacier during the last ice age that filled with meltwater and now offer some fantastic fishing in the rolling hills of the Kettle Moraine. Located between Highways 41 and 45 a few miles southwest of West Bend, Big Cedar is easily accessible from anywhere in southeastern Wisconsin. It covers just under 1,000 acres and consists of two basins separated by a shallow narrows at its midsection.

The north basin has a maximum depth of 37 feet, but most of it is a lot shallower, with extensive weedbeds that hold plenty of largemouths, crappies and northerns. Gilbert Lake, a shallow, 44-acre basin attached to the north end of Big Cedar by a navigable channel, is used by spawning pike, crappies and bass, and provides additional fishing for these species.

Big Cedar's southern basin is much deeper, with shorelines that drop off sharply to a maximum depth of 105 feet. Weed growth here extends out to the main breakline, providing excellent cover for gamefish and panfish alike. A honey of a gravel bar rises to within eight feet or so of the surface near the middle of the south basin, and another one comes up out of a 20-foot saddle at the mouth of the outlet bay to Cedar Creek, along the south basin's east shore. Both of these humps and the entire east shore fall off so abruptly that a mountain goat would have trouble keeping its footing here if this were dry land.

In addition to the usual forage base of perch, suckers and assorted minnows, Big Cedar has a good population of ciscoes, and rainbow smelt have also found their way into the lake somehow. These latter species, especially ciscoes, provide the kind of feed that puts pounds on pike.

Big Cedar isn't exactly overrun with northerns, as are many southern Wisconsin lakes that have too many "hammer handles" and not enough bigger fish, but the population here is well-balanced and includes many pike over 10 pounds. Bob Bergstrom of West Bend can attest to this, as he spent some 15 years pursuing Big Cedar's big pike, taking and releasing many from 10 to 15 pounds and several larger ones. According to Bergstrom, trolling Spoonplugs along the weed edges or casting weedless baits closer to shore will yield 3- to 5-pound pike in the north basin, while cisco-imitating baits fished in the deeper south basin produce most of the trophy fish.

Bergstrom says white and silver baits work best on the south basin's big pike, and recommends spinner-baits, crankbaits and plastics. His favorite lure is an eight-inch silver Reaper rigged on a large swimming jighead with a trailer hook looped over the jig's main hook. In May and June, this bait is deadly when jigged along the sandy lip between the weedline and the sharp dropoff to deep water, where big pike ambush the schools of ciscoes that move along the break.

Big Cedar develops an unusually deep thermocline in summer, according to DNR fish manager John Nelson, providing good oxygen down to about 40 feet. Once this occurs, the ciscoes suspend in a narrow band from 35 to 40 feet or so over deeper water, and the big pike follow them. To get them now, first locate the schools of ciscoes, then troll with wire line and Spoonplugs or downriggers and silver Bagleys, or backtroll with an eight- or 10-inch sucker on a quick-strike rig.

Bob Bergstrom of West Bend hefts a pair of big bass from Big Cedar Lake. Bergstrom fishes bass tournaments now, but used to specialize on Big Cedar's pike. Photo courtesy Bob Bergstrom

Big Cedar has a good largemouth population, and Bergstrom has joined a number of anglers who've turned their efforts from pike to bass in recent years. Early in the year, weedy Gilbert Lake and the weed-beds of Big Cedar's north basin produce good catches of bass, as do the north and west shores of the southern basin. Look for inside turns on the breaks and work these with diving crankbaits or plastics. Spinnerbaits often produce bass in the flats around the two islands in the north basin. Bass from two to four pounds are common, and some over five pounds are taken every season.

As good as the bass and pike fishing can be on Big Cedar, the real news is that now there are walleyes here as well. DNR crews have planted 45,000 fingerlings annually since 1986. By the winter of 1993, anglers were taking walleyes up to seven pounds. Look for them on the sharp drops and bars along the south basin's eastern shore, where there is good structure for both perch and walleyes.

Another new addition to Big Cedar's fishery is lake trout. The DNR stocks some 15,000 fingerling lakers every other year. When I talked to John Nelson in January 1993, anglers were taking trout up to 26 inches or so on cut bait near bottom in the deep southern basin. Nelson anticipates these trout will in time provide a trophy fishery. The season runs from early January through September, with a daily bag limit of two trout over 17 inches.

There are plenty of small perch and bluegills in Big Cedar, but crappies dominate the panfish scene. Kewaskum taxidermist Al Broecker and tackle designer Jim Roe took me and the *Outdoor Wisconsin* camera crew out for crappies one mild spring day a few years back. We worked the north basin's west shore, using tiny white and yellow jigs to take a mess of nice fish suspended along the weedline there. Broecker also caught and released one of the biggest white bass I've ever seen -- it must have weighed three pounds.

Just after ice-out, crappie action is hot at the north end of the lake and in Gilbert Lake. Most anglers use minnows, but light line and ultralight swimming jigs tipped with tube tails or grub tails will take just as many. Speaking of ice, Big Cedar also produces good pike and crappie action in the winter months. Big golden shiners on tip-ups fished along the breaks near the narrows and throughout the north basin will take pike, while tiny teardrop jigs tipped with mousies and small jigging spoons, like a Rembrandt, will take crappies at the extreme north end and in Gilbert Lake. The secret for fast action on big crappies is to use very light line -- Trilene Cold Weather in one-pound test is ideal.

The best boat launch is the public ramp next to Fischer's Lakeshore Resort on Gonring Drive off Highway 144. Fischer's provides docking facilities, bait, tackle, gas and minor repairs, in addition to a tavern and restaurant; telephone: (414) 338-1999.

You can also get bait, tackle and guide service at Kettle Moraine Bait, 1720 North Main St., West Bend, WI 53095, telephone (414) 338-9455. For information on lodging, restaurants and other area facilities, contact: West Bend Area Chamber of Commerce, P.O. Box 522, West Bend, WI 53095, telephone (414) 338-2666.

BIG CEDAR LAKE

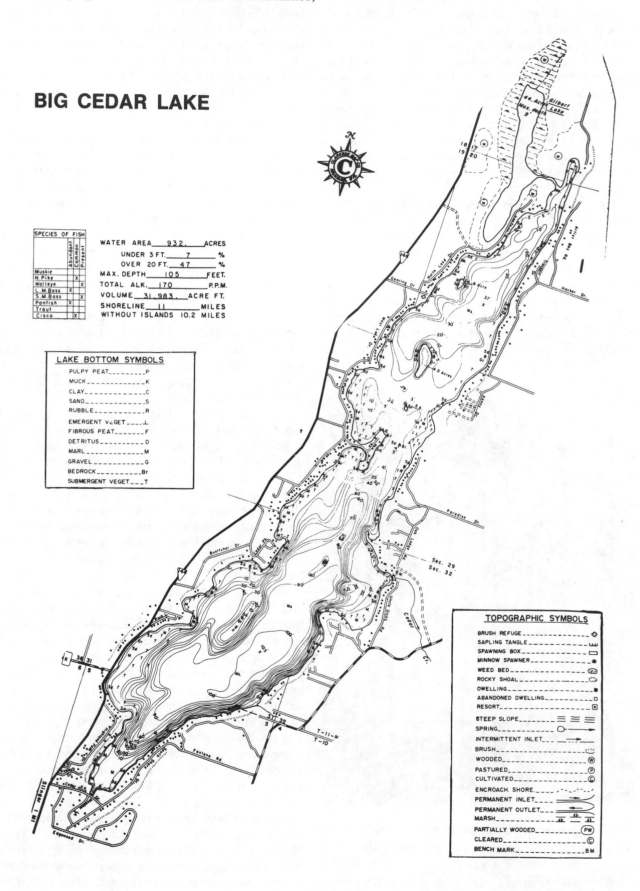

SPECIES OF FISH	Abundant	Common	Present
Muskie			
N. Pike			X
Walleye			X
L.M.Bass	X		
S.M.Bass			X
Panfish	X		
Trout			
Cisco			X

WATER AREA ___932.___ ACRES
UNDER 3 FT. ___7___ %
OVER 20 FT. ___47___ %
MAX. DEPTH ___105___ FEET.
TOTAL ALK. ___170___ P.P.M.
VOLUME ___31,983.___ ACRE FT.
SHORELINE ___11___ MILES
WITHOUT ISLANDS 10.2 MILES

LAKE BOTTOM SYMBOLS
PULPY PEAT _____ P
MUCK _____ K
CLAY _____ C
SAND _____ S
RUBBLE _____ R
EMERGENT VEGET ____⊥
FIBROUS PEAT _____ F
DETRITUS _____ D
MARL _____ M
GRAVEL _____ G
BEDROCK _____ Br
SUBMERGENT VEGET ___ T

TOPOGRAPHIC SYMBOLS
BRUSH REFUGE _____ ⊕
SAPLING TANGLE _____ �
SPAWNING BOX _____ ▭
MINNOW SPAWNER _____ ✳
WEED BED _____
ROCKY SHOAL _____
DWELLING _____ ■
ABANDONED DWELLING _____ □
RESORT _____
STEEP SLOPE _____
SPRING _____
INTERMITTENT INLET _____
BRUSH _____
WOODED _____ Ⓦ
PASTURED _____ Ⓟ
CULTIVATED _____ Ⓒ
ENCROACH. SHORE _____
PERMANENT INLET _____
PERMANENT OUTLET _____
MARSH _____
PARTIALLY WOODED _____ PW
CLEARED _____ Ⓒ
BENCH MARK _____ B.M.

Chequamegon Bay

Lake Superior, Ashland and Bayfield Counties

Chequamegon Bay

From the old lumbermill dock pilings west of Ashland at the head of the bay, north to Madeline Island and Bayfield, Lake Superior's Chequamegon Bay supports a diverse fishery that rivals any you'll find in the Great Lakes. Trout and salmon head the list, but there is excellent fishing for northerns and walleyes as well, not to mention perch, smallmouths, and a spring smelt run that draws enthusiasts from all over the Midwest.

Chequamegon Bay is sheltered from all but northeast winds, but this is a big body of water and storms may blow in from Lake Superior at any time. It's a good idea to venture out in at least a 16-foot deep-V boat with a motor of 25 horsepower or larger, just in case you get caught out in rough weather. A smaller auxiliary motor will reduce your chances of being stranded if your primary motor fails. Safety flares are required on boats using the Great Lakes, and you may want to stow some foul weather gear as well.

Soon after ice-out, which usually occurs by mid-April, trollers do well on splake, browns, cohos and the occasional chinook along the west shore from Barksdale to Bayfield and on the Ashland side of the bay. The rainbow trout and smelt spawning runs, along with warmer water temperatures, bring all the salmonid species into the shallows. In the 1980s, trollers began taking more rainbow trout than the wild population could stand, so the bag limit for rainbows was reduced to one fish over 28 inches to help maintain a viable brood stock of wild fish. The DNR stocks browns, splake and chinooks, but cohos and rainbows reproduce naturally.

Trout and salmon move around a lot, so you may have to try different depths to find them. Early and late in the day, they are often a block or less from the beach in four to 10 feet of water, while at midday you may have to troll in 30 feet to connect. Tributary mouths are especially productive. Many trollers concentrate on the stretch of shoreline north of Washburn between Houghton and Van Tassel's points, where the Sioux and Onion rivers enter the bay.

Most anglers go with medium-action spinning rods, open-face reels and 12-pound test line, but some prefer the longer trolling rods and level-wind reels common on Lake Michigan. Floating crankbaits, such as jointed Rapalas, Shad Raps, Rebels, Rebel Fastracs and similar lures in fluorescent orange, chartreuse, silver or blue work well in shallow water, while weighted spoons in the same colors do the job when the fish are deeper. Most anglers drag a combination of shallow- and deep-running baits. Side-planers, outriggers and other devices that take lines away from the boat's wake will increase your strike rate. Fish that are spooked by a boat passing overhead will often hit a lure trolled 20 yards or so to one side or the other.

Once the smelt run is over in early May, perch fishing picks up all around the bay. On the east side of the bay, Oak Point, Brush Point and Sand Cut are popular spots. On the west side, the weedbeds off Barksdale and VandeVenter Bay at Washburn's West End Park produce well. Pier fishermen can get in on the action, but most perch are taken by boat anglers. Small shiners or fathead minnows are the preferred bait, and you can also catch perch on jigs tipped with live bait or plastic grub tails.

Jake LaPenter watches as Jon Small pulls a nice splake onto the ice of Chequamegon Bay. Photo by Dan Small

Northern pike run big in Chequamegon Bay, though their numbers have been depleted of late for a variety of reasons. A few years ago a Mercer fisherman caught one measuring more than 50 inches and weighing over 25 pounds, and Washburn veterinarian Steve Schmidt caught one weighing 24 pounds.

Pike in the 15- to 20-pound class are taken every spring. The same places that produce perch are good spots to try for northerns using large spoons or dead smelt. The shallows off the Highway 2 bridge (known locally as "Short Bridge") at Prentice Park Slough are another good spring pike spot. Passing motorists are often treated to the sight of an angler fighting a big northern here. In midsummer, the deep cabbage beds between Ashland's ore dock and breakwall yield some nice pike. Heavy jigs tipped with plastic Reapers, Creatures or Sassy Shads work well.

Walleye anglers have a field day on the bay in May and June. Slow trolling around the Oak Point and Brush Point flats with a crawler harness sporting fluorescent chartreuse or orange spinner blades often yields limits of three-pound-plus walleyes. Anglers with small boats take plenty of walleyes on jigs and crawlers in the deep holes in the Fish Creek Slough, known locally as Prentice Park Slough.

Heavy stockings of walleyes by the DNR and local sports clubs has resulted in an improving walleye fishery throughout the bay. Large schools of walleyes constantly follow schools of baitfish, and trollers have good success working the area from the coal dock to the breakwall lighthouse.

Most smallmouths caught in the bay are taken incidentally by pike and walleye anglers, but a few anglers in the know take bronzebacks up to six pounds in the flats around Brush Point on crankbaits, spinners and flies.

Summer trout action is hottest in the ship channel between the Ashland breakwall and the Chequamegon Point Lighthouse on Long Island. This is an eight-mile trip one way, so bring plenty of gas and plan to spend the day. The sand flats south of Madeline Island produce good catches of lake trout in the summer, but you'll need a bigger boat to fish safely outside the protective shelter of Long Island. Charter boats operating out of Ashland, Washburn and Bayfield will take you out for a day or half-day of fishing on the flats or among the Apostle Islands, and they provide all the gear you'll need.

Chequamegon Bay probably yields as many fish through the ice as it does during the open-water months. Armed with tip-ups, jig rods and a bucket of shiners, you're likely to catch a mixed bag most anywhere on the bay in winter. The flats west of Oak Point produce good catches of perch, northerns and walleyes, as does the area off the Ashland breakwall. The Washburn shore boasts good perch and trout action off West End Park and Memorial Park. The weedbeds off Barksdale are noted for excellent pike and early brown trout and splake action. Splake and trout tend to follow the edge of new ice as it moves north and east from the head of the bay. The waters off the mouths of Bono's Creek and the Sioux and Onion rivers are winter trout and splake hotspots.

The smartest thing a newcomer to ice fishing on the bay can do is to go where the locals fish. Even then, it's wise to exercise extreme caution on the ice because conditions can change rapidly. Early and late in winter, the ice can be especially treacherous. One December before the entire bay had frozen over, my son Jon and I, along with about 40 other fishermen, were stranded briefly on a large sheet of ice that broke away from shore at Barksdale in a strong southwest wind. On another occasion, this time in March, we were on our way out to fish with a friend when his truck broke through the ice two miles offshore near Brush Point and sank to the bottom in eight feet of water. Fortunately, we escaped injury both times, but we learned to respect the lake, and now I always inquire about ice conditions before venturing out.

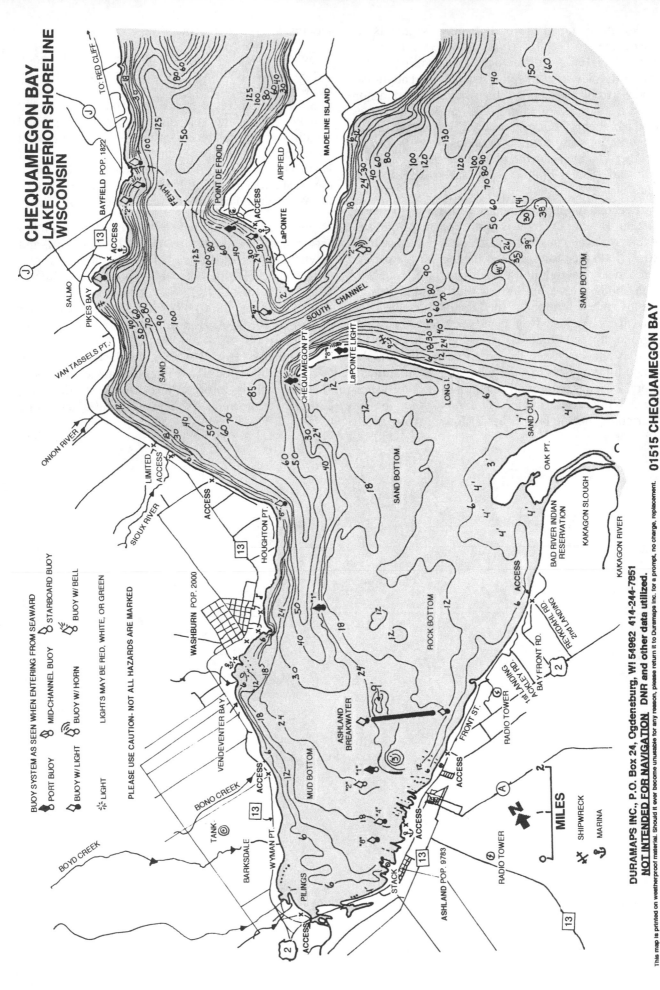

CHEQUAMEGON BAY
LAKE SUPERIOR SHORELINE
WISCONSIN

BUOY SYSTEM AS SEEN WHEN ENTERING FROM SEAWARD

Port Buoy   Mid-Channel Buoy   Starboard Buoy

Buoy w/ Light   Buoy w/ Horn   Buoy w/ Bell

Light   LIGHTS MAY BE RED, WHITE, OR GREEN

PLEASE USE CAUTION- NOT ALL HAZARDS ARE MARKED

MILES

SHIPWRECK   MARINA

DURAMAPS INC., P.O. Box 24, Ogdensburg, WI 54962 414-244-7851

NOT INTENDED FOR NAVIGATION — DNR and other data utilized.

This map is printed on weatherproof material. Should it ever become unusable for any reason, please return it to Duramaps Inc. for a prompt, no charge, replacement.

01515 CHEQUAMEGON BAY

BAYFIELD POP. 1822

TO: RED CLIFF

MADELINE ISLAND

AIRFIELD

POINT DE FROID

LaPOINTE

LaPOINTE LIGHT

SOUTH CHANNEL

CHEQUAMEGON PT.

SAND BOTTOM

SAND CUT

LONG I.

OAK PT.

BAD RIVER INDIAN RESERVATION

KAKAGON SLOUGH

KAKAGON RIVER

2ND LANDING

RED CLIFF RD.

BAY FRONT RD.

1ST LANDING

LAKEY RD.

FRONT ST.

RADIO TOWER

ASHLAND POP. 9783

RADIO TOWER

ASHLAND BREAKWATER

ROCK BOTTOM

MUD BOTTOM

VENDEVENTER BAY

BONO CREEK

WASHBURN POP. 2000

SAND

HOUGHTON PT.

SIOUX RIVER

LIMITED ACCESS

ONION RIVER

VAN TASSELS PT.

PIKES BAY

SALMO

SAND BOTTOM

BOYD CREEK

BARKSDALE

WYMAN PT.

TANK

PILINGS

STACK

ACCESS

FERRY

We have taped several fishing segments on Chequamegon Bay for *Outdoor Wisconsin*. On our first outing, Frank Roman took us out trolling for lakers on the flats off Madeline Island. We caught two modest trout, but pulled lines and headed ashore when a sudden wind shift kicked up six-foot waves. Two members of our camera crew had already turned green and chummed their breakfast long before the weather change, and the rest of us hung on to our gear and wished Frank greater speed back to Ashland.

A second attempt for lakers with Bayfield charter captain Howie Dietz was cut short by high seas before we even caught a fish. In between those trips, Roger LaPenter took me ice fishing for splake and perch near the lighthouse. We caught a couple of each, along with a big lawyer (burbot) that Roger's friends ribbed him about for months after the show aired. Last August, Roger and I taped a fly fishing segment for smallmouths. We caught some nice fish on flies and discussed the proposed regulations that would limit anglers to a daily bag of one smallmouth over 22 inches, essentially creating a trophy fishery here. While some anglers feel this would be too restrictive, most agree the bay's slow-growing small-mouths deserve such protection.

Several excellent boat launches provide good access to Chequamegon Bay. On the Ashland side, the Kreher Park launch is located at the foot of Prentice Avenue, there is a smaller launch site behind Anglers All on the east end of town, and Second Landing is several miles east of town on Reykdal Road. Small boats can launch off Highway 13 at Bono's Creek near Barksdale. In Washburn, launch at the Washburn Boat Club landing in West End Park or the Washburn Marina at the foot of Central Avenue.

Food, lodging, marinas, fishing charters and other services are available in Ashland, Washburn and Bayfield. For recreation guides and more information, contact: Bayfield County Tourism and Recreation Department, P.O. Box 832, Washburn, WI 54891, telephone (800) 472-6336; Bayfield Chamber of Commerce, P.O. Box 138, Bayfield, WI 54814, telephone (800) 447-4094; or Ashland Area Chamber of Commerce, P.O. Box 746, Ashland, WI 54806, telephone (800) 284-9484. For bait, tackle, guide service and fishing information, contact: Anglers All, 2802 E. Front Street, Ashland, WI 54806, telephone (715) 682-5754.

Chetek Chain Of Lakes

Chetek, Barron County

You say your family's been bugging you to find a new vacation spot far enough away from home to know you've been someplace, with beaches, ski shows, one-of-a-kind gift shops, nearby canoeing rivers, and of course a variety of good, easy fishing opportunities so the kids can actually catch something this time? Well, I think I've got the place: the Chetek Chain of Lakes. Never heard of it? Let me describe it for you.

Located just off Highway 53 in southeastern Barron County about a half-hour north of Chippewa Falls, this chain of six lakes hugs the small, northern city of Chetek and is actually one 3,800-acre flowage on the Chetek River, a tributary to the Red Cedar River. The chain boasts some 30 resorts and campgrounds, many miles of sandy beach, and a wide range of four-season family recreational opportunities that include good fall hunting and camping, snowmobile and ski trails, and a golf course for days when the fishing is slow.

Many resort communities hold annual fishing contests in the summer, but Chetek's Fish-O-Rama is scheduled for the month of May each year to coincide with the opening of the inland fishing season. That's a hint: the fishing here is good right from opening day on.

Lake Chetek, Prairie Lake and Pokegama Lake are the largest and most centrally located of the six. Ojaski Lake connects with the north end of Pokegama via a channel that passes under Hwy. M, while Ten Mile and Moose Ear lakes connect with Lake Chetek to complete the south end of the chain. The lakes are relatively shallow, with lots of bays, gravel shorelines and extensive weedbeds that hold both gamefish and panfish. Navigable channels connect the lakes, allowing you to explore the entire chain without having to launch your boat more than once.

According to fish manager Rick Cornelius, the Chetek Chain's largemouth bass fishery can be rated right up near the top, while walleye and northern pike numbers are good, but more modest. Panfish, however, are the chain's forte, and the main reason so many families keep coming back here for summer vacations year after year.

★ **Chetek Chain Of Lakes**

The DNR stocks about 30 walleye fingerlings per acre annually, scattered among the six lakes. That adds up to over 100,000 per year. Other species take care of themselves, as there is adequate spawning habitat for bass, panfish and northerns.

Weedbeds make up the primary structure on the chain, but the Chetek Lake Protection Committee has installed over 300 fish cribs in 10 to 12 feet of water in Prairie, Chetek and Pokegema lakes to provide more structure for panfish and walleyes.

Prairie Lake suffered several small winter kills in the 1980s, which followed a severe kill there in the late 1970s, prompting the installation of an aeration system in 1992 off Veterans Park at the lake's north end. Four townships, Barron County and the city of Chetek teamed up with the DNR to fund the aeration project. "It looked as though oxygen depletion was becoming a common problem in the northern third of the lake," says Rick Cornelius, "so now we run the aerators from December through February. The system worked well in its first two winters, but it's hard to say how successful it will be in the long run."

Walleye action is good early in the year, but then slows considerably as summer wears on and forage becomes more abundant. Walleyes grow fast on the chain, and while you shouldn't expect to catch a mess of them, your chances of taking a trophy fish are as good here as on any inland lake. Big walleyes frequent the weedbeds, where you'll need weedless lures like a Slo-Poke jig with a Texas-rigged plastic tail, or the Mepps Timber Doodle, a black, silver or gold spoon that can be rigged with a Mister Twister Split Double Tail to run weedless.

Work the dropoffs, sand bars and gravel bars of Chetek, Pokegema and Prairie lakes and the narrows between Chetek and Pokegema early in the season with jigs and minnows. As soon as the weeds are up, switch to the weedless baits mentioned above. You'll also take some nice largemouths while after walleyes in the weeds, but that's the price you'll have to pay. Trolling is legal on the entire chain, and some anglers do well trolling crawler harnesses along sharper dropoffs. Trolling -- or, if the wind is right -- drifting parallel to shoreline dropoffs is a good way to fish Prairie Lake. Backtrolling with crawler rigs and leeches is also worth a try in the deeper channels and narrows. The Panther Martin blade of the new Infiltrator in-line spinner rig keeps spinning at very slow trolling speeds, making it ideal for backtrolling.

Some of the biggest walleyes -- 10-pounders and better -- are taken right after ice-up in December. Tip-ups and big shiner minnows fished along weed edges and wherever there are structure breaks will do the job.

Did someone mention bass? Any of the bays on the chain will yield good bass action, but Moose Ear, Ten Mile and nearby Bass Lake probably have the best bass water overall. Early in the season, go with plastics and shallow crankbaits, like floating Rapalas. Once the weeds are up, topwater baits, buzzbaits and spinnerbaits will take more fish. Don't neglect the piers of cottages and resorts, as bass often use these for cover in summer.

You'll find northerns in many of the same places as bass. Look for the bigger pike along deep weed edges and off the mouths of bays where they prey on small panfish. Shallow crankbaits, big, flashy spinnerbaits and weedless spoons will take them, or you can drift a live sucker on a bobber line while you cast for bass.

Bluegills, the most abundant panfish, are literally everywhere on the chain. Nine- and 10-inchers are fairly common, and once in awhile you'll find one that pushes a pound in weight. The two best times to get the big ones are when they are on the beds in early to mid-June, and then later in summer when

Look for big bluegills and sunfish like these on the beds in the Chetek Chain in June. Photo by Dan Small

PRAIRIE LAKE

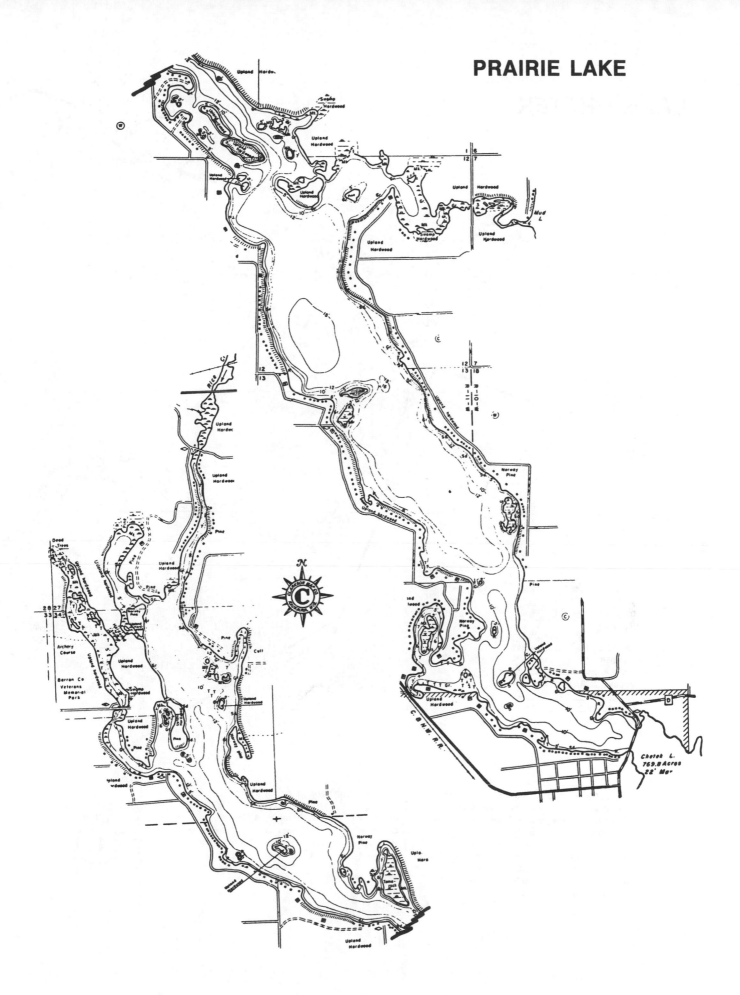

LAKE CHETEK

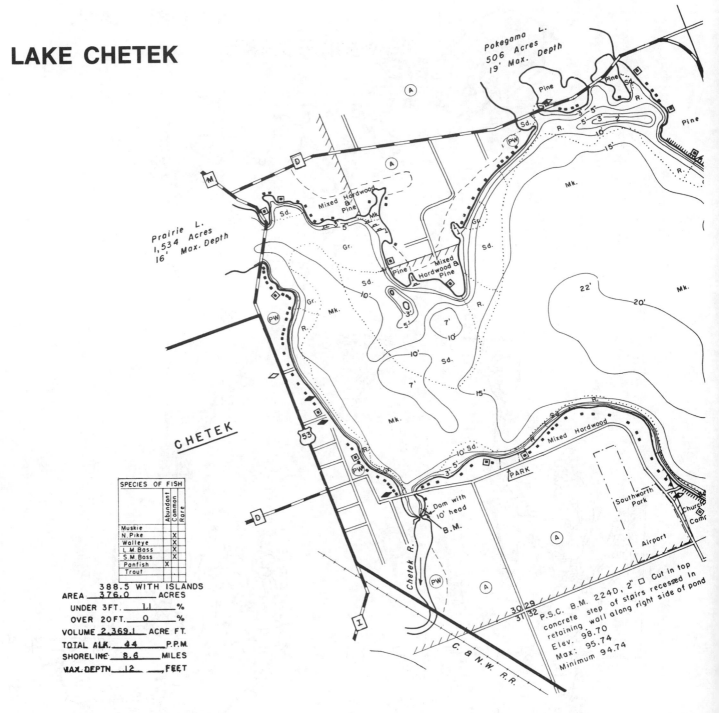

SPECIES OF FISH

	Abundant	Common	Rare
Muskie			X
N. Pike		X	
Walleye		X	
L.M. Bass		X	
S.M. Bass		X	
Panfish	X		
Trout			

388.5 WITH ISLANDS
AREA __376.0__ ACRES
UNDER 3 FT. __11__ %
OVER 20 FT. __0__ %
VOLUME __2,369.1__ ACRE FT.
TOTAL ALK. __44__ P.P.M.
SHORELINE __8.6__ MILES
MAX. DEPTH __12__ FEET

CHETEK

Pokegama L.
506 Acres
19' Max. Depth

Prairie L.
1,534 Acres
16' Max. Depth

P.S.C. B.M. 224D, 2" □ Cut in top
concrete step of stairs recessed in
retaining wall along right side of pond
Elev. 98.70
Max: 95.74
Minimum 94.74

Dam with
10' head
B.M.

Southworth
Park
Airport

Mixed Hardwood

PARK

Chetek R.

C. & N.W. R.R.

TOPOGRAPHIC SYMBOLS

- (B) Brush
- (PW) Partially wooded
- (W) Wooded
- (C) Cleared
- (P) Pastured
- (A) Agricultural
- B.M. Bench Mark
- ■ Dwelling
- ▣ Resort
- ▣ Camp

- iIIIIIi Steep slope
- ‒‒‒ Indefinite shoreline
- Marsh
- Spring
- Intermittent stream
- Permanent inlet
- Permanent outlet
- Dam
- D.N.R. State owned land

LAKE BOTTOM SYMBOLS

- P. Peat
- Mk. Muck
- C. Clay
- M. Marl
- Sd. Sand
- St. Silt
- Gr. Gravel
- R. Rubble
- Br. Bedrock

- B Boulders
- Stumps & Snags
- Rock danger to navigation
- T Submergent vegetation
- Emergent vegetation
- Floating vegetation
- Brush shelters

CLARKSON MAP CO.
KAUKAUNA, WIS.

34

TEN MILE LAKE

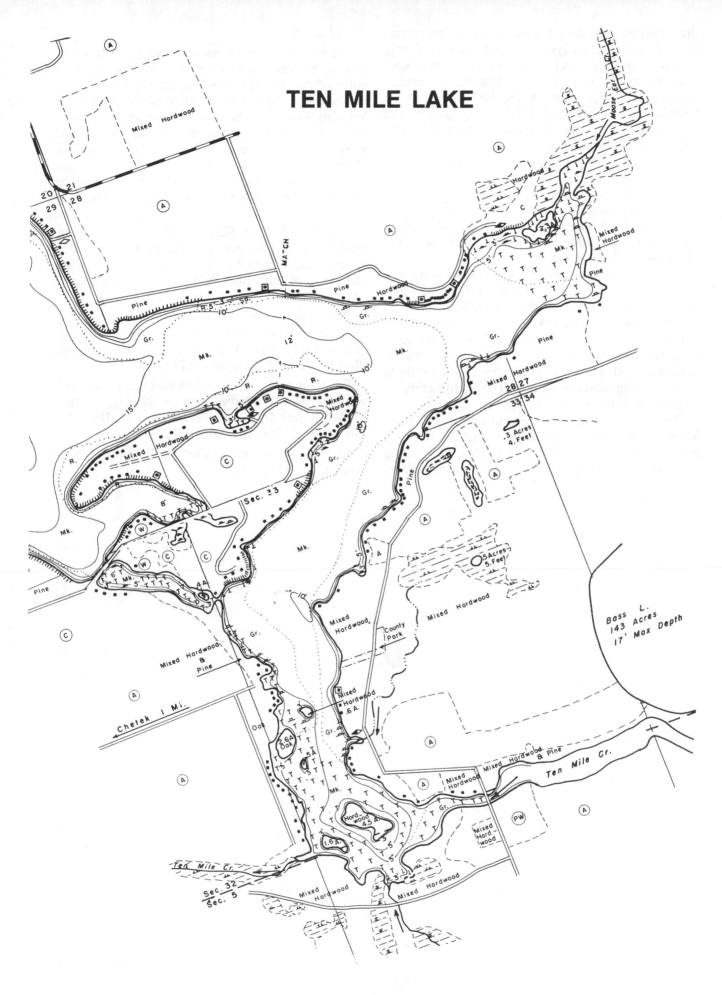

they suspend over deeper water. Look for concentrations of 'gills in the bays at the far north end of long, skinny Prairie Lake and along both shores of Pokegema, north of the narrows to Chetek. Remember where you found them on the beds along shore, because later in summer you'll take big 'gills off the mouths of these same bays and over deeper water beyond the shoreline drop-offs.

Live bait, such as redworms, chunks of nightcrawler or waxworms will take bluegills fished on a teardrop ice jig over the beds and with a Bait Rigs panfish spinner rig or a swimming jig when they are suspended. If you can get hold of some small leeches, try them on a 1/32-ounce swimming jig and see if the bluegills don't clobber them.

There are strong year classes of crappies on occasion, but you'll have to hunt for them. Try deep water off the mouths of bays in May, then look for them around brush and fish cribs at spawning time and suspended over deep water or off sharp-breaking dropoffs later in the summer. Small, live minnows work well, but I like to finesse them with ultralight swimming jigs and plastic tails. The chain's crappies run big, with many over a pound.

Perch are present, but nothing to get excited about. There are some good bullheads, though, if you've a mind to soak crawlers on the mud flats in the evening or on bottom off the mouths of bays and weedlines almost any time.

There is a new state-owned landing with a concrete slab, deep water and plenty of parking a mile north of the city of Chetek on the southeast end of Prairie Lake. There are also good public landings at Veterans Memorial Park on the northwest shore of Prairie Lake near Cameron, another on Chetek Lake at Southworth Park near the airport, and another one off Highway D on the east shore of Ten Mile Lake. There is also a handicapped-accessible fishing pier on the southwest end of Pokegema Lake off Highway D.

The Rod & Gun Shop in Chetek carries bait, tackle, maps and can give you the latest word on fishing conditions, as well as register your catch for local and regional contests. Address: 513 2nd Street, Chetek, WI 54728, telephone (715) 924-4181.

If you get hungry while fishing, dock at Pete's Landing on Lake Chetek for a pizza or anything from burgers to T-bones. Address: 121 Lakeview Drive, Chetek, WI 54728, telephone (715) 924-3100.

For information on accommodations, restaurants, guide service and other area highlights, contact: Chetek Resort Owners Association, P.O. Box 172, Chetek, WI 54728, telephone (715) 924-4440.

121 Lakeview Drive, Chetek, WI 54728, telephone (715) 924-3100.

Chippewa Flowage

Central Sawyer County

Chippewa Flowage

After 35 years, the Chippewa Flowage can once again lay claim to the world record musky. The 69-pound, 11-ounce giant taken by Louis Spray in 1949 was knocked out of first place by a fish taken in New York's St. Lawrence River in 1957, but a recent investigation spearheaded by Chippewa Flowage guide John Detloff revealed the New York State fish was a bogus entry that weighed only 49 pounds. The Freshwater Fishing Hall of Fame reinstated Spray's musky as the world record in 1992.

Even without a world record, Sawyer County's Chippewa Flowage is impressive. A Northern States Power Company hydroelectric dam near Winter at the confluence of the East and West Forks of the Chippewa River flooded 10 lake basins back in 1923, creating the "Big Chip," and life in the North Woods has not been the same since.

The flowage encompasses over 15,000 acres, with 233 miles of near-wilderness shoreline, 140 islands and six major tributaries. Anglers catch more muskies here every year than on any other lake in the state.

The Chip also has plenty of walleyes, northerns and bass, and an awesome population of big crappies besides.

In 1988, in a land deal that some say is the most important in Wisconsin in the last 50 years, the state spent nearly $7 million to purchase 6,900 acres of land surrounding the flowage from the Northern States Power Company, saving it from possible commercial development. Most of the remaining land on the flowage belongs to the federal government (Chequamegon National Forest) and the Lac Courte Oreilles Chippewa Indian Tribe. Unlike the Hayward area's many resort-ringed lakes, the Chippewa Flowage breathes easy, and so do its many visitors who can expect its shores to remain undeveloped for generations to come.

The flowage's water is stained brown and relatively infertile. There is deep water in some areas, but most of the flowage runs from 15 to 25 feet deep at summer levels. A winter drawdown lowers water levels 16 feet and creates dangerous ice conditions but does not appear to have an effect on fish.

Sand and gravel dominate the bottom types, although there are areas of rock and muck as well. Vegetation is scattered and sparse, but there are weedbeds near some creek mouths and in shallow bays. Large floating bogs, pushed around by the wind, create moving fish cover and sometimes make navigation confusing. Bars, sunken islands, stump fields and reefs abound, supplemented by many hundreds of log fish cribs, providing excellent structure for muskies, walleyes, bass and panfish. Fish here also frequent the dropoffs of former river channels and lake beds.

It would take many years to explore thoroughly even a portion of the Chip. As a newcomer, you would be wise to choose one or two basins to begin with or hire a guide to ensure you'll at least be fishing productive water.

Muskies put the Chip on the map, and muskies continue to draw large numbers of anglers from all over the world every year. The adult musky population is in good shape, bolstered by catch-and-release fishing. DNR fish manager Frank Pratt says half of those taken are over 40 inches. Muskies topping 20 pounds are landed every week here, and a few over

30 pounds are taken each season. A recent DNR radio-telemetry study found more musky spawning activity than anticipated, but Pratt plans to keep stocking 2,500 musky fingerlings annually as a hedge against northern pike.

Musky action starts off slowly in spring and improves steadily throughout the season. In spring, work the dark-bottomed bays and shallow inlet areas that warm up sooner than the main basins, and use smaller baits. "Twitching" small suckers and chubs on light tackle is a proven method for early-season flowage muskies. It consists of casting a lip-hooked minnow in likely spots and working it back to the boat in very slow jerks. This technique also produces some dandy walleyes.

Summer hotspots include offshore bars and deeper bays, especially those in the eastern half of the flowage. More muskies are probably taken on bucktails here than on all other baits combined. Most guides prefer orange, yellow or black bucktails. Those with large fluted or tandem blades will send out more vibrations to attract fish from a greater distance. Noisy surface baits are also effective in summer, especially at night over shallow bars. Casting is about the only option, since motor trolling is prohibited.

Al Denninger, one of the Chip's more consistently successful guides, has his best luck in fall. When the weather cools in late September, he switches from Skimmer bucktails and surface baits to jerk baits and suckers. When the water temperature is 55 degrees or warmer, he uses Suicks, Bobbies or Hi-Fin Foolers, all jerk baits with an up-down motion. Below 55 degrees, he finds Eddies or Strikers more effective because a musky can catch these glider-type jerk baits with less effort. After mid-October, he fishes suckers almost exclusively, often setting up between two cribs and soaking a sucker on a bobber over each one. Denninger finds muskies near weeds, stumps, rock bars and old river channels, as well as over dropoffs. His best fish on the Chip was a 40-pounder taken in a downpour in September of 1984 on one of his own bucktails. That was the biggest musky recorded in the state that year.

Muskies grab bigger headlines than walleyes do here, but the Chip's walleye fishery is as good as any in the state. Frank Pratt says the population is healthy, at over five adults per acre, but numbers are down somewhat, due to several years of poor reproduction caused by low water levels in spring. There are plenty of older fish, however, with some 20-year-old females reaching 31 inches. Pratt expects walleye numbers to increase when spawning conditions improve, based on the Chip's past history.

The Chip is exempt from the statewide 15-inch size limit on walleyes, but most anglers have no problem taking walleyes that big or bigger anyway. Spring action is best in the tributaries and near their mouths, as well as along gravel shorelines. Jigs and minnows account for most walleyes, but artificials can also be productive.

Come summer, most walleyes head for deep water. Offshore structure and river channels are good places to try backtrolling or drifting with a jig and leech or crawler. If you mark fish over deep structure, try teasing them with a leech on a slip bobber. Most big walleyes are taken in the fall along gravel shorelines and weed edges. Chief Lake and Tyner Lake, at the west end of the flowage, are good bets for fall 'eyes.

The same weather conditions that hamper walleye spawning efforts are a boon to bass, and Frank Pratt says both smallmouth and largemouth numbers have really taken off in the last few years. Smallmouths are more common in the eastern half of the flowage, while largemouths dominate in the western half. These are relatively young populations, but there should be plenty of big bass within five years or so. Try jigs and small crankbaits off the river mouths and rubble shorelines for bronzebacks. In the weedy bays, surface baits will take some nice largemouths and may draw action from muskies or northerns as well.

Guide Al Denninger with a 35-pound 10-ounce musky, the largest caught from the Chippewa Flowage in 1991. Photo by Al Denninger

38

Pratt reports that northerns are now the second-most abundant gamefish, at about three adults per acre. When they showed up a few years ago, biologists feared they might hurt the flowage's musky population, but their impact so far is negligible. Pike in the 25- to 30-inch range are common and are often taken in shallow, weedy areas on smaller musky baits and live minnows.

Of the panfish, crappies and bluegills are the current standouts. The Chip has long been noted for its incredible crappie fishing, which seems at its best in fall. Anglers took some 200,000 crappies here in 1990 and triple that number in '91. Try minnows or tiny swimming jigs, like the Slo-Poke Mini or Swimmin' Ratt, on a slip bobber near the floating bogs and off creek mouths and you should be able to fill a basket with 10- to 14-inch slabs. Since 1990, bluegills have become an important part of the fishery, thanks to stable spring weather during their spawning period. The bluegill harvest jumped from 30,000 in 1990 to 300,000 a year later. This population is still young and should provide good fishing for years to come.

Good public landings provide access to all portions of the flowage. On the west half, there are two off Highway CC, one on Crystal Lake at the north end and one on James Slough at the south end, and a private but free ramp at Pat's Landing Resort on the west shore of Chief Lake on Chief Lake Road. Near the center of the flowage, the public ramp next to Herman's Landing Resort and Campground on Highway CC has been moved a half mile south of the causeway to relieve traffic congestion there. Plans call for the construction of two handicapped-accessible fishing piers in this area by 1995. On the east half, there is a public ramp at the north end at Hay Creek with an expanded parking lot on Highway F and another at the Winter Dam.

Pat's Landing also has a bait shop and boat rental. Address: Route 5, Box 5377, Hayward, WI 54843, telephone (715) 945-2511. So does Herman's Landing: Route 9, Box 9344, Hayward, WI 54843, telephone (715) 462-3626. The flowage area's most complete bait and tackle shop and headquarters for guides is Jenk's Bait & Tackle on Highway B, 1/4 mile west of Highway CC, telephone (715) 462-3055. Most resorts and bait shops in the area can also book guides. To fish with Al Denninger, contact him from May through November at Indian Trail Resort, Route 1, Box 93, Couderay, WI 54828, telephone (715) 945-2665. Winter residence: 10251 W. Leon Terrace, Milwaukee, WI 53224, telephone (414) 353-5760.

For a brochure listing more resorts, campgrounds, tackle shops and other services, contact: Hayward Lakes Resort Association, P.O.Box 1055, Hayward, WI 54843, telephone (800) 826-FISH, or (715) 634-4801.

East Fork Chippewa River

Glidden, Ashland County to Chippewa Flowage, Sawyer County

Tell me you're looking for a northwoods river to float, one that wanders for many miles between road crossings through wild and uninhabited land, where you're as likely to see a bear or even a wolf around the next bend as some more commonplace critter, like a beaver or deer. A river not so fast that you have to spend all your time dodging boulders and running rapids, and one that's not so wide that you can't check out the far bank now and then as you work your way downstream. Come take a closer look at the East Fork of the Chippewa.

The Chippewa River proper begins below Winter Dam on the Chippewa Flowage, and from there downstream it's a pretty hefty chunk of water, but in its upper reaches, the East Fork of the Chippewa is manageable as a canoe river and not hard to take as a fishing stream either. The East Fork rises in Iron County just below the spine of the Penokees, once a towering mountain range and today a series of rugged ridges where played-out iron and copper mines have given way to ski hills in a region that remembers the last bust and waits patiently for the next boom.

**East Fork
Chippewa River**

Trace the state line on any road map southeast from Hurley and Ironwood until the rivers start running in both directions, then go west between the headwaters of those that flow to Lake Superior and those that drain south. This is the Continental Divide between watersheds that lead to the Atlantic on one slope and the Gulf of Mexico on the other. The streams that flow north from here feed the Great Lakes and eventually the St. Lawrence River, while those that flow south and west spend their nickel in the Mississippi. The Chippewa is one of the latter.

But don't dally too long here at the headwaters. Head on downstream into Ashland County and find Glidden on Highway 13. Drop your canoe in here or at one of 17 landings and bridge crossings spread out over the next 50 miles or so, and you can paddle and fish as the river courses through the Chequamegon National Forest. What is there to catch? Well, mostly muskies, walleyes, smallmouths and panfish, with a northern or two tossed in to keep you on your toes. River muskies are like nothing you've ever hooked before. They don't run big for muskies, but they use the current like a bass or trout, and anything three feet long is big when it's on your line and you're in a moving canoe.

DNR fish manager Dennis Scholl reports that muskies are stocked annually at several points along the river, but other species are self-sustaining. Surveys in the river and Bear Lake, one of several natural lakes the river flows through, revealed muskies up to 42 inches long, walleyes to 23 inches, smallmouths to 18 inches and crappies to 15 inches. Most fish were smaller, but these larger fish give some indication of the potential of this fishery, a potential that not many people take advantage of.

When fishing rivers for gamefish, the more attention you pay to seasonal movements the more successful you are likely to be. DNR surveys suggest that many muskies spend the winter and early spring in Bear Lake, then move into the river for summer and fall. Walleyes and smallmouths are known to migrate long distances in other rivers, so it is likely they do the same here.

The first 20 miles of river from Glidden to the National Forest Campground at Stock Farm Bridge are pretty easy going, but this is a long day's float without stopping to fish, so you may want to break it into two legs. The deepest holes and best cover occur between Glidden and Kenyon Road, a couple miles below Shanagolden. The rapids along this stretch are easy, but you may have to wade and drag your boat in some places during low water, and you may have to portage around fallen trees.

You'll find muskies wherever there is cover. Look for them in the shadow of logs, boulders and other instream obstructions, as well as in deeper holes and along grassy banks. Small jerk baits, bucktails and noisy topwater lures, such as Mudpuppies, spinner-baits and others that create a commotion, will draw strikes in shallow areas and near bank cover. Try crankbaits in the deeper holes and runs. River muskies are opportunists that will eat almost anything, regardless of size, so don't be surprised to catch one on a smaller bait. I took my best Chippewa River musky on a Shad Rap while casting for walleyes.

The late "Musky Pete" Peterson's favorite style of musky fishing was to drift down the Chippewa in a small boat, casting a bucktail or Mudpuppy with one rod and trailing a sucker on a bobber with the other. This tactic will work all year, but it is especially productive in fall. Pete's wife Shirley still operates Musky Pete's Tackle Shop on Highway 13 at the south end of Glidden.

You'll also take an occasional northern on musky baits, especially along eelgrass beds and in the wide-spread lakes. These pike make good eating and they have become more numerous in recent years. Keeping the pike you catch will help improve life for the river's muskies.

As a rule, walleyes hold in deep holes during the day. Drift a crawler or leech or bounce a jig and minnow along with the current, but stay in touch with the bottom. Concentrate on deep, shaded holes where the water slows down or swirls into eddies. Sometimes bumping bottom with crankbaits will trigger inactive walleyes to strike. Cast these quartering upstream and retrieve them slowly across and downstream, letting them bang into rocks and debris as they come. I have taken many a river walleye on Shad Raps and Rebel "R" Series baits fished this way.

Come evening, walleyes often move up onto shallow bars and into riffles to feed. In-line spinners can be deadly now. Cast a small Mepps quartering upstream and retrieve it just fast enough to keep your line taut and the blade flashing and ticking bottom as it comes, and you'll take walleyes in the riffles and behind sand bars. Floating Rapalas also work well in the shallower riffles. Some fly fishermen even take walleyes on big streamers, such as Muddler Minnows, Zonkers and fur leeches.

These same flies will take smallmouths, but most anglers use crankbaits, spinners and jigs. Look for bass in the faster water below rapids, among boulders and in riffle areas. Any place you have trouble negotiating in a canoe or johnboat is worth fishing for bronzebacks. I like to shoot a riffle or easy rapids, then beach my boat and work slowly back upstream, casting Rapalas, Mepps spinners or Beetle-Spins as I go. Bass hold right against cover, so lob your casts as close to logs and boulders as you can. Sometimes I'll cast a spinner right up onto shore or a rock, then twitch it to drop it gently into the water. This move often draws a strike.

As shadows grow long in late afternoon, bass move into the shallowest riffles, where you can sometimes see them herding schools of minnows against rocks and right up onto sand bars. Drop a No. 5 floating Rapala or a No. 0 Mepps into such spots and let your bait hang in the current for a moment. You shouldn't have to wait long for a hit.

Panfish are most abundant in the lakes, but some are found throughout the river. DNR surveys in Bear Lake revealed good numbers of perch up to 11 inches, although most were smaller, and a fair population of big crappies. Try small spinners, jigs and minnows along weed edges and in the deeper holes. Bear Lake covers some 200 acres but is only 9 feet deep, so fish should be easy to locate.

The river flows through three more lakes between the Sawyer County line and Winter Dam, all of which become very weedy in summer: Blaisdell (340 acres), Hunter (113 acres) and Barker (215 acres). The lakes offer decent fishing for the same species, but a difficult set of rapids between Blaisdell and Hunter (Snaptail Rapids) makes floating this stretch impossible in anything but a canoe, and even then you'll have to portage around a small dam to continue below the rapids.

It's wise to release big smallmouth bass in almost any water in the state, but especially in smaller bodies of water like the Chippewa River where angling could have a negative impact on quality fisheries. Photo by Dan Small

41

Wear waders in cool weather and an old pair of tennies in summer so you can wade and fish wherever you want along the way. A small anchor will hold you below rapids and riffles and let you fish them thoroughly. Polarized glasses will help you spot submerged rocks in the river's dark water.

There is a campground at Stock Farm Bridge, and primitive camping is allowed along the river in the Chequamegon National Forest. Maps are available at the District Ranger's Office, P.O. Box 126, Glidden, WI 54527, telephone (715) 264-2511.

For bait, tackle, guide service and fishing information, stop at Musky Pete's, P.O. Box 194, Glidden, WI 54527, telephone (715) 264-5225. For more information on area facilities, contact: Ashland Area Chamber of Commerce, P.O. Box 746, Ashland, WI 54806, telephone (800)-284-9484.

Upper And Lower Clam Lakes

Siren, Burnett County

Upper and Lower Clam Lakes

Get out your Wisconsin road map and follow the heavy red line of I-94 northwest from Madison to Eau Claire. Now swing north on Highway 53 -- don't worry, you're still on a four-lane -- past Rice Lake and on into Spooner. One thing you discover rather quickly up here in the Northwest is that all roads eventually lead to Spooner.

Now get off the four-lane and head west on Highway 70 through town, past the DNR District Headquarters on the right and the fish hatchery on the left. That's the largest muskellunge hatchery in the world, by the way. Go another 20 miles or so, pull off at the wayside and take a look around. You're at Clam Lake Narrows. That's Upper Clam Lake on the south side of the road, and Lower Clam Lake on the north. Right there in front of you, on the Lower Clam Lake side, is the best boat landing on either lake. You can get to Upper Clam by boat through the channel under the Highway 70 bridge. There's a tackle shop right across from the landing -- Big Mike's Outdoor Sports Shop. Ask Mike Henricksen how the fishing's been. He's fished these lakes for over 35 years and ought to

know.

Upper Clam Lake covers some 1,200 acres, while Lower Clam covers 340. Both are shallow and weedy -- you'd have a hard time finding a 10-foot hole in either of them. These are drainage lakes on the Clam River, a nifty stream that winds through Burnett County to the St. Croix. They'd both be shallower still if it weren't for a dam on the river a few bends downstream from the outlet of Lower Clam Lake. You can motor right to the dam in a 14-foot boat, and the inlet to Upper Clam is navigable as far as the first log jam, although boaters sometimes find the going tough for the first few hundred yards in either channel.

Impenetrable weeds would make both lakes virtually unnavigable in summer, but the Clam Lakes Protection District keeps two weedcutters going fulltime from June until October to control vegetation in the midsection of both lakes. One machine harvests weeds right to the lake bottom, creating weed edges that make good fishing structure, while the other chops them off just deep enough to clear boat props and let you get around.

These fertile lakes harbor excellent populations of largemouths, bluegills and northerns. The bluegills are not huge, but the bigger ones average a half-pound or so, and as district fisheries operations supervisor Stan Johannes puts it, "they have shoulders -- they're not skinny little things." Anglers take good catches of bluegills practically everywhere on both lakes on waxworms and other live bait.

While there is always a good supply of bluegills, crappie numbers rise and fall as they do on many lakes. Crappie action is best in early spring, when small minnows and jigs both produce fish. The trick for good success on crappies is to fish the river channel and midlake open-water areas near, but not in, the weedbeds. Anglers take both bluegills and crappies through the ice in good numbers. Look for the small city of ice shanties on Upper Clam for an idea of where the panfish action is hottest.

Largemouth bass turn on early in the season and remain active all summer long. Both lakes produce good bass, but newcomers may do better on Upper Clam because there is more open water. Both lakes yield bass up to eight pounds each summer -- try to catch a bigger one somewhere else in Wisconsin! Topwater baits seem to work best, because of all the weeds. Try a Moss Boss, Weed Walker or a spinnerbait. Henricksen says scented worms are especially productive, but you have to rig them weedless. Look for holes in the weedbeds and you'll find bass.

Highway 70 is the line separating the northern and southern bass zones, which creates a bit of a problem. Upper Clam lies in the southern zone, where bass season opens the first Saturday in May and bass have a 14-inch size limit. But Lower Clam lies in the northern zone, where catch-and-release fishing only is allowed until June 20 and the size limit is 12 inches. Fish manager Larry Damman says this glitch should soon be remedied, as he has recommended Lower Clam be included in the southern zone. Watch for this regulations change within a year or so.

Most pike taken in the summer months run on the small side, averaging two to three pounds. There are plenty of bigger ones, but they stay deep in the weeds where it's hard to get at them. Once the weeds start to die back in fall, you'll have better luck on larger pike. The best pike, running six to 10 pounds or so, are taken through the ice by anglers using shiners on tip-ups.

Anglers take channel cats up to 10 pounds right from shore on summer evenings, using a dead minnow fished on bottom. There are also plenty of cats and the occasional sturgeon in the deep holes above the dam on the outlet. Sturgeon season is open only in the fall and you must have a sturgeon tag (free at any DNR office) before you keep one, but you may keep catfish all year. The *Wild Harvest Cookbook* has a couple great catfish recipes, by the way, including one with pineapple sauce that is an unusual taste treat.

There are smallmouths in the river below Lower Clam and above Upper Clam. Work the deeper bend holes and instream cover with Mepps spinners. The smaller sizes with squirrel-tail dressing are deadly. Beetle Spins and dark crankbaits are also effective.

Mike Henricksen let me in on a local secret: there are some big walleyes in the lakes. He has two on his wall that weighed 11 pounds 8 ounces and 10 pounds 6 ounces. Not bad for a bass lake! The walleyes spawn on rock riprap near bridges. Try for them with a jig and minnow after dark at bridge holes, in deep water by the dam or on bottom in open water.

Henricksen also reports that many local anglers fish for suckers right after ice out from the bridges that cross the Clam River. This time of year, suckers have firm flesh and taste great smoked.

If you're up for a float-fishing canoe trip, the Clam River is worth a try in June, unless another drought comes along. On the upper river, you can put in at either the Malone Road or Lynch Road crossing and work your way down to the landing at the southeast end of Upper Clam. To fish the lower river, put in

below the dam at Clam Dam County Park and make the half-day float to Meenon County Park at Highway 35. You can camp at both parks.

From Highway 35, the river meanders another 20 miles to the St. Croix. Ice House Road is the halfway point and the only bridge crossing. It'll take all day to float and fish either half of this stretch, but the smallmouths will keep you occupied. Before it reaches the St. Croix, the river enters Clam Flowage, where largemouths, northerns and panfish again make up the fishery.

Fish Wisconsin author Dan Small hefts a nice largemouth from Upper Clam Lake. Try spinnerbaits in holes in weedbeds to take bass. Photo by Dan Small

You can get everything you'll need to fish the lakes or river at Big Mike's. Mike has the only on-water bait and tackle shop on the lakes with access by boat or car. When I spoke with Mike in March 1993, he was planning to add a boat and motor rental in the next year or two. Address: 6659 Highway 70 (at The Narrows), Siren, WI 54872, telephone (715) 349-2400.

There are a number of fine resorts on both lakes. For information on these and other area services, contact: Burnett County Resort & Campground Owners Association, 6420 Highway 70, Siren, WI 54872, or call their accommodations hotline number: (715) 349-2000.

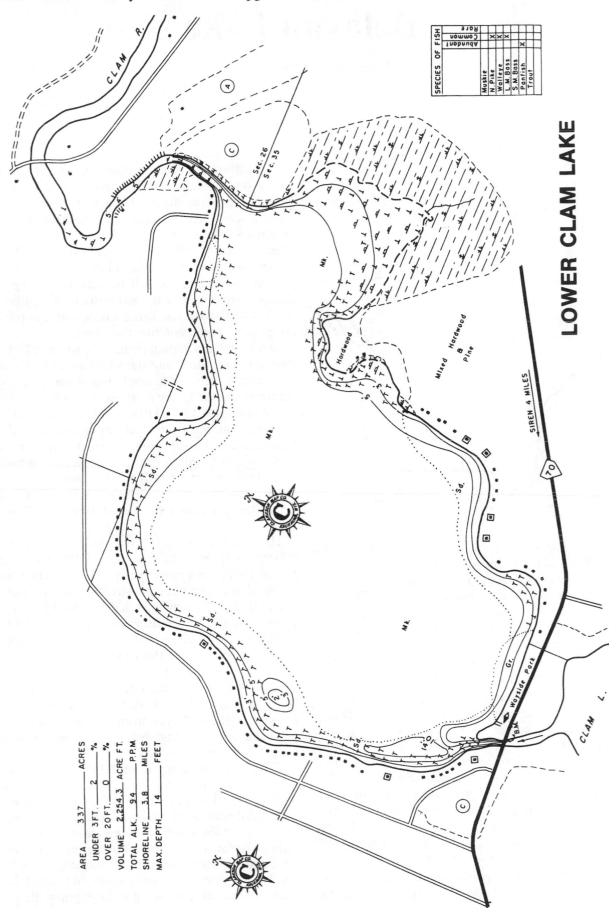

LOWER CLAM LAKE

SPECIES OF FISH	Abundant	Common	Rare
Muskie		X	
N. Pike		X	
Walleye		X	X
L. M. Bass		X	
S. M. Bass	X		
Panfish	X		X
Trout			

AREA	337	ACRES
UNDER 3 FT.	2	%
OVER 20 FT.	0	%
VOLUME	2,254.3	ACRE FT.
TOTAL ALK.	94	P.P.M.
SHORELINE	3.8	MILES
MAX. DEPTH	14	FEET

Delavan Lake

Delavan, Walworth County

Delavan Lake

I don't know if anyone submitted this one to the *Guinness Book Of World Records*, but somebody should. Walworth County is home to the largest lake reclamation project ever attempted. At 2,076 acres, Delavan Lake is the second-largest lake in the county. Until a couple years ago, it was also the stinkiest. Today, you'd be hard-pressed to find a cleaner lake, or one with a more diverse and exciting fishery, anywhere in southern Wisconsin.

Historically, Delavan Lake was clean and clear, with a gracious wooded shoreline that invited Native American encampments. The setting appealed to modern settlers as well, and today private homes, resorts and condos surround the lake. The influx of nutrients from all those lawns and septic systems fed a growing algae problem, and water clarity dropped. An abundant population of carp and bigmouth buffalo did the rest. By the mid 1980s, you couldn't see three feet down on a good day. Swimming was banned, and fishing was a waste of time.

Then, a number of public agencies and citizens' groups teamed up with the DNR to try to save the lake. By the late 1980s, the plan was ready for implementation. Gamefish were removed and relocated, then the lake was drawn down to remove as much water as possible. Area residents describe the scene as other-worldly, with mud flats and only puddles where there had been deep water before. DNR technicians then treated the remaining water with 50,000 gallons of rotenone to kill off any remaining fish, most of which were carp and buffalo. A fish barrier was constructed at the Turtle Creek outlet to prevent rough fish from re-entering the lake.

During the drawdown period, the town of Delavan dredged a section along the south shore and built a new boat launch at the north end of the lake. After the treatment the lake was allowed to refill itself, and in the spring of 1990, DNR crews began restocking the lake. During a two-year restoration period, the lake was closed to all fishing. DNR fisheries manager Doug Welch faced an exciting challenge: to build a sustainable fishery literally from scratch.

"To restore Delavan's fishery, we knew we had to get a strong predator base established first," Welch says.

He began by stocking two million walleye fry, 400,000 northern pike fry, and 100,000 true musky fry in 1990. That same year, crews stocked about 1,300 adult largemouth and smallmouth bass ranging from 11 to 15 inches in length. In 1991, crews planted another two million walleye fry and 17,860 musky fry. An additional 12,074 fingerling northerns were planted between 1990 and 1992.

The bass spawned the same spring they were stocked and have established a stable population. Northerns have also established themselves and are growing well. Walleyes from the first planting are abundant and growing, but those from the second year class have disappeared.

"They were probably eaten by everything else out there," Welch says. He plans to continue stocking walleyes until a second year class becomes established. All walleyes introduced here will be from the Pike Lake strain which are able to reproduce successfully in some southeastern Wisconsin lakes. In the past, algae blooms smothered walleye eggs on Delavan Lake before they could hatch, but Welch hopes to establish a self-sustaining walleye population here.

Panfish reintroduction began in 1991, with the planting of 70,800 three-inch bluegills, 95,564 three- to five-inch perch, and 6,270 five- to seven-inch crappies. Similar numbers of perch and bluegills were planted in 1992, and both species have really taken off.

Delavan Lake was reopened to fishing in 1992, with restrictive regulations to help the lake continue its transition. On bass the minimum size is 14 inches and the daily bag is five fish. Walleyes must measure 18 inches and only three may be kept. The daily limit on northerns is one fish over 32 inches, and on muskies, one fish over 40 inches. There is no size limit on panfish, but the daily bag is 25 fish.

Anglers who flocked to Delavan Lake in 1992 to sample its reborn fishery were far from disappointed. Limits of panfish were common all summer and into the winter as well, with perch and bluegills running to 10 inches or better. Every point and dropoff yielded sublegal walleyes, and by fall, a few legal-sized northerns were showing up. Good numbers of both species should reach legal size some time in 1993, but most Delavan anglers are so tickled over their "new" lake they're planning to throw back every gamefish for another year or two.

Catching and releasing 50 bass in an afternoon is a piece of cake. Don Frost, who lives on Delavan and loves to fly fish for bass, told me he has a ball working the weeds and piers with poppers and bass bugs. Tom Newbauer taped an *Outdoor Wisconsin* segment on Delavan Lake last summer and caught so many bass videographer John McKay had to tell him to quit fishing!

Doug Welch is pleased with the lake's progress, but there's more work to be done. "It's still a new fishery working toward a balance," he says. In addition to working toward a self-sustaining walleye population, Welch is concerned about Delavan's muskies. "We caught only one musky in our first two years of surveys, so I'll be looking for them in 1993 and '94."

Now that it's once again full of water, Delavan Lake has a maximum depth of 56 feet and an average depth of 25 feet. In June, 1992, the water was so clear that DNR crews took Secchi disk readings at depths of 28 feet. For now at least, algae blooms are a thing of the past. A summer thermocline develops, with low oxygen levels at depths of 30 feet or more. The bottom is mostly muck, gravel and sand, and there are extensive areas of rock, riprap and gravel along the shoreline. Many shoreline areas and bays support good coontail and elodea weedbeds and there are areas of bulrushes as well.

Look for walleyes along steep shoreline dropoffs, such as those along the southeast and northwest shores. You'll also find walleyes on the rocky humps off the large point known as The Island at the southwest end of the lake and on the bar off Browns Channel inlet on the southwest shore. Jigs and minnows should produce, as should crankbaits trolled along the breakline.

You'll find smallmouths in some of the same areas frequented by walleyes, and anywhere there is shoreline riprap with adequate depth to hold fish. Small artificials will take them.

Look for largemouths in the shallow bays, along weed edges and under piers. They'll slam topwater baits all day long, but to get bigger fish you may need to go deeper with soft plastics and diving crankbaits. The Jackson Creek inlet and Turtle Creek outlet hold lots of bass and northerns in spring. Try spinnerbaits and weedless spoons for both species.

Bluegills are everywhere, but in spring you'll find them in the shallow flats, while in summer they favor the south shore's riprap. You'll find perch along the shallow rock bar on the north side of the outlet bay mouth in spring, and over the rocky flat just east of the outlet bay all summer. Crappies favor bulrushes and deep shoreline areas in spring and deep weed edges in summer.

Sue Pfeiffer pulls a dandy hybrid bluegill through the ice of Delavan Lake. Photo by Dan Small

Ice fishermen did well on panfish and northerns in the winter of 1992-93, especially in the bays at the lake's southwest and northeast ends.

The new town of Delavan landing on South Shore Drive just off Highway 50 at the lake's northeast end has a four-lane concrete ramp, loading piers, a large gravel parking lot, picnic area, swimming beach, restrooms and shore fishing sites. There is another smaller public launch site with limited parking on the south shore off Bluegill Lane, and a private ramp at American Marina on the south shore. There is another public shore fishing site on North Shore Drive off Highway 50 at the Turtle Creek outlet.

Bait, tackle and boat rentals are available at Sportsman's Park, located an the inlet on Highway 50, telephone (414) 728-6037. Brahm's Service Station in Delavan also sells bait, telephone (414) 728-3660. Geneva Lake Bait & Tackle, at the intersection of Highways 50 and 67, offers boat rentals and guide service, in addition to bait and tackle, telephone (414) 245-6150.

For information on resorts and other area facilities, contact the Delavan Chamber of Commerce, 52 E. Walworth Avenue, Delavan, WI 53115, telephone (414) 728-5095.

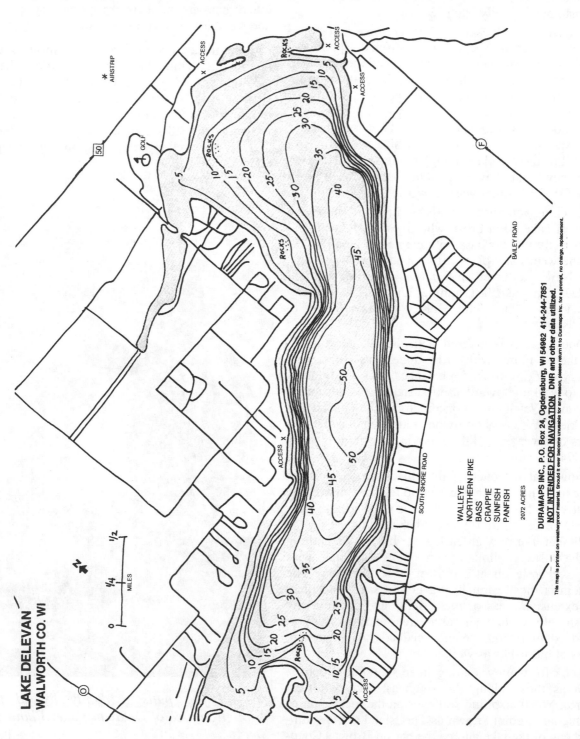

LAKE DELEVAN
WALWORTH CO. WI

WALLEYE
NORTHERN PIKE
BASS
CRAPPIE
SUNFISH
PANFISH

2072 ACRES

DURAMAPS INC., P.O. Box 24, Ogdensburg, WI 54962 414-244-7851
NOT INTENDED FOR NAVIGATION DNR and other data utilized.

Lake DuBay

Marathon/Portage Counties

Lake DuBay

Lake DuBay guide Pat Pierce has done what most entrepreneurs would love to accomplish -- he has developed a business that serves an untapped clientele while keeping his regular customers happy at the same time. All it took was a positive attitude and the purchase of a new piece of equipment. The attitude part comes naturally to Pierce, whose knowledge of this sprawling Wisconsin River flowage and its tremendous fishery are unmatched. The equipment part wasn't hard, either. In the market for a new guide boat several years back, Pierce decided against a sleek, over-powered model that cruises at freeway speeds with trolling motors fore and aft, aerated livewells and all the other trappings that have most anglers salivating, and opted instead for a pontoon boat. That's right, one of those flat-decked party barges you often see chugging along on calm evenings, hauling a resort full of revelers for a look-see at the water.

But Pierce's clients don't party, they catch fish -- lots of them. Pierce's new clientele are disabled folks -- many of them wheelchair-bound -- who have a dif-ficult time getting in and out of conventional fishing boats, let alone fishing from them. The pontoon boat will handle up to four wheelchairs, which can be fastened to the side rails or move freely about the 24x8-foot deck. Pierce added extra-wide side gates to accommodate motorized chairs, and he carries a cellular phone to keep in touch with onshore services.

"The whole point of fishing is to have a good time," Pierce says. "So I aim to keep my customers comfortable and see that they catch fish."

Pierce's disabled clients often come with family members and friends who fish with them or just enjoy the day on the water. And, of course, Pierce also caters to able-bodied anglers as well. His pontoon boat provides the comfort of charter-boat fishing for small groups, yet allows Pierce to devote the personal attention fishing clients expect from a guide.

"Going to that pontoon boat was the greatest thing I ever did," says Pierce. "Families and corporate groups love it because they can all fish out of one boat. It's not only safer and drier in rough water than a conventional boat, it's also easier to control when backtrolling and following a break or contour, and the wind doesn't affect it as much on a drift. You just have to plan well ahead of time when making a turn, just as an airline pilot does."

This season Pierce is adding another boat with larger, more stable pontoons to his fleet, in order to accommodate larger groups. His wife, Leone, will captain the second boat.

Just how successful have his clients been? Well, in the past five years, they have boated 24,994 walleyes, 1,826 northerns and 110 muskies, along with literally tons of smallmouths, largemouths and panfish. Highlights from his 1992 season included 19 walleyes over 10 pounds (and that doesn't count two that might have threatened the state record that clients lost at the boat), 13 northerns over 20 pounds, and 11 muskies topping 20 pounds. To the credit of Pierce and his clients, most of those fish are released. Pierce's phenomenal catch record reveals the potential of this fertile flowage that awaits anglers ready to explore its many bays, shoals and channels.

Lake DuBay was named for John Baptiste DuBay, an early settler who ran a trading post on the Wisconsin River here. The site of DuBay's trading post, along with a lot more central Wisconsin real estate, was covered with water in 1942 when a Consolidated Water Power Company dam on the Wisconsin River about 10 miles north of Stevens Point created this 6,830-acre flowage. Other tributaries include Johnson Creek and the Big Eau Pleine, Little Eau Pleine and Little Eau Claire rivers.

Lake DuBay has a maximum depth of 47 feet in the river channel just above the DuBay Dam, but much of the flowage ranges from five to 10 feet deep. There are areas of rubble, gravel and muck, but the bottom is predominantly sand, which shifts considerably during high-water periods. Pat Pierce counted 35 major changes in bottom structure when the power company drew down the lake one recent winter.

Stumps, snags and flooded timber line the shore and shallow bays in many places, especially above the Highway 34 bridge crossing. The sparse vegetation is limited to bays and backwaters. Like that of most flowages, DuBay's water is stained brown, limiting visibility but affording good fishing during daylight hours.

For those who like to take home a few fillets, DuBay's fish are safe to eat and taste good, too. The lake's numerous tributaries flush out contaminants from the sandy bottom, and there are currently no PCB or mercury advisories on fish here.

The DNR has not surveyed DuBay since 1983, but fisheries manager Al Hauber reports that the fishery appears to be holding up well. Natural reproduction sustains an abundant walleye population and growth rates are exceptional. Hauber cites angler-caught walleyes up to 29 inches, northerns to 45 inches, smallmouths to 21 inches and muskies to 40 pounds and better. Panfish here are also abundant and big. Crappies in the 14- to 15-inch range are common, as are 10-inch bluegills and perch.

Local musky clubs planted some hybrid muskies in the late 1980s, but the DNR doesn't stock any and has no plans to manage the flowage for muskies. True muskies are native to the Wisconsin River system, and they grow fast in DuBay. Pat Pierce says Dubay's muskies are heavy for their length, with 40-inchers easily topping 20 pounds. Pierce attributes the apparent increase in their numbers to low fishing pressure aimed at them.

DuBay is one of the few lakes in Wisconsin capable of producing trophy northern pike, so DNR management efforts are geared to this species. When Consolidated Water Power Company's dam license came up for renewal a few years ago, the DNR got the company to voluntarily manage spring water levels to favor northern pike spawning.

There is a lot of good structure here, but it is scattered throughout the lake, so it pays to keep moving to find fish. Walleyes especially roam from one stump field or rock pile to another, and you have to intersect them. Pat Pierce says some walleyes run up

the rivers just after ice-out to spawn, while others remain in the lake and spawn later. In early spring, he fishes the deep edges of river channels for pre-spawn lake walleyes. When the river walleyes have finished spawning, he targets them in the flats and wood found in the inlet arms.

In summer, the only time Pierce works deeper water is when lightning storms that precede a cold front chase walleyes into the deeper channels, otherwise he concentrates on the major flats and back bays in the lower portion of the lake, staying in water that is six feet deep or less.

"July and August are top months for walleyes here," says Pierce, who likes to backtroll or cast with a jig and minnow. "Emerald shiners, the most common forage species here, spawn in shallower water in summer, so the walleyes simply follow them in to feed, making fishing for them pretty easy."

Fishing guide Pat Pierce (right) and a happy client show off a whopper walleye from Lake DuBay. Photo courtesy Pat Pierce

Most of the northerns Pierce and his clients catch (and for that matter, many other species as well) come while fishing for walleyes using these same methods, but to target muskies he switches to conventional musky tackle. He likes bright lures -- large, noisy bucktails and shallow-running crankbaits. In spring, he throws these baits in the inlets and bays. In summer, Pierce trolls the river channels and flats in the lake's large, south basin, where the larger muskies roam in search of baitfish, especially schools of carp. Topwater baits don't do much during the day, but often produce fish on calm summer nights.

Pierce sticks with bright bucktails and crankbaits in fall, but now fishes flooded timber, inlets and the many cuts around Big Island at the lake's north end. Jerk baits and live bait are a waste of time here, he says.

Pierce takes most of his largemouths using walleye tactics in congested stump fields, but says his neighbor does well on largemouths using plastic worms and spinnerbaits. When after smallmouths, Pierce casts or jigs vertically over small, isolated rock piles, many of which don't appear on any maps.

"Some of these rock piles are as small as a couple picnic tables," Pierce says. "But in May and June, smallies spawn on visible shoreline riprap, making them easier to find then."

For crappies in spring, Pierce works very shallow bays and shoreline pockets. In summer, he takes big crappies in the bays and flats on quarter-ounce jigs and small minnows. To target post-spawn bluegills, he drifts slowly through bays at the eight- to 12-foot depth with ice-fishing jigs and maggots below slip bobbers.

Pierce has seen an increase in 10- to 13-inch perch over the last four years, but he releases most of those he catches, hoping the population will keep growing. In summer, they hang out over wooded humps in the river channels.

DuBay offers a great ice fishery as well. Walleyes bite during daylight hours in the river channels, the back bays east of Highway DB and near the county park at the south end off Highway E. Jigging produces more walleyes than tip-ups, and night fishing is a waste of time.

The back bays and inlet mouths produce good catches of big crappies and bluegills in winter. Pierce favors small jigging spoons for crappies and teardrops for the 'gills. Fish move to deeper water when the power company draws down the lake in February. Be careful in winter, as the river channel may be ice-covered one day and open the next.

There are public landings at the DuBay Dam and the Big Eau Pleine Dam, as well as several on Highway DB, one on Highway E and one off Highway 34. Eleven in all serve the lake, so take your pick.

To book a trip with Pat Pierce's Lake DuBay Guide Service, contact him at 2330 Lakeshore Drive, Mosinee, WI 54455, telephone (800) 348-1434.

You'll find plenty of accommodations to choose from in Mosinee, Stevens Point or Wausau. DuBay County Park on Highway E at the southwest end of the lake offers 24 campsites and a boat landing. Lake DuBay Shores Campground, 1713 DuBay Drive, Mosinee, WI 54455, located just south of the Highway 34 bridge, has 220 sites with electricity and water. Telephone: (715) 457-2484.

Eagle River Chain Of Lakes (Lower Chain)

Eagle River, Vilas County

Eagle River Chain of Lakes

It is a warm Sunday morning in August on Catfish Lake. A screen door slams and boom-box rock blares out across the bay, as three teenagers in bright, form-fitting life jackets tote water skis and a tow rope down to the dock. Moments before, only the drone of two lawnmowers broke the stillness, but heavy metal conquers all. Standing in the stern, George Langley nudges his trolling motor with one foot to keep us moving parallel to shore as we parade slowly past a motley assortment of rock gardens, piers and boathouses, where summer residents sort gear, clean up after last night's pontoon boat party, or set up lawn chairs to read the *Trib* or *Journal* in the morning sun.

"I've taken a lot of nice muskies right out from under this sort of man-made cover," says Langley, as he lobs a bucktail into the open door of a vacant boathouse. Docksiders wave. We wave back and swing out to skirt a swimming raft, then resume our course past piers, pontoons and people. "They always enjoy the show when somebody hooks one right in front of their place," he continues, "and I guess I get a kick out of catching a big musky right under their noses."

But the muskies haven't read the script this morning, and as speedboat wakes rock us more frequently with the approach of noon, we move. Lily pads carpet most of this quiet bay on Voyageur Lake, but out near the mouth there are pockets of open water wide enough to work a surface bait. In one of them, a fin emerges in the middle of a large ring.

"There's an active fish," George says, pointing to the ring I've been staring at without understanding what I was seeing. "Throw your bait over there."

I obey and crank three times to retrieve my black Hi-Fin Creeper, when the surface boils and a toothy mouth gapes in apparent slow motion behind the lure. With a reaction time that would impress any drivers license examiner, I yank the lure away from the fish just before its jaws clamp down.

"Throw it back there," George shouts, as he casts where the receding ripple marks the near-miss. The musky surfaces again, 20 yards away, and we both cast and retrieve furiously to cover the entire open pocket while this fish is still here. Then, without any warning wake at all, the musky inhales Langley's bait and the fight is on.

Five minutes later, some 15 pounds of green and gold fury lie in the net, gills pumping, reddened fins split from the struggle. A roving eye looks to be searching for something soft and vulnerable for those nasty jaws to clamp onto, but the fish is soon freed from the hook and swims slowly away.

"Don't feel bad," Langley explains, as he checks the hooks on his Cisco Kid Topper. "That's a common mistake with a surface bait. You've got to wait for them to take it. A lot of bass and trout fishermen pull a bait away before a musky has it because they react too quickly to the surface boil. Ironically, it's often the people who've never held a rod who hook muskies on topwater baits."

Hey, I didn't mind. I thanked George and that fish for a well-taught lesson. Besides, I was having a ball, lawnmowers, rock music and all.

Catfish and Voyageur are two of 11 lakes on the Lower Eagle River Chain in southern Vilas County. You can navigate through the entire Lower Chain and the 17 lakes of the Upper Chain a few miles upstream near the city of Three Lakes in Oneida County.

A hydro dam on the Wisconsin River a half mile west of the city of Eagle River forms the Lower Chain. The lakes are relatively shallow, with the deepest holes around 30 feet. The water is stained dark and very fertile. There are a few scattered rock and gravel bars and pronounced shallow shoreline weedbeds on all the lakes, but no deep weed flats to speak of. Although this is an older flowage, there is still plenty of wood along the shore in many areas, supplemented by many large cribs scattered throughout the chain by the Eagle River Guides Association. Both make good cover for crappies, walleyes, smallmouths and muskies.

DNR fish manager Harland Carlson reports that walleyes and muskies are in good supply throughout the chain. When we spoke in February 1993, he was planning a spring walleye population estimate, followed by a creel census scheduled to run through the winter of 1994. Walleyes reproduce naturally and are not stocked, but muskies are stocked annually. The chain also harbors a fair number of largemouth and smallmouth bass, loads of big crappies, and a decent perch population, although these are sometimes hard to locate.

Summer boat traffic is as intense here as anywhere in northern Wisconsin, making daytime fishing difficult during the peak vacation period. Many serious anglers have resorted to fishing early in the morning or after dark with surprisingly good results on all species. George Langley, who runs Eagle Sports in downtown Eagle River, fishes the chain extensively year-round. He and his clients boated 50 legal muskies on the chain in 1992, many of them during "off-peak" hours. In summer, he says, when most fishing and boating pressure occurs, all fish species concentrate on the shoreline weedbeds, so anglers should do the same.

"Eurasian milfoil, which grows all the way to the surface, is gradually replacing native cabbage, which remains submerged," Langley told me. "That means we have to fish along weed edges now, rather than over the tops of weedbeds, as we were accustomed to doing."

Cranberry and Catfish, the two uppermost lakes on the Lower Chain, offer good walleye and perch fishing and excellent musky action throughout the season. In addition to casting the shorelines with bucktails and topwater baits, musky anglers would do well to try crankbaits in the few deep holes on Cranberry. Both lakes hold good numbers of big crappies. The flats behind the big island on Cranberry produce good hauls of crappies on small minnows in May and June.

Voyageur, the next lake downstream, is just a widening of the Eagle River. It is always worth stopping here on your way up or down to throw a topwater bait near the dense weedbeds for muskies, as Langley proved to me that August morning.

"Ranger" Rick Krueger (left) and Bob Craft with a nice musky taken from the Eagle River Chain in October. The musky was later released. Photo by Dan Small

Eagle, the deepest lake on the Lower Chain, is the best bet for big walleyes and muskies, according to Langley. He and a client boated a 48-incher there in the fall of 1989, and they saw a bigger fish. Spring walleye fishing with 1/8-ounce jigs or slip bobbers and fathead minnows can be hot in new weedbeds here. Once the weeds are up, try the 10- to 15-foot breaklines along the south and west shores for muskies and walleyes, and a rock bar just west of the river outlet for walleyes and smallmouths.

Another good spring walleye spot is the narrows between Eagle and Scattering Rice Lake. On Scattering Rice, the weedbeds around the island and along the north shore are good spots to try for spring muskies.

Most anglers bypass Yellow Birch Lake on their way upstream or down, but Langley says it's a sleeper for summer muskies at night. Yellow Birch also produces some nice catches of crappies in spring and good walleyes through the ice. One recent winter, a newcomer to the area filled a bucket with 10-inch perch while ice fishing on Yellow Birch. He had no idea how deep he was fishing, and when asked how he found them, he simply said: "I just went out there and drilled a hole." Good advice. Hard to catch 'em watching the Super Bowl.

Another sleeper is Watersmeet Lake, the lowest on the chain. The fact that you have to putt-putt down the river through a mile-long no-wake zone to get there from the upper lakes ought to indicate this lake is not fished as heavily as the others. Langley caught a 35-pound musky here a few years ago. "Go ahead and name the lake," he told me. "Nobody believes that's where I caught it anyway." That's the price you pay when the whole world suspects you and your buddies of using code names for lakes half the time. Watersmeet is the best northern pike lake on the chain, with most of its chunky pike coming through the ice on tip-ups.

There is a definable edge in Watersmeet where the darker, clearer water of the Wisconsin River merges with the greener, murkier water of the Eagle River. This current break produces some fantastic musky action, especially in fall. When the dam is open, as it is sometimes in fall, the river channel in Watersmeet Lake and in the Eagle River in town produces good fishing for walleyes and muskies. Apparently the increased current flow pulls everything in the food chain, from micro-organisms, minnows and panfish, on up to gamefish, into the channel, creating a smorgasbord for big predator fish.

There are good boat landings on the east side of the river at the mouth of Yellow Birch Lake, one on the north shore of Eagle Lake off Chain-O-Lakes Road, next to Boat S'Port Marina just west of the Highway 70 bridge across the Catfish Lake narrows, on the west bay of Catfish off Highway 45, and on the south shore of Cranberry off Meta Lake Road.

For bait, tackle, supplies and to book one of the 20 guides in the Eagle River Guides Association, contact: Eagle Sports, 702 Wall Street, P.O. Box 367, Eagle River, WI 54521, telephone (715) 479-8804.

For information on the many resorts, campgrounds, restaurants and other family vacation services on the Lower Chain, contact: Eagle River Information Bureau, P.O. Box 218, Eagle River, WI 54521, telephone (800) 359-6315.

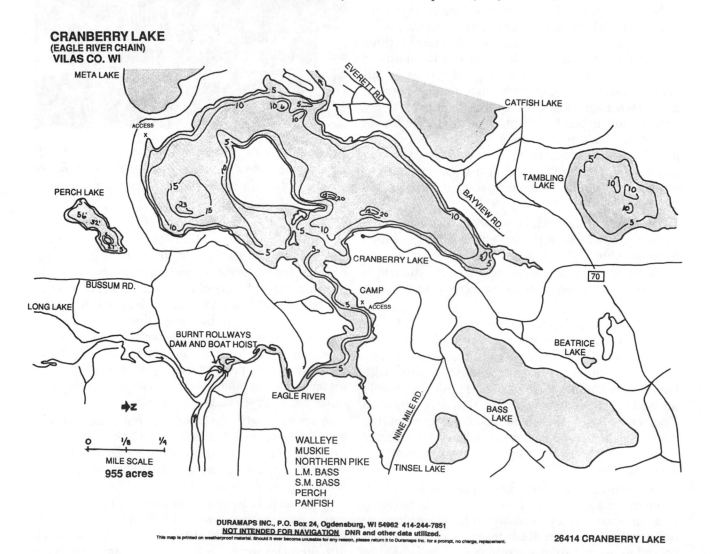

CRANBERRY LAKE
(EAGLE RIVER CHAIN)
VILAS CO. WI

META LAKE

EVERETT RD.

CATFISH LAKE

ACCESS

TAMBLING LAKE

PERCH LAKE

BAYVIEW RD.

CRANBERRY LAKE

70

BUSSUM RD.

CAMP
ACCESS

LONG LAKE

BEATRICE LAKE

BURNT ROLLWAYS
DAM AND BOAT HOIST

EAGLE RIVER

N

NINE MILE RD.

BASS LAKE

0   ⅛   ¼

MILE SCALE
955 acres

WALLEYE
MUSKIE
NORTHERN PIKE
L.M. BASS
S.M. BASS
PERCH
PANFISH

TINSEL LAKE

DURAMAPS INC., P.O. Box 24, Ogdensburg, WI 54962 414-244-7851
NOT INTENDED FOR NAVIGATION DNR and other data utilized.
This map is printed on weatherproof material. Should it ever become unusable for any reason, please return it to Duramaps Inc. for a prompt, no charge, replacement.

26414 CRANBERRY LAKE

54

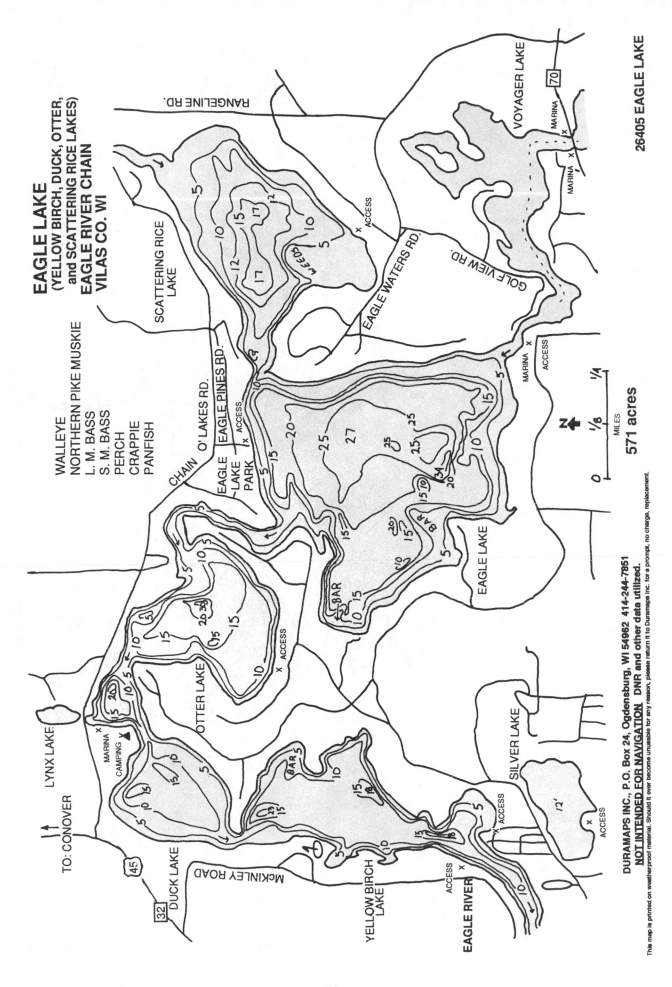

EAGLE LAKE
(YELLOW BIRCH, DUCK, OTTER, and SCATTERING RICE LAKES)
EAGLE RIVER CHAIN
VILAS CO. WI

WALLEYE
NORTHERN PIKE MUSKIE
L. M. BASS
S. M. BASS
PERCH
CRAPPIE
PANFISH

Scattering Rice Lake

Chain O' Lakes Rd.
Eagle Pines Rd.
Eagle Lake Park

Eagle Waters Rd.

Golf View Rd.

Voyager Lake

MARINA

26405 EAGLE LAKE

571 acres

N

0 1/8 1/4
MILES

Eagle Lake

Silver Lake

Otter Lake

Lynx Lake
TO: CONOVER

Duck Lake

McKINLEY ROAD

Yellow Birch Lake

EAGLE RIVER

Eagle River

RANGELINE RD.

DURAMAPS INC., P.O. Box 24, Ogdensburg, WI 54962 414-244-7851
NOT INTENDED FOR NAVIGATION   DNR and other data utilized.

This map is printed on weatherproof material. Should it ever become unusable for any reason, please return it to Duramaps Inc. for a prompt, no charge, replacement.

55

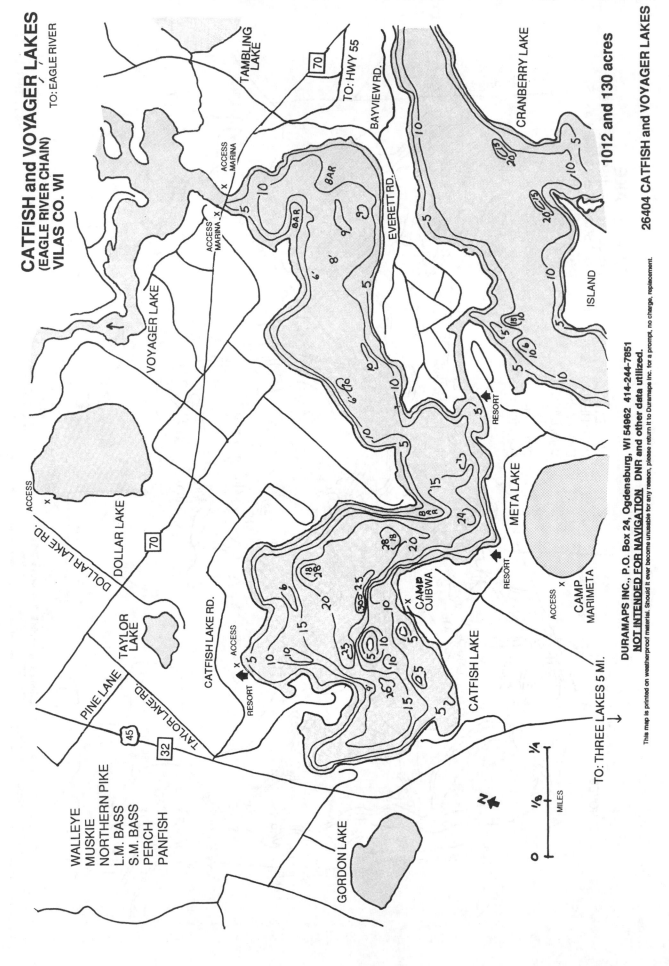

CATFISH and VOYAGER LAKES
(EAGLE RIVER CHAIN)
VILAS CO. WI

TO: EAGLE RIVER

WALLEYE
MUSKIE
NORTHERN PIKE
L.M. BASS
S.M. BASS
PERCH
PANFISH

VOYAGER LAKE

DOLLAR LAKE

DOLLAR LAKE RD.

ACCESS x

70

TAYLOR LAKE

PINE LANE

45

32

TAYLOR LAKE RD.

CATFISH LAKE RD.

RESORT ◄ x ACCESS

CAMP OJIBWA x

CATFISH LAKE

RESORT ◄

ACCESS x

CAMP MARIMETA

META LAKE

TO: THREE LAKES 5 MI. →

GORDON LAKE

TAMBLING LAKE

ACCESS MARINA x

ACCESS MARINA x

70

BAR

BAR

BAR

EVERETT RD.

BAYVIEW RD.

TO: HWY 55

70

RESORT ◄

ISLAND

CRANBERRY LAKE

N ↑

0   1/8   1/4
MILES

TO: THREE LAKES 5 MI. →

DURAMAPS INC., P.O. Box 24, Ogdensburg, WI 54962 414-244-7851
NOT INTENDED FOR NAVIGATION   DNR and other data utilized.

This map is printed on weatherproof material. Should it ever become unusable for any reason, please return it to Duramaps Inc. for a prompt, no charge, replacement.

1012 and 130 acres

26404 CATFISH and VOYAGER LAKES

Eau Claire Chain Of Lakes

Southwestern Bayfield County

Eau Claire Lakes

Many of us dream of building a hideaway cabin on that perfect lake somewhere, far from our everyday concerns, a place hard enough to get to so that when we do go, we will stay awhile, and one where the air is clean, the water clear, and the fish eagerly receptive to our offerings. Gordon MacQuarrie made his dream a reality on Middle Eau Claire Lake with a split-log cabin that he built back in the early 1930s.

MacQuarrie, managing editor of the Superior Evening Telegram and later outdoor editor for the Milwaukee Journal, was a feisty redhead who played as hard as he worked. No matter where his newspaper duties took him, his heart always brought him back to the cabin and his favorite playground, the Eau Claire Lakes region of Bayfield County. MacQuarrie paid all of $142 for the load of cedar logs he used to build that cabin, but for years it was his headquarters and jumping-off point for many a hunting and fishing adventure.

A few years ago, I made a sort of pilgrimage to the old place. The cabin has changed hands several times since MacQuarrie's death in 1956, but it stands today

as a monument to the poet laureate of Wisconsin's northwoods. Sitting before the massive stone fireplace built by Mac's friend Hank Koehler, it is easy to imagine MacQuarrie and hizzoner, "Mr. President," plotting their next sortie in quest of spring steelhead on the nearby Brule River, November bluebills on a secluded pothole, or midsummer muskies on the Eau Claire Lakes themselves.

Today there are many more private cabins, several resorts and two campgrounds, but the lakes remain largely unchanged since MacQuarrie's day. The Eau Claire Chain consists of 11 interconnected lakes that cover a total area of some 3,200 acres. The lakes are all spring fed and most have extremely clear water. The largest, Upper Eau Claire, covers 1,030 acres and has a maximum depth of 90 feet. Middle Eau Claire is next in size, at 900 acres and 66 feet, followed by Lower Eau Claire, at 800 acres and 42 feet.

These lakes have sand and gravel bottoms and abundant rocky shoals, as do Bony Lake (200 acres and 52 feet) and Robinson Lake (90 acres and 36 feet), two of the smaller lakes on the chain with good fishing. There are navigable channels connecting Upper Eau Claire with Birch and Robinson lakes to the west and Smith, Schunenberg and Sweet lakes to the north. The Eau Claire River outlet from Upper to Middle Eau Claire Lake is too rocky and steep to navigate in a motor boat. A navigable outlet connects Bony Lake to Middle Eau Claire Lake, and there is a roller dam and small-boat lock on the Eau Claire River between Middle and Lower Eau Claire lakes.

The upper lakes (Upper Eau Claire, Sweet, Schunenberg, Smith and Bony) are hard-water lakes, with scant vegetation and fewer, but larger, fish. Middle and Lower Eau Claire are soft-water lakes, with more weeds and larger fish populations. Summer thermoclines develop in all the lakes, restricting fish activity to the upper 25 feet or so.

DNR fish manager Dennis Scholl reports good walleye reproduction in all the lakes. Walleye fingerlings are stocked in Upper (50,000) and Middle Eau Claire (23,500) annually, but at present none are stocked in the other lakes. A cooperative rearing program with the Eau Claire Lakes Conservation Club and another with the Lake Superior Chippewa tribes adds thousands more walleye fingerlings to the chain each year. In addition, musky fingerlings are stocked in Upper, Middle and Lower in alternate years. As of this writing, all three lakes were scheduled for comprehensive population surveys in the spring of 1993.

Walleye fishing on the chain has improved considerably in recent years, according to Jim Nieckula, owner of Jim's Bait and Sport Shop on Highway 27 between Bony and Middle Eau Claire. Upper Eau Claire produces consistently bigger walleyes than the other lakes. Spring walleye action is good along gravel shorelines and over the shallower reefs, such as those at the north end of Middle Eau Claire, where jigs and minnows will take them. In summer, walleyes hug bottom in deeper shoal areas, where slip-sinker fishing with leeches and crawlers can be effective.

Nieckula has designed a slip sinker that really hugs bottom and works well on the steep dropoffs here. Called "Let-M-Run," this sinker comes in a variety of sizes and has a design that puts most of its weight right on bottom, with a narrow keel that resists planing in current or when trolled or drifted. Its small eyelet opening resists snagging and is chamfered to allow the line to slip through it smoothly. It is effective in weeds and in river current as well. Nieckula and his clients have taken good catches of large walleyes in summer with his rig.

In fall, Nieckula takes walleyes in very deep water (down to 60 feet at times) with his Let-M-Run sinker or in shallow water, where Rapalas and other crankbaits work well.

The Eau Claire Lakes have produced some big

Guide Bruce Shumway (left) and Steve Gearhardt release a heavy 46-inch musky to the Eau Claire Chain. It was taken on a Fuzzy Duzzit. Photo courtesy Bruce Shumway

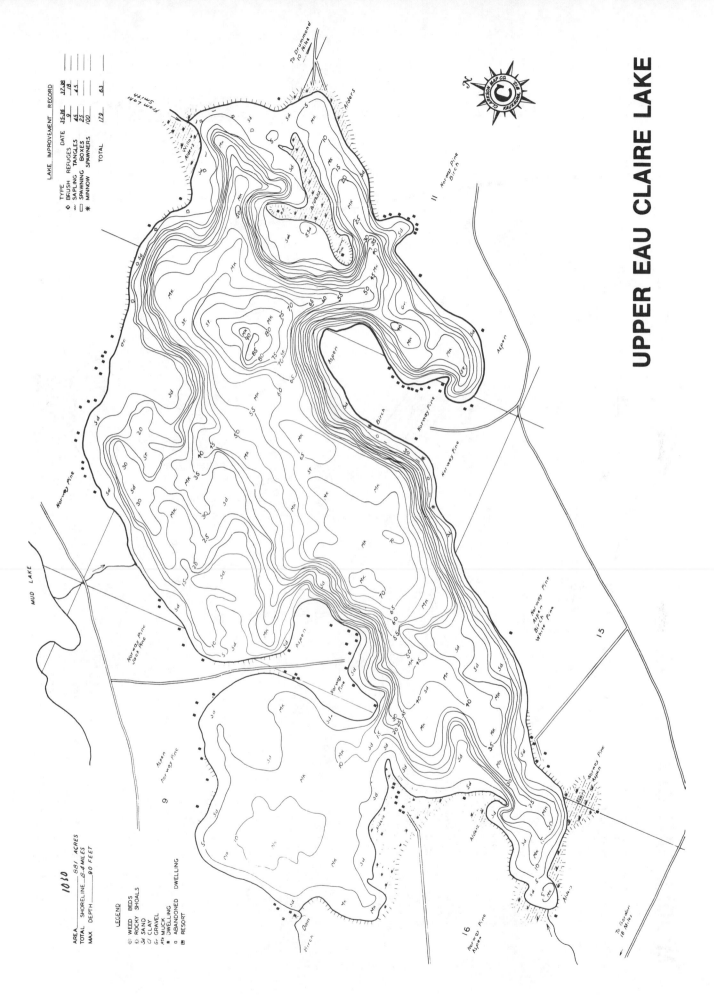

UPPER EAU CLAIRE LAKE

1080

AREA _____ 881 ACRES
TOTAL SHORELINE __ 8.4 MILES
MAX DEPTH _____ 90 FEET

LEGEND

Wb WEED BEDS
Ry ROCKY SHOALS
Sd SAND
Cl CLAY
Gr GRAVEL
Mk MUCK
□ ABANDONED DWELLING
◼ DWELLING
◼ RESORT

LAKE IMPROVEMENT RECORD

TYPE		DATE	35-36	37-38
◇ BRUSH REFUGES			9	18
∿ SAPLING TANGLES			45	45
▭ SPAWNING BOXES			25	
✳ MINNOW SPAWNERS			100	
	TOTAL		179	63

MUD LAKE

To Drummond 10 Miles

From Lake Smith

To Gordon 18 Miles

11

15

16

9

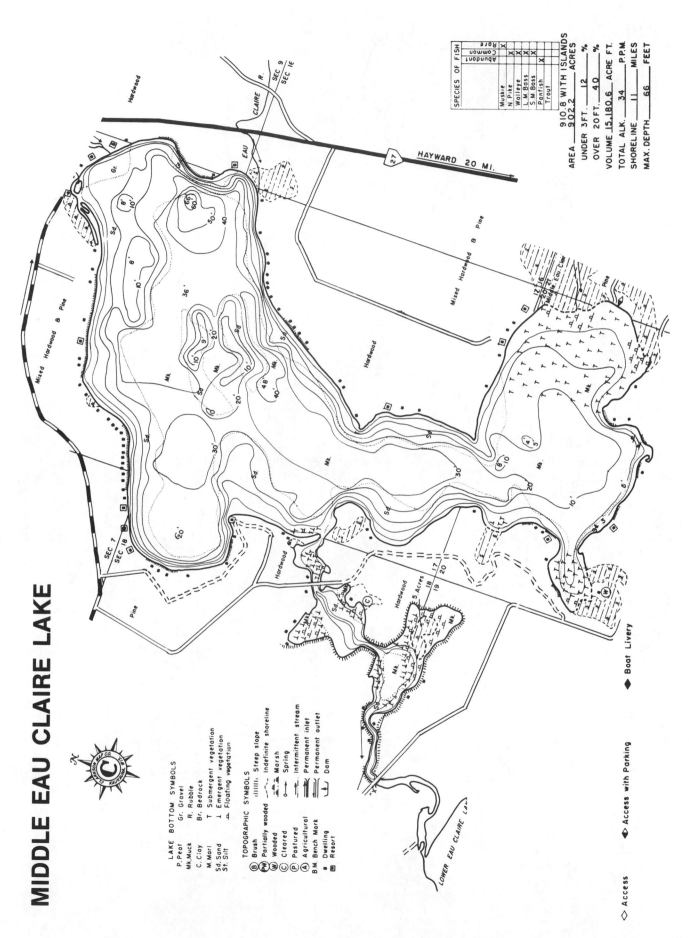

MIDDLE EAU CLAIRE LAKE

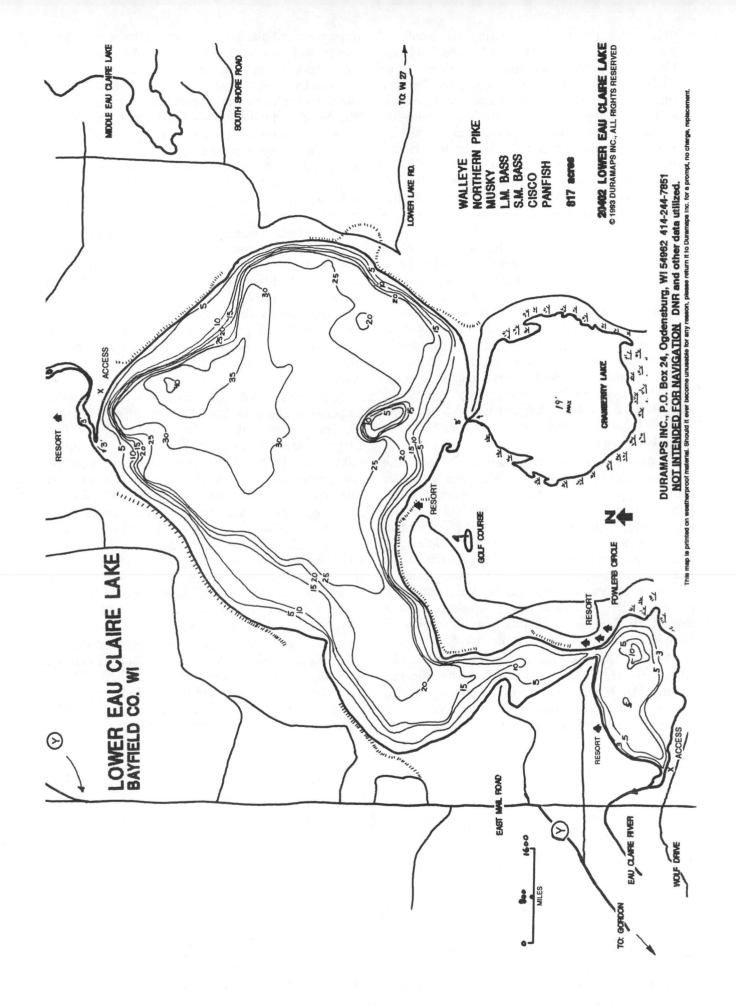

LOWER EAU CLAIRE LAKE
BAYFIELD CO. WI

MIDDLE EAU CLAIRE LAKE

SOUTH SHORE ROAD

TO W 27

LOWER LAKE RD.

WALLEYE
NORTHERN PIKE
MUSKY
L.M. BASS
S.M. BASS
CISCO
PANFISH

817 acres

20482 LOWER EAU CLAIRE LAKE
© 1993 DURAMAPS INC., ALL RIGHTS RESERVED

ACCESS

RESORT

CRANBERRY LAKE

19'
MAX

RESORT

GOLF COURSE

FOWLERS CIRCLE

RESORT

N

RESORT

ACCESS

EAST MAIL ROAD

EAU CLAIRE RIVER

WOLF DRIVE

TO: GORDON

1600
MILES

DURAMAPS INC., P.O. Box 24, Ogdensburg, WI 54962 414-244-7851
NOT INTENDED FOR NAVIGATION DNR and other data utilized.

This map is printed on weatherproof material. Should it ever become unusable for any reason, please return it to Duramaps Inc. for a prompt, no charge, replacement.

muskies over the years, including the unofficial world-record 70-pounder taken on Middle Eau Claire in 1954 by Robert Malo. (If you want the whole story behind this controversial fish, stop at the National Freshwater Fishing Hall of Fame in Hayward.) Despite their reputation, Jim Nieckula reports the lakes are not heavily fished for muskies and visiting anglers have a good chance at a trophy fish. He has taken four muskies over 30 pounds himself, and many fishermen are releasing muskies over 20 pounds, a practice unheard of just a few years ago. Nieckula says several 49-inchers have been released in recent seasons.

Look for muskies over newly formed weedbeds and shallow bars in spring, where they will hit bucktails, shallow crankbaits and topwater baits. Muskies are deep and tough to come by in summer, but Nieckula does well in fall using jerk baits weighted down with lead on the leader so they dive straight down and bounce back vertically. Since smaller fish in distress often trigger strikes from muskies, Nieckula's goal is to imitate a hooked walleye struggling to free itself. He says Bobbies, Suicks, Smitys and Eddies all will take muskies, but since these are large, wooden baits, they may need to be tuned to make them work properly.

Muskies feed on the abundant cisco population here, especially in summer and fall, when these baitfish are suspended over deep water. Another guide, Bruce Shumway of Drummond, has had good success on deep-water muskies in fall using live suckers. A few years back, Shumway's brother Bill designed a large jigging spoon called a "Fuzzy Duzzit" that is deadly on suspended muskies. Shumway locates a school of ciscoes, then stays above them and works the Fuzzy Duzzit with a steady lift-drop, lift-drop motion. His best fish with this new lure was a 26-pounder a client took on one of the Eau Claire lakes.

The Eau Claire Chain also produces some nice bass, both largemouths and smallmouths. Nieckula has recorded bronzebacks up to six pounds. Try jigs with minnows and leeches on the rocky shoals of any of the three larger lakes for smallmouths, while top-water baits and plastics worked over the weedbeds of Lower, Robinson and Birch lakes produce the best largemouth fishing. The new no-kill early season on northern bass waters saved the life of a 24-inch largemouth an angler took on Lower Eau Claire in June of '92. As far as anyone knows, that bass is still there.

The largemouth lakes also hold some nice bluegills. When they're on the beds, you can take them on fly-rod spiders or live bait. Look for big 'gills to suspend over deep water in summer, when small jigs and Bait Rigs spinner rigs tipped with waxworms or red worms should take them.

For crappies, concentrate on Lower Eau Claire and Robinson. In spring, you'll find them in the shallows, but later in the year they hang out near the many cribs that line the shore on Lower Eau Claire in 12 to 15 feet of water. Small minnows, tiny swimming jigs, and in-line spinners, such as Mepps in sizes 0 and 00, all produce good catches of crappies. A Mepps Crappie Kit comes with an assortment of tiny spinners and plastic tails that are effective for crappies.

There are two public landings on the east shore of Upper Eau Claire, both on Lake Road off Highway 27. The landing at the southeast end of Middle Eau Claire is just off Highway 27, two miles south of Lake Road. There are also a boat ramp, campground and picnic area at the Douglas County park at Mooney Dam near the outlet on Lower Eau Claire.

For bait, tackle and guide service, stop at Jim's Bait & Convenience Store at the intersection of Highway 27 and Lake Road; address: HCR 61, Box 6315, Barnes, WI 54873, telephone (715) 795-2413. Bruce Shumway also guides on the chain. Contact: Shumway's Guide Service, Route 1, Box 82, Drummond, WI 54832, telephone (715) 798-3441.

For information on the chain's many fine resorts, restaurants and other vacation services, contact: Eau Claire Lakes Business Association, Route 1, Box 90, Gordon, WI 54838, telephone (715) 376-2722 or (715) 795-2750; or Bayfield County Tourism & Recreation Dept., P.O. Box 832, Washburn, WI 54891, telephone (800) 472-6338 or (715) 373-6125.

Escanaba Lake

5 Miles Southeast of Boulder Junction, Vilas County

In the past few years, Wisconsin anglers have faced the most restrictive fishing regulations in over a generation. Walleyes especially are subject to stricter limits now, with a 15-inch minimum size imposed on most waters and daily bag limits reduced on some lakes in response to proposed Chippewa treaty-harvest quotas. New rules in recent years also call for larger minimum size limits on bass and muskies, and some managers are calling for reduced bag limits of panfish on certain waters.

Angler response to this tightening of the regulatory belt so far is mixed. Most who understand the reasons for these changes support them in the interest of improving the resource now and in the future, but some grumble about what they see as unreasonable restraints on their harvesting privilege, and unfortunately there will always be a minority who will violate the new rules and manage to convince themselves they are right in doing so.

I would never argue that we should toss out altogether rules such as season dates and bag and size limits, but regulations bring with them several side effects that sometimes divert our attention away from the real reasons we go fishing. Too many restrictions can turn sport into a numbers game and rob us of the chance to act responsibly. A law-abiding angler is not necessarily an ethical sportsman.

Against this backdrop of greater restrictions, Escanaba Lake stands out as a place of opportunity. Since the 1940s, there have been no harvest restrictions here whatsoever -- no closed season, no minimum size, and no bag limits for any species. Here, the rules are suspended, putting anglers in a position to write their own. A daily limit of five walleyes has no meaning here, so if you normally see a limit as a goal, you'll have to find another reason to keep fish. Take home 100 walleyes a day if you want -- if you can catch them -- or set limits on your kill according to your own conscience and needs. Whichever way you respond to the freedom allowed here, you'll find a trip to Escanaba a worthwhile experience.

Located in the heart of the Northern Highland State Forest in central Vilas County, 288-acre Escanaba Lake is one of five lakes that make up the DNR's Northern Highland Fishery Research Project, where experiments are conducted that may eventually lead to improved management on other lakes in the state. Harvest restrictions were lifted here as part of an ongoing study to determine what effects doing so would have on fish populations.

When you arrive at Escanaba, you must check in at the DNR office at the landing and obtain a free permit before you may fish. Then, when you quit fishing, you turn in the permit and a census clerk measures and weighs any fish you have kept and asks about fish you released. Researchers use this information to monitor angling pressure and exploitation rates.

Walleyes are the dominant species here. They have always enjoyed excellent natural reproduction and good growth, and for the first 30 years or so, unrestricted harvest did not appear to have any significant effects. In the past few years, though, that has begun to change.

The walleye harvest has dropped dramatically since the late 1980s. Annual records are kept here from ice-out in April to ice-out in April of the following year. In 1987-88, anglers fished a total of

12,689 hours and creeled 5,027 fish, including 2,939 walleyes. In 1988-89, anglers fished 15,350 hours and creeled 8,465 fish, including 4,398 walleyes. Looking at just the walleye harvest in both years, anglers fished about four hours to creel one walleye, which does not seem like excessive exploitation, but the total harvest for this two-year period amounted to 7,337 walleyes, or 25 per acre. That is a lot of fish! Anglers caught and released an additional 2,336 and 4,926 walleyes in these two years, most of them under 12 inches.

Jumping ahead to 1991-92, anglers fished 11,366 hours and creeled 1,033 walleyes. Through March 1 of the 1992-93 season, anglers fished 10,200 hours and creeled 1,569 walleyes. It took 11 hours to creel a walleye in 1991 and 6.5 hours in 1992. In these two recent years, anglers caught and released an additional 504 and 1,231 walleyes, respectively, most of them under 15 inches.

Steve Newman, DNR fisheries biologist in charge of Escanaba, says this kind of fluctuation is normal. Over the last 20 years, Escanaba's walleye population has averaged 14 to 16 adults per acre, with a high of 49 per acre. Newman attributes the current level of six to seven per acre to several years of less successful reproduction.

"Escanaba experiences good natural reproduction most years, with some phenomenal year classes now and then," says Newman. The large 1990 year class, for example, should boost the adult population back up into the range of 15 to 20 per acre in a year or so. Even a level of six or seven walleyes per acre, though, is well above average for walleye lakes throughout the state. Newman says Escanaba currently holds a good number of walleyes over 20 inches, even though the angler exploitation rate has hovered right around 35 percent of the total adult population annually -- that's as much as most biologists feel walleyes can stand without hurting natural reproduction.

Researchers recently completed gathering data in a long-term natural reproduction study on Escanaba. When the report is released, researchers hope to be able to predict annual natural reproduction rates so managers may set stocking quotas on other lakes to meet the specific needs of a given lake in that year. Other studies still in the planning stages include looking at how many walleyes can be safely harvested before the quality (size), as well as the quantity, of the fish taken begins to decline.

The best times to catch walleyes here are from about 10 days after ice-out until the end of May, and

Fish Wisconsin author Dan Small took his first legal musky from Escanaba Lake near Boulder Junction. He was guided by Pat Shields. Photo by Dan Small

ESCANABA LAKE

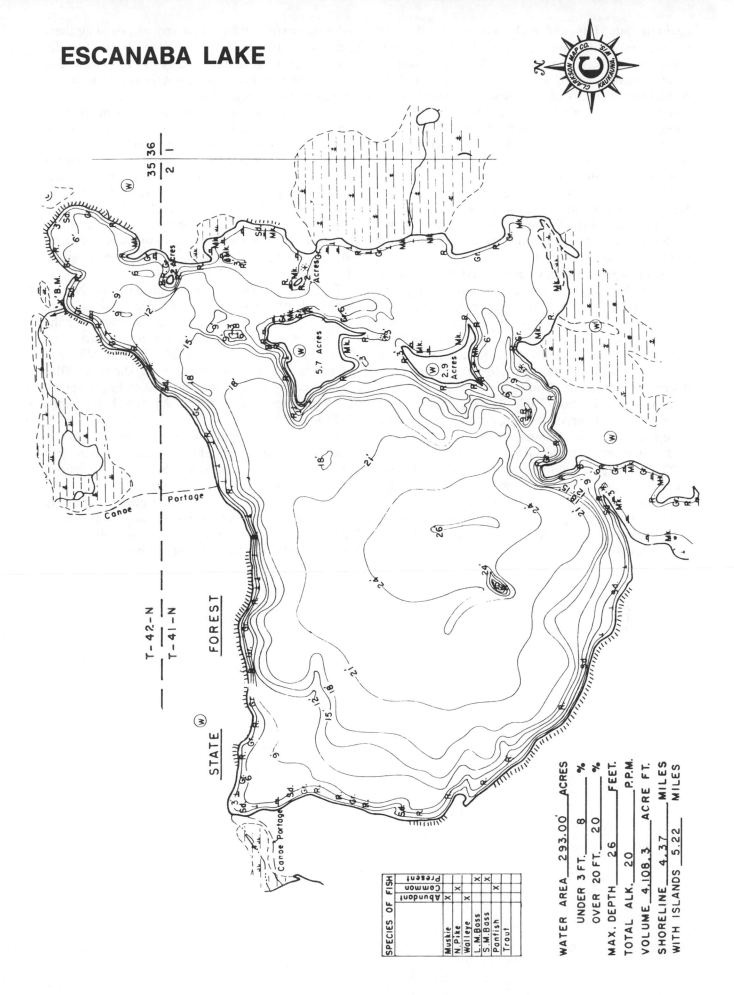

SPECIES OF FISH	Abundant	Common	Present
Muskie	X		
N.Pike		X	
Walleye	X		
L.M.Bass			X
S.M.Bass			X
Panfish		X	
Trout			

WATER AREA __293.00'__ ACRES

UNDER 3 FT. __8__ %

OVER 20 FT. __20__ %

MAX. DEPTH __26__ FEET.

TOTAL ALK. __20__ P.P.M.

VOLUME __4,108.3__ ACRE FT.

SHORELINE __4.37__ MILES

WITH ISLANDS __5.22__ MILES

again in late July and early August. In the first period, you'll find walleyes along the lake's gravel shorelines, where the traditional jig-and-minnow combo, floating crankbaits like Rapalas and Rebels, or Mepps spinners will take them. The late summer action comes when a heavy algae bloom blocks out enough sunlight to allow walleyes to move into shallow water (four to eight feet deep) and feed actively at midday. Try crawlers and leeches, or artificials like crankbaits and spinners now.

The worst times to fish walleyes here? In June and early July when walleyes are deep and small forage abundant, and through the ice in midwinter. Some walleyes are taken during first ice in December and last ice in March, however.

I'll confess that I have not fished Escanaba for walleyes. But I have a special fondness for the lake because I did catch my first legal musky here. No, I'm not going to tell you in what year, although Steve Newman could look it up in his records. I was fishing with Eagle River guide Pat Shields on a rainy, blustery day in August during the field trip part of an outdoor writers meeting. (You can have your Las Vegas conventions -- I'll take Eagle River any day!) I had caught plenty of shorties before, but the pressure was on me and Shields to come up with a legal fish to enter in the annual writers fishing contest.

The rain had let up temporarily, but wind gusts were churning up the water, so we worked along a shoreline that was taking a good pounding from the waves. I was tossing a jointed perch-finish Believer of Shields' that looked like it had been munched by quite a few fish in its day. The musky smacked it just under the surface, then rolled and sort of hung there in the water the way they sometimes do, as if totally confused by this strange turn of events. I landed it without much of a struggle, but it measured an honest 36 inches and I was jubilant.

Shields took several photos of me with the fish, then we released it. Putting a fish back never made me feel better than that time, when nothing was forcing me to do it. Back at the conference, we found out no one else had caught a musky that day, so my name went on the plaque that hangs at Trees For Tomorrow. I made Shields give me the Believer, then bought him a new one at Eagle Sports and told him to start putting tooth marks in it. I still have that bait, but I haven't caught another musky on it since. Maybe I should give it back to Pat.

To reach the landing at Escanaba, take Nebish Road east off Highway M near Trout Lake or south off Highway K west of Star Lake, and look for the big fish research project signs with a walleye on them. The nearest town is Boulder Junction. You can get bait and tackle in lots of little shops in Vilas County, but none is as well stocked as Eagle Sports, 702 Wall Street, Eagle River, WI 54521, telephone (715) 479-8804.

You can book a guide at Eagle Sports, but if you want to fish with Pat Shields, contact him directly at 1290 Tyson Road, Eagle River, WI 54521, telephone (715) 479-FISH. Tell him I sent you.

For information on resorts and other services in Vilas County, contact: Vilas County Advertising Dept., Vilas County Courthouse, P.O. Box 369, Eagle River, WI 54521, telephone (715) 479-3649.

Flambeau River And Dairyland Reservoir (Lake Flambeau)

Ladysmith, Rusk County

Wisconsin's many lakes present a variety of challenges to DNR fish managers whose job it is to maintain or enhance the quality of our state's fisheries. Some lakes are loaded with stunted panfish and need more gamefish to thin them out, some have an overabundance of carp that root up bottom vegetation, muddy the water and generally raise havoc with game fish populations, and some actually have too many walleyes for their own good. As hard to believe as that may be for anglers who face 15-inch size limits and reduced bags on many walleye lakes in northern Wisconsin, that was the case on Dairyland Reservoir just a few years ago.

Also known as Lake Flambeau, this 1,700-acre reservoir on the Flambeau River's midsection near Ladysmith in Rusk County has as high a density of walleyes as you'll find just about anywhere. Small forage fish were scarce, though, and the walleyes grew slowly. DNR fisheries crews, with a lot of help from the Rusk County Wildlife Restoration Society and Dairyland Property Owners Association, went to work to remedy that imbalance and after 10 years, their combined efforts are showing positive results indeed.

According to DNR fish manager Frank Pratt, most of the restoration effort went into two activities: stocking panfish and installing artificial habitat. Large numbers of perch and other panfish were planted in the 1980s to help restore a diverse forage base and to add another dimension to the fishery. Today, panfish numbers are up and anglers are catching some nice-sized perch, crappies and bluegills. Walleyes are abundant, and channel catfish are increasing in number every year. There are also lots of good-sized black bullheads, providing a fishery that is underutilized.

Some 400 fish cribs, including 50 space-age plastic cribs, supplemented by a veritable underwater forest of Berkley artificial fish habitat, have been placed around the lake in 12 to 16 feet of water. Fish have flocked to these structures, and everyone concerned -- fish managers, local club members, and anglers -- is pleased with the success of the project. In addition, after the reservoir was drawn down in 1983, natural weedbeds appeared where none had existed before, providing still more cover. The lake's dark water shades weeds from sunlight and prevents their growth much below five feet, though, so shallow bars and humps hold more fish than deeper ones do.

There's even more good news. Muskies have been stocked since the late 1950s and are doing quite well, thanks to adequate forage in the form of suckers, redhorse and walleyes. According to Frank Pratt, there is some natural reproduction, but not enough to sustain the fishery, so alternate-year stocking will continue at the rate of one fingerling per acre. The flowage yields fish in excess of 30 pounds annually, and Clark James, of James Sport Shop in Ladysmith, calls Dairyland "as good a lake for big muskies as you'll find." Northern pike are less important here than muskies, but some nice fish are taken every year, especially through the ice.

Flambeau River & Lake Flambeau

Walleye fishing is good early in the season below the four hydro dams. Parking is available at each dam, and you can fish right from shore. Dairyland Dam, which creates the reservoir, is the most popular of the four. Work the eddies and slower side-currents with jigs and minnows, or cast crankbaits and retrieve them slowly across the current, bumping bottom where possible. The tailwaters of Big Falls Dam, the farthest upstream of the four, are easier to fish from a small boat. You can troll here with crankbaits or backtroll with river rigs and live minnows, but watch for boulders. This stretch is tricky to navigate if water levels are down.

In the lake itself, there are several hot spots for spring walleyes: the flats around the island in Groothausen Bay, the east shoreline north of the airport, and the mouth of Crooked Creek on the west shore. These are spawning areas where walleyes hang out well into May. Spend some time around the cribs concentrated in Groothausen Bay. Jigging with minnows, and casting or long-line trolling with shallow-running crankbaits are all effective techniques in these spots.

Later in the season, Clark James recommends casting Rapalas and Shad Raps or drifting leeches over the shallow rock bars and weedbeds scattered all around the lake. The larger of two humps in the main basin, located about 300 yards northeast of the dam, is broad and tops out at about 10 feet, with a 20-foot-deep saddle in the middle of it. Many cribs and artificial weeds have been placed here, making it attractive to walleyes.

Frank Pratt says the lake's smallmouth bass population has exploded in recent years, due apparently to low water levels that have created good spawning conditions for them, and they're growing well. Walleye anglers take smallmouths by accident in the spring, but to concentrate on smallies, work the island shoreline in Groothausen Bay or the river holes below Big Falls Dam. Most are modest in size, but each year a few in the four- to five-pound range are taken. James also says the river between town and the Thornapple Dam makes a dandy summer float trip for bass and walleyes.

Musky anglers work the weedbeds and bars, along with cribs and creek mouths. Since trolling is legal, diving crankbaits and bucktails dragged across these areas should get results, but casting shallow-running crankbaits, jerk baits and bucktails is a lot more fun.

Big Falls Flowage, just upstream from Big Falls Dam, now has a fishable population of flathead catfish. No one knows where they came from, but Frank Pratt says they're abundant and big. For a change of pace, skewer a live carp on a stout hook and dunk it in one of the flowage's deep holes. When a 30-pound cat inhales your bait, it may tow your boat around awhile before you land it.

To reach the boat ramp at Community Park just south of the Dairyland Dam, take Highway 8 east out of town and turn north on Community Park Road. There are smaller ramps on the west shore north of the dam, on the south shore on Groothausen Bay and

Nice walleyes make their home in both the Flambeau River and Lake Flambeau. Photo by Dan Small

two on Manedowish Point, reachable off "A" Street in Tony. To fish the north end of the lake up to Big Falls Dam, use the new ramp at Josie Creek County Park on the east shore off Highway X.

To reach Big Falls Dam, take Highway X past Josie Creek Park. Ladysmith Dam (also called Papermill Dam) is located in town off Worden Avenue, just below the Highway 8 bridge. To get to Thornapple Dam, take Highway 27 south to Highway P, then turn west. There are campgrounds at Community Park, Josie Creek Park, Big Falls Park and Memorial Park right in Ladysmith.

Clark James reports that ice fishermen have done well on walleyes, northerns and big crappies for the past several years. You can drive onto the lake at either access near the dam or at Josie Creek Park. Tip-ups baited with shiners set in the shallows near weeds and rock bars do the trick, although some anglers take walleyes on jigging Rapalas and Swedish Pimples.

James Sport Shop, 120 Lake Avenue, Ladysmith, WI 54848, telephone (715) 532-6016, is headquarters for bait, tackle and fishing information. For information on lodging, other area facilities, recreational opportunities and seasonal events, contact: Rusk County Information Center, 817 W. Miner Avenue, Ladysmith, WI 54848, telephone (715) 532-6222, or (800) 535-7875.

North Fork Flambeau River

Park Falls, Price County, to Highway W, Sawyer County

North Fork Flambeau River

A century ago, lumber camps along the upper Flambeau River swarmed with men and horses in winter. One by one, the great white pines of this virgin forest fell to the lumberjacks and were dragged to the frozen riverbanks, where they lay stacked until spring. Then, the headlong rush of the river drive flushed them down the Flambeau to the Chippewa and on to the sawmills of Chippewa Falls and Eau Claire.

On a lonely stretch of the Flambeau today, you can almost hear the wheeze of a well-oiled crosscut in the sighing of wind through pines or the ghostly shout of a long-gone river driver in the roar of an approaching rapids. But where pine and hemlock once choked the river from bank to bank, now the Flambeau carries a much lighter burden of kevlar and aluminum, and the riverman in lug-soled boots who struggled daily to keep his footing and his life has given way to the modern float-fisherman whose only goal is a sleek bronzeback waiting around the next bend to give him a sporting tussle.

The North and South Forks of the Flambeau River offer over 100 miles of superb canoeing that draws whitewater enthusiasts from many states, but if you like to cast as well as paddle, you can enjoy both sports at their finest on the 35-mile midsection of the North Fork. Between Park Falls and a place called Babbs Island in the middle of the Flambeau River State Forest, the North Fork calms down enough to let you relax at the paddle and concentrate on the fishing. Depending on which portion of this stretch you choose, you can catch muskies, walleyes, sturgeon or catfish, with smallmouths a sure bet all along the river.

Three dams on this stretch, one at Park Falls just above Highway 182, and the other two within ten miles downstream, also offer you the option of camping in one spot and fishing a small flowage. You can camp at Memorial Park in Park Falls or at Pixley Dam, west of Fifield on Highway 70, or begin a trip downriver at any of the three dams. The flowage at Park Falls receives more fishing pressure than the rest of the river, so if you prefer seclusion and a chance at fish that haven't been hassled, head downriver.

Below Crowley Dam, the last of the three flowages, the North Fork runs unhampered through state forestland to join the South Fork near the Sawyer/ Rusk county line. Two bridge crossings at 10-mile intervals, one on Highway 70 at Oxbo and the other at Highway W about 12 miles southeast of Loretta, let you choose either of two one-day floats or a weekend adventure on the entire section.

The river runs high in early spring, but by the opening of the inland fishing season in May, water levels are usually just right for canoeing and fishing. In summer, if the river is too low for good canoeing, you can still find good fishing in the deeper holes above or below any of the bridge crossings or access points.

Designated sites along the river provide camping opportunities reserved for canoeists, so you won't find a dozen car-campers where you had planned to spend the night. You can get information on water levels and detailed canoe trail maps that show every campsite, rapids and other feature of interest at State Forest Headquarters, located at the Highway W take-out point. Write: Superintendent, Flambeau River State Forest, Star Route, Winter, WI 54896, telephone (715) 332-5271.

As an alternative plan, you might want to set up a base camp at one of the state campgrounds on Connors Lake or Lake of the Pines and then make day trips on the river. Both campgrounds are located on good fishing and swimming lakes off Highway W just east of Forest Headquarters, and neither is crowded, even on busy weekends.

Smallmouths are the primary species on the North Fork, and the summer months are the best time to fish for them. The flowages yield good numbers of bass, as do the deeper sections above Highway W, but every riffle, hole and boulder run will hold smallmouths. Work instream cover and deeper holes with small jigs tipped with leeches, crawlers or plastic tails, small spinnerbaits, such as Beetle-Spins, or floating Rapalas and similar lures.

Flyfishing can also produce lots of action. Try a seven- to nine-weight rod with a floating or sink-tip line and a three- to five-foot leader. Black marabou leeches, Zonkers and streamers will take bass, but my favorite is a Dahlberg Diver tied with deer hair and rabbit fur. This fly pops on the surface and dives when strip-retrieved. Bass love it and sometimes come from yards away to smash it as it flutters in the current or dances just under the surface.

Walleyes inhabit the same water as bass, but they often hang back a few feet from obstructions, while bass tend to jam themselves tight to cover. Side pockets, eddies and backwaters, no matter how small, often yield walleyes in spring and early summer. Jigs and minnows account for most of the walleyes, but a swimming jig like the Slo-Poke ought to work as well. Try the 1/4-ounce size in chartreuse or orange, tipped with a shad tail.

If you've never caught a river musky, the Flambeau is a good place to accomplish that goal. The stretch between Oxbo and Highway W has the best cover in the form of large boulders and deep bend holes, but any place you can't see bottom is worth trying. Most people toss bucktails for muskies, but topwater baits can provide a lot more excitement. Scale down your tackle for more sport. A sturdy bass baitcasting rig with 12-pound test line will do just fine.

Stop at Bridge Bait & Tackle in Park Falls, telephone (715) 762-4108, for supplies and information. You'll see fewer canoes on the river on weekdays or after Labor Day, but even in summer you'll have plenty of fishing spots to yourself. To help plan a trip, write: Park Falls Area Chamber of Commerce, P.O. Box 246, Park Falls, WI 54552, telephone (715) 762-2703.

A float trip down the North Fork of the Flambeau River can yield exciting fishing action. Photo by Dan Small

Lower Fox River

De Pere Dam to Green Bay, Brown County

Every few years, the Packers have a miraculous comeback season that is welcomed like an old friend by ecstatic fans of the Green and Gold, but Lambeau Field is not the only site in the city by the bay where comebacks have worked their magic. Long before most of today's Packers played their first college football game, cleanup efforts on the Lower Fox had begun to transform this essentially dead river into a viable fishery. By the early 1980s, the turnaround was well on its way, and today, from the De Pere Dam downstream to the bay, the fishing is better than it has been for as long as anyone can remember.

Sediments in the river and in Green Bay still carry a heavy load of contaminants, the legacy left by decades of waste effluents dumped into the river by the industries that still line its banks, but the water itself runs clean enough now to support a mix of fish species that had been absent for a generation or more. Walleyes are the main attraction here, but smallmouths, white bass, crappies, northern pike, catfish, and even trout and salmon now frequent the river and are taken regularly by anglers. Muskies, too, are beginning to show up in the catch.

Lower Fox River ★

"We're currently promoting the Lower Fox as an urban recreational fishery," says DNR fish manager Terry Lychwick. "Walleyes 15 inches and under now pose the lowest health risk, but our health guide still warns people not to eat some fish species taken in the river. There's no reason why they can't have fun catching and releasing them, though."

As part of that philosophy, from early March until the general inland opener in May, anglers may keep only one walleye in the Lower Fox below the De Pere Dam, and it must measure at least 28 inches. These restrictions protect most of the active spawners and still allow anglers to try for a trophy. Stocking is no longer needed, since walleyes are reproducing successfully now, and all age classes are showing up in spring survey nets. The biggest walleye surveyed to date was a 16-1/2-pounder caught in the spring of 1989. Anglers have taken walleyes from 12 to 16-1/2 pounds, and the next state record walleye may already be swimming in the river.

Lychwick reports that the 1991 walleye hatch was the best ever, with at least ten times as many fish produced as any year since the surveys began. He anticipates this year class will produce record numbers of big fish a few years down the road.

In spring, most walleye anglers fish just below the De Pere Dam and anywhere there is riprap farther downstream. Jigs and minnows are the traditional baits, the lighter the better to avoid snags in the shallow, rocky water. Crankbaits and other artificials also work well. On a good day you can catch and release 20 or more walleyes below the dam. We've taped several spring walleye segments there for *Outdoor Wisconsin*, including one with Rick Winans in an April snowstorm that produced a number of heavy fish. As of this writing, I'm planning another TV trip -- this time in quest of a fly-fishing world record.

Walleyes also make a fall run upriver to feed on the schools of shad that move in from the bay. On a brisk October day, tournament anglers Ralph Brunner, Ken Ellis and I had a picnic catching three- to five-pound walleyes below paper company discharge pipes on the east and west banks, in the Wisconsin Electric Power Company outflow at the mouth of the river, and along several rocky points along the way. We used 3/8-ounce jigs with Gitzit tube tails and shad-imitation crankbaits right in the flow, and 1/4-ounce Slo-Pokes with shad tails in slower eddies. These same baits took several nice smallmouths and white bass, all of which we released.

White bass and crappies are showing up in good numbers in spring after the walleye action tapers off, and again in fall when it's time to eat shad. Look for them in deep holes and along rocky shorelines. They'll hit minnows, smaller jigs and crankbaits readily. Smallmouths are also in good supply wherever you find rocks and dropoffs, as well as in the eddies and pockets of slower water around outflow pipes. Lychwick would like to see more anglers take advantage of another recent discovery on the Fox, channel and flathead catfish, whose numbers are on the rise here as elsewhere in the state. Big flatheads are aggressive predators of young carp and could help keep these rough fish in check.

Northern pike are present, but not in great numbers, since the marsh habitat along the Green Bay shoreline where they spawn has deteriorated in the past 40 years. Successful hatches occur in high water years, but when water levels are low, recruitment is poor. In tagging studies throughout Green Bay, Lychwick has found that pike are very migratory. Fish tagged in the Lower Fox may show up just about anywhere, making population monitoring and management difficult.

Seasonal spawning runs of trout and salmon make it upriver to surprise anglers targeting bass and walleyes. The day I fished with Brunner and Ellis, we watched another angler fight and lose a big chinook that hit a chartreuse Shad Rap near the Fort Howard discharge pipe. I know what bait he was using because it floated downstream to our boat after the fish broke his line and shook free of the hook. I returned it, of course, but dug into my tackle box for something similar.

The most exciting recent news on the Fox is the introduction of muskies. Hybrids stocked above the dam several years ago have made their way downstream, and anglers catch them now and then. Two area musky clubs, The Packerland Musky Club and Dave's Musky Club, have helped fund the introduction of true muskies in the Lower Fox and Green Bay. The DNR obtains eggs from Michigan Great Lakes strain spotted muskies under a cooperative agreement with the Michigan DNR, raises them to fingerling stage, then plants them in the bay. These fish spawn on offshore reefs and gravel shoals and like areas with current, so they should do well in the bay and river. Terry Lychwick expects anglers to start catching legal spotteds within two years.

Biologists are watching two exotic species to see what effect they may have on the rejuvenated Fox River fishery: sea lampreys and white perch. After considerable debate, the Rapide Croche lock, upstream from the De Pere Dam, was closed to prevent sea lampreys from entering the Wolf River/Lake

Winnebago system, where it is feared they could harm populations of sturgeon and other fish. U.S. Fish and Wildlife Service nets set at the De Pere Dam each spring have already caught a few lampreys, suggesting the closing of the Rapide Croche lock was a wise move. If they got into the upper lakes, eradicating them would cost millions, Lychwick says.

There are several harmless native species of lampreys in the system already, and biologists cannot tell by looking at a lamprey scar on a fish which variety made it. If you catch a fish with a lamprey attached to it, take both prey and lamprey to the area DNR office at 200 N. Jefferson Street, Green Bay, WI 54301, telephone (414) 497-4020.

An April snowstorm didn't prevent Rick Winans from catching this 10-pound walleye from the Lower Fox River at DePere. Photo by Dan Small

White perch, another undesirable from the lower Great Lakes, have increased dramatically since 1988, when four were taken in the river. In the spring of 1992, survey nets caught 7,600 white perch, so they're here perhaps for good. White perch compete for food with yellow perch, walleyes and white bass, and they can hybridize with white bass, which could jeopardize the gene pool of this desirable species in the Winnebago system. The main strategy for their control now is to maintain high populations of predators, such as walleyes, muskies and northerns.

There are three good boat landings on the Lower Fox, with several paved ramps and loads of parking. The largest is located on the west bank off Highway H in De Pere at the Brown County Fairgrounds. The city ramp at the mouth of the river on the east bank has been improved and more parking spaces added, and there is a new landing on the east bank just north of Voyageurs Park.

Bob's Bait and Tackle in Green Bay, open daily, carries a complete line of supplies for fishing the river or bay. Address: 1504 Velp Avenue, Green Bay, WI 54303, telephone (414) 499-4737. For information on lodging, food, campgrounds and area events, contact: Green Bay Area Visitors and Convention Bureau, P.O. Box 10596, Green Bay, WI 54307-0596, telephone (414) 494-9507 or (800) 236-3976. Plan well in advance for a fall trip when the Pack is in town.

Geneva Lake

Lake Geneva, Fontana, Williams Bay, Walworth County

Of all the gamefish that swim Wisconsin's waters, it's tough to pick a favorite. I love to flyfish for trout, and the sight of a 45-inch musky turning on a dime behind a bucktail at boatside is almost too much for me to take. But go ahead, push me into a corner and I'll admit that I'd rather catch smallmouths than anything. Tell me about a hot "bass" lake and I'm likely to stifle a yawn. Good largemouth lakes are a dime a dozen. But mention that the bass therein are of the leaping bronze persuasion and I'm already halfway to the boat landing.

It's partly because of the places they live: amber rivers that roll through some of the prettiest woodlands in the state, and clear lakes with gravel bars that melt away out of sight into depths as green as the eyes of a lady I once shared a canoe with long ago. And it's partly because of their spunk. Their big-mouthed cousins don't exactly slouch from a fight, but after a few sluggish head-shakes and a dive into the nearest weeds, most largemouths remind me of an aging prize-fighter in a half-hearted comeback attempt, while smallies battle you from strike to net like a charging welterweight.

But it's mostly because when hooked, they go instantly airborne as though flying will save them from the sting of this thing in their mouth. Sure, chinooks jump, and so do rainbow trout. Rainbows of the Skamania strain put on an aerial display that'll rattle your teeth, but just imagine what a smallmouth could do if it grew to 20 pounds!

A 20-pound smallmouth is a creature that lives only in dreams, but enough four-pounders swim the crystal waters of Walworth County's Geneva Lake that catching 20 pounds of bronzebacks in a summer afternoon is not an impossible feat. A challenge, but not out of the question, for the state's sixth-largest natural lake is right at the top of the list of top smallmouth waters.

This might come as some surprise to those who pay a casual visit to the lakeside towns of Lake Geneva, Williams Bay and Fontana, with their upscale summer homes and classy resorts where sailboats and sleek runabouts seem to outnumber humble fishing boats. Geneva Lake is a playground to many, but it is undeniably one of the top fisheries in southern Wisconsin.

Geneva Lake

Geneva Lake covers well over 5,200 acres, with depths to 135 feet. The bottom is about two-thirds gravel and rock and one-third sand, with some areas of muck in the shallower bays. Structure is abundant, ranging from natural points, reefs, rock ledges and sand flats to man-made cribs supporting the many elaborate private piers that line the lakeshore. The main forage species are ciscoes in deep water areas and shiners on shallow bars and along shorelines.

Most of this structure is prime smallmouth habitat. Many of the bars have extensive sandgrass beds that extend out to the 15- or 20-foot depths. Smallmouths feed heavily on the abundant crayfish in these weeds and on shiners, and trolling or casting diving crankbaits that imitate either can be very productive. It is illegal to fish with live crayfish, of course, but Brian Gates of Geneva Lake Bait & Tackle has good luck with Nature jigs in perch and crayfish patterns. He casts these toward shore, then rips them back in three- to six-foot jumps in eight to 10 feet of water to trigger strikes.

There are weedy bars on both shores at the mouth

of Geneva Bay at the east end of the lake, and another along the north shore at the narrows that attract smallmouths. Other smallmouth hotspots include the pier cribs west of Conference Point on the north shore and the shoreline near the military academy between Fontana and Black Point on the south shore.

Hefty rock bass provide a bonus for the smallmouth angler on Geneva Lake. You'll find these scrappy fighters in the same areas as bronzebacks, and they'll take the same baits. Some run to a pound or more, and they're good eating, so you may want to release smallmouths and keep rockies if a fish fry is one of your goals.

Largemouths are also common in Geneva Lake, although fewer anglers fish for them. The extensive cabbage beds just inshore from the sand grass along many gravel bars are worth trying. Williams Bay and The Flats east of the narrows on the south shore are good spring largemouth spots. In the summer, weedlines and the many piers provide good largemouth cover.

Jim Schillinger caught this smallmouth bass which weighed 5 pounds, 3-1/2 ounces from the productive waters of Geneva Lake while using a Mepps spinner. Photo courtesy Jim Schillinger

Northern pike also frequent the bays, but in summer the largest pike hang out along sharp dropoffs and over deep structure, where they feed on schools of ciscoes. Brian Gates has his best summer luck on pike backtrolling Lindy Rigs baited with four- to six-inch chubs in 30 to 50 feet of water. He also picks up walleyes, brown trout and white bass this way. In fall, trolling the shallow flats can be productive. Ice fishing for pike is usually good for the first few weeks of the season in the weedy bays. DNR fisheries technician Rick Dauffenbach reports that ice fishermen caught a number of pike in the 20-pound class in the winter of '93.

The lake's management plan calls for regular stocking of gamefish to maintain a healthy balance of predator and prey species and to enhance the fishery. The DNR stocks 100,000 fingerling walleyes every other year, up to 5,000 fingerling northerns, along with some largemouths and brown trout. When disease-free fingerlings are available, lake trout are stocked as well. In 1992, 20,000 splake were stocked for the first time, along with 30,000 lake trout.

Walleyes grow quickly in Geneva Lake, and many large fish are taken annually. Cedar Point, just east of Williams Bay, and the gravel shoreline directly across the lake are walleye spawning areas that sometimes still hold fish when the inland season opens in May. Later in spring, try the weedbeds along the east shore of Williams Bay. Night fishing is productive on the many shallow bars and flats, while in the daytime, sharp dropoffs hold fish. In fall, big walleyes and pike follow spawning ciscoes into the rocky shoreline areas around Conference Point.

Lake trout stay deep and can be taken on flashing spoons either jigged or trolled on downriggers or wire line. Some browns are taken by trollers after lake trout and by ice fishermen seeking northerns. Ice fishing for lakers has been quite good the past few years, especially off Williams Bay, Cedar Point and The Narrows.

Crappie action can be hot in the spring, especially in Abbey Lagoon at the lake's west end. Dan Dattilo, of Kenosha, does well on spring crappies using tiny "Yummies" -- a 1/32-ounce jig with a chenille body and marabou tail. He fishes them on ultralight spinning tackle below a small bobber. Look for crappies off bay mouths later in the summer. You can take good catches of bluegills over weedbeds in spring and summer, although the larger 'gills suspend over deep water when the lake stratifies. Perch fishing is usually best in winter. You'll find schools of one- to two-pound white bass suspended deep in summer and fall, where vertical jigging with a 3/4-ounce Hopkins Spoon or Swedish Pimple will take them.

Public access on this popular lake has been a source of controversy for years, with high fees the main problem. The DNR worked out an agreement under which municipalities provide a total of 70 parking spots at 5 sites where boaters pay only $3.50

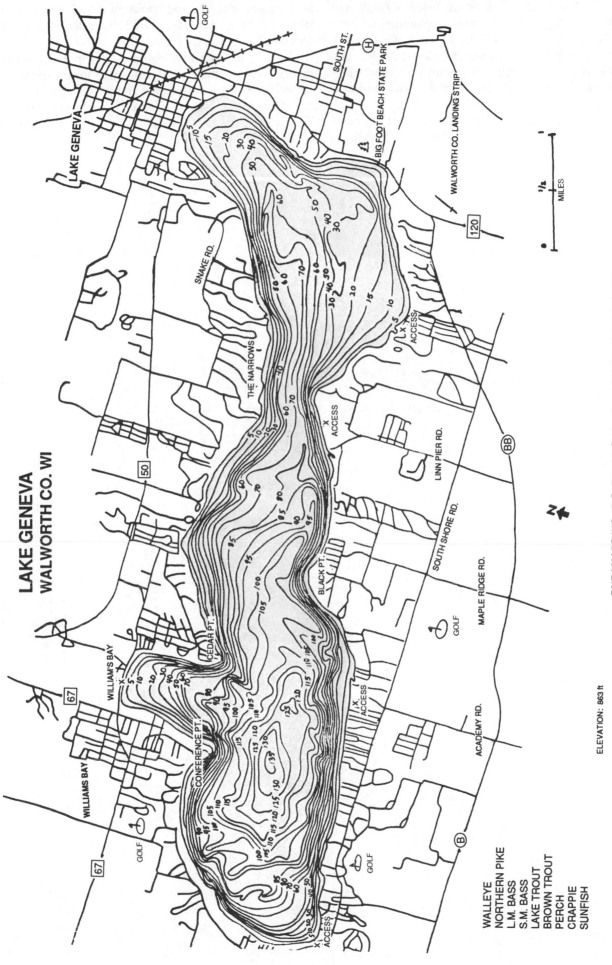

LAKE GENEVA
WALWORTH CO. WI

ELEVATION: 863 ft

WALLEYE
NORTHERN PIKE
L.M. BASS
S.M. BASS
LAKE TROUT
BROWN TROUT
PERCH
CRAPPIE
SUNFISH

DURAMAPS INC., P.O. Box 24, Ogdensburg, WI 54962 414-244-7851
NOT INTENDED FOR NAVIGATION DNR and other data utilized.

This map is printed on weatherproof material. Should it ever become unusable for any reason, please return it to Duramaps Inc. for a prompt, no charge, replacement.

26503 LAKE GENEVA

77

to launch. Once these spaces are filled, though, you must pay the higher fee. There is one municipal ramp each in Fontana, Williams Bay and Lake Geneva, and two in the Town of Linn off Linn Pier Rd. and Hillside Rd. This agreement expires in the fall of 1993, but boaters can probably look forward to new statewide rules regarding launch fees.

Geneva Lake Bait and Tackle, located at the intersection of Highways 67 and 50 north of Williams Bay, carries supplies and books guides. Address: P.O. Box 822, Williams Bay, WI 53191, telephone (414) 245-6150.

For a complete travel package that includes a recreation guide, map, and information on lodging, camping, resorts, restaurants and guide service, contact: Geneva Lake Area Chamber of Commerce, 201 Wrigley Drive, Lake Geneva, WI 53147, telephone (800) 345-1020 or (414) 248-4416.

Gile Flowage

Southwest of Hurley, Iron County

Gile
Flowage

Here's a Wisconsin fishing-trivia question for you: What lake holds the state record for a species that doesn't even live there? Give up? Back in 1967, Allen Dollar caught a four-pound, eight-ounce crappie in Gile Flowage. That was the biggest crappie anyone has ever reported taking in Wisconsin. Trouble is, somehow that fish was recorded as a white crappie, a species that does not exist in the Lake Superior watershed, according to George Becker's *Fishes Of Wisconsin.*

Fish biologists now concede that the record is probably in error. Dollar's crappie is actually the state record black crappie by a pound and a couple ounces, a hefty margin for any panfish species. Record keepers for the DNR will probably make the correction quietly sometime soon. Even if they don't, now at least you know the truth. Earth-shattering? Hardly, but darned interesting to northwoods crappie anglers.

Wedged in between Highways 51 and 77, southwest of Hurley and Ironwood, Michigan, Gile Flowage is a long drive from just about anywhere else in

Wisconsin. It's also one of the newest lakes in the state. A power dam on the Montreal River created it in 1941. The flowage covers some 3,300 acres and has a depth of 35 feet at maximum pool size, but a fall drawdown reduces both figures considerably. Gile's water is soft and stained brown. The bottom is primarily sand, but there are extensive areas of rubble, gravel and muck as well.

Gile has very little vegetation, but structure is abundant in the form of sand and gravel bars, former creek and river channels, stump fields and even a submerged roadbed and railroad grade near the Highway C dike. Riprap along the dike draws walleyes, crappies and smallmouths, but fishing on or within 200 feet of the dike is prohibited until May 15 to provide a refuge for spawning walleyes. Several dozen fish cribs sunk in 15 to 20 feet of water by the Gile Flowage Fishing Association have created new cover for fish and areas for anglers to target.

According to DNR fish manager Dennis Scholl, 2,500 musky fingerlings are stocked here annually to supplement natural reproduction that has declined from the heyday of the 1950s and '60s. When available, a few extra muskies are stocked. A 40-inch size limit now applies here on muskies.

An abundant walleye population sustains itself through outstanding natural reproduction and good growth rates. Walleyes here are exempt from the statewide 15-inch limit. Mercury levels are high in larger fish, and officials want to encourage the harvest of smaller walleyes.

Scholl is enthusiastic about Gile's new smallmouth fishery. Smallies were introduced here in 1985 and they have done well, thanks to good spawning cover. A two-fish bag and 15-inch size limit have helped them get established and produced a quality fishery in just a few years. Most area anglers support this effort, Scholl reports, and many are releasing all the bass they catch now as an investment in the future.

Gile is trophy musky water, according to Scholl. Anglers should not expect a lot of action, but there is a good chance of taking a fish over 20 pounds. A number of 30-pounders show up every year, and one 40-pounder was taken in 1988. Since weeds are scarce, muskies hang out over deep bars and near stumps. Forward motor trolling is not permitted, so most musky anglers cast these spots or drift with suckers. Dark-colored bucktails and jerk baits are the preferred artificial lures. Shallow-running bucktails with large, noisy blades will attract more attention in this dark water.

Early in the year, work the creek mouths, standing timber and shallower stump fields at the south end and along the west shore, then move out to deeper structure as summer progresses. Diving crankbaits and weighted jerk baits should produce in deep water. In fall, try drifting with large suckers over river and creek channels and off the mouths of bays where the mud bottom runs into sand.

Walleye action is hot right when the season opens, as walleyes have normally just finished spawning. Work the inlets, gravel shorelines and around the islands. A swimming jig tipped with a minnow will take walleyes now, as will shallow crankbaits like floating Rapalas and Rebels.

Downstream from the flowage, the Montreal River itself provides a flurry of walleye action in May. You can wade in places, but the water is fast and deep and footing is treacherous in the first half-mile below the dam. You can get on the river at several road crossings in Gile and Montreal and fish for walleyes with ultralight spinning tackle in a setting that looks more like a trout stream than a walleye river. When I lived only an hour's drive from Gile, I made it a point to collect a few river walleyes for fish fries here every spring.

Summer walleye action is slow during the day, although you can usually pick up a fish or two with leeches over the deeper bars. Once the fishing ban is lifted on the Highway C dike, anglers take some nice walleyes here in the evening. In fall, walleye action picks up again, and you'll find fish just about anywhere on the flowage and in the river below the dam. Crankbaits produce well now, as walleyes go on the feed when the weather cools. Try a Bait Rigs Slo-Poke jig rigged Texas-style or with a shad tail right in among the stumps on overcast days.

The flowage's northerns run bigger than those found in most area lakes. Dennis Scholl reports pike up to 37 inches, and there are few "snakes" to pester anglers. Spoons and spinnerbaits will take them in the shallow bays and stump fields, and you'll also pick up northerns while fishing for muskies or walleyes.

Gile's crappies run big and there are plenty of them. Don't expect to catch a four-pounder, but those you take will average 12 inches or better. After May 15, the dike is as good a spot as any on the flowage to take crappies on minnows, small jigs and spinners.

There are also some nice perch here if you can find them. Look for them over the deeper bars and near fish cribs, but be prepared to move to stay with a school. Worms and minnows should take good catches.

The relatively-untouched waters of the Gile Flowage produce some awesome muskies. Many trophies over 20 pounds and monsters in excess of 40 pounds have been taken there. Photo by Dan Small

The best boat launch is located at Gile Park in Gile near the dam at the north end of the flowage. There is another paved ramp at the north end of the Highway C dike. The ramps at the 4-H park on the west side and near the Montreal River inlet at the south end are suitable for small boats, but low water levels may render them unusable. You can reach them both off Spring Camp Road.

Paige's Bait Shop, 101 Cary Road, Hurley, WI 54534, telephone (715) 561-5116, is closed in winter, but Giovanoni's True Value Hardware, 303 Silver Street, Hurley, WI 54534, telephone (715) 561-4141 carries bait and tackle year-round.

Camping is permitted at the 4-H park and on any of the flowage's islands. For information on resorts, maps, guide service and other area services, contact: Hurley Area Chamber of Commerce, Highway 51 South, Hurley, WI 54534, telephone (715) 561-4334. The chamber also has a 24-hour fishing and sports information hotline number: (715) 561-3866.

Big Green Lake

City of Green Lake, Green Lake County

If you think ice fishing means hunching over an upturned bucket somewhere on a vast, frozen wasteland, squinting at tip-ups that haven't sprung for hours, with your back to an arctic wind that drives THE BIG CHILL into the very core of your being and threatens to turn you into a block of the stuff you're sitting on, then you need to spend a January day catching lake trout and ciscoes on Big Green Lake with Mike Norton.

Mike operates a year-round guide service on Big Green, but the highlight of the year is the ice fishing season. We taped an *Outdoor Wisconsin* segment with Mike a couple years ago, after I had read about this style of fishing and decided I just had to try it myself. Mike helped us load our camera gear onto a flatbed trailer with heavy sled runners instead of wheels, then towed us a mile or so out onto the ice with a Jeep. There waited a red shanty as big as a one-car garage, its wood stove cranking out the BTUs.

"I like to be comfortable when I fish," Mike said, as we shed our parkas. A wooden bench lined the shanty's inside walls within comfortable reach of the dozen holes cut into its plywood floor. An emerald glow lit the shanty, emanating from holes cut through the ice below each hole in the floor. Mike switched on an electronic fish locator and handed me a simple jigging stick, notched at each end and wound with dacron line. Several yards of monofilament were tied to the end of the dacron line and to that was attached a snap-swivel and a large silver Swedish Pimple.

We lowered our lures to the bottom through 120 feet of water and began jigging. It wasn't long before I caught a lake trout, but it was short of the minimum 17-inch legal size, so back down the hole it went. The locator showed an occasional fish near bottom which turned out to be lake trout. If any ciscoes swam into the locator's cone, they would appear as marks well off bottom, Mike told me, and we would raise our lures to that depth and try for them. No ciscoes showed up, but we soon had our limit of four lakers, and Mike announced it was time for lunch.

Mike filleted some ciscoes he had caught earlier in the day, seasoned them with butter, salt, pepper, celery seed and sliced onions, then wrapped them in foil and baked them over a charcoal fire right outside the shanty. The crew and I gobbled them up, along with some homemade bread and cole slaw, and pronounced that the best offshore lunch we could remember. I vowed to return to Big Green soon for another go at the ciscoes!

At 237 feet, Big Green is Wisconsin's deepest lake, and it holds a greater volume of water than any other inland lake in the state, including Lake Winnebago. Its 7,325 surface acres make it the state's fifth or 11th largest lake, depending on whether or not you count flowages.

Big Green's south shore drops off sharply into deep water, while the west end, north shore and east end slope more gradually and support good weed growth out to depths of 25 feet or more. Several rock bars provide offshore structure along the north side of the lake's eastern half. Abundant springs provide cold water with good oxygen levels down to considerable depths, making this perhaps the best inland lake trout water in the state. Walleyes, both largemouth and smallmouth bass, and a variety of panfish round out the fishery.

Big Green Lake

The DNR has stocked lakers in Big Green for many years, but disease outbreaks in state hatcheries cut back sharply the number available for stocking in recent years. Some 45,000 lake trout fingerlings are scheduled to be stocked in 1993. Fishing for lakers has improved somewhat in the last couple years, according to DNR fish manager Jim Congdon. Anglers are taking many smaller lake trout and a fair number of big ones.

For several years, brown trout were planted to supplement the lake trout fishery, but few browns showed up in the harvest, so browns have been replaced by rainbows. Anglers began reporting catches of 14- to 18-inch rainbows in 1992. Rainbows have been stocked at the rate of 10,000 per year since 1988, but Congdon plans to double that number in 1994 and may consider stocking up to 40,000 rainbows annually eventually. He says anglers should expect to see some big rainbows in the years ahead. Most will be taken in open water by white bass and walleye anglers, he believes.

Ice fishermen began to target ciscoes when lake trout numbers slumped, and now this fishery has become very popular. Small jigging spoons will take them from suspended schools.

If you ice fish for lakers, as I did with Mike Norton, note that it is illegal to fish with minnows (alive, dead or as cut bait) through the ice here in water over 50 feet deep. Trolling with flashing spoons during open-water months is also effective for taking lakers. Soon after ice-out in spring, look for them as shallow as 50 feet, but later in summer they will be in 70 to 150 feet of water off the Sliding Rock and Sandstone Bluff areas of the south shore and along the south side of the Heidel Bar at about midlake near the east end. You'll need lead-core line or downriggers to reach the trout, or you can charter a pontoon trolling boat with Mike Norton or another of the area's guides.

Big Green's walleyes grow big and fat on ciscoes and other forage. Early in spring, some are taken near the Silver Creek inlet at the east end and the Spring Creek inlet at the west end. Stay out of the posted fish refuge at the Silver Creek inlet. Later in the year, you'll find walleyes in weedbeds along the north shore and over deep offshore structure. In warm weather, they will hold as deep as 35 or 40 feet, where downrigger trolling with diving crankbaits, drifting with slip bobbers and live bait, or back-trolling with Bait Rigs spinner rigs and leeches will take them.

Big Green holds some dandy smallmouths, but you'll have to work for them. Try the rock reefs close to the south shore in June and July, and work deeper in the same areas later in summer. Steep dropoffs, like those at Sugar Loaf Point on the north shore, sometimes produce big bronzebacks in the fall. Dark-colored jigs tipped with leeches or plastic tails bumped down the steep breaks should draw strikes.

Guide Mike Norton lowers a Swedish Pimple jigging spoon in to the waters of Big Green Lake. A growing pile of lake trout and ciscoes lays on the floor of the heated ice shack. Photo by Dan Small

You don't hear much about Big Green's largemouths, but Dartford Bay attracts some hefty prespawners early in the year, and the shallower weedbeds hold largemouths any time of year. Bigmouths find a jig and pig or silver floating Rapala tough to resist.

Northern pike, like walleyes and lake trout, chow down on ciscoes and run big. Troll or cast for them over weedbeds in spring and early summer, but later the big pike suspend off structure as deep as 50 feet, where drifting with big suckers on quick-strike rigs or trolling with deep-diving crankbaits and Spoonplugs on downriggers will take them.

Several species of panfish are abundant here. Good catches of perch are taken on hellgrammites on Heidel Bar and other weedy shoals. Bluegills school off inlet mouths and weedbeds and in Dartford Bay, where tiny ice jigs tipped with grubs and fished on slip bobbers will take them. Watch for large schools of white bass just about anywhere on the lake -- sometimes shallow, but often suspended in deep water. True to their voracious nature, they will nail just about anything you cast, jig or troll near them.

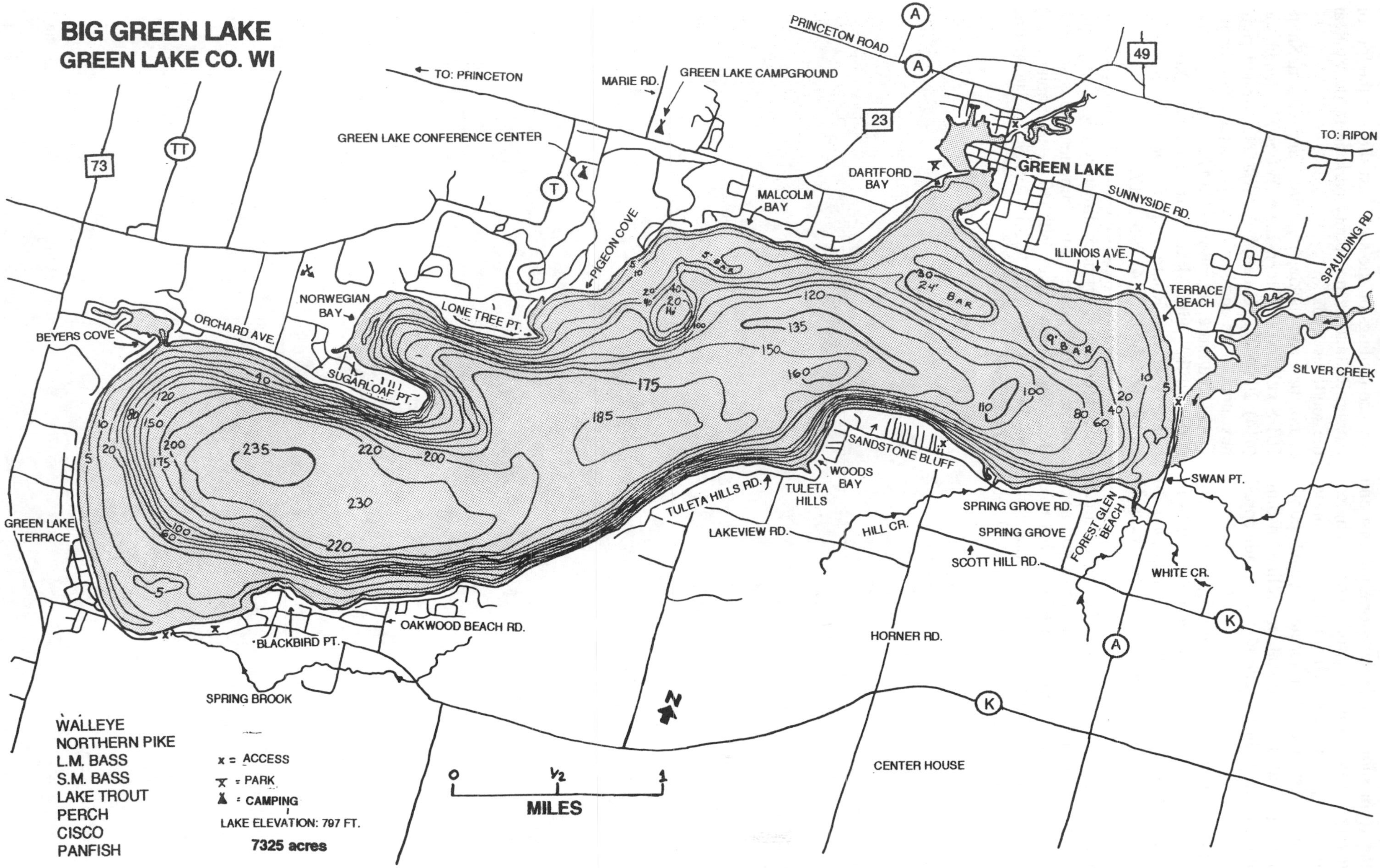

BIG GREEN LAKE
GREEN LAKE CO. WI

WALLEYE
NORTHERN PIKE
L.M. BASS
S.M. BASS
LAKE TROUT
PERCH
CISCO
PANFISH

x = ACCESS
⚲ = PARK
⛺ = CAMPING

LAKE ELEVATION: 797 FT.

7325 acres

DURAMAPS INC., P.O. Box 24, Ogdensburg, WI 54962 414-244-7851
NOT INTENDED FOR NAVIGATION   DNR and other data utilized.

This map is printed on weatherproof material. Should it ever become unusable for any reason, please return it to Duramaps Inc. for a prompt, no charge, replacement.

22401 BIG GREEN LAKE

MILES

83

Fishing from shore is popular along the east end off Highway A, and Jim Congdon told me anglers there are taking some nice channel cats in spring, along with panfish and other species. A new public pier there provides additional shoreline fishing opportunities, including access for handicapped anglers.

To supplement natural structure, Big Green Lake Fishing, Inc. has placed several hundred fish cribs in 18 to 30 feet of water around the lake and plans to sink more. Maps showing their location are available at local sport shops.

There are two public landings in the city of Green Lake, one at the marina and the other off Illinois Avenue. The county-owned landing on Highway A near Silver Creek features a new ramp and expanded parking lot, in addition to the public fishing pier. There are also landings on the southeast shore at the foot of Horner Rd. and at the county park on Highway K at the southwest end.

For bait and tackle, try Schroeder's Sport Shop, 501 South Street, Green Lake, WI 54941, telephone (414) 294-6462. Green Lake Marina, located right next door, rents and services boats, sells bait, books guides and more; telephone: (414) 294-6221 or 294-6760. To fish with Mike Norton, contact: Norton's Charter Service, Route 1, Box 396, Princeton, WI 54968, telephone (414) 295-3617.

The Green Lake Area Chamber of Commerce provides a complete services directory and map, along with a county guide in the summer. Address: P.O. Box 386, Green Lake, WI 54941, telephone (414) 294-3231 or (800) 553-7354. WI 54968, telephone (414) 295-3617.

High Falls Flowage

10 Miles Northwest of Crivitz, Marinette County

Until Bob La May caught a 50-pound musky there in October 1983, few people outside of Crivitz had ever heard of High Falls Flowage. La May was fishing for walleyes at the time, but that's beside the point. That fish is still a line-class world record on six-pound test line. Now a lot of Wisconsin anglers know what a handful of High Falls regulars have been hushing up for a long time: this is one heck of an exciting fishery!

At 1,700 acres, High Falls is the largest of several reservoirs created by power dams that tame the brawling Peshtigo River as it grinds through the sand and bedrock of Marinette County on its way to Green Bay. Wisconsin Public Service Corporation of Green Bay built the dams and controls much of the land surrounding the reservoirs, so there is very little development on the water itself.

The flowage, like the river that feeds it, is stained light brown, limiting visibility to four feet in spring and fall, and less during midsummer algae blooms. This place is not kind to fishing tackle and boat propellers, for there are countless jagged rock bars and reefs that lurk a few feet below the surface to snag lures, abrade lines and beat on lower units. This same craggy structure is a haven to the flowage's primary gamefish: bass, walleyes and muskies.

That muskies are even present here is something of an accident, according to DNR fish manager Tom Thuemler. Stocked in Caldron Falls Flowage, the next reservoir upstream, but not in High Falls itself, some have come over the Caldron Falls dam to make their home in the lower flowage. Since fewer people target muskies here, says Thuemler, your chances of taking a trophy are better on High Falls than on Caldron Falls. Bob La May's fish and several in the 30- to 40-pound class taken in recent years are testimony to that notion.

The DNR does no fish stocking on High Falls, and none is planned. Natural reproduction sustains good populations of walleyes and bass, with one dominating for a time, then the other. Walleye numbers have been down somewhat for the last few years, while smallmouth bass have held their own and largemouths have come on strong. Thuemler says the bass population is about equally split between largemouths and smallmouths now. He reports seeing largemouths over 20 inches in a 1991 survey. There are also a fair number of northerns, although many are small.

The drop in walleye numbers is due in part to fluctuating water levels in the river below Caldron Falls Dam, where walleyes from High Falls spawn. In spring, WPSC often raises water levels during the day to run its turbines, then lowers them at night, leaving walleye eggs high and dry. When WPSC's license comes up for renewal before the Federal Energy Regulatory Commission in late 1993, Thuemler hopes a solution to this problem can be built into the power company's new 30-year license.

Motor trolling is legal on High Falls and can be an effective way to locate fish. The lake is also popular with boaters and water skiers, however, so you may find yourself sharing the water with other recreationists.

Mike Mladenik is the only active licensed guide who regularly fishes High Falls. Smallmouth bass are his specialty and he'll gladly show you a stack of photos of his grinning clients with a live-and-kicking four-pounder in their fist. Rocky points and sunken islands throughout the lake hold smallmouths all season long, says Mladenik, but the best time to catch them is in May and June when they are in shallow water. The shallower upper end of the flowage warms up sooner in spring, so the pre-spawn and spawning periods stretch out here for three or four weeks. Mladenik prefers in-line spinners, like Mepps, and lightweight jigs with grub tails for this shallow-water fishing.

After spawning, smallies simply go deeper but remain in the same areas. Fishing is best early and late in the day, when bass are not disturbed by boat traffic. Mladenik switches to crawlers and leeches now, fishing them on a plain No. 6 hook with as little weight as he can get away with because of all the rocks and snags. Weedlines are distinct and easy to locate here, and in fall, Mladenik works the deep edges in seven or eight feet of water with diving crankbaits.

Mladenik's clients have taken more largemouths in the last few years. For largemouths and northerns, try spinnerbaits, surface lures and plastics in any of the shallow, weedy bays at the north end of the flowage.

Walleyes move around a lot on High Falls, as they do on many flowages. In May and June, they're concentrated in the upper half of the flowage, above the Highway X bridge. Mladenik likes to work up the channel toward the Caldron Falls dam or fish the many stump fields of the flowage's north end. A slip bobber or lightweight leadhead jig with a small fathead minnow will take nice walleyes here in spring. Go with the lightest jig you can manage, says Mladenik, to avoid snagging in rocks and to help you feel a pickup.

In summer, walleyes move back into the river channel and relate to deep structure around the bridge and near the High Falls Dam. Look for humps that come to within 10 or 15 feet of the surface and fish slowly with jigs and leeches. Walleyes scatter in fall and are tough to locate, but some nice ones are taken every year after Labor Day. Big minnows ought to entice big walleyes on a fall feeding binge. Try a Dragon Fly jig to fish deep water and avoid getting hung up. Made by Skipper's Jigs of Fond du Lac, the Dragon Fly's two heads give it snag resistance and stability, keeping the hook in an upright strike-ready position.

Most people who fish for muskies on High Falls pound the weedlines, and that, says Mladenik, is a mistake. You'll take muskies there, all right, but the bigger ones haunt the deeper structure of rocky points and sunken islands. Deep-diving crankbaits, like the mid-size Bagleys, work well on muskies here from early in the season right on into fall. If Mladenik's success is any indication, musky numbers here are on the rise. He and his clients boated several muskies over 30 pounds in 1992.

Mike Mladenik guided this young angler to a dandy smallmouth on High Falls Flowage. Photo courtesy Mike Mladenik

Crappies are abundant and relatively easy to find. In spring, they frequent the inlets, mouths of bays and wood at the upper end of the flowage, while in summer many suspend five to 10 feet down over deep water near the High Falls Dam at the south end of the flowage. Tiny jigs or small minnows will take them in either location. For suspended crappies, it's tough to beat slip bobbers and swimming jigs like the Swimmin' Fool or Slo-Poke Mini tipped with plastic tails and wax worms. The shallower bays at the north end produce good bluegill action on live bait.

Ice fishing can be very productive for walleyes along weedlines, dropoffs and bars in December, but by January it slows down considerably. Later in winter, crappie fishing is hot in the main basin south of the bridge. Here, crappies suspend as they do in summer, and small minnows or jigging spoons on very light line will take them.

The eight public landings maintained by Wisconsin Public Service Corporation are all numbered and indicated on an excellent free map you can get by contacting Wild Shores Brochures, Public Affairs Department, WPSC, P.O. Box 19002, Green Bay, WI 54307-9002, telephone (414) 433-1116. There are

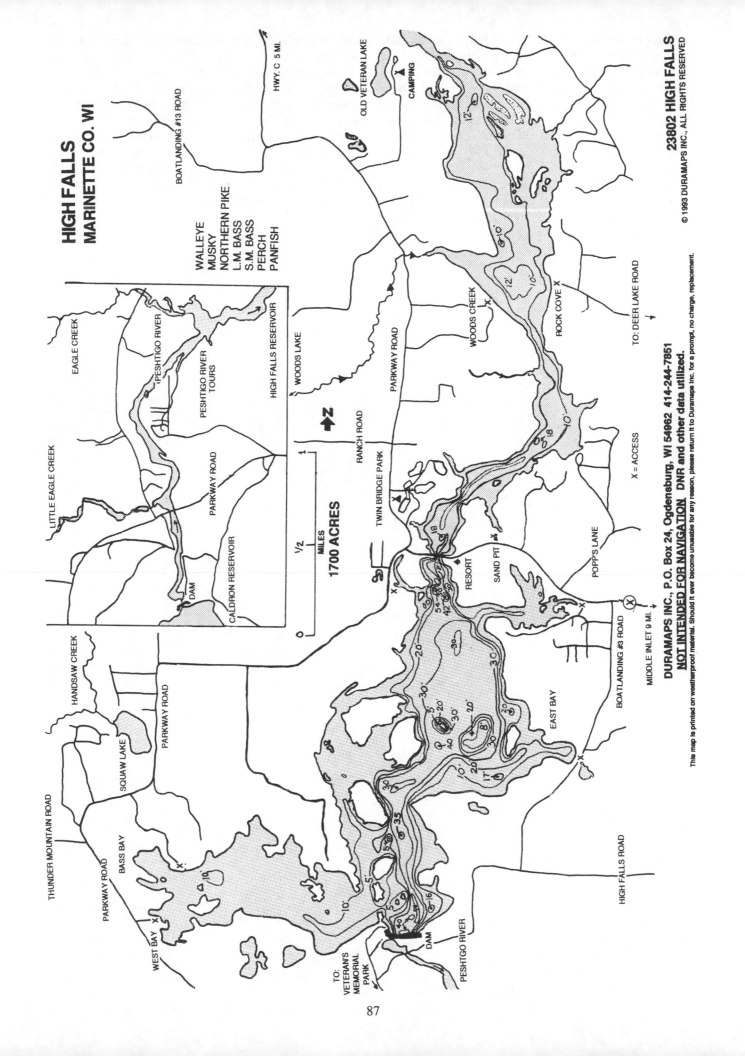

HIGH FALLS
MARINETTE CO. WI

WALLEYE
MUSKY
NORTHERN PIKE
L.M. BASS
S.M. BASS
PERCH
PANFISH

1700 ACRES

MILES
0   1/2   1

N

EAGLE CREEK

LITTLE EAGLE CREEK

PESHTIGO RIVER

PESHTIGO RIVER TOURS

HIGH FALLS RESERVOIR

PARKWAY ROAD

CALDRON RESERVOIR

DAM

BOATLANDING #13 ROAD

HWY. C 5 MI.

OLD VETERAN LAKE

CAMPING

WOODS LAKE

WOODS CREEK

PARKWAY ROAD

RANCH ROAD

TWIN BRIDGE PARK

ROCK COVE X

TO: DEER LAKE ROAD

RESORT

SAND PIT

POPP'S LANE

X = ACCESS

EAST BAY

BOATLANDING #3 ROAD

MIDDLE INLET 9 MI.

HANDSAW CREEK

SQUAW LAKE

THUNDER MOUNTAIN ROAD

PARKWAY ROAD

PARKWAY ROAD

PARKWAY ROAD

BASS BAY

WEST BAY X

TO: VETERAN'S MEMORIAL PARK

DAM

PESHTIGO RIVER

HIGH FALLS ROAD

DURAMAPS INC., P.O. Box 24, Ogdensburg, WI 54962 414-244-7851
NOT INTENDED FOR NAVIGATION   DNR and other data utillized.

23802 HIGH FALLS

two good landings on the west shore: one at Twin Bridge County Park and Campground north of the Highway X bridge, and one south of the bridge. There are two more on the east shore: one on a back bay at Popp's Resort, and another on Boat Landing No. 7 Road near Wolf Rock Motel and Campground. This last landing has a wheelchair access. A handicapped-accessible fishing pier is also slated for the Twin Bridge area.

A five-mile stretch of trout water on the Peshtigo River below Johnson Falls Dam, the next reservoir below High Falls, is open to fishing with artificials only. Water levels here fluctuate depending on power production, but you can call WPSC's toll-free number for water level information: (800) 236-7341.

Popp's Resort, Route 3, Crivitz, WI 54114, telephone (715) 757-3511, has the only bait and tackle shop right on the flowage, although there are others nearby and in town. To book a guided fishing trip, contact: Mike Mladenik, Route 2, Crivitz, WI 54114, telephone (715) 854-2055. For a complete list of area services, contact: Crivitz Recreation Association, Crivitz, WI 54114, telephone (715) 757-3651.

Lake Kegonsa

Stoughton, Dane County

Maybe my mind is warped, but when I first heard that Beach Boys tune from a few years back, the one that catalogs all those tropical paradises that the singer invites his sweetie to visit with him, the first thing that came to mind was a Wisconsin version featuring the Madison chain of lakes: "Mendota, Monona, come on Babe we're gonna ... Kegonsa, Yahara, it sure beats the Sahara ... Waubesa, Wingra, come on girl we'll linger ... Cherokee, Upper Mud ... " Oh well, it sort of loses its rhythm there at the end. I don't know where that notion came from, but I'll always be indebted to Brian, Mike and Carl for helping me remember the names of our Capitol City's lakes and the river that threads them together. Now if I could only recall which is which ...

In case you have the same problem, here they are, from north to south (upstream to downstream), but with no attention to rhythm or rhyme: Cherokee, Mendota, Monona, Upper Mud, Waubesa, Lower Mud, Kegonsa. Spring-fed Wingra has an outlet to Monona, but is not on the Yahara River, while all the others are. That makes Kegonsa the last lake in the chain. From its outlet at Kegonsa, the Yahara River wanders aimlessly through southern Dane and Rock counties on its way to merge with the Rock River downstream from Indianford. Now that you know more than you need to about the Yahara and the Madison chain, let's look more closely at Kegonsa.

At 3,200 acres, Kegonsa is about the size of Monona, but it is somewhat shallower and murkier, with a heavy summer algae bloom and less abundant submergent vegetation. The lake bottom is mostly sand and muck, but there is extensive gravel and rock along the entire shoreline except for the marshy north end east of the Yahara River inlet.

Kegonsa receives less recreational boating and fishing pressure than the upper lakes, and it is harder to fish, since fish tend to be scattered. Panfish are less abundant than on Mendota or Monona, but they run bigger. The current crop of perch and crappies includes a good number of 12-inchers, and bluegills that push nine or 10 inches are common. White bass, too, have come on strong in recent years.

According to DNR fish manager Scot Stewart, walleyes are doing well here, thanks to massive stocking efforts. Stewart planted over 250,000 wall-eye fingerlings from 1989 through 1992. To supplement fingerling stocking, the Madison Fishing Expo funded a portable fish hatchery for use on the Madison Chain. Dubbed the "walleye wagon," this 20-jar mini-hatchery produced a million walleye fry in 1991 and again in '92 using eggs and milt taken from Kegonsa fish. The fry are held in the walleye wagon until they reach swim-up stage, then they are released in the Yahara River below Lake Waubesa. From there, currents take them home to Kegonsa.

Northern pike are fewer in number, but Kegonsa holds some nice fish. The DNR stocks some 2,500 fingerlings in alternate years, supplemented by several large plantings of fry. Since pike spawn earlier than walleyes, the walleye wagon does double duty and produces a half million northern fry annually as well.

The most exciting news on the game fish management front here is the introduction of hybrid muskies to the lake beginning in 1985. Anglers are already catching legal fish in good numbers.

Lake
Kegonsa

Big northern pike practice their tackle-busting ways in the waters of Lake Kegonsa.

Stewart's management plans for Kegonsa include continued stocking of muskies, northerns and walleyes and improvement of the marsh at the north end of the lake as spawning habitat. In addition to the walleye wagon, proceeds from the annual Madison Fishing Expo have helped improve spawning areas on the Yahara River between Kegonsa and Lake Waubesa. Stewart is hopeful that more of Kegonsa's walleyes will spawn there to bolster the population.

Expo proceeds and the Friends of Lake Kegonsa have funded the placement of 250 fish cribs in the last few years. The cribs are all in about 10 to 15 feet of water in the following locations: off Williams Point on the northeast shore, on a bar south and west of the inlet, on the east side of the shallow rock bar off Calladay Point on the west shore, about midway across Calladay Bay between Calladay Point and the inlet, and along the southeast shore. These cribs are already producing good catches of panfish and walleyes and should continue to do so.

Moving around the lake counter-clockwise from the inlet on the north shore, other traditional walleye hotspots include the river mouth and nearby rock bar in spring, the turns and breaks on the bar off Calladay Point, the gravel bar off Lund's Point (the major point along the south shore), the rocky shoreline and sloping gravel bottom off Nichols Point, several small humps off Williams Bay west of the Yahara River outlet, and the dropoff all around Williams Point.

Try the shallower parts of these areas early in the year and in the evening in summer, and the deeper portions and steeper dropoffs during the day in summer. Walleyes may be scattered over a large area, so troll weedlines with diving crankbaits to find them, then try vertical jigging with live bait or drifting with a leech on a slip bobber.

Northerns and muskies hang out in the shallower bays, especially where there are weeds and flat shelves near dropoffs. Don't neglect the inlet bay for pike. Try flashy spinnerbaits and noisy topwater lures for both.

A few smallmouth bass are present, but hardly enough to worry about. Largemouths are fairly common in the shallow bays and on humps. Try Lincoln Park Bay and Barbers Bay in the southwest corner, and Atkinson Bay in the southeast corner. Floating Rapalas, stickbaits and plastic worms should take bass. Some nice largemouths show up every year. A young angler hauled in a 6-1/2-pounder during the Stoughton Conservation Club's Ice Fisheree in February 1990.

Kegonsa's panfish are often worth the trip in themselves. For a taste of bluegill fishing at its best, work the beds in the bays off Kegonsa State Park or Lincoln Park with a fly rod and little poppers and spiders in May. Try the outside weedlines for crappies in summer. They suspend at about mid-depth and will hit small jigs and Willy Worms, Slo-Poke Minis with tube tails, or small fathead minnows on a slip bobber.

There are several public boat ramps, starting at the inlet and moving clockwise around the lake: one off Fish Camp Road at the Yahara inlet, one off Sugar Bush Avenue on the northeast shore, and one with a wheelchair-accessible pier just east of there in Lake Kengonsa State Park. The state recently purchased the landing off Quam Drive on Dewey Bay east of Lund's Point and put in a concrete slab and a paved parking lot.

Quam's Marina has been a fixture on the lake for as long as anyone can remember. Address: 1896 Barber Drive, Stoughton, WI 53589, telephone (608) 873-3366. Another long-time service just down the road is Brown's Bait, 1958 Barber Drive, Stoughton, WI 53589, telephone (608) 873-6770.

The nearest well-stocked tackle shops are in Madison. For reliable information on fishing, contact: Dorn Hardware, 5503 Monona Drive, Madison, WI 53716, telephone (608) 222-4157; or D & S Bait,

1411 Northport Drive, Madison, WI 53704, telephone (608) 241-4225. Anglers coming from the Milwaukee area often stop at Dick Smith's Live Bait & Tackle in The Barn at the Hartland-Wales exit on I-94 at Highway 83, telephone (414) 646-2218. Jim Zielinski guides on Kegonsa and the rest of the Madison Chain. Contact him at 630 Rogers Street, Fort Atkinson, WI 53538, telephone (414) 563-8282.

There are 80 campsites at Lake Kegonsa State Park on the east shore, and one resort on the lake: Sunnyside Resort, 3097 Sunnyside Street, Stoughton, WI 53589, telephone (608) 873-9484. For information on restaurants and other area facilities, contact: Stoughton Chamber of Commerce, 532 E. Main Street, Stoughton, WI 53589, telephone (608) 873-7912.

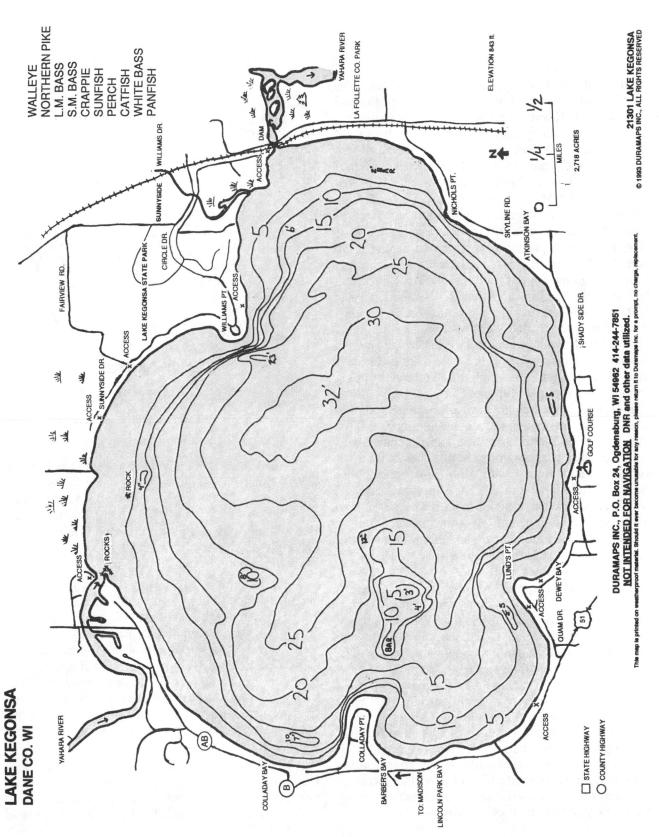

LAKE KEGONSA
DANE CO. WI

WALLEYE
NORTHERN PIKE
L.M. BASS
S.M. BASS
CRAPPIE
SUNFISH
PERCH
CATFISH
WHITE BASS
PANFISH

ELEVATION 843 ft.

21301 LAKE KEGONSA
© 1993 DURAMAPS INC., ALL RIGHTS RESERVED

2,718 ACRES

☐ STATE HIGHWAY
○ COUNTY HIGHWAY

Lake Koshkonong

Southwestern Jefferson County, Northern Rock County

The first time I laid eyes on Lake Koshkonong was on Valentine's Day a few years back when the late "Musky Bill" Klanchar invited me to sample the fantastic crappie fishing there. The lake was frozen, of course, and Bill had been doing well on Koshkonong's slab crappies for several weeks when I joined him. I took North Shore Road off Highway 106 out of Fort Atkinson and drove to a tavern called The Lamp as Bill suggested, then put the Jeep in four wheel drive and struck out south across the ice.

Aside from a pressure ridge or two a mile or so out, the driving was easy and tracks left by other vehicles told me I was heading in the right direction. Bill told me to give the Rock River mouth a wide berth and said I'd find him close to shore in Haight's Bay. There are no road signs on Koshkonong, but I soon spotted a knot of cars and ice fishermen and had no trouble locating Bill's big blue Buick. He was glad to see me and the supply of Rembrandt jigging spoons I had brought with me.

Bill showed me how to work a Rembrandt on light line, starting just below the ice and jigging it lightly, lowering it six inches at a time until I found fish. I marveled at how those crappies just sucked up a silver Rembrandt tipped with a hot pink rubber boot without any bait on it at all. The supply of crappies, which all seemed to be cast from the same 12-inch mold, was unending, and we soon had a dozen or more flopping on the ice. Anglers all around us were filling buckets with them, using Rembrandts, minnows and who knows what other baits.

Most of those crappies are gone now, and there has not been a good hatch to equal the production of a couple years in the early 1980s that were responsible for that bonanza. Such is the nature of the cyclic highs and lows that panfish populations experience. Fortunately, some other species often fills the void left by a decline in one, and the beat goes on.

Koshkonong's perch are still strong, but white bass were practically wiped out by a 1989 winterkill. Enough white bass survived and spawned in the river to bring off a good hatch that same year, and their offspring spawned successfully in '92, so in another three or four years white bass may replace perch as the mainstay of Koshkonong's panfishery, and by then it may be the crappies' turn again.

Lake
Koshkonong

Formed by the Indianford Dam on the Rock River, Koshkonong is a shallow, dark water flowage that covers some 10,000 acres in the southwestern corner of Jefferson County and spills over into Rock and Dane counties as well. At normal pool level, Koshkonong's maximum depth is all of seven feet, but fluctuations of up to two feet occur at times.

The lake bottom is mostly sand, with some gravel and muck. Fish-holding structure is limited to several gravel and rock bars that extend north from Thibeau's Point and Bingham's Point on the south shore, rock and rubble at the mouth of the Rock River and around Blackhawk Island on the east shore, an area known as the Shoal Bars a half mile north of Bingham's Point, and a ridge of sand that extends across the lake just west of Thibeau's Point. Subtle differences in depth anywhere on the lake can also hold fish.

A high carp population kept weed growth in check for years, but carp, too, experienced poor reproduction for nearly a decade, allowing vegetation to recover nicely. Carp pulled off a couple successful hatches in a row in the late '80s, however, and according to fish manager Don Bush, commercial fishermen are removing as many carp as they can to prevent them from taking over again.

Walleyes are the dominant game fish on Koshkonong and the main target of the DNR's management plan for the lake. Some 4 million walleye fry were planted in even-numbered years from 1982 through 1990 to supplement natural reproduction. In 1992, the walleye allocation was lowered to a half million fry. According to Bush, there is some successful natural reproduction every year. Occasional fish over eight pounds are caught, primarily by ice fishermen, indicating a well-balanced population.

Just after ice-out, look for pre-spawn walleyes near the mouth of the Rock and on all the structure along the east shore. Walleyes run up the river as far as the dam in Jefferson, where many are taken in spring. Swimming jigs, like the Slo-Poke and Swimmin' Ratt, tipped with minnows or plastic tails should produce well over shallow structure in spring.

After spawning, walleyes head for the deeper structure off Thibeau's and Bingham's points, where drifting with slip bobbers and leeches or trolling with fluorescent crankbaits will take them. Walleye action slows in summer, but picks up dramatically in September along all the structure mentioned above. Late in the fall, fish big minnows slowly in deep water for a crack at a real wall-hanger.

DNR crews stocked 300,000 sauger fry for the first time in 1989, and Bush says they're doing well, adding a new wrinkle to walleye fishing now that the 15-inch size limit is in effect. The combined daily bag limit is five walleyes and saugers, but the size limit at the time of this writing applies only to walleyes. Saugers have a spotted dorsal fin and lack the walleye's white-tipped lower tail lobe. Better learn to tell the difference between a sauger and a walleye, or else toss 'em all back if they're under 15 inches.

Recent dry springs have hurt northern pike production and their numbers are down. DNR crews planted 2.4 million pike fry in 1990, but not many of those fish survived. There are a fair number of pike in the 24- to 28-inch class, but most of the big pike are gone. Traditional pike hotspots include Stinker's Bay north of the Rock inlet, the inlet area itself, Lalk's Bay between Thibeau's and Bingham's points, and the entire northwest bay. Try trolling large flashy spoons in these areas, especially along the edges of weedbeds.

Several area fishing clubs have helped fund a hatchery on the Rock River at Fort Atkinson. "Starting in 1993, we'll be taking our own eggs from northerns, walleyes and saugers," says Bush. Like the walleye wagon on the Madison Chain, this hatchery will raise fry to the swim-up stage, then let them drift down to the lake. Bush hopes to produce 4 mil-

Koshkonong crappies, close up and personal. Photo by Dan Small

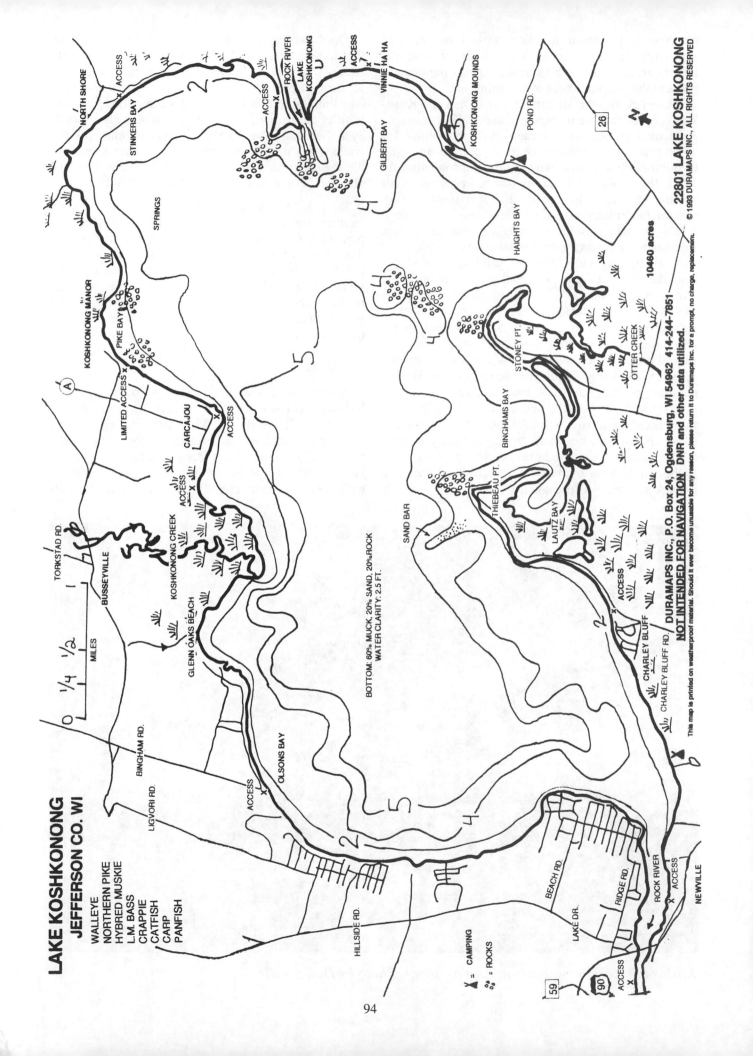

LAKE KOSHKONONG
JEFFERSON CO. WI

WALLEYE
NORTHERN PIKE
HYBRED MUSKIE
L.M. BASS
CRAPPIE
CATFISH
CARP
PANFISH

BOTTOM: 60% MUCK, 20% SAND, 20% ROCK
WATER CLARITY: 2.5 FT.

= CAMPING
= ROCKS

22801 LAKE KOSHKONONG
© 1993 DURAMAPS INC., ALL RIGHTS RESERVED

DURAMAPS INC., P.O. Box 24, Ogdensburg, WI 54962 414-244-7851
10460 acres   NOT INTENDED FOR NAVIGATION   DNR and other data utilized.

This map is printed on weatherproof material. Should it ever become unusable for any reason, please return it to Duramaps Inc. for a prompt, no charge, replacement.

94

lion walleyes, 4 million sauger and a million northerns each year here.

Muskies have been stocked here since 1989, when 400,000 hybrid fry were put in. Since then, 2,500 muskies have been planted annually, with true muskies supplanting hybrids as of 1992. Since many Koshkonong muskies migrate down the Rock River to Illinois, the Illinois DNR provided 5,000 fingerlings for stocking in Koshkonong. Northerns are legal all year and there is no size limit, while true and hybrid muskies can only be taken after the general inland opener in May and must measure 32 inches.

Weedbeds in any of the bays are the place to look for bluegills, largemouths and perch. These species have all done well in recent years, thanks to effective carp control.

Channel catfish are also in good supply and increasing every year. More anglers are turning to them for year-round action. You'll find them close to shore as the water warms in spring and in deep water areas of the Rock River both above and below the lake. Don Bush admits he takes an occasional cat during lunch breaks fishing right from shore by the DNR office in Newville, about a mile downstream from the lake. His favorite bait? Uncle Josh Cheese Bait with blood added, smeared on a corrugated Doc's Getter Worm. He fishes this rig with a slip sinker so a cat can mouth the bait with no resistance.

Another recent Illinois contribution to Koshkonong's fishery was a half ton of flathead catfish. Commercial fishermen on the Rock River in Sterling provided 125 flatheads weighing up to 25 pounds that were released in the lake and the river upstream as far as Johnson Creek. Hook one of these babies and you'll know you're into something! Hint: they eat live carp.

There are two state-run boat landings on the Rock River, one off Groeler Road at the public hunting ground a mile upstream from the lake, and one downstream from the outlet on Ellendale Road that was improved in 1992 with a new concrete ramp, paved parking lot and dusk-to-dawn light. A second pier is slated for installation there in 1993. The Groeler Road landing will be moved a half mile upstream and upgraded to coincide with the construction of the Highway 26 bypass, probably in 1994. There is another state landing on Kuehn Road at Carcajou Point on the lake's north shore, and a county park landing on the south shore at Dallman's Park, on Charley Bluff Road off Highway 59. Several resorts, taverns and marinas also operate private landings.

There are two marinas on the Rock River in Newville: Denna Marine, Edgerton, WI 53534, telephone (608) 884-9415, and Harbor Recreation, 807 Harbor Road, Milton, WI 53563, telephone (608) 884-6007. On the Fort Atkinson side, Patten's Marine operates a full-service marina with 42 boat slips, boat rentals and a bait and tackle shop. Address: W6745 Highway 106, Fort Atkinson, WI 53538, telephone (414) 563-5350. Geno Johnson at Patten's is a good source of fishing information on the lake.

Jim Zielinski guides anglers on Koshkonong and the Rock River from ice-out until mid-June, when he heads up to Sawyer County for the summer. Contact him at 630 Rogers Street, Fort Atkinson, WI 53538, telephone (414) 563-8282.

For information on area resorts, campgrounds, restaurants and other facilities, contact: Edgerton Area Chamber of Commerce, P.O. Box 5, Edgerton, WI 53534, telephone (608

Lac Courte Oreilles

Eight Miles South of Hayward, Sawyer County

Lac Courte Oreilles

There is probably no lake in the Hayward area -- or anywhere, for that matter -- that has produced more big muskies over a longer time period than Lac Courte Oreilles. Back in the 1940s, when the world was waking up to Wisconsin's musky potential, Lac Courte Oreilles gave up two fish over 60 pounds, the biggest of which was the world-record 67-1/2-pounder Cal Johnson caught there on July 24, 1949. That fish is still on display at the Moccasin Bar in Hayward. The ink on Johnson's world record certificate was barely dry when Louis Spray nailed a bigger fish on the Chippewa Flowage three months later, but Spray's fish did nothing to diminish Lac Courte Oreilles' reputation as a trophy musky lake.

That reputation still stands today. No one has taken another 60-pounder, but according to DNR fisheries manager Frank Pratt, Lac Courte Oreilles has produced more muskies over 30 pounds (including a number of fish topping 40 pounds) in the last decade than any other lake in the area. Why? At least two reasons: its size and its forage base of ciscoes. At 5,039 acres, LCO is the largest natural lake in the

county. Its deepest point is 91 feet and its mean depth is 34 feet. That amount of water gives muskies a better chance of evading anglers while they grow older, heavier and more selective in their feeding habits.

Big muskies here roam the open lake, feeding heavily on the large schools of cisco that inhabit its depths. Deep-water muskies typically suspend lethargically near the bottom of the thermocline, keeping track of roving schools of ciscoes. When hunger calls, they simply slash into a school, knock a bunch of ciscoes silly, pick them off one at a time until they've had their fill, then resume their suspended watch. Even if you can locate them, you can drag any number of baits past inactive fish to no avail.

Whitefish, redhorse, white suckers, perch and small walleyes round out the forage base here, which produces some whopper northerns and walleyes as well. Growth rates for all three species are high.

Northerns spawn successfully here, but both muskies and walleyes need help. The DNR stocks some 2,500 fingerling muskies per year to supplement natural reproduction. The lake's abundant northerns spawn earlier than muskies and use the same areas, so young northerns eat most of the musky fry that manage to hatch.

Fisheries crews currently stock some 100,000 two-inch walleye fingerlings every other year, double the rate of recent years. "The adult walleye population is between two and three per acre, but there is no natural reproduction to speak of," explains Pratt. "There is some bioenergetic feedback within the fish community that inhibits reproduction at this population density -- it may be as simple as ciscoes feeding on walleye fry. Our goal is to boost the walleye population to the point where natural reproduction kicks in."

That happened on nearby Grindstone Lake when the density reached three adult walleyes per acre, and Pratt hopes the same thing will occur here.

Fishing strategies here follow the seasons. In spring, you'll find muskies and northerns in the warmer, shallow waters of Musky and Stukey bays at the west end or Barbertown Bay at the far east end of the lake. Try shallow-running crankbaits like a Grandma or Crane in the smaller sizes, or slow-moving bucktails. Natural colors work best. If these spots don't produce, troll over the tops of the larger, shallower bars, like Winter Bar off the north shore or Blue Goose Bar at the northeast end.

In summer, you'll still find some fish along deep weed edges, where you can reach them with diving crankbaits or big jigs and plastics, but the biggest fish will be suspended in deep water. Use your locator to find a school of ciscoes, then look for larger blips which indicate predators -- pike, muskies or even big walleyes. Troll weighted flashers, silver spoons or deep-diving crankbaits through these areas or try vertical jigging with a Fuzzy Duzzit or Bullet.

When heavy recreational boat traffic makes daytime fishing difficult in summer, switch to night fishing. You won't catch pike at night, but muskies often prowl the shallow bars and weedbeds after dark. Start on top with a Hawg Wobbler, Cisco Kid Topper, Globe or other splashy bait, then try shallow-running bucktails with oversize blades -- the kind that really thump when they turn. Retrieve them just below the surface and be prepared for a crashing strike, often at boatside. If the shallows don't produce at night, troll or throw deep-diving crankbaits along the deep weed edges. This is tricky fishing, but it can produce big fish. Before fishing at night, clean up your boat and stow all unnecessary gear. It's no fun trying to untangle a net or jerk a hook out of your arm in the dark. Wear a headlamp to assist in boating and releasing fish.

In fall, muskies zero in on spawning ciscoes, then most head for deep water. Troll or cast silver baits along the north shore west of Moccasin Point, or soak a big sucker along steep dropoffs. Good late-season spots include Wismo Point on the southwest shore, Blue Goose Bar and Frenchman's Bar, both on the north shore.

Spring walleye action is hot along the Victory Heights shoreline west of the Wismo Point boat landing. Try drifting with a jig and minnow or trolling diving crankbaits. In summer, drift over the steep sides of sunken bars with leeches or crawlers. Several hundred brush and concrete fish cribs were placed in shoreline areas back in the 1960s. Some of these still hold walleyes and panfish. DNR crews recently placed 50 space-age plastic fish cribs near the mouth of Musky Bay which should be better prospects for walleyes.

The smallmouth population is on the rise, according to Frank Pratt, and the lake produces some real trophies. Try gravel shorelines throughout the lake early in the year and bars and dropoffs along the north shore later in summer. Live bait on slip-sinker rigs or small crankbaits will take them. Largemouths are also increasing in number, but they are primarily confined to weedy bays.

Of the panfish species, perch and crappies stand out. Perch numbers are increasing, and anglers take fair catches of fish in the eight- to 10-inch range on

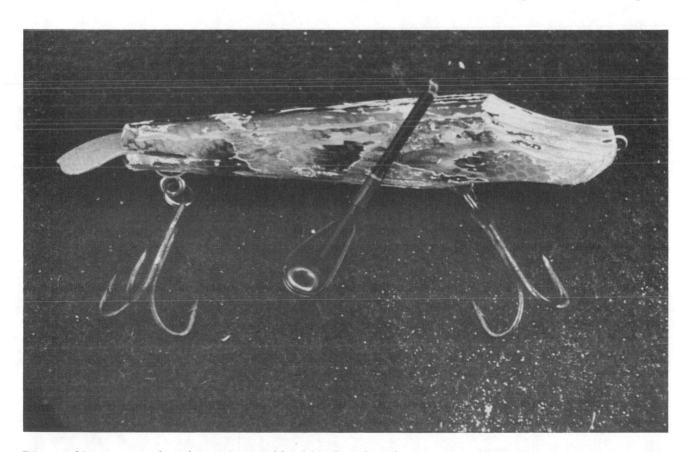

Big muskies are good at damaging tackle. It's what they do. Lac Courte Oreilles is full of big muskies, so bring plenty of gear. Photo by Dan Small

live bait along deep weed edges and over shallow bars. Crappies are hard to locate, but they run big. Look for suspended schools off bay mouths in spring and in deeper water later. Tiny jigs on light line work well. Ice fishermen concentrate in and near Musky Bay, where they take good catches of perch and crappies, along with some bluegills.

Navigable channels connect Lac Courte Oreilles with Whitefish Lake, Grindstone Lake and Little Courte Oreilles Lake, all of which harbor the same mix of fish species.

There are two public landings off Highway K on the north shore. The best of these, at Chicago Bay, features two concrete ramps, restrooms and plenty of paved parking. The other is located just west of the Grindstone Creek inlet. On the south shore, there is another landing with a paved ramp west of Wismo Point on the Victory Heights Peninsula.

For bait and tackle, try Pastika's Sporting Goods, 217 Dakota Avenue, Hayward, WI 54843, telephone (715) 634-4466. For information on resorts, campgrounds and other area services, contact the Hayward Lakes Resort Association, P.O. Box 1055 Hayward, WI 54843, telephone (800) 826-FISH.

No trip to the Hayward area is complete without a visit to the National Freshwater Fishing Hall of Fame, located just east of downtown. You can't miss it, because the Hall's main building is actually a gigantic leaping musky over four stories tall. You can walk up inside the fish and survey all of Hayward from the viewing platform in its mouth. Address: P.O. Box 33, Hall of Fame Drive, Hayward, WI 54843, telephone (715) 634-4440.

Long Lake

Southeastern Washburn County

On our way home from a busy week up in Bayfield, taping segments for *Outdoor Wisconsin* a couple summers ago, Nancy Frank, Jerry Luedkens and I swung through Sarona to visit the Hunt Hill Audubon Camp just east of town. We had been doing some rather strenuous stuff -- sea kayaking among the sandstone caves of the Apostle Islands and trolling for lake trout off Madeline Island, among other things. After battling the heavy swells of Lake Superior, we needed to relax, but we were fresh out of ideas.

"I hear the bluegills are biting on Long Lake," the caretaker told us, eyeing the camera boat we had in tow.

That was all the suggestion we needed. An afternoon of bluegill fishing seemed like just the thing, and nearby Long Lake seemed just the place. We launched our wave-weary boat at the public landing across the road from the laundromat on Highway M and headed up the lake between Kunz Island and the west shore.

Long Lake

Long Lake certainly lives up to its name, stretching in a lopsided "U" for some 16 miles along two county highways in southeastern Washburn County. Wedged into a narrow, steep-sided valley, this deep, clear lake covers some 3,300 acres and harbors good populations of panfish and gamefish. The southern end of the lake has all sorts of structure in the form of sunken islands and gravel points that drop off precipitously into 40 to 60 feet of water, creating superb habitat for walleyes and smallmouths. Countless small bays all along the shoreline are filled with submergent and floating vegetation that harbors largemouths, northerns and panfish.

No area lake produces more winners in local and regional fishing contests, but on that warm August day, competitive fishing was not what we had in mind. Pulling up onto a weedy bar that runs north and south off a much smaller island near the north end of Kunz Island, we rigged up our ultralight spinning rods with slip bobbers and Bait Rigs panfish rigs, baited up with small chunks of nightcrawler, and soon began catching bluegills to beat the band.

Most of the 'gills were on the small side, but along the dropoff where the weeds ended, we picked up an occasional fish that bent our rods double and made us whoop and holler, as we derricked them one after another into the boat. We released the majority, but those that were hooked too deeply to survive were kept for dinner. I had hoped for at least a slight breeze to push us along in a slow drift, but the lake's surface mirrored the sky, unbroken but for our dancing bobbers. After Lake Superior's brutal pounding, this was idyllic. We caught no real bragging fish, but after a couple hours motored back to the landing completely refreshed.

Many lakes could call themselves the "Walleye Capital of Wisconsin," but the Long Lake Chamber of Commerce had the foresight to register the title with the Secretary of State, and so this is the state's only "official" walleye capital. Long Lake certainly merits the designation, though, as it produces some of the biggest walleyes of any inland lake in the state. The state stocks some 60,000 walleye fingerlings annually to supplement natural reproduction. A good forage base, consisting mainly of white suckers and ciscoes, along with plenty of deep water and weeds

LONG LAKE

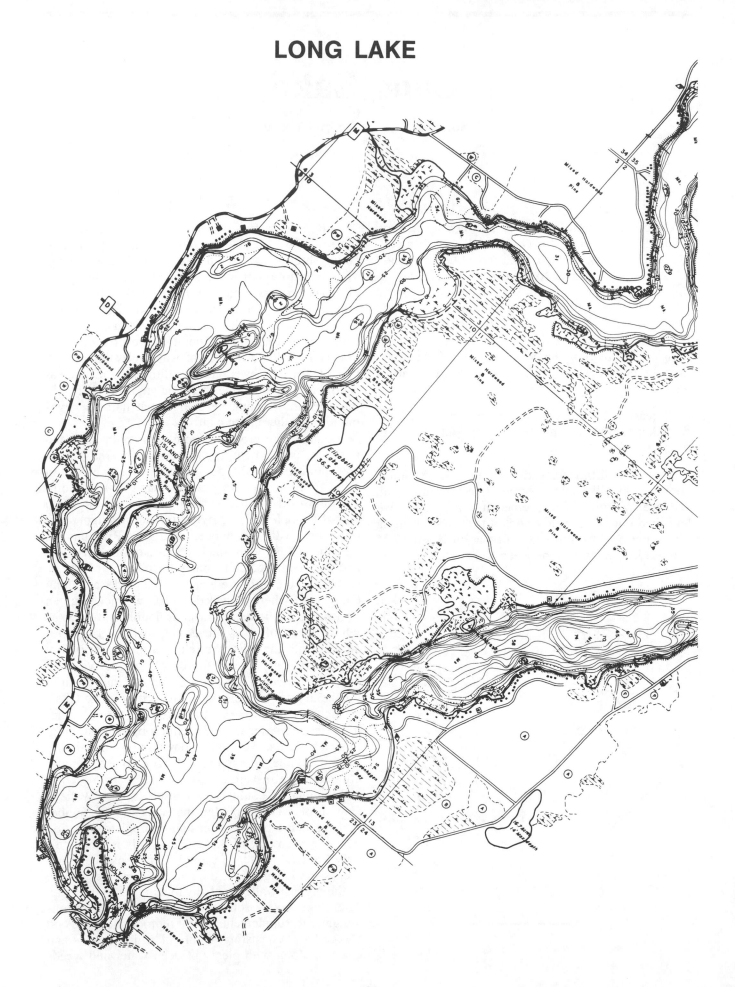

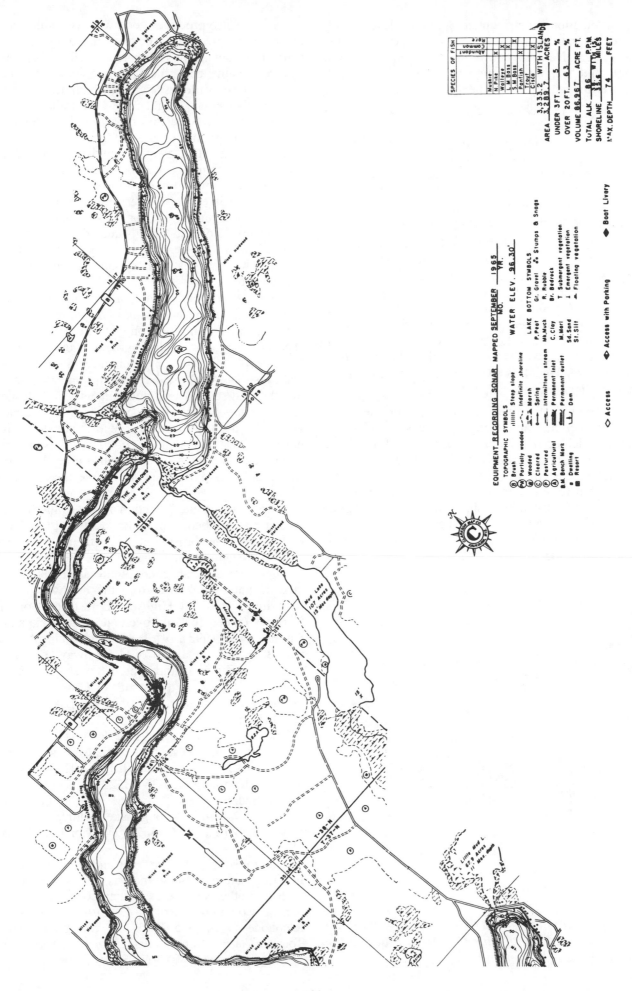

EQUIPMENT RECORDING SONAR MAPPED SEPTEMBER 1965

WATER ELEV. 96.30'

TOPOGRAPHIC SYMBOLS

Ⓑ Brush
ⓅⓌ Partially wooded
Ⓦ Wooded
Ⓒ Cleared
Ⓒ Pastured
Ⓐ Agricultural
B.M. Bench Mark
● Dwelling
■ Resort

ıllıllı Steep slope
˙˙˙˙ Indefinite shoreline
Marsh
Spring
Intermittent stream
Permanent inlet
Permanent outlet
Dam

LAKE BOTTOM SYMBOLS

P. Peat   Gr. Gravel   Stumps & Snags
Mk.Muck   R. Rubble
C. Clay   Br. Bedrock
M. Marl   T Submergent vegetation
Sd. Sand   ⅄ Emergent vegetation
Si. Silt   ⩘ Floating vegetation

◇ Access   ◈ Access with Parking   ◆ Boat Livery

SPECIES OF FISH	Abundant	Common	Rare
Muskie			X
N. Pike	X	X	
Walleye	X	X	
L.M. Bass	X		
S.M. Bass		X	
Panfish	X		
Trout			
Cisco		X	

AREA 3,333.2 WITH ISLAND
 _____ ACRES
UNDER 3FT. 5 %
OVER 20FT. 63 %
VOLUME 86,967 ACRE FT.
TOTAL ALK. 86 P.P.M
SHORELINE 31.6 WITH ISLAND MILES
MAX. DEPTH 74 FEET
3,289.7

for protection, contribute to good walleye growth here. Numerous fish over eight pounds are taken every year. Natural walleye reproduction was poor in 1990 and '91, but a strong year class in 1992 should bolster the fishery for the next few years.

Early in the season, the bars and gravel points of the lake's southern basin produce good walleye fishing. Becky Martino, proprietress of The Bait Shop on Long Lake, says local anglers use jigs tipped with three- to four-inch red-tailed chubs for walleyes in spring. The chubs are not available everywhere, but she keeps a good supply because the lake's walleyes seem to prefer them over other minnows.

Later in summer, drifting with leeches on spinner rigs produces well over deep structure, where many big walleyes are taken during daylight hours. On days with a light breeze, try a Bait Rigs Finicky Walleye Rig or an Infiltrator by Ray's Custom Tackle. The spinners on both these rigs revolve at slow speeds. Panfishermen also take enough big walleyes in the weeds to suggest this phenomenon is not a fluke. Weedless swimming jigs with plastic or pork trailers ought to take fish here.

A summer thermocline develops in the lake's deeper sections, and many species suspend in the oxygen-rich epilimnion anywhere from 10 to 25 feet deep. Schools of ciscoes frequent Gruenhagen Bay, the lake's eastern arm, and big walleyes and northerns often follow them around for an easy meal. To catch these suspended fish, troll with downriggers and diving crankbaits or flasher-and-minnow rigs. Watch your graph for schools of baitfish with larger blips below them.

Many anglers thrill to a nice batch of hand-sized bluegills, and Long Lake is a great place to find them. Photo by Dan Smal

Early ice also produces good walleye action. From ice-up until there is snow cover, most Long Lake regulars jig or set tip-ups with red-tailed chubs. After snow covers the ice, shiners seem to work better, perhaps because walleyes can see them from farther away in the reduced light. The best walleye action through the ice comes from sunset until midnight.

Pike fishing on Long Lake is almost an afterthought for most anglers, even though the lake's northerns are chunky and good eating. Several 20- to 25-pounders show up every season. Most, it seems, are taken on live chubs (the same redtails used for walleyes, in a larger size) or suckers hung below a big bobber and drifted along weed edges on a second or third rod by anglers after panfish. Some anglers cast the weed edges with spoons or troll for suspended fish.

DNR fish manager Larry Damman says smallmouth numbers are increasing in response to the new bass regulations, and foot-long fish are common here, especially around shallow gravel shoreline areas. Most people take them by accident while fishing for walleyes. The shallow bays hold some nice largemouths, and several bass tournaments are held here each summer. Mud Lake, accessible through a navigable channel off the east side of Long Lake just north of The Narrows, is a good early-season largemouth lake. It warms up sooner in spring than Long Lake, and pre-spawn bass are active there early in May.

Crappie and bluegill action is good all over the lake along weedbeds and in the mouths of bays. Two hotspots are The Narrows at the north end of the lake, and Holy Island Flats, at the extreme south end.

There are several good public landings on the lake. Counter-clockwise from the northwest shore, they are located: off Highway B just north of The Narrows (slated for improvement and an expanded parking lot in 1993), off Todd Road south of Highway B, east of the Highway M-Highway D intersection near Kunz Island on the west shore, off Schnacky Road near the mouth of Gruenhagen Bay on the southeast shore, and off Long Lake Road on the northeast shore.

The Bait Shop on Long Lake, located on Highway M along the southwest shore, can also match you up with a guide. Address: Route 1, Box 192, Sarona, WI 54870, telephone (715) 354-3322. Dan Lubinsky, at Marawaraden's Resort, is one of the best local authorities on fishing Long Lake. Address: Route 1, Box 228, Sarona, WI 54870, telephone (715) 354-3855.

Many resorts also carry bait and some rent boats. For information on the numerous resorts, area restaurants and other services, contact: Long Lake Chamber of Commerce, Route 1, Sarona, WI 54870, telephone (715) 635-3976; or Washburn County Tourism Association, Route 1, Box 327, Sarona, WI 54870, telephone (800) 367-3306.

McKenzie Lakes

Washburn-Burnett County Line

McKenzie Lakes

Every time I get an invitation to spend a day in the field with professional fish and wildlife managers, I jump at the chance because I know I'm going to learn something and more than likely come back with enough ideas and photos for a good story or two. On one of my first such outings, I met DNR fish managers Tom Beard and Stan Johannes one chilly April morning in 1981 on Big McKenzie Lake, about 10 miles northwest of Spooner on the Washburn -- Burnett county line.

They arrived at the landing with two large, green johnboats in tow. I had my camera, notebook and a winter parka to ward off the cold wind. They were wrapping up the field work for a fish population estimate, and their task that day was to check a series of fyke nets set around the lake for muskies, walleyes and northern pike. Beard and fish technician Don Stafford took off in one boat, while I hopped in the other boat with Johannes and technician Gary Lund.

As we headed out to check the first net, Johannes explained that they had fin-clipped every walleye, musky and northern captured during the first phase of the survey and had also put metal tags on a number of walleyes and muskies. In this second phase, they would note the percentage of marked fish recaptured to help them estimate the total population of each species.

Funnel-type fish traps, like most good tools, are simple and efficient, and they have always fascinated me. As Lund secured the first net to the boat and prepared to open it, I recalled my anticipation as a kid when I lifted my minnow traps out of the creek near home. On a good haul, the wire-mesh baskets would be full of fat-bodied chubs and minnows, wiggling frantically as the water drained away. Our first net was a good haul, and these critters were a lot bigger than my minnows. I stared bug-eyed and speechless, as Lund dip-netted over 150 chunky walleyes from the net bag and dumped them into a galvanized tub.

In the course of that day, the two crews handled well over 300 walleyes, some of them up to 27 inches in length, a couple dozen pike and muskies, and a handful of bass and panfish. They measured each fish, checked them for fin clips and noted their spawning condition. Every fish was returned to the lake, apparently none the worse for the experience. I shot several rolls of slides, took tons of notes, and just plain enjoyed the opportunity to see more big walleyes than I had ever observed in one place before.

Later, Johannes sent me the survey results. He estimated the lake held a total of 4,332 walleyes over 13 inches in length, or 3.8 fish per acre. Males captured averaged 18 inches, while females averaged 22 inches. Big McKenzie's musky population was estimated at 346 fish over 20 inches, or .3 fish per acre. The average female musky seen in the survey was 40 inches long, while males averaged 30 inches. The best musky the crew handled was a 47-inch beauty. Pike (both sexes) averaged 20 inches, but the sample size was too small to estimate the overall population.

Another survey conducted in 1987 showed an estimated population of 2,777 adult walleyes, or 2.3 per acre. While a significant drop from the 1981 level, this was still above the average for northwest Wisconsin lakes. The biggest fish marked in that survey was a 28.8-inch female. A 1990 follow-up survey showed little change in either the walleye or musky population, although northerns seemed to be down somewhat, perhaps due to poor spawning conditions during the drought of the late 1980s.

Fishing license revenues, along with Dingell-Johnson funds, pay for this work, and DNR fisheries crews conduct similar surveys every spring on as many lakes as possible to provide data that will help managers establish safe harvest limits. Surveys of northern Wisconsin lakes have been stepped up in the last few years, due to increased sport-fishing pressure and the Native American spear harvest, but the work is too labor-intensive and time-consuming to permit each crew to survey more than a few lakes during the brief spawning period each spring.

These surveys also help determine stocking levels. Currently, musky fingerlings are stocked every other year at a rate of one per acre, while 40,000 walleye fingerlings are stocked annually. Populations of both species appear to be doing well, according to fish manager Larry Damman, with no dramatic changes in the past few years.

At 1,185 acres and a maximum depth of 71 feet, Big McKenzie is the largest of three drainage lakes on McKenzie Creek. Middle McKenzie covers 530 acres and has a maximum depth of 45 feet, while Lower McKenzie is much smaller and shallower at 185 acres and 18 feet. Big and Middle McKenzie have similar structure, water quality and fish populations which move freely between the lakes via McKenzie Creek. Walleye, musky and northern pike are the dominant species. Middle McKenzie receives 25,000 walleyes every other year, but no muskies are stocked here. Both largemouth and smallmouth bass are present in moderate numbers, and crappies are the most abundant panfish. A fair cisco population in the deeper portions of both lakes helps put beef on gamefish.

Both of the larger lakes stratify in summer, and both have extensive gravel bars and enough vegetation to provide cover and structure for gamefish. Small boats can use McKenzie Creek to move from Big to Middle McKenzie, but the channel to Lower McKenzie is too shallow for fishing boats.

Walleye fishing is very good on the larger lakes when the season opens in May. Minnows work well now, since baitfish populations are low at this time. Look for walleyes along gravel bars at the north end of Big McKenzie and the south end of Middle McKenzie. In summer, walleyes move to deeper structure. In Middle McKenzie, a midlake hump due west of

DNR biologist Tom Beard (left) and fish technician Don Stafford tag a walleye during a spring population survey on Big McKenzie. Photo by Dan Small

the grassy island is a good spot to try, while the south end of Big McKenzie has a lot of similar structure. Slip bobbers and leeches or bait rigs and crawlers should produce well now. Motor trolling is allowed here and can be an effective way to locate walleyes in summer.

Ice fishing can be very productive in December, especially over the bars on both lakes and near the Big McKenzie outlet, but watch for thin ice there early in the season.

Creel census results reveal that August, September and October are the best months for muskies. Some anglers troll the bars and deep structure with bucktails or diving crankbaits, while the purists stick with casting and work shorelines, weedbeds and shallow humps. Most northern pike are taken incidentally by walleye and musky fishermen, but you can take fair catches of 20- to 30-inch pike in the weedbeds on live bait and spoons.

Crappies can provide decent action early in spring if you locate a suspended school. Later, look for them along dropoffs closer to shore or over the many shallow bars on either lake. Live minnows or small swimming jigs, especially in red and white patterns, will produce.

Unlike the two upper lakes, Lower McKenzie is very shallow and weedy, with a few small gravel bars. Largemouth bass are the primary gamefish here, and bass action can be very good in spring and early summer. Try the sandy north and south shorelines early in the year, then work the weedbeds with weedless lures. Surface baits can be productive along weed edges and over humps on warm summer evenings.

There is one public landing on each lake. On Big McKenzie, launch on the northeast shore off Highway E at the county line. The landing on Middle McKenzie is on the west shore off McKenzie Road. To reach the ramp on Lower McKenzie, continue north from Middle McKenzie on McKenzie Road, then go east on Zehm Road and south on Lower McKenzie Landing Road. The landing is near the outlet on the north shore.

For bait, tackle and guide service, try A & H Outpost and Bar at the intersection of Highways A and H west of Middle McKenzie Lake. Address: 2397 Highway A, Spooner, WI 54801, telephone (715) 635-3145. For information on area resorts, campgrounds and other services, contact: Burnett County Resort & Campground Owners Association, 6420 Highway 70, Siren, WI 54872, telephone (715) 349-2000; or Washburn County Tourism Association, Route 1, Box 327, Sarona, WI 54870, telephone (800) 367-3306.

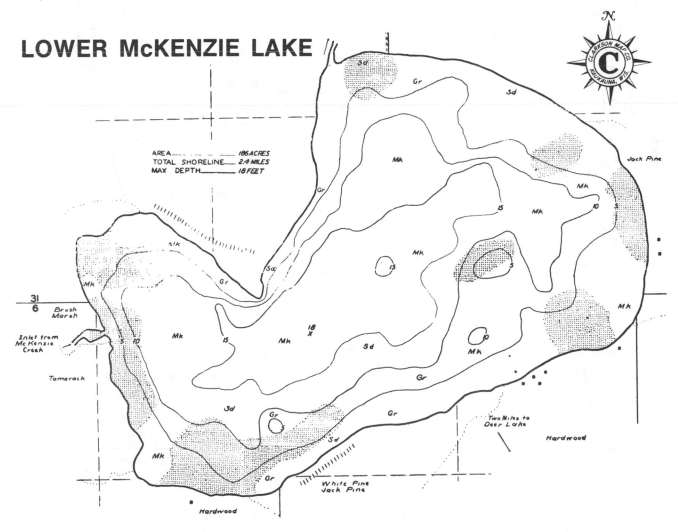

LOWER McKENZIE LAKE

AREA _____ 186 ACRES
TOTAL SHORELINE ___ 2.4 MILES
MAX DEPTH _____ 18 FEET

MIDDLE McKENZIE LAKE

SPECIES OF FISH	Abundant	Common	Present
Muskie			X
N. Pike	X		
Walleye			X
L.M.Bass	X		
S.M.Bass			
Panfish	X		
Trout			

WATER AREA _____ 529.7 _____ A(
UNDER 3 FT. _____ 7 _____
OVER 20 FT. _____ 56 _____
MAX. DEPTH _____ 45 _____ F
TOTAL ALK. _____ 67 _____
VOLUME _____ 10,782 _____ ACRE
SHORELINE _____ 3.96 _____ MI
SHORELINE 4.11 MILES WITH I:

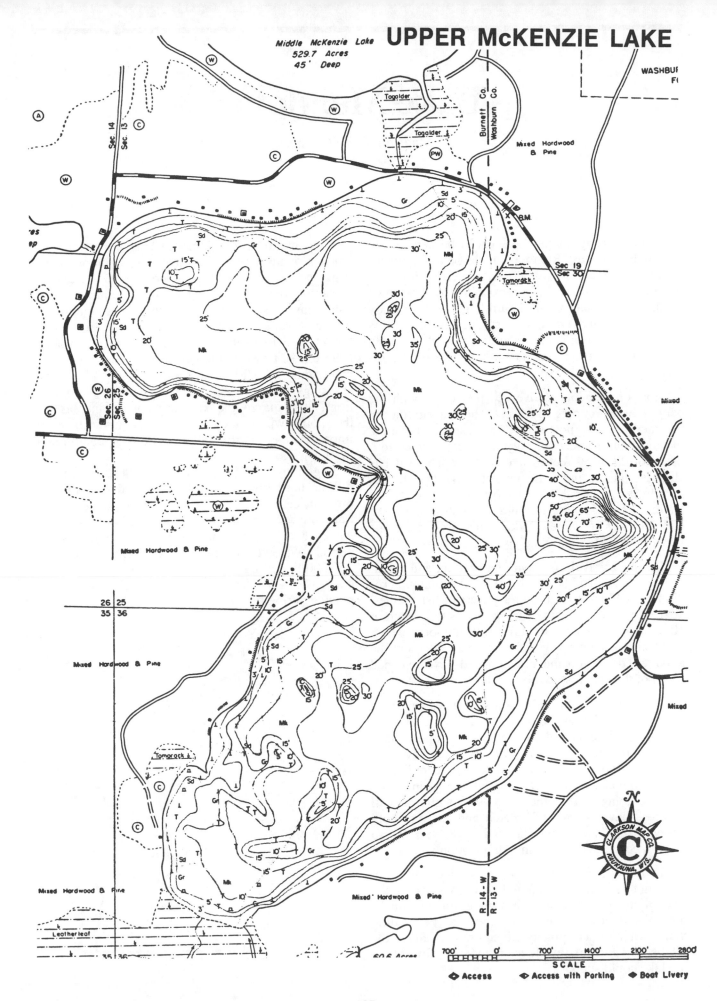

UPPER McKENZIE LAKE

Middle McKenzie Lake
529.7 Acres
45' Deep

SCALE
◆ Access   ◆ Access with Parking   ◆ Boat Livery

Lake Mendota

Madison, Dane County

A more cosmopolitan lake you'd be hard put to find in the Midwest. Mendota, the largest of the Madison Chain and at over 9,800 acres the fourth-largest natural lake in the state, is surrounded by downtown Madison, the State Capitol Building, the University of Wisconsin and a couple classy suburbs. Still, it is one of the best panfish lakes around, and it is rapidly becoming just as spectacular in the gamefish department.

Most of Mendota is over 20 feet deep, with the deepest hole dropping to 83 feet. The lake stratifies in summer, causing most species to suspend above the thermocline. There is usually adequate oxygen to a depth of 25 or 30 feet in late summer. The water is slightly murky, and a heavy summer algae bloom greatly reduces visibility in most years. The Yahara River enters Mendota through a marsh at the north end and exits at Tenney Park on the east shore on its way to lakes Monona, Waubesa and Kegonsa.

Sand and gravel dominate the bottom, and extensive rock reefs and humps break up the contour, providing excellent structure for a variety of fish species. Vast weedbeds cover the shallow areas to a depth of 10 feet or so. Eurasian milfoil, a noxious exotic, crowded out native vegetation in the 1960s, but the good weeds are on the rebound and have regained much of the area lost to the invader.

Over the years, different panfish species have succeeded each other as the primary fish in the lake and the creel. White bass, then perch, then crappies have assumed this role, while bluegill numbers have also risen and fallen in a cyclic pattern. According to DNR fish manager Scot Stewart, white bass in particular are doing well in the early '90s, while bluegill numbers have tapered off. Perch and crappies both pulled off abundant year classes in 1989 and '91, so these species should remain in good supply.

Gamefish populations, too, have fluctuated, but their numbers have remained low considering the size of the lake and availability of forage. Smallmouth and largemouth bass appear to be holding their own. Northern pike declined dramatically in the 1980s, however, and walleyes number far fewer than the lake could support.

Low numbers of gamefish, an abundance of smaller panfish, and a nuisance algae bloom have triggered a joint DNR-University of Wisconsin research project whose main goal is to improve sportfishing and restore adequate natural reproduction of pike and walleyes in Lake Mendota. Funded largely by Dingell-Johnson and Wallopp-Breaux money from excise taxes on the sale of sport fishing equipment, this $900,000 study aims to see if massive stockings of gamefish will reduce panfish populations, allowing zooplankton numbers to increase to the point where they will eat enough algae to improve water clarity. Talk about a food-chain reaction!

Beginning in 1987, 20 million walleye fry and 10 million northern pike fry were planted annually for three successive years. These were supplemented by fingerling plants of about 1-1/2 million two-inch walleyes and 45,000 nine-inch pike in that same period. Walleye stocking levels were reduced to 250,000 fingerlings annually from 1990 through '92, and just over 50,000 pike fingerlings were also planted during that period.

Annual electroshocking surveys and an on-going creel census will help researchers determine the effects of the project. To help these predator species become reestablished, a three-fish bag limit was imposed on walleyes with an 18-inch minimum size. The pike bag limit was cut to one fish over 32 inches per day. Stewart reports that both species are growing quickly and the pike fishery is on its way back to what it was in the 1960s. Sub-legal walleyes are abundant, but anglers are cropping them off quickly once they reach 18 inches.

Madison area fishing clubs have enthusiastically endorsed the project, and some have provided money and manpower to help with the restocking effort. In addition, proceeds from the annual Madison Fishing Expo held in February have helped with a variety of research and habitat improvement projects, including the construction of an artificial northern pike rearing marsh upstream from Lake Mendota.

All this effort appears to be paying off, as 1992 saw the first significant reproduction of northerns in Cherokee Marsh, Sixmile Creek and University Bay in many years. Stewart also cites improved cooperation with the Dane County Public Works Department to maintain adequate water levels during the critical ice-out spawning period for northerns. Stewart says the data gathered from this study has already

spawned one book, and knowledge gained here will help managers determine appropriate stocking levels, size limits and other regulations elsewhere.

DNR crews also stocked some 18,500 hybrid musky fingerlings during the 1980s. No more have been stocked since 1987, but some of those fish are pushing 30 pounds or better. Stewart told me of a 47-incher released by an angler in 1991 and a 48-incher handled in a DNR spring survey. Where can anglers try for them? Stewart says they're scattered near the better weedbeds, for example along the north shore, off Tenney Park, in the bay off Warner Park east of Governors Island, and all along the north shore from the Yahara River mouth west.

Walleye hotspots, especially through the ice, include dropoffs at Picnic Point and the huge Second Point Reef on the south shore, and Warner's Bay and Governors Island on the north shore. But why not let the walleyes fulfill their predator role and instead cash in on Mendota's fantastic panfish opportunities?

Take perch, for example. Local anglers report a brief flurry of fast action on tiny white or yellow plastics in new weeds in five or six feet of water during the spawning period in late April. Then in summer and fall they often roam the 15- to 30-foot depths in huge schools. Try drifting with long greens or other live bait on a plain No. 6 or 8 hook or 1/32-ounce jig head tipped with a strawberry-colored plas-

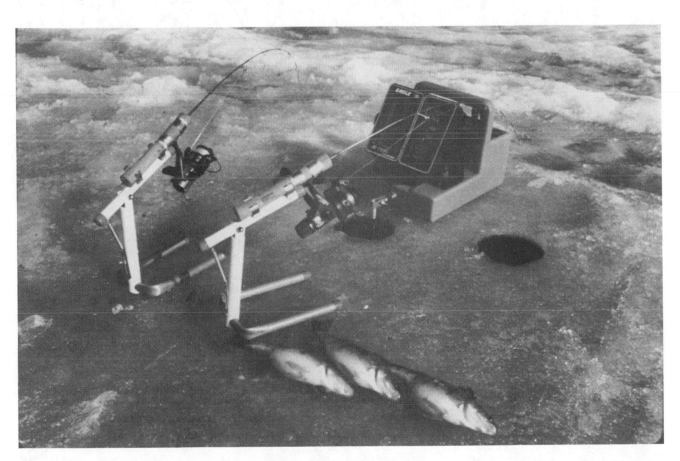

Here's the perfect deep water rig for taking Mendota's big perch — ultralight rods and reels and a sensitive locator to find schools. Photo by Dan Small

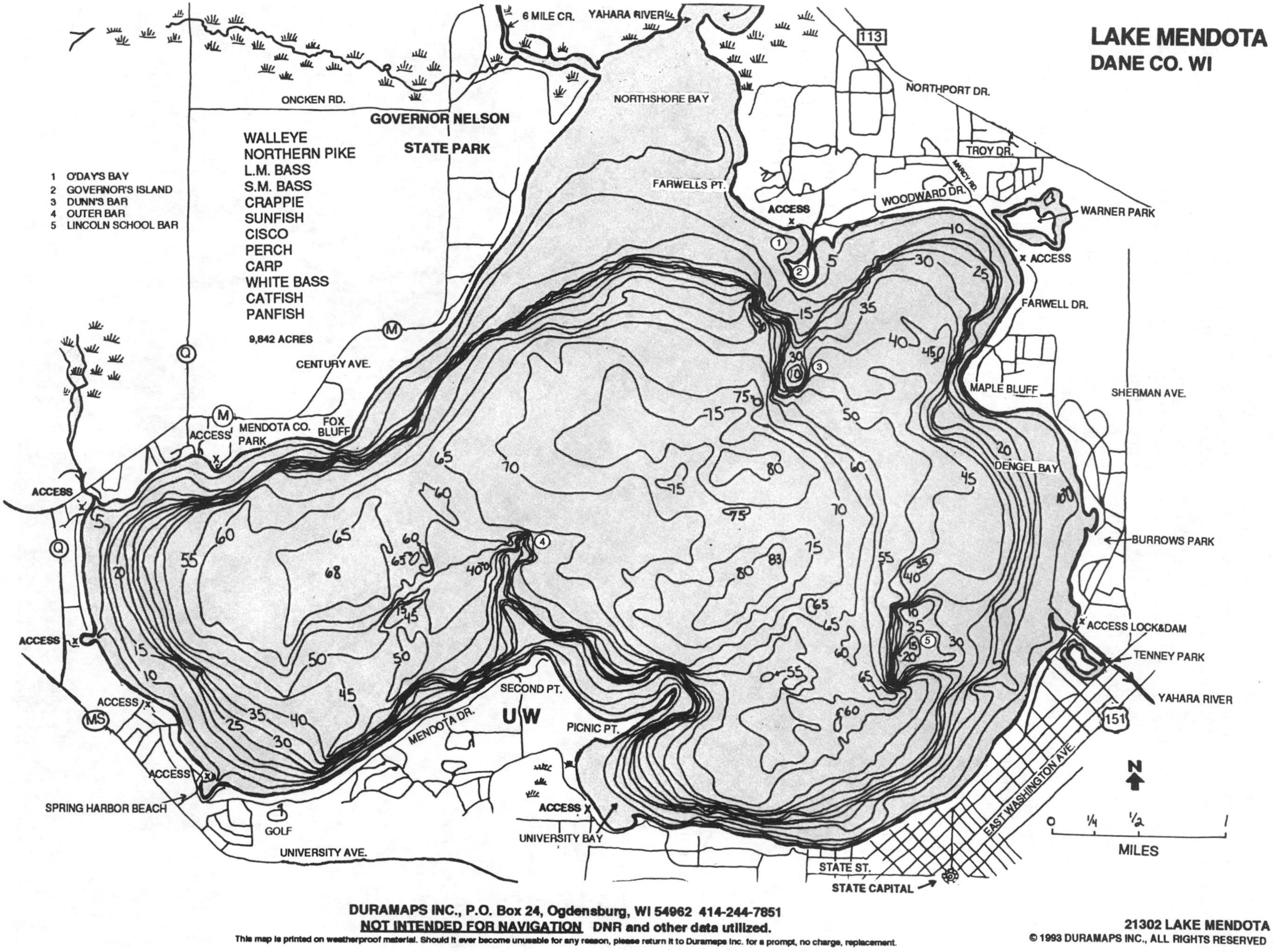

LAKE MENDOTA
DANE CO. WI

WARNER PARK

x ACCESS

SHERMAN AVE.

FARWELL DR.

BURROWS PARK

MAPLE BLUFF

DENGEL BAY

x ACCESS LOCK&DAM

TENNEY PARK

YAHARA RIVER

151

N

NORTHPORT DR.

113

TROY DR.

MARCY RD.

WOODWARD DR.

FARWELLS PT.

ACCESS x

1 2

6 MILE CR.

YAHARA RIVER

NORTHSHORE BAY

GOVERNOR NELSON
STATE PARK

ONCKEN RD.

WALLEYE
NORTHERN PIKE
L.M. BASS
S.M. BASS
CRAPPIE
SUNFISH
CISCO
PERCH
CARP
WHITE BASS
CATFISH
PANFISH

9,842 ACRES

1 O'DAYS BAY
2 GOVERNORS ISLAND
3 DUNN'S BAR
4 OUTER BAR
5 LINCOLN SCHOOL BAR

M MENDOTA CO.
PARK
ACCESS X

Q

CENTURY AVE.

FOX BLUFF

SECOND PT.

PICNIC PT.

UNIVERSITY BAY

ACCESS X

U/W

MENDOTA DR.

UNIVERSITY AVE.

GOLF

SPRING HARBOR BEACH

ACCESS X

MS

ACCESS X

Q

ACCESS

STATE ST.

STATE CAPITAL

EAST WASHINGTON AVE.

MILES

0   1/4   1/2

DURAMAPS INC., P.O. Box 24, Ogdensburg, WI 54962 414-244-7851
NOT INTENDED FOR NAVIGATION DNR and other data utilized.

This map is printed on weatherproof material. Should it ever become unusable for any reason, please return it to Duramaps Inc. for a prompt, no charge, replacement.

21302 LAKE MENDOTA

110

tic Willy Worm and waxworms or spikes. One effective drifting rig consists of an egg sinker threaded on the line above a simple barrel swivel, with the hook or jig tied to a 10-inch leader. The rig does double duty for Mendota's big bluegills, which you'll find suspended above the thermocline in summer.

I had a taste of Mendota's great winter perch action when I joined La Brant Pikalek, Jerry Honeyager and Jim Lindsey to tape an *Outdoor Wisconsin* segment on light-tackle ice fishing. We trudged out a mile or so off Governors Island and set up in about 75 feet of water. A fish locator helped us find perch suspended five to 10 feet off bottom, and we could actually watch our sinkers take our baits right to their depth. Using ultralight jigging rods, Berkley Trilene Cold Weather line in two-pound test, and Star-Glo ice jigs tipped with spikes, we iced over a dozen 10- to 11-inch perch in about an hour, while other anglers fishing nearby with conventional heavier tackle were skunked. Pikalek told me Mendota's perch used to come easy on the heavy gear, but they've become tough to catch on anything but the lightest tackle in the last few years.

After a break for lunch, we moved across the lake to try for bluegills along shore just off the UW campus. Parking here is at a premium, but ice fishermen adapt. That was the first time I have ever parked in a university ramp to go ice fishing! In another hour, we caught a mess of big bluegills using tiny ice jigs tipped with -- get this -- nothing but a bit of purple plastic cut from the skirt of a Gitzit tube tail. One Gitzit will last all winter at that rate. Here, even

lighter line was the ticket -- we used one-pound test Trilene and half-pound test sewing thread. Other anglers had fish, but caught them at a slower rate than we did.

Crappies spawn in late May or early June in the shallows (four feet if the water is cloudy, six feet if clear) along new weedbeds, such as those on Mendota's south shore between the Edgewater Motel and James Madison Park. Wait for a west wind and you can drift this entire shoreline, casting Willy Worms, Slo-Poke Minis or tube jigs and minnows. In summer, you'll find them suspended over deep water or off weed edges.

There are excellent public landings with good concrete ramps and oodles of parking in several city parks around the lake, including Warner on the northeast shore, Tenney at the Yahara River outlet to Lake Monona, and Marshall on the southwest shore, as well as at Mendota County Park on the northwest shore and Governor Nelson State Park off Highway M on the north shore. The state park landing features four concrete ramps, three piers, a fishing pier with handicapped-accessible fishing stations and a fish-cleaning station.

D & S Bait, Tackle and Archery, 1411 Northport Drive, Madison, WI 53704, telephone (608) 241-4225, is headquarters for supplies, bait, fishing information and guide service. Gene and Sandy Dellinger, who run the shop now, keep tabs on what's biting where. If you're coming from out of town, accommodations and excellent restaurants are everywhere in Madison.

111

Menominee River

Florence and Marinette Counties

The Menominee River snakes along between Wisconsin and Michigan from just north of Florence, all the way to the city of Marinette. Ten hydro dams slow it down on its descent to Green Bay, creating a wide range of habitat for a variety of fish species and a recreational resource that relatively few people use. Many town roads dead-end on both banks, but in some stretches the river flows for miles between bridge crossings. Here, within easy reach of Green Bay and the Fox Valley, is as wild a setting as you'll find for a river its size.

As on all Wisconsin boundary waters, special fishing regulations apply on the Menominee, so be sure to check your rules booklet before venturing out on the river for the first time. The season is open year-round for all species except sturgeon, which may be taken during a fall season each year. You'll need either a Wisconsin or Michigan license to fish the river, but not both, regardless of where you get on the water.

Fed by many trout streams, the upper Menominee flows full and cold all summer long. In its upper reaches, its dark waters harbor an abundant population of smallmouth bass. Smallies lurk under downed logs and undercuts, behind boulders and in deep holes at the outside of bends. Smallies here average 10 to 15 inches in length, but occasional fish run to five pounds. If you tangle with one that size on light tackle, you'll remember it for some time to come.

Crivitz guide Mike Mladenik reports catches of 50 fish or more on good days. Smallmouth action starts in mid-June and gets better as the summer progresses. When area lakes warm up and fishing slows in late summer, the Menominee's smallmouths remain aggressive in the river's cooler water. Smallmouths love spinnerbaits and jigs in smaller sizes. Work these below rapids and near instream cover early and late in the day and bump them slowly through deep holes at midday. In fall, small crankbaits take some of the biggest fish. Stick with bright colors: chartreuse, yellow and orange will show up best in this dark water.

Mladenik often prospects with leeches or other live bait, then switches to artificials once he finds active fish. I plan to try a fly rod on the Menominee's smallies this season. To assure the continuation of

this prime fishery, release the bass you catch. There are plenty of walleyes, catfish and pike if you want fish to eat.

Walleyes congregate below the river's many dams in spring and again in fall, where you can take good catches on jigs and minnows or crankbaits. Some walleyes in the 10-pound class show up in anglers' catches every year. In summer, work the deeper holes with crawlers or leeches during the day and probe riffles below sandbars and above bridges in the evening. The river's big northerns also move upstream in spring and fall, where you can take them on large artificials.

Menominee River ★

In summer, channel catfish provide good sport in the deeper holes and below dams, where shore fishing is often productive. The best action comes at night. Try live minnows, nightcrawlers or a commercial stinkbait.

Before you fish for sturgeon, pick up a free tag for the Wisconsin-Michigan boundary waters. The season runs from early September through October, but check the regulations booklet for the exact dates. The current limit is one sturgeon measuring 50 inches or better per year. Most anglers fish sturgeon just for the fun of fighting them on spinning tackle, since the vast majority of fish caught are undersized. Bank fishing with a gob of nightcrawlers is the traditional method. Sturgeon hold in deep holes near bends and bridges.

Poorly marked and unimproved landings make access to the upper river difficult for large trailered boats, but you should have no trouble finding a spot to launch a cartopper. Like many rivers, the Menominee is chock full of boulders that can swamp you or stop your motor cold, so take care when motoring on unfamiliar stretches.

There is better access below the hydro dam at White Rapids. From this dam downstream 26 miles to Grand Rapids Dam, Wisconsin Public Service Corporation maintains a total of seven public landings, two of them on Grand Rapids Flowage just west of Ingalls, Michigan. Grand Rapids Flowage itself covers some 260 acres and has a maximum depth of 21 feet. The reservoir has extensive shallow areas and numerous stump fields.

A recent DNR survey, conducted in preparation for the Federal Energy Regulatory Commission relicensing of the Grand Rapids Dam scheduled for 1993, revealed an excellent fishery for smallmouths and northerns, along with a fair population of walleyes, largemouths and panfish. Walleyes migrate upriver to spawn, but the other species appear to spawn in the reservoir.

For smallmouths, work the rocky shoreline of the upper arm of the flowage. Look for summer walleyes in the deeper holes between the landings and among the stumps. The extensive stumps and large, weedy bay on the Michigan side should hold largemouths, northerns and panfish.

For information about camping and other facilities near the Grand Rapids Dam, contact the Menominee Area Chamber of Commerce, 1005 10th Avenue, Menominee, MI 49858, telephone (906) 863-2679.

Some 15 miles downstream, the Menominee suddenly becomes an urban river in the twin cities of Marinette and Menominee. Two dams maintained by the Scott Paper Company created the Upper and Lower Scott Flowages. The larger of the two, Upper Scott Flowage covers 586 acres and has a maximum depth of 16 feet. The river channel averages eight feet or so in depth, but backwaters, side channels and sloughs are shallower. The bottom here is 50 percent sand, 30 percent muck and 10 percent gravel. Weeds are abundant in the flowage and its back bays. There is a state-owned access off Highway 180 just above the dam.

The DNR has not surveyed the fish population here recently and the flowage is not stocked, but good populations of gamefish and panfish sustain a varied fishery.

Mike Mladenik reports taking largemouths up to seven pounds in the shallow backwaters, where they are active from shortly after ice-out through July. He likes spinnerbaits and jig-and-pig combos until the weeds get too thick, then he favors weedless spoons. In fall, he finds largemouths along channel edges where jigs and crankbaits take them. Northerns seem to follow the same seasonal patterns.

Mladenik says smallmouths are scattered here along shoreline cover and around the island near the dam. He recommends prospecting with crankbaits in natural patterns, then switching to jigs and plastics or live bait for precise work close to cover.

Walleyes are also scattered here, so Mladenik likes to vertical jig over bottom structure to keep his presentation precise. He tips jigs with leeches in summer and shiners in fall and uses his trolling motor to stay over fish he has marked.

You'll find good-sized perch, crappies and bluegills here as well. Try live bait or crab tails in the deep holes and along weed edges for perch, ice jigs baited with waxworms in the bays for bluegills, and drift the channel with small swimming jigs or minnows for crappies.

Lower Scott Flowage, also known as Menominee Flowage, was created by the first dam upstream from the mouth. It covers a mile of water and approximately 120 acres and has a depth of 20 feet near the dam. Most of the flowage is under 10 feet deep and numerous navigational hazards require boats to travel at slow speeds. Weeds are plentiful along the shore. Scott Paper Company maintains a landing on the Michigan side at the end of 11th Avenue, just above the power house.

Guide Mike Mladenik (right) and client with some nice smallmouth bass from the Menominee River. Photo courtesy Mike Mladenik

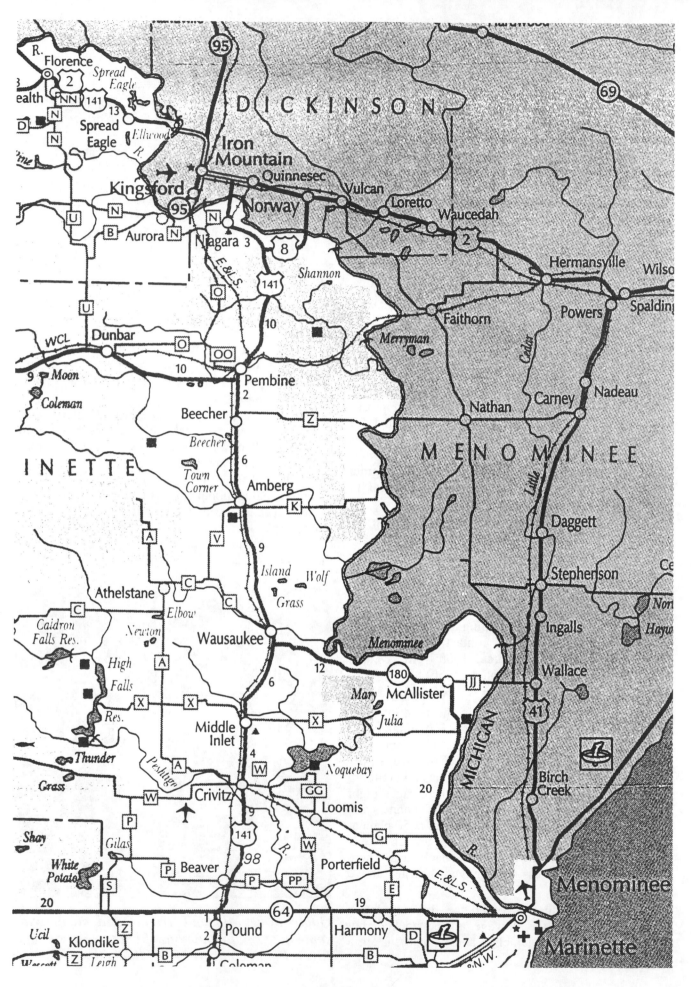

A recent DNR survey found a good population of smallmouths and northerns, with some walleyes and largemouths. Rock bass are the dominant panfish species, but there is a mercury advisory on both rock bass over 10 inches and walleyes over 15 inches. Relatively few anglers fish here because of the better angling opportunities immediately upstream and downstream, but those who do seem to focus on northerns.

If you've stayed with me this far, the last three miles, from the Lower Scott Dam to the mouth, are by far the most exciting part of the Menominee River. Here, the river's warmwater fishery blends with the coldwater fishery of Green Bay to create year-round angling opportunities.

Structure here consists of the river channel, which plunges to 25 feet in places, bridge abutments, rock piles, deep holes, rubble and scattered old pier pilings.

The lower river's walleye population has always been good, according to DNR fisheries biologist Brian Belonger, but it has literally exploded in the last few years. Most of the current crop are at or over the 15-inch size limit, but Belonger says they are so abundant that there will be plenty of big walleyes for years to come. Anglers now take walleyes topping 10 pounds every year.

Walleyes move in and out of the river from Green Bay, but some stay in the river all year. Walleyes spawn all along the river shoreline, not just at the dam, where most anglers fish. Both Mladenik and Belonger recommend jigs tipped with white or yellow plastic tails or shiners. In summer, Mladenik works the holes behind humps and rock piles, while Belonger likes to jig the channel at the river mouth. In fall, many walleyes move back into the river, where spring tactics will take them.

Northern pike action peaks in spring, when big pike move into the river to feed on smelt and anything else they can get their jaws around. Fish up to 20 pounds or so are not uncommon. Big crankbaits, small musky bucktails, live suckers and dead smelt all take northerns.

Belonger reports there is a fair population of good-sized smallmouths here, although few people target them. Mladenik likes to work jigging spoons near bridge pilings and other cover. Anywhere there are rocks, you should be able to find smallies.

Belonger says anglers harvest an average of 20 legal sturgeon each fall from the river's large population. A recent midsummer survey turned up 830 sturgeon in the first few hundred yards below the dam. These fish move freely between the river and the bay.

According to Belonger, crappies and suckers are two underutilized species here. He says good numbers of large crappies hang out near pilings and bridges in May, where minnows and jigs will take them. Dipnetting suckers is legal here, and a few local anglers take good catches from the walkway beneath the downstream side of the Hattie Street Bridge.

Finally, there are good runs of steelhead upriver to the dam in spring and fall. Browns, chinooks and, in odd years, pink salmon join the steelhead in fall, providing a salmonid smorgasbord in the riffle area below the dam, where many anglers take mixed catches on spawn, spoons, spinners and flies.

There are two good ramps on the Michigan side of the river and three in Marinette, one at Stevenson Island just above the Highway 41 bridge, one at Boom Park just upstream from the Marinette Marina, and one at 6th Street next to Nestegg Marine. There are also public ramps on Green Bay, north of the river at Menominee Marina and south at Red Arrow Park.

You can contact Mike Mladenik at Route 2, Crivitz, WI 54114, telephone (715) 854-2055. For a map and brochure listing boat ramps and area services, contact the Marinette Area Chamber of Commerce, P.O. Box 512, Marinette, WI 54143, telephone (715) 735-6681.

Lake Michigan Kenosha/Racine Area

Kenosha and Racine Counties

It is no secret that Lake Michigan offers some of the finest trout and salmon fishing to be found anywhere in North America, but this has not always been the case. Lake Michigan once supported a population of native lake trout, but today exotic species figure heavily in the catch, their numbers sustained artificially through a vigorous stocking program here in Wisconsin and in the other states that border the lake.

Wisconsin anglers can thank two unwelcome invaders from the Atlantic Ocean for getting the party started. The first of these, the sea lamprey, entered the Great Lakes through the St. Lawrence Seaway and wiped out Lake Michigan's native lake trout population. Next, alewives found their way into the lake. In the absence of major predators, their numbers exploded, leading to massive die-offs in the 1960s that left beaches windrowed with their reeking bodies.

Lake Michigan, Kenosha-Racine

Seeking a solution to this ecological imbalance, fisheries biologists began planting rainbow trout in Lake Michigan in 1963. In the years following, stocking of brown, brook and lake trout, splake, and coho and chinook salmon was begun. Today, Wisconsin alone annually stocks some 5 million trout and salmon in Lake Michigan.

Measured from north to south, Lake Michigan is roughly 300 miles long, but the 30-mile stretch from the Illinois line north to Oak Creek along the coast of Kenosha and Racine counties produces more trout and salmon per angler/hour of effort than anywhere else on the big lake. Stocking is one reason for this, but fish migration patterns and the geology of the lake are also responsible. Salmon tend to winter at the shallow southern end of the lake, then move north along the coast as spring progresses, making them available to anglers in the Kenosha/Racine area sooner and for a longer time. Underwater glacial structure starts appearing near the state line, providing fish-holding deep water close to shore within reach of anglers in small boats.

Charter boats take their share of the harvest, but shore and pier anglers, as well as those in private boats, account for the bulk of the catch. At both Racine and Kenosha, public fishing piers and deep harbors provide some spectacular fishing for trout and salmon during much of the year and good opportunities for perch in the summer.

Soon after ice-out, anglers start taking good catches of browns, cohos, chinooks and steelheads. April is the best month for browns. As inshore water temperatures rise above 40 degrees, the action occurs close to shore, where small boats and light tackle are all you need. May has proven to be the best month overall for taking numbers of fish. Coho fishing peaks in May, and chinooks start to come on strong as well. Spawned-out steelheads have returned to the lake from tributary streams and feed voraciously now. Lake trout begin to show up more consistently in the catch.

June is the transition month between hot inshore spring fishing action and the slower but steady summer pattern when fish are more scattered throughout the lake. Early in the month, salmon action is good close to shore, but as the lake warms into the low 50s, comfortable water is available over a larger area and fish spread out. Many cohos move farther up the coast, while chinooks and lake trout head for the edges of deep-water structure. The series of glacial ridges that begin a mile or so offshore of Racine produce good numbers of both species.

Lake trout action is usually best in July, when large schools of lakers that average six to 10 pounds hang out near bottom in 50 to 150 feet of water, often near structure. When strong west winds bring cooler water inshore, brown trout and coho action picks up in shallow water. Skamania steelheads, which run up into tributary streams in summer, make up a good portion of the catch now. Most fishing is done from larger boats several miles from shore, where downriggers and sturdy trolling gear are needed for lakers and chinooks, while flatlining near the surface takes steelheads.

In August, chinooks, cohos, browns and lakers begin feeding more heavily and staging prior to fall spawning. Lakers will be found near reefs, while the other three species begin to move into shallower water and can often be taken just off harbor mouths when temperatures are right. Inshore chinook and brown trout action remains good into September and early October, as these species move into tributary streams to spawn. Cohos spawn later in October, and some of the largest cohos of the year are taken as they move into shoreline areas. Fall-run steelhead action improves right up until it becomes impractical to fish.

Early and late in the season, you can fish close to shore from a small boat with no special tackle other than long, sturdy rods capable of handling a big king. Spool your reels with plenty of 12- to 17-pound test mono and make sure your drags run smoothly. Flatline trolling directly behind the boat works well, but side planers or skis take your lures out away from your wake where you'll get more strikes. Inexpensive Yellow Bird or Wille Side-Liner planer boards attach directly to your line and are the easiest to use. To fish deeper water in summer, you'll need at least a 16-foot boat, and longer is better. Downriggers, a good fish locator and some basic safety equipment are essential for deep-water fishing.

You'll need an assortment of lures to fish at different depths and times of the year. J-Plugs, crankbaits such as Rapalas, Rebel Fastracs and Shadlings, a variety of spoons like Andy Reekers, Crippled Alewives, Flutter Chucks and Little Cleos, and dodger/fly rigs will take most trout and salmon. When browns and kings are in the harbors, you can take them on lighter tackle and jigs tipped with minnows or cut bait.

Pier anglers can get by with seven-foot, heavy-duty spinning rods. Match them with quality spinning reels that hold at least 250 yards of line in case you hook a big chinook. You'll also need a long-handled net and something to sit on. Pier anglers either cast heavy spoons or soak spawn or alewives on slip

bobbers or three-way swivel rigs for trout and salmon. In summer, perch hit well on minnows and small jigs.

A number of fully-equipped charter boats will take you out from either port. I've fished out of Kenosha at least once each season and have never failed to catch fish. On more than one trip, we managed to take a grand slam -- at least one of each species, coho, chinook, brown, rainbow and laker. Once, outdoor writer and tackle designer Dan Gapen and I took some nice lake trout using Gapen's Bait Walker (he calls it a "poor man's downrigger.") to bump bottom with dodgers and flies. Another time a 12-pound steelhead nailed a crankbait on the surface and jumped a half-dozen times before we landed it.

Fish Wisconsin author Dan Small hefts a dandy chinook salmon caught off Kenosha. Photo by Dan Small

To book a charter out of Kenosha, contact: Kenosha Charter Boat Association, P.O. Box 981, Kenosha, WI 53141, telephone (800) 522-6699. In Racine, contact: Fishing Charters of Racine, P.O. Box 1393, Racine, WI 53401, telephone (800) 475-6113 or (414) 633-6113.

The Kenosha public boat ramp is located on the inner harbor at 45th Street and Kennedy Drive. In Racine, you can launch at Pershing Park on 5th

Street. Both port cities sponsor annual fishing derbies and offer a complete array of services, including excellent marinas. Racine's Reefpoint Marina (the largest of six marinas here) can accommodate 1,000 boats, address: 2 Christopher Columbus Causeway, Racine, WI 53402, telephone (414) 633-5244. Of seven marinas in Kenosha, the largest is Southport Marina, which will soon feature 520 slips at 57th Street and 3rd Avenue, telephone (414) 656-8107. For more information, contact: Racine County Convention and Visitors Bureau, 345 Main Street, Racine, WI 53403, telephone (414) 634-3293; or Kenosha Area Tourism Corporation, 800 55th Street, Kenosha, WI 53140, telephone (800) 654-7309 or (414) 654-7307.

Lake Michigan's Nuclear Power Plants

Point Beach, Manitowoc County; Kewaunee, Kewaunee County

Lake Michigan, Nuclear Power Plants

Wisconsin's two nuclear power plants, located five miles apart on the Lake Michigan coast between Kewaunee and Two Rivers, have provided the communities of Northeastern Wisconsin with electrical energy since the early 1970s. Their excellent service and safety records have calmed the fears of many who thought these modern plants were a pair of nuclear disasters just waiting to happen. Today, while most lakeshore residents have more or less made their peace with the plants, Lake Michigan anglers have accepted them with enthusiasm because of the fantastic fish-drawing power of their warm water discharges.

Both plants use Lake Michigan water to cool their nuclear reactors, drawing it in through offshore pipes, then discharging it again close to shore. The water does not come into contact with radioactive material. It is simply warmed up by the heat-transfer process of cooling the reactors. Where it re-enters the lake, the warmed water forms a plume whose temperature, current flow and added oxygen all attract baitfish and, in turn, trout and salmon. These effects are at their peak whenever the water near shore is colder, as it is in late fall or early spring, and again in midsummer, when offshore winds blow warm surface water out into the lake, allowing colder water to well up close to shore.

The smaller Kewaunee plant, run by the Wisconsin Public Service Corporation, operates a single unit that circulates 435,000 gallons of water a minute. Wisconsin Electric Power Company runs the Point Beach plant, whose two reactors each take in and discharge 375,000 gallons of water a minute. During most of the year, at least one of the plants is in operation. The Kewaunee plant runs around the clock, except for a two-month period each spring (March and April) when it is shut down for inspection and maintenance. The Point Beach plant shuts down one unit in spring and the other in fall for a six-week refueling period.

Browns, rainbows and chinooks are all taken around the power plant discharges, but just which species you'll find in the area at any given time depends on a number of factors, the first of which is water temperature. Each species has a preferred water temperature, and by moving closer to or farther from a discharge plume, trout and salmon can stay in their preferred temperature range and maintain an efficient metabolism that keeps them feeding more frequently. The more often they eat, the more vulnerable they are to fishermen.

Browns seek out warmer water than the other two, so they are more likely to be found right in the discharge plume or close to it most of the year. Their preferred temperature range is 65 to 75 degrees. Salmon like water temperatures of 54 to 62 degrees and rainbows prefer 58 to 62 degrees, so these species are often found right in the plume in spring or fall, when the surrounding water is much colder. In summer, Lake Michigan warms up and a thermocline develops, just as in deep inland lakes. A west wind blows warmer surface water offshore, causing a wedge of cooler water to flow toward shore, bringing rainbows and chinooks with it. An east wind blows warmer surface water onshore, pushing cooler water, and those same species, farther out into the lake.

Spawning patterns also play a role in determining which species you're likely to catch. Browns and chinooks spawn in fall, so they will be found moving along the shoreline at this time looking for tributary streams. Several strains of rainbows, or steelheads, are now stocked in the lake. All are spring spawners, but some move into tributary streams in summer, some in late fall and some in late winter and early spring. When not inshore for their spawning run, rainbows tend to roam the open lake where they are inaccessible to most anglers.

Both plants provide parking and access for anglers who fish from shore, pier or boats. The Kewaunee Plant access is open from 4 a.m. until 11 p.m. daily. To get there, take Sandy Road off Highway 42 to the power plant, then turn right at the main parking lot and follow the road around to the fishermen's access parking lot. There is no boat ramp, but you may carry a small boat down a 200-foot paved path and launch it on the beach. Many fishermen simply don chest waders and wade out to fish, or cast right from shore.

The Point Beach access hours are 5 a.m. to 11 p.m. daily. Take Nuclear Road off Highway 42 and follow signs to the Energy Information Center, then take the turnoff to the fishermen's parking lot. You may drive down to the lake to unload gear, but you must park in the lot. There is a fishing pier built over one of the discharge pipes with room for a dozen or so anglers. You'll need a long-handled net to land fish from the elevated platform. On a slow fishing day, the Energy Information Center is an interesting place to visit.

The public ramp in Two Creeks, midway between the plants, will handle boats up to 16 feet in length. Larger boats must launch at Two Rivers or Kewaunee and run about 10 miles to the nearest plant.

You'll find fish at depths of five to 15 feet, shallower early and late in the day or on overcast days, deeper at midday or on bright days. When fishing from shore or the pier, you'll need sturdy tackle capable of controlling a 20-pound chinook. Some anglers use surf-casting rods, while others go with seven-foot heavy-duty spinning rods and large-capacity reels spooled with 12- to 20-pound test line. Boat fishermen can get by with lighter gear. Some boat fishermen troll back and forth across the discharge plume, while others drift or anchor and cast.

Spawn sacks are a favorite bait, but live minnows -- especially alewives -- also produce. Fish them on a Wolf River-type dropper rig with enough weight to keep your line where you want it. Light-tackle enthusiasts can have a ball vertical jigging with jigs and minnows or plastic tails. Hook a big king or husky brown on this gear and you'll remember the battle for some time to come.

Casting from shore or the pier requires a heavy spoon. Some favorites include Little Cleos, Krocodiles, KO Wobblers, Crippled Alewives and others in chrome, green or blue. Jointed crankbaits, such as Rebel Fastracs, Rapalas and others in chartreuse, fluorescent orange and silver work well for casting if there is no wind. Trollers drag these same lures either flatlined behind the boat or off to the side on planer boards.

For more information on fishing at the Kewaunee plant, contact: Corporate Communications, Wisconsin Public Service Corporation, P.O. Box 19002, Green Bay, WI 54307-9002, telephone (414) 433-5543. For water temperature information at the Kewaunee Plant, call WPSC'S public relations office at (414) 433-5528. For information on the Point Beach fishing facility, contact: Point Beach Nuclear Plant, Energy Information Center, 6600 Nuclear Road, Two Rivers, WI 54241, telephone (414) 755-4334.

There are tackle shops, full-service marinas, charter boat associations, restaurants, motels, campgrounds and areas of historic and cultural interest in the Kewaunee and Two Rivers-Manitowoc areas. For more information, contact: Manitowoc-Two Rivers Area Chamber of Commerce, P.O. Box 903, Manitowoc, WI 54220, telephone (800) 262-7892; or Kewaunee Chamber of Commerce, 308 N. Main Street, Kewaunee, WI 54216, telephone (414) 388-3430.

You can camp in Point Beach State Forest for a nominal fee and get more fishing information at the DNR office there: Point Beach State Forest, 9400 Highway O, Two Rivers, WI 54241, telephone (414) 794-7480.

The Francis Lee heads out of Two Rivers for a day of trolling action. Photo by Dan Small

Milwaukee Harbor

Lake Michigan, Milwaukee County

One of the great success stories of *Outdoor Wisconsin* has been our long association with Captain Jack Remus, of Jack's Charter Service in Milwaukee. Jack has guided us to some phenomenal Lake Michigan trout and salmon action on The Leader over the years.

Our very first outing with Jack set the standard for Lake Michigan trolling segments. Pauline Kilsdonk had purchased the charter trip donated by Jack to WMVS-TV's auction fund-raiser as a surprise birthday gift for her friend, Laura Wojciuk. Neither lady had done much Great Lakes fishing, so Jack instructed them in the basics as we headed out in an early morning fog.

The salmon were in close that day, and it wasn't long before we got into them. Laura, Pauline and I took turns fighting fish and shouting words of encouragement to each other, while Captain Jack coached us in the finer points of playing a big salmon from a moving boat. We had each taken and lost a couple fish, when three rods bucked in rapid succession -- a triple!

Lake Michigan, Milwaukee Harbor

Jack cleared the other lines and yelled to us to keep our fish away from each other -- fat chance with fresh chinooks. While we struggled to tire the fish and keep them apart, videographer Mike Kuklinski ran up the ladder to the flying bridge so he could get us all in the frame at once.

As our fish neared the boat, Pauline's sounded and mine went under both her line and a downrigger cable. To get our lines straightened out, I had to pass my rod under the downrigger arm, keeping enough tension on it to avoid losing the fish, then hug Pauline and pass the rod from one hand to the other in front of her, while she raised her arms and rod high over her head. Kuklinski did a great job of capturing that maneuver, and it made a super shot. We finally led the fish one after the other into Jack's waiting net and he lifted them into the boat all together.

After a round of triumphant cheers, we set about untangling the lines and sorting out who had caught what. Laura and I each had a decent king, while Pauline had caught a 10-pound coho. Later, a passing tour boat bullhorned this message: "Show us your fish, or we'll blow you out of the water!" We obliged, with tape rolling of course.

Pauline caught a 20-pound chinook that same day, and on other trips with Jack we've taken chinooks to 24 pounds, lots of cohos, some big rainbows and a mess of gorgeous brown trout in their rich spawning colors. On two outings, for a change of pace, Jack tied The Leader up to the breakwall and we caught enough perch for several fish fries. Jack has helped us show off the diversity of an urban fishery, for every one of those segments was shot within sight of Milwaukee Harbor.

Milwaukee Harbor might not appear to be the kind of place you'd go on purpose to catch fish, but then looks can be deceiving. From early in the season right through fall, the harbor and outlying waters hold great numbers of trout and salmon and provide some superlative action that the charter boat fleet, small private boats, and even pier anglers can cash in on.

The seasonal fish movements, angling techniques and effective baits discussed in the chapter on the Kenosha-Racine area also hold true for Lake Michigan's Milwaukee shoreline, so I won't repeat them here. Spring salmon action may start a couple weeks later here as fish move north from their wintering grounds, but otherwise the patterns are very similar. There are so many ways to approach this fishery, however, that it is worth looking at them in some detail.

The main feature of the Milwaukee waterfront is the extensive system of breakwalls -- 5 miles in all -- that enclose the harbor, provide structure, funnel currents and fish, and create a transition area from warm zone to cold zone. In spring and fall, the water inside the breakwall can be as much as 10 degrees warmer than the water outside, drawing baitfish and in turn, trout and salmon. Early and late in the year, trolling inside the harbor itself can be productive, especially for browns and kings. Later, salmon hang just outside the harbor, often right along the breakwalls, where they pick off injured baitfish in the current outflows. Trolling along the breakwalls or in and out of the gaps can be productive -- just be sure to watch for boat traffic in the gaps and rocks close to the walls.

Several new developments have increased fishing opportunities in the harbor and the Milwaukee River.

New riprap around Harbor Island just off the Marcus Amphitheatre on the north side of the Hoan Bridge holds baitfish most of the year, creating a superb brown trout fishery accessible to small boat and shore anglers. The opening of the North Avenue Dam and other cleanup efforts have helped flush contaminants out of the Milwaukee River, and trout and salmon now make spawning runs as far upstream as Estabrook Park. This river fishery will only get better in the years to come.

Outside the harbor, Black Can Reef, about 1-1/2 miles offshore from the South Gap, is a good spot for chinooks. Farther south, the outflow pipes at the sewage treatment plant south of Grant Park and the Wisconsin Electric Power Company plant in Oak Creek at the Milwaukee-Racine county line both attract fish when the surrounding water is colder. Troll parallel to shore here or cast and jig at the edge of the outflow plumes. These are great spots for browns as soon as open water lets you get to them.

North of Milwaukee Harbor, structure and deep water close to shore provide some good fishing in spring and fall and when offshore winds bring cool

Pauline Kilsdonk, Captain Jack Remus, Dan Small and Laura Woijciuk (left to right) with a day's catch aboard Remus' boat, The Leader. The catch was made during the taping of an Outdoor Wisconsin segment. Photo by Dan Small

water inshore in summer. Flatline and planer-board trolling close to shore early and late in the day from just north of McKinley Marina all the way to Doctors Park at Fox Point will take trout and salmon when the temperatures are right. Later in the day, or whenever inshore water is warm, you can move less than a mile offshore and troll for salmon with downriggers in 50 feet of water. Depths run to 100 feet another mile offshore, where you'll pick up kings and lakers near bottom.

Rainbow numbers have increased in recent years, and in summer large schools of rainbows cruise the surface at the "scum line" where warm and cold currents meet, often 10 miles or more offshore over 150 or 200 feet of water. Most charter boats can find them, but Steve Cedarburg and Maxine Appleby of Seagull Charters specialize in rainbows. One of their clients, Eric Leibold of Monroe, caught a state-record 25.8-pound rainbow on July 29, 1992. Steve and Max hope to offer rainbow flyfishing charters in another year or so. Bill Schreiber, who runs the Orvis Shop at Laacke & Joys on Water Street, and I will be helping them get that option rolling. Trout and salmon offer plenty of flyfishing opportunities in the harbor and off piers as well.

There are several good places where shoreline anglers can get in on the action. From north to south, Doctors Park, Klode Park and Atwater Beach all provide public access to beach or jetty fishing. Government Pier, accessible from McKinley Park, is a popular walk-on fishing spot, as is the south end of Summerfest Grounds, accessible from the foot of Erie Street. On Jones Island, accessible off the end of I-794, you can fish along the entire face wall from just north of the Coast Guard station to the freight docks. There are jetties and shoreline accesses north and south of the South Shore Yacht Club (including a floating pier on the north side accessible to wheelchairs), at Sheridan Park, and at Grant Park. The South Metro Pier south of Grant Park provides 1,500 feet of public access. All these spots provide fair to good fishing for trout and salmon early and late in the year, and in summer when west winds prevail.

Throughout the summer, perch fishing can be excellent at many of the places mentioned above. Boat fishermen can take perch most any time in summer along the north-shore beaches and inside the har-

bor, while pier and shore fisherman can catch them whenever the onshore water is too warm for trout and salmon. Tiny jigs, tipped with any type of live bait or plastic tails will take perch.

Northern pike are one species overlooked by many Milwaukee anglers. While not abundant, there are some dandies that hang out along jetties, piers, near creek mouths and anywhere you find weedbeds, such as those off the War Memorial and along North Harbor Drive. Try for them with big spinnerbaits, spoons or even musky jerk baits.

Excellent public boat ramps with ample parking, fish-cleaning stations and restrooms are located at McKinley Park on Lincoln Memorial Drive, and just south of South Shore Yacht Club off Nock Street. There is a smaller, very steep ramp on South Water Street, just north of Duchow's Harbor Marina. The only free boat ramp is located at Grant Park on Oak Creek in South Milwaukee.

There are numerous bait and tackle shops in and around Milwaukee. At McKinley Marina, Steve Cedarburg and Maxine Appleby of Seagull Charters operate Lakeside Lures, a bait and tackle shop that also stocks a complete line of Ray Troll (of "Spawn 'Til You Die" fame) books, hats and t-shirts. Steve and Max also rent 17-foot Boston Whalers equipped with downriggers, rods and reels for do-it-yourself trolling. Address: P.O. Box 92024, Milwaukee, WI 53202, telephone (414) 224-7707. On the south side, try Ski Brothers Bait, 5334 S. Packard Avenue, telephone (414) 744-1996. On the west side, stop at Tom Newbauer's Live Bait and Tackle, 13680-A W. Capitol Drive, telephone (414) 783-6546.

Jack Remus also runs his boat out of McKinley Marina. Contact: Jack's Charter Service, 2545 S. Delaware Avenue, Milwaukee, WI 53207, telephone (414) 482-2336.

Milwaukee Harbor is used primarily by local anglers making one-day trips, but for those coming from out of town, the Greater Milwaukee area offers plenty of lodging and every sort of restaurant imaginable. And if you're in town during one of the many summer festivals, you may want to take in the show after a day on the water. If you fish into the evening hours close to Summerfest Grounds, you'll be able to enjoy the music right along with those on shore.

Mink River And Rowley Bay

Lake Michigan, Door County

Mink River and Rowley Bay

"There's not much to the Mink River," Wayne Larson told me, as we set out across Rowley Bay in a rented boat. "It rises in a springfed wetland and flows only about two miles before dumping into Rowley Bay, but it draws big pike like a magnet, and only a few locals fish for them."

I thought Wayne was putting me on, but he had been right about the fantastic ice-out brown trout action, so I humored him and agreed to this side trip for northerns. As we crossed a sandbar at the river mouth and motored slowly up the winding channel, I noticed the clarity of the water and the weed growth that seemed lush for so early in the year. Rounding a bend, we saw two old timers fishing from a dock. One of them was tending two handlines, while the other added a northern of about ten pounds to a stringer that held two more just like it. That was all the inspiration I needed. Around the next bend we were alone in this mini-wilderness. We cut the motor and began to cast.

Soon we were both into pike that hammered our floating Rapalas. We caught and released several

strong, silver-green fish of about three or four pounds, then switched to spoons hoping for bigger fish, but had no hits. I then snapped on a magnum floating Rapala and heaved it toward a weedbed. On my third cast, it disappeared in a titanic swirl. For a brief moment, the biggest pike I have ever seen lay on the surface as I watched, too stunned to set the hook. Then it simply opened its mouth and swam back into the weeds.

Shaken, but wired, I frantically cast the big Rapala at every weedbed as we drifted with the slow current. We saw several more big pike, but caught only the "little" ones up to five pounds or so. Still, I had seen enough in two hours to put Mink River's pike fishery high on my list of exciting spring outings.

I made that first trip back in 1985. Wayne is gone now, but the Mink River still holds monster northerns and Rowley Bay still offers some of the fastest ice-out brown trout action on the Door Peninsula, all in a setting as isolated and pristine as any you'll find on the shores of Lake Michigan. Rowley Bay was once northern Door County's main port for lake schooners, but today it serves vacationers and fishermen.

To get there, take Highway 42 up the west side of the peninsula, then drive east from Sister Bay on Highway Z. The road ends at the Wagon Trail Resort, which also has the only marina and boat launch in the area. Adjacent to the Wagon Trail, there is a modern campground. Across the bay from the Wagon Trail, Newport State Park features wilderness camping, but has no launch for trailed boats.

Ice-out usually occurs here in early April, and for the next few weeks, trollers take good catches of browns. The bay itself is shallow, with numerous rocks, humps and reedbeds close to shore. Troll floating crankbaits along the breaklines early in the morning or late in the afternoon for browns. Because of the clear water, you'll get more strikes on six- or eight-pound test line. Run flatlines well behind the boat and use planer boards or skis to drag baits close to shore, islands and other shallow structure.

Our pike adventure occurred during a three-day brown trout outing with Greg Bambenek ("Dr. Juice") which we taped for *Outdoor Wisconsin*. Wayne, Juice and I trolled flatlines up and down the shore and took some nice fish, but had more fun fly-fishing for them from belly boats. Just getting into the water was a production in itself. Wearing neoprene waders and diving flippers, we somehow wriggled into our float-tube harnesses and waddled across the deck of Juice's boat, then clambered down the stern ladder and fell backward into the frigid water, looking about as graceful as overweight bullfrogs wedged into donuts.

Once in the water, though, a belly boater rides the swells and waves. The ten-foot rod Wayne loaned me made casting a sinking 8-weight line easier than I thought it would be from just above the water. We took a couple browns on streamers and smelt imitations and ended up with one of the most unusual fishing segments we've ever aired.

Captain Jerry Stumpf hefts a nice brown trout taken while trolling on Rowley Bay, using a jointed Rapala behind a Wille ski. Photo by Dan Small

Northern pike move into the Mink River to spawn just after the ice leaves and are ready to feed by mid or late April. The pike fishing lasts through May, but tapers off as the water warms in summer. Large spinnerbaits and spoons also take fish, but twitching a floating crankbait is more exciting. Sturdy tackle and a wire leader are a must for pike. Some anglers soak big smelt or shiners on bobbers or slip-sinker rigs in the deeper holes. Trollers often hook into northerns in the bay itself, but most of them break off on the light tackle used for trout.

In late spring and summer, you'll take both perch and smallmouths in Rowley Bay. Try wigglers, small minnows and crab tails near the reedbeds for perch. For bass, use small spinners and crankbaits early and late in the day. On calm days, you can have a ball catching bass on streamers and hair bugs. Cast near rocks, reed beds, islands and anywhere there is cover.

If your boat is equipped for offshore trolling, you can sometimes take chinooks and lake trout around several offshore shoals in May and again in fall. East winds can churn up the bay in a hurry, so pay attention to weather changes. The bay's many rocks can also pose a navigational hazard.

As the second edition of this book goes to press early in 1993, I'm planning another trip to Rowley Bay, this time with Captain Jerry Stumpf of Reel Pleasure Charters, who specializes in ice-out browns. As before, we'll be staying at the Wagon Trail Resort, which, in addition to a bait shop, marina, boat ramp, mooring slips, RV hookups, a swimming beach and miles of hiking trails, features a superb restaurant and the finest Scandinavian bakery I've found in Wisconsin.

For lodging reservations or information, call (414) 854-2385 or (800) 99-WAGON. To reach the campground adjacent to the Wagon Trail, call (414) 854-4818. For camping information at Newport State Park, call (414) 854-2500. For information on other area facilities, contact the Door County Chamber of Commerce, P.O. Box 346, Sturgeon Bay, WI 54235, telephone (414) 743-4456 or (800) 527-3529. Mac's Sport Shop, 33 South Madison Avenue in Sturgeon Bay, telephone (414) 743-3350, has bait, tackle and information on fishing conditions. To book an outing with Reel Pleasure Charters, call (414) 478-2027.

Lake Monona

Madison, Dane County

Lake Monona is the second-largest lake on the Madison Chain, covering 3,274 acres just a few blocks downstream from Mendota. Several parks save Monona's upland shoreline from complete residential and commercial development, but downtown Madison's imposing skyline, dominated by the bright dome of the State Capitol, is visible from just about anywhere on the lake, reminding us that Monona is just as urbane as her big sister.

Monona's fishery complements that of Mendota. Panfish are the biggest draw, but there are good opportunities for walleyes, northerns and bass, and muskies have really come on strong in recent years.

The Yahara River enters the lake on the northwest shore and exits at Squaw Bay on the southeast shore. Two other major inlets also feed Monona: Starkweather Creek enters the lake at Olbrich Park on the northeast shore, and Murphy Creek, the Lake Wingra outlet, comes into Monona directly across the lake at Olin Park. Monona is quite fertile and somewhat murkier than Mendota, with a definite summer thermocline that restricts oxygen and fish activity to the top 25 or 30 feet of water.

Sand dominates the bottom type, but there are areas of muck in the shallow bays and some gravel in places. Extensive weedbeds develop in late spring and early summer in the shallow bays and on several bars out to a depth of 10 feet or so, with some areas of sandgrass running out to 15 feet or more. Weedlines make up much of the important structure that fish relate to. Several major offshore bars also hold fish: a broad, flat bar off Murphy Creek and a long, skinny bar off the Yahara River. Both are separated from the mainland by a deep, narrow trough, while between the Capitol dome and Squaw Bay Point a midlake gravel hump rises to 14 feet, and on the same line just off the mouth of Squaw Bay, there is another, shallower bar.

Proceeds from the Madison Fishing Expo funded the installation of 27 fish cribs on the west side of the last bar mentioned in the winter of 1989. Fish began using them immediately, and local anglers report taking good catches of crappies and bluegills from around these cribs.

Lake Monona

DNR fish manager Scot Stewart reports that muskies have the longest history of any species stocked in Monona in recent years, and Monona is fast becoming the best musky lake on the Madison chain. Since 1976, several thousand fingerlings have been stocked nearly every year, and anglers are taking some nice fish on a regular basis. Early plantings were mostly hybrids, but a now more true muskies are planted. Trues live longer and grow bigger. The Portage musky Club has provided some of the fish, and Stewart plans to keep planting muskies.

Early in the year, Squaw Bay and shallow Monona Bay (west of the railroad trestle on the west shore) should hold muskies. Try bucktails and shallow jerk baits. Later, muskies relate to weedlines and bars, where deep trolling or casting with diving crankbaits and jigs tipped with large plastics should get results.

No walleyes have been stocked here since 1986, but there are some larger fish left from the 100,000 fingerlings planted that year and some natural reproduction. Walleyes up to 10 pounds or so are taken every year, but the current health guide recommends women and children avoid eating Monona walleyes over 18 inches long. Some of the millions of walleyes planted in Lake Mendota find their way downstream to Monona, and Stewart reports good movement of fish between the lakes.

When the season opens in May, try the bars and shoreline dropoffs for walleyes. As summer progresses, work the deeper edges with Bait Rigs spinner rigs and leeches or crawlers by day and shallow, weedy flats at night with floating Rapalas and other shallow lures. Tip-ups baited with golden shiners often produce walleyes in the evening along the sharp dropoffs at Law Park (close to the Capitol) and directly across the lake along the east shore north of Squaw Bay.

Largemouth bass are common in the bays, and they run big, up to six or seven pounds. Stewart reports more bass tournaments here every year, so don't be surprised to find a hundred or more gadget-and-glitter bass boats powering around Monona on a spring or summer weekend. Watch the guys in the logo-laden jumpsuits and you'll learn more about catching bass in one day than you will fishing all summer by yourself. Don't horn in on their spots -- just make a mental note to try them later.

Monona Bay and Squaw Bay, especially the channels on the north side, are super spots for early bass, while Turville Bay is good for summer sloppin' with a jig and pig or other weedless contraption.

Monona has a fair population of northerns, but Stewart is concerned that anglers are overharvesting smaller fish. He stocks some fingerlings when they're available, but most Mendota pike are naturally reproduced or migrants from elsewhere in the chain. Ice fishermen haul in a few in the 15- to 20-pound range every winter off weed edges. Bait tip-ups with big golden shiners and forget wire leaders -- that way you'll have a good chance of taking walleyes as well as northerns. Just play a big pike carefully and let it run if it wants to. Before you gaff a northern through the ice, make sure it's not a hybrid musky. Hybrids are active all year and sometimes hit as well as pike in winter, but it is not legal to keep them until the first Saturday in May.

Monona's crappies currently run bigger than those on Mendota, though their numbers are down somewhat from their levels in the early 1980s. Try the Yahara River mouth in spring, where crappies seek warmer water. Another spring hot spot is near the railroad trestle at the mouth of Monona Bay. Tiny plastics on 1/32- or 1/64-ounce swimming jigs, like the Slo-Poke Mini, are dynamite for pre-spawn and spawning crappies. Later, work the deeper holes in Turville Bay's weedbeds with small jigs and minnows.

The shoreline at Hudson Park, just north of the Yahara inlet, is a primary bluegill spawning area. Expect good action here in late May or early June on tiny ice jigs tipped with waxies or spikes, or on fly-rod artificials. In summer, most of Monona's bigger 'gills, crappies and perch suspend over deep water in the middle of the lake.

Joe Puccio, of the Bait Rigs Company in Madison, introduced me to this midlake fishery a couple years ago, and it is nothing short of phenomenal. Puccio did his homework and learned from UW limnologist Jon Magnuson that large schools of panfish feed on zooplankton -- tiny crustaceans -- that drift about in the middle of the lake in huge clouds. He then designed a spinner rig to imitate the translucent colors of these zooplankton, using a small fluorescent or hammered-gold blade and custom-ground beads.

Joe Puccio of Bait Rigs Tackle unhooks a dandy bluegill taken from the deep water of Lake Monona while using a Bait Rigs panfish rig. Photo by Dan Small

Joe and I baited his rigs with spikes, red worms and waxies and drifted with slip bobbers on ultralight tackle over the 40-foot depths, where we caught buckets of big 'gills eight to 12 feet below the surface. If we let our baits go deeper, we took crappies, and down about 20 feet we ran into perch. You can use small jigs and plastics, but panfish hit the almost-weightless spinner rigs more readily because they can inhale them with no effort.

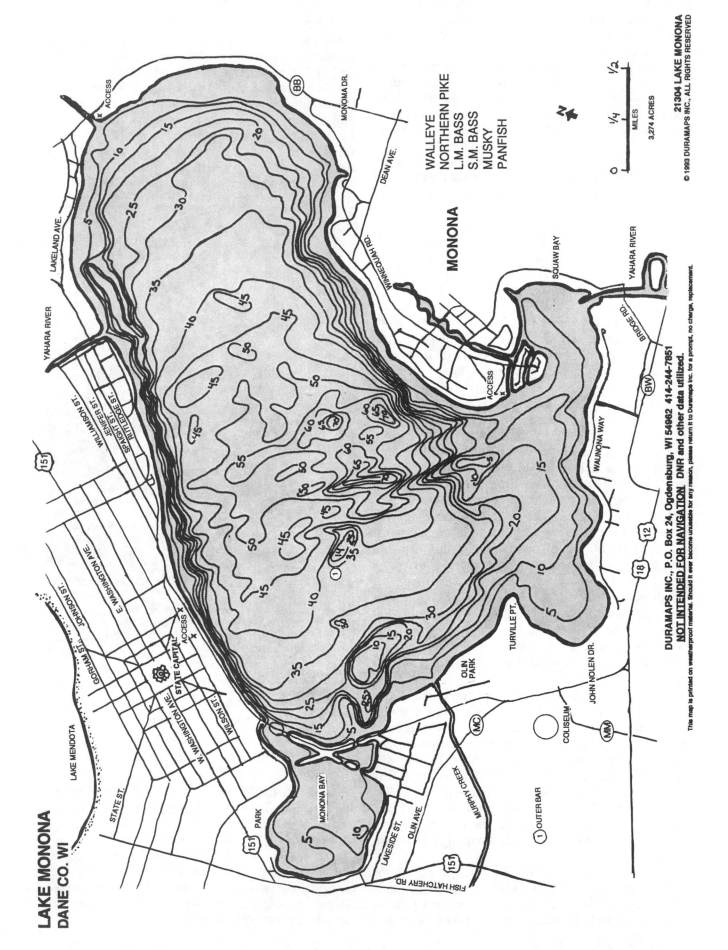

LAKE MONONA
DANE CO. WI

MONONA

WALLEYE
NORTHERN PIKE
L.M. BASS
S.M. BASS
MUSKY
PANFISH

MILES

0   ¼   ½

3,274 ACRES

21304 LAKE MONONA

DURAMAPS INC., P.O. Box 24, Ogdensburg, WI 54962 414-244-7851
NOT INTENDED FOR NAVIGATION   DNR and other data utilized.
This map is printed on weatherproof material. Should it ever become unusable for any reason, please return it to Duramaps Inc. for a prompt, no charge, replacement.

① OUTER BAR

128

There are good public landings with plenty of parking and wheelchair-accessible piers in Law, Olin and Olbrich Parks, as well as two more on the east shore at the end of Winnequah Trail and on Fairchild Street off Winnequah Road. There is also a public fishing barge, funded by the Yahara Fishing Club, moored on the north shore next to the causeway. Cliff Robertson runs Lake Monona Bait and Tackle, located near the Fairchild landing. Address: 4516 Winnequah Road, Monona, WI 53716, telephone (608) 222-1929. Cliff carries a full line of Bait Rigs tackle and other gear for fishing Monona. He reports watching right from his store window as anglers take muskies, perch and bluegills in summer and pike through the ice. From anywhere on the lake it's just a short drive to the many restaurants and motels on East Washington Avenue (Highway 151).

Nagawicka Lake

Delafield, Waukesha County

As it retreated through what is now Waukesha County some 10,000 years ago, the Wisconsin glacier left a dozen or so lakes in its wake, among them 917-acre Nagawicka Lake, located in the town of Delafield, just north of I-94 and west of Highway 83. The Bark River flows through the lake, with an inlet at its northeast end and an outlet to Upper Nemahbin Lake at its southwest end. There is a water control dam at the outlet, but more about that later.

Much of Nagawicka is over 50 feet deep, and its deepest point is 90 feet. An extensive marsh with many small bays lines the shallow west shore, while the east shore is primarily upland. Weed growth is extensive to a depth of 15 feet or more, but from there the bottom drops off rapidly. There are large shoreline areas of sand and gravel, but muck covers most of the lake bottom. A small lake known as the "Kettle" connects with the main basin at its north end via a narrow, but navigable, channel.

Fishermen tend to forget that lakes are dynamic ecosystems that can sometimes change dramatically from one year to the next. We may remember the way fishing was a few years ago on our favorite lake and wonder why it "just ain't the same" anymore. The interaction of many different fish and forage species, changes in water quality, and the increase or decrease in fishing pressure are a few major factors that can bring about changes, but there are others at work as well.

Nagawicka is a prime example of a lake whose fishery has changed over the past dozen years or so. Panfish fluctuate in both size and abundance in many lakes. On Nagawicka, crappies dominated panfish catches briefly a number of years ago, but today, the bluegill is again the number one panfish species, as it was before the crappie heyday. The biggest changes in the last decade, however, have occurred in walleye and northern pike numbers. Walleyes have replaced northerns as the primary gamefish species.

Nagawicka was once THE place to go for lots of northerns, but pike fishing there has declined steadily to reach a level comparable to that of other area lakes. Spring runoff once flooded marshlands adjacent to the lake, providing prime spawning habitat for northern pike. In the early 1980s, anglers on Nagawicka harvested three northerns per acre, or about 3,000 fish per year, and DNR fish manager Randy Schumacher estimates the lake supported a population of about nine adult pike per acre.

Since that time, though, the Town of Delafield has controlled the outlet flow at the dam on the Bark River to avoid spring flooding. As a result, water levels are now too low in marshy areas, greatly reducing northern pike spawning habitat. Schumacher estimates the pike population is down to around two adult fish per acre. The average size of a pike caught here today is larger than it used to be, but you'll wait a lot longer between fish.

Pike anglers are about evenly divided between hardware slingers and live bait fishermen. Area bait shops keep a good supply of golden shiners and suckers, both of which produce well on pike when fished along weed edges. Crankbaits, spinnerbaits and weedless spoons do the trick over submerged weedbeds at both the north and south ends of the lake. Some large pike suspend over deep water in summer in both the main lake and the Kettle, where deep trolling near the bottom of the thermocline is the best way to reach them.

Nagawicka Lake

Ten years ago, Nagawicka was a mediocre walleye lake at best, with a small walleye population and some natural reproduction. Today Nagawicka has one of the top walleye fisheries in southeastern Wisconsin, thanks to regular stocking since 1981 that has bolstered the native population. Walleyes are now the lake's most sought-after gamefish. Anyone who doubts the size of Nagawicka's walleyes missed the segment we did for *Outdoor Wisconsin* with Randy Schumacher and technician Sue Beyler during a spring population assessment there. They showed us netfuls of walleyes, some of them topping seven pounds, and an assortment of other species as well.

Top walleye spots include the sharp dropoffs along the east shore and rock bars located on the north side of the lake's lone island and off the mouth of the large, shallow bay about midway up the east shore. Try walking a jig and Twister tail down the dropoffs and along the rocks in spring. In summer, vertical jigging with a 1/4-ounce Swimmin' Ratt tipped with a minnow should take walleyes suspended off the deep weed edges.

Nagawicka's largemouths run big. Schumacher told me he receives more reports of bass in the six- to eight-pound range from Nagawicka than from any other area lake, and his spring netting surveys have turned up some dandies as well. Early in spring, the shallow back bays along the northwest shore produce some good action for prespawn bass. If you fish for prespawners, stick to artificials and release any large females. In summer, the outlet bay and the bays and coontail beds along the northeast shore are great bass spots. Try weedless lures by day and surface baits at night.

Schumacher reports that Nagawicka's smallmouths have come on strong in the last few years. There is good natural reproduction and anglers are taking fair numbers of them.

While not as abundant as they once were, Nagawicka's crappies run big. The same areas that produce bass in spring are worth trying for early crappies. Another good crappie spot is the channel leading to the Kettle. Use minnows to locate them, then switch to 1/32- or 1/64-ounce jigs or Slo-Poke Minis tipped with plastic Gitzit tubes or tails for more fun. You can't go wrong with a selection of yellow, white, hot pink, chartreuse and orange jigs with tails in matching or contrasting colors.

DNR survey nets turn up some real jumbo perch, but relatively few are caught by anglers. Ice fishermen catch some nice perch in 25 to 35 feet of water at the lake's far south end, around the island and in the Kettle. Any of the lighter swimming jigs tipped with a mousie or waxworm will entice winter perch to bite.

Bluegills write most of the panfish headlines on Nagawicka. 'Gills measuring eight to nine inches are common, and an occasional 10-inch bull shows up in fish baskets. Two favorite spots are the mouth of the

outlet bay and along the weedline in the Kettle. Bluegill action remains hot from mid summer through mid fall. In winter, most ice fishermen concentrate on the Kettle, where bluegills from all over the lake congregate. For a change of pace from weedline fishing in summer, try drifting for suspended bluegills over deep water in either basin, using the Bait Rigs panfish rigs that have proven so effective on suspended panfish on the Madison lakes.

Tom Newbauer landed this big largemouth bass during a trip to Nagawicka. DNR biologist Randy Schumacher receives more reports of six- to eight-pound bass from Nagawicka than any other lake. Photo courtesy Tom Newbauer

The public launch site at Naga-Waukee County Park, on the lake's southeast shore, has paved ramps and plenty of parking. There is a paved ramp access to the Kettle off Nagawicka Road and also a state-owned walk-in access at the northwest end of the Kettle used primarily by ice fishermen.

For bait, tackle and lake maps, stop at Dick Smith's Live Bait & Tackle, located right under the smile in the big yellow barn at I-94 and Highway 83, address: 2420 Milwaukee Street, Delafield, WI 53018, telephone (414) 646-2218. On a sad note, the last of the on-water boat rentals and bait shops was replaced by a row of condos a couple years ago, so now anglers must have their own boats and come prepared with gas and bait.

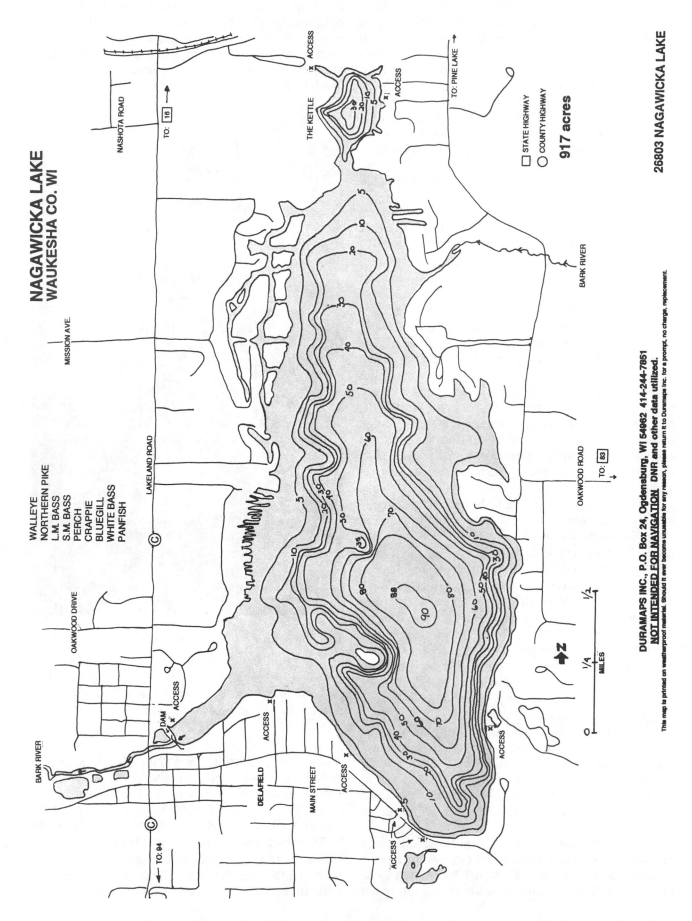

NAGAWICKA LAKE
WAUKESHA CO. WI

WALLEYE
NORTHERN PIKE
L.M. BASS
S.M. BASS
PERCH
CRAPPIE
BLUEGILL
WHITE BASS
PANFISH

☐ STATE HIGHWAY
○ COUNTY HIGHWAY

917 acres

26803 NAGAWICKA LAKE

DURAMAPS INC., P.O. Box 24, Ogdensburg, WI 54962 414-244-7851
NOT INTENDED FOR NAVIGATION DNR and other data utilized.

This map is printed on weatherproof material. Should it ever become unusable for any reason, please return it to Duramaps Inc. for a prompt, no charge, replacement.

Lake Namekagon

Southeastern Bayfield County

There used to be a big pile of driftwood on the east side of Chief Namekagon Island. For all I know, it may still be there, but I haven't been back to that spot since Lee Merrill and I used it for a blind during the late bluebill season a number of years ago.

November is a special time on a northwoods lake like Namekagon. A sullen sky hangs so low you can almost touch it. Pale bulrushes, drained of their green life, lean away from the wind and shake their heads with that steady beat that tricked the mythological Ojibwa hero Winneboujou into dancing all night on a beach, thinking he had come upon a powwow. The same wind wakens water as dull as the sky, kicking life into a spread of black and white decoys that bob and nod in the gray chop. Not so long ago, it also swept great flocks of scaup down from Canada, just ahead of the ice sheet that skips southward from lake to lake, sealing them for another season.

On that day, though, the wind brought only singles past our makeshift blind, and we let them pass. Far out in the lake, we watched an eagle swoop down repeatedly on a small knot of ducks that dove but

would not fly. The eagle, apparently looking for cripples, lumbered off to perch on a dead snag. Lee and I marveled at this little drama, then wandered around to the opposite end of the island where scattered red, green and yellow hulls behind another driftwood pile told of better shooting days.

A lone fishing boat headed out as we paddled back to the landing. The two occupants hunched their shoulders against the cold spray as their bow bounced on the waves. Their stout rods were rigged with jerk baits that showed signs of past encounters with toothy fish. They certainly had picked the right kind of day for muskies, and now that we were leaving, they would have at least this portion of Lake Namekagon all to themselves.

November and perhaps March and April are about the only times of year you'll find this Bayfield County lake so deserted. In spring, summer and early fall, fishermen and recreational boaters make heavy use of its waters, while in winter, ice fishermen and snowmobilers leave their tracks in every bay and basin. Permanent homes, summer cottages and resorts take up most of the wooded upland shoreline, but the lake is saved from ring development by 1,000 acres of wetlands that provide habitat for the full gamut of northwoods wildlife species.

At 3,200 acres, Namekagon is Bayfield County's largest lake. Surrounded by rugged terrain, the lake has a very irregular shoreline, with many bays and pockets that invite exploration. Four large basins make up Namekagon: Upper, Middle, Lower and Garden lakes. A shallow channel connects Upper Lake to 142-acre Jackson Lake. There are two permanent inlets, Castle Creek and Taylor Creek, and an outlet that forms the headwaters of the Namekagon River. A concrete roller dam with a three-foot head at the outlet controls the lake level and keeps connecting channels navigable.

Namekagon's light brown water is rather fertile. Submergent vegetation is extensive in some areas, with an outside weedline at a depth of six to 10 feet, providing excellent cover for many fish species. The east half of the lake usually has darker water, while the west side is often clearer. Summer algae blooms can obscure visibility throughout the lake, however. The deepest hole is 51 feet in Middle Lake. Sand and

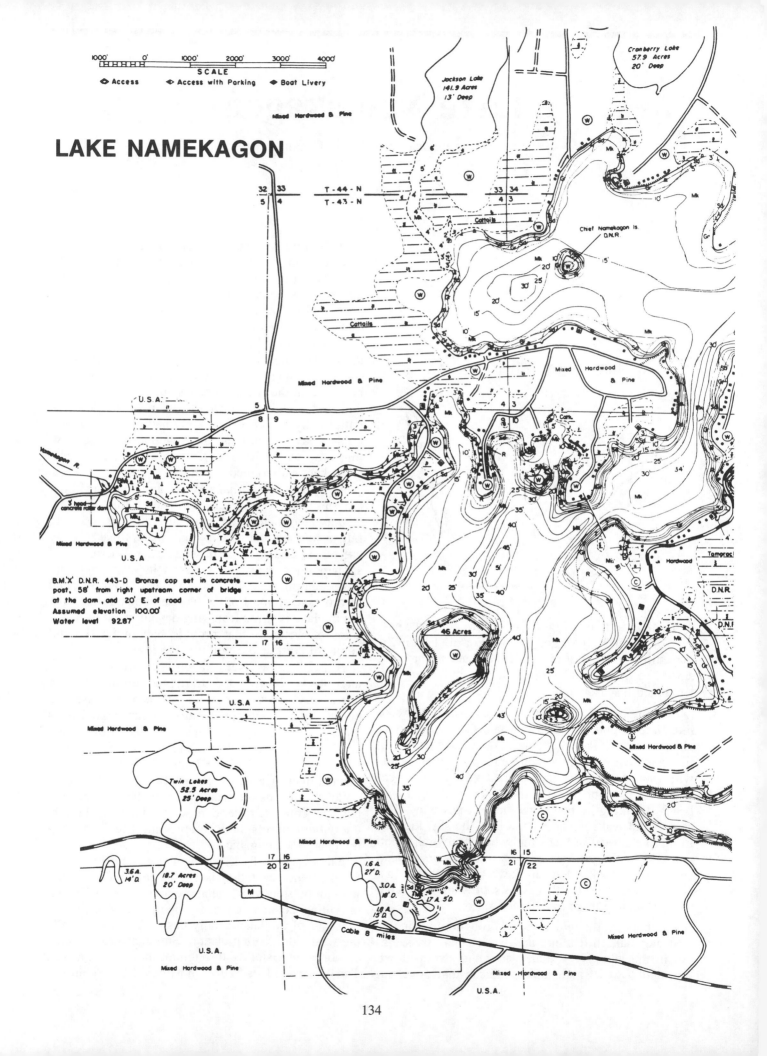

LAKE NAMEKAGON

SCALE

◆ Access   ◆ Access with Parking   ◆ Boat Livery

Cranberry Lake
57.9 Acres
20' Deep

Jackson Lake
141.9 Acres
13' Deep

Chief Namekagon Is.
D.N.R.

Mixed Hardwood & Pine

Cattails

Mixed Hardwood & Pine

T-44-N
T-43-N

U.S.A.

Namekagon R.

3' head concrete roller dam

Mixed Hardwood & Pine

U.S.A.

B.M.'X' D.N.R. 443-D Bronze cap set in concrete
post, 58' from right upstream corner of bridge
at the dam, and 20' E. of road
Assumed elevation 100.00'
Water level 92.87'

46 Acres

U.S.A.

Mixed Hardwood & Pine

Twin Lokes
52.5 Acres
25' Deep

Mixed Hardwood & Pine

3.6 A.
14' D.

18.7 Acres
20' Deep

1.6 A.
27' D.

3.0 A.
18' D.

1.8 A.
15' D.

17 A. 5' D.

Cable 8 miles

U.S.A.

Mixed Hardwood & Pine

Mixed Hardwood & Pine

Mixed Hardwood & Pine

U.S.A.

134

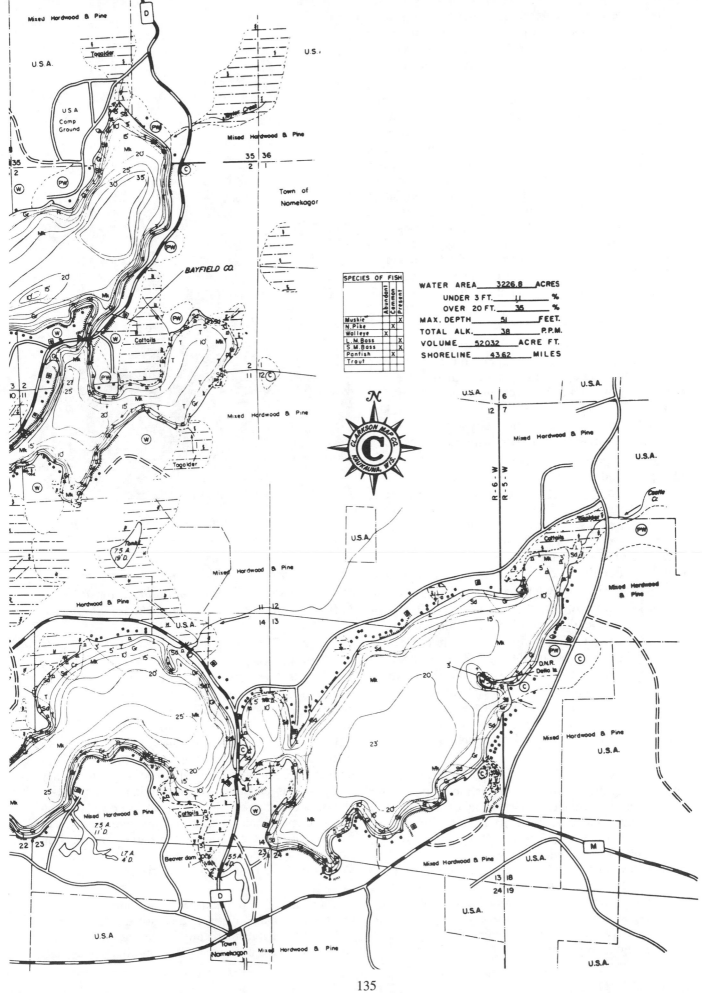

SPECIES OF FISH	Abundant	Common	Present
Muskie			X
N. Pike		X	
Walleye	X		
L. M. Bass			X
S. M. Bass			X
Panfish		X	
Trout			

WATER AREA _____3226.8_____ ACRES
UNDER 3 FT. _____11_____ %
OVER 20 FT. _____35_____ %
MAX. DEPTH _____51_____ FEET.
TOTAL ALK. _____38_____ P.P.M.
VOLUME _____52032_____ ACRE FT.
SHORELINE _____43.62_____ MILES

gravel cover most of the bottom, but there are areas of rubble and muck as well. Several bars on Upper and Middle lakes and dropoffs along some shorelines and around points and islands provide fish-holding structure.

Walleyes dominate Namekagon's diverse fishery. The DNR does not stock walleyes here, since natural reproduction maintains a good population density and size structure, but a local conservation group called Fish For The Future planted 11,000 fingerlings in Namekagon in 1992. Some anglers complain that walleyes are declining, but recent spring population estimates by DNR and Great Lakes Indian Fish and Wildlife Commission biologists indicate Namekagon has plenty of walleyes. It's just a tough lake to fish because the habitat is so diverse. DNR fish manager Dennis Scholl has scheduled a comprehensive survey of Namekagon's fish population for 1993 which ought to answer most questions about the status of walleyes and other species here.

When the season opens in May, look for walleyes near the creek inlets on Upper and Lower lakes because these areas warm up sooner than the rest of the lake. Lower Lake's gravel shorelines are another spot worth trying. Motor trolling is legal here and on all Bayfield County lakes, and many anglers troll bait harnesses or shallow crankbaits with good success.

Later in spring, the sunken bars and rocky points of Upper and Middle lakes hold good numbers of walleyes. Look for them at depths of 15 to 20 feet. Troll with diving crankbaits or backtroll with leeches and crawlers. In summer, some walleyes relate to the steeper, rocky dropoffs, where leeches on slip bobbers, jigs or diving baits will take them. Other walleyes hang out along deep weedlines and in weedbeds themselves, where a jig and leech can be productive.

Muskies are probably the best thing that has happened to Namekagon, but this news is slow in reaching the musky-fishing public. There have always been muskies here, but until the DNR began stocking them in 1982, their numbers were low. Since then, 2,500 fingerlings have been planted annually, supplemented by additional plants when available. The few anglers who target muskies here quietly admit to catching and releasing good numbers of legal-sized fish.

Bruce Shumway is the best-known musky guide on Namekagon. He and his clients have boated and released many muskies over 40 inches, including a couple each year that push 50 inches. Shumway's personal best was a 53-inch, 40-pounder taken in 1985. Shumway's advice to newcomers here is simple and straightforward: "Fish weeds and keep prospecting." He works weeds and shallow structure exclusively, leaving deep water alone altogether. Namekagon is a good lake to fish early in the season, Shumway says, and it also produces well in the summer, despite heavy boating traffic.

Ray Townsend caught this 48-inch, 27-pound musky on a chartreuse Hot Head while fishing with guide Bruce Shumway on Lake Namekagon in September of 1992. He also caught and released fish of 40 and 34 inches. It was Ray's first musky trip. Photo courtesy Bruce Shumway

When muskies are active, Shumway's primary bait is a bucktail he designed called the "Bootail," which uses a generous swatch of marabou feathers and a large Colorado blade. What color? Black or fluorescent orange. He started making a giant 12-inch Bootail a couple years back and took near-twin 30-pounders on it on a flat, sunny post-cold-front September day. Shumway has also had good luck early in the season and again in September with the new Hot Head spinnerbait he designed, especially along weed edges. When muskies are inactive, he likes to throw jerk baits, the bigger the better. He likes an Eddie, the original jerk bait, because it moves with a slow glide. He has taken a couple 30-pounders on Eddies.

There is a fair population of northerns here, and DNR survey nets have turned up some as large as 37 inches. You'll find them anywhere there are weeds, and should have no trouble catching them. The shallow bays hold some nice largemouths, but they are largely ignored. Try topwater baits or weedless spoons and plastics in areas of thick emergent vegetation.

Panfish are abundant here and they grow well. Crappies attract the most attention, but bluegills are also worth trying for. In spring and summer, look for crappies off the mouths of bays and over submerged bars. During fall electrofishing surveys, DNR crews have found large numbers of 10- to 12-inch crappies along shore almost everywhere on the lake. Try drifting the shoreline with a slip bobber and minnow, or cast with small spinners and jigs. The lake's best-known fall crappie hotspot is near where the Highway D bridge crosses the narrows on the east side of Upper Lake. Anglers take some very nice catches here in the evening on minnows.

There are several good boat landings on the lake. On the north side, there are two landings off Highway D on Forest Roads 209 and 212. There is also a National Forest Campground at the first of these. Another ramp on Highway D, 1 1/2 miles north of Highway M provides access to Lower Lake, and there is one on Garden Lake's east shore off Highway M on Forest Road 192.

Several resorts also have landings, including Lakewoods off Highway M at the southern tip of Middle Lake, which also features a full-service marina, boat ramp, boat rentals, guide service and some of the best food in the North Woods. Address: Lakewoods, Cable, WI 54821, telephone (800) 255-5937 or (715) 794-2561.

Many resorts carry some bait and tackle, or you can stop at Rondeau's Shopping Center in Cable, telephone (715) 798-3211, or Big Brook Bait, just south of Cable on Highway 63, telephone (715) 798-3310. For guided musky fishing, contact: Shumway's Guide Service, Route 1, Box 82, Drummond, WI 54832, telephone (715) 798-3441.

For more information on area resorts and services, contact: Bayfield County Tourism Department, P.O. Box 832, Washburn, WI 54891, telephone (800) 472-6336 or (715) 373-6125; or Cable Area Chamber of Commerce, P.O. Box 217, Cable, WI 54821, telephone (800) 533-7454, or (715) 798-3833.

Namekagon River

Cable, Bayfield County, to Riverside, Burnett County

From its unpretentious beginnings as the outlet of Lake Namekagon in southern Bayfield County, the Namekagon River follows a hundred-mile course to rendezvous with the St. Croix in northern Burnett County. Winding through a succession of small towns that have traded logging for tourism as their major industry, the Namekagon is protected forever as part of the St. Croix National Scenic Riverway. For those who love to combine float-camping and fishing, the Namekagon offers some of the finest canoeing water in the state and angling opportunities as varied as you're likely to find in one stretch of river.

Bridge crossings and public landings every few miles provide easy access and help you plan a trip. Make a leisurely half-day float between two bridges or spend several days on the river, camping at your choice of primitive or developed campgrounds along the way. If you can spare a whole week, you can float and fish the entire river from Cable to the St. Croix. If you do plan an extensive trip, bring along an assortment of tackle, because there will be opportunities to fish for trout, bass, walleyes, northerns, muskies, catfish and, in the fall, even sturgeon. The Ojibwa word from which the river takes its name means "place where sturgeon are plentiful."

For its first few miles, the Namekagon is a shallow, warm-water stream with few gamefish, but near the village of Cable several spring-fed brooks cool its waters enough to support trout. From Cable downstream to Hayward the river offers excellent fishing for brown and rainbow trout. Highway 63 follows the river along this stretch, and there are over a dozen access points along the highway and at town road bridge crossings. Wading is easy and the river is wide enough to permit fly casting.

The best trout fishing occurs on a 6.6-mile stretch in Sawyer County in the Township of Lenroot. Here, artificials only are permitted and a slot-size limit requires anglers to release trout between 10 and 15 inches in length. According to DNR fish manager Frank Pratt, angler use has increased on this stretch, but the number of trout over 15 inches has doubled. Most fly fishermen practice catch and release here even on larger fish, taking only an occasional trophy trout over 20 inches.

The stretch from the Lake Hayward Dam downstream to the Sawyer-Washburn County line harbors some large trout and is also subject to special regulations. From the May opener through September, the limit here is three trout over nine inches, but from October 1 until the next May opening date, catch-and-release fishing with artificials only is permitted. The only winter fishery of its kind this far north, this stretch offers some fabulous fishing for big browns and rainbows, especially on mild days in March and April.

Since natural trout reproduction is sporadic, Pratt hopes to raise the offspring of wild Namekagon browns for restocking here and elsewhere. The Namekagon's predatory browns grow fast and have a high resistance to warm water, making them prime candidates for such a project.

An eight- or nine-foot rod in 4, 5 or 6 weight will do nicely for trout. If you bring only one rod and plan to fish for smallmouths on downstream stretches as well, go with the 6-weight rod. Two lines, one floating and one sink-tip, will handle all your fly fishing. You'll need a full range of leader tippets from 0X to 7X, depending on the size of the flies you use.

Traditional evening mayfly hatches in May and June provide most of the Namekagon's trout fishing opportunities, although on some sections there is a heavy hatch of giant Hexagenia mayflies after dark for a week or so in late June and a reliable daily morning hatch of the diminutive Tricorythodes later in the summer. When there is no surface activity, try a nymph or scud imitation fished dead-drift on your sink-tip line. In the fall, large streamers and bucktails worked along undercut banks and cross-current in deep runs often draw strikes from hungry browns.

Three warmwater flowages between Cable and Hayward — Pacwawong Lake, Phipps Flowage and Lake Hayward — offer some limited opportunities for bass, northerns, muskies and panfish, but most anglers skip these small lakes. Below Hayward, four 15-mile stretches of river offer a variety of canoeing and fishing opportunities. It takes about five hours of steady paddling to traverse each stretch, but if you fish seriously you can spend a day or two on any one of them.

The first stretch runs from Hayward to Spring-brook. Put in below the Hayward Dam or behind the DNR Ranger Station on Highway 27 just south of town. The fast runs and shallow riffles here make for fun canoeing, but you may want to portage around one tricky set of rapids located about 11 river miles downstream from Hayward at Groat Landing.

Walleyes and smallmouths are the main species on this stretch. During the day, concentrate on the deeper runs, bend holes and instream cover like boulders and logs. Try live bait, jigs, small spinners and crankbaits on ultralight spinning tackle for both species. In the evening when both bass and walleyes move into shallower riffles to feed on minnows, shallow-running crankbaits and spinners produce well. You can also take both species on fly tackle, using streamers and fur-bodied flies on a sink-tip line and short leader. Dark colors — black, bronze and brown — seem to work best.

Between Springbrook and Trego, the Namekagon slows down and deepens. This is an easier float and the fish tend to run bigger. On several occasions, fishing for an hour or so just before dark below the highway bridges on this stretch, I have caught numerous walleyes and smallies in the one-to-two-pound class, along with an occasional bigger fish, on small Mepps spinners and floating Rapalas. You may run into an occasional northern along weedy shorelines in the

Fish Wisconsin author Dan Small fly-fishes on the Namekagon between Hayward and Spooner. Photo by Dan Small

wider portions of this stretch. Take out at the Trego Wayside Landing just above Trego Flowage. There are two campsites below the Trego Landing and two more on the flowage itself.

Trego Flowage holds walleyes, panfish, northerns and bass. You'll find walleyes and smallmouths in the river channel by day and along shallow bars in the evening. Panfish and northerns frequent the bays of this five-mile-long flowage. Portage to the left around the dam at the lower end of the flowage.

Below Trego Flowage, the Namekagon flows through 30 miles of near wilderness. The current is moderate, but there are no rapids. Walleyes, smallmouths and channel catfish frequent the deeper holes and runs, and muskies are common here. Catfish will take deep-running crankbaits, but you'll do better on these fighters with live bait or cheese fished right on bottom. Muskies lurk near boulders, logs and other cover and will often strike large, splashy topwater lures, bucktails and spinnerbaits.

If you fish the lower Namekagon in September or October, you may want to try for a sturgeon. Concentrate on deep runs and fish right on bottom with a gob of nightcrawlers on heavy spinning tackle. It's a good idea to release sturgeon, but if you do plan to keep one, be sure to pick up a free hook-and-line sturgeon tag at any DNR office before you fish. The season limit is one fish over 50 inches.

Whispering Pines (Byrkits Landing) is the halfway point on this final stretch of river, but there are alternate take-outs at Howell Bridge, three miles downstream and at the State Highway 77 bridge, another 2 1/2 miles downstream. The final take-out is located at the Namekagon Trail bridge, 16 miles below Byrkits Landing. Primitive camping is permitted anywhere along the river, but canoeists are encouraged to use established sites.

Services ranging from restaurants and motels to campgrounds and canoe rentals are available in Hayward, Trego and Spooner. For information on these and other area attractions, write Hayward Chamber of Commerce, P.O. Box 762, Hayward, WI 54843, telephone (715) 634-8662; or Hayward Lakes Resort Association, P.O. Box 1055, Hayward, WI 54843, telephone (715) 634-4801, or (800) 826-FISH. For bait, tackle and fishing information: Big Brook Bait, Route 2, Box 334, Cable, WI 54821, telephone (715) 798-3310; Pastika's Sporting Goods, P.O. Box 687, 217 Dakota Avenue, Hayward, WI 54843, telephone (715) 634-4466.

For river maps and camping information, write St. Croix National Scenic Riverway Headquarters, P.O. Box 708, St. Croix Falls, WI 54024, telephone (715) 483-3284. The Park Service also maintains a summer office (May-October) on the river at Trego: National Park Service, P.O. Box 100, Trego, WI 54888, telephone (715) 635-8346.

Nelson Lake

Six Miles North of Hayward, Sawyer County

Nelson Lake

Sawyer County's Nelson Lake doesn't get the attention lavished on the area's better-known musky waters -- Grindstone, Lac Courte Oreilles, Teal, Lost Land, and of course the mighty Chip -- but locals know Nelson is tough to beat for walleyes, bass and bluegills. Home of the former state record bluegill and current state record black bullhead, Nelson is a likely candidate to break the long-standing state largemouth record as well, if any lake can in this era of sophisticated methods and heavy fishing pressure.

Created as a recreational facility in 1937 by the damming of the Totagatic River, Nelson Lake has certainly lived up to its potential. Its 2,500 acres harbor a wide range of fish-holding habitat. Its deepest point is 33 feet in the basin of former Lake 25. Most of the lake is quite shallow, with extensive areas of stumps that provide great cover for fish but can mess up your motor's lower unit if you run about heedlessly at full throttle.

Vegetation is sparse, but there are floating bogs and some lily pads and bulrushes in bays. The old Totagatic River channel, marked on most maps and

easily found with a locator, provides good holding structure as well. The bottom is largely sand, rubble and gravel, with areas of muck and some huge boulders in places. The water is stained brown and quite murky, with extensive algae blooms in late summer.

I caught my first Wisconsin walleye on Nelson Lake, fishing with Charlie France of Hayward many years ago. Charlie, his son Chuck, and I would launch at Gerlach's Landing on the southeast shore, run around the east side of Big Island, and cast floating Rapalas among the stumps east of Eagles Nest Pass. In those days, limits of pan-size walleyes were easy to come by. If that spot didn't produce fish, we'd run up the inlet into Bass Bay and drift the river channel or work the stumpy bays along the east shore. Whenever there was a fair wind, we'd find a rocky shoreline and cast right up against the rocks, often taking walleyes in only a foot of water.

Today, Nelson still holds plenty of walleyes, although the population has declined somewhat in recent years. A 1992 survey there showed about 15 adult walleyes per acre. These fish averaged 17 inches, but anglers have had a hard time catching them because there is so much forage, they're rarely hungry. Unfortunately, there are virtually no young walleyes coming along to replace the current stock, thanks to three consecutive years of poor natural reproduction.

"We've seen the same phenomenon on a number of area lakes," says DNR fisheries manager Frank Pratt. "The walleye population is on the verge of collapsing. If we have another poor reproductive year, we may have to stock walleyes again to bring them back." Stocking was curtailed some years ago, once the population became self-sustaining.

Largemouths, on the other hand, are doing well. Their numbers have increased as walleyes have declined. Largemouths average 16 inches here, and there are plenty of trophies running well over six pounds. While no longer a secret, Nelson's great largemouth fishery attracts far fewer anglers than do its golden-flanked walleyes.

Northerns are far less abundant, but they too run big. Pratt knows of nine pike over 20 pounds that came out of Nelson Lake in 1992 alone. Some anglers target them, but most pike are taken incidentally by anglers after walleyes or panfish. Nelson also harbors a few muskies, and they're doing well, says Pratt, thanks to a good population of large white suckers.

Nelson's bluegill fishery is one of the state's best, although anglers have overharvested large 'gills in recent years. In the mid-1980s, 55 percent of the bluegills harvested measured over eight inches, but that percentage has declined since then. Even so, every summer, Nelson produces a few 'gills weighing in at over a pound. Bluegills here reach eight inches in only four summers, and Pratt thinks the lake could once again yield two-pounders, if anglers would only let them grow up. Like bass, bluegills have increased as walleyes have declined, as have crappies. Nelson now harbors a substantial populations of crappies ranging up to 14 inches in size.

In early spring, walleyes head for the Totagatic River inlet, riprap near the outlet and rocky shorelines throughout the lake. Casting with crankbaits produces good action, as does drifting with jigs and minnows. Snags are common, so floating baits are preferable. In summer, work the wood, bog edges and river channel with diving crankbaits or jigs and leeches. Fish cribs also hold walleyes in summer.

You'll find log and brush cribs located along the river channel at the west end, in deep water around the smaller island off the southwest side of Big Island, and between Big Island and the red beacon on the south shore. There are also 50 new plastic cribs in the main lake and in Lake 25 that are worth trying. Forward trolling is legal here, so you may want to drag diving crankbaits along the river channel in summer or fall.

For spring bass, work close to weed cover in the shallow bays. West Bay and North Bay at the lake's west end are good spring spots. Spinnerbaits, soft stick baits and plastics all produce well. Later in the year, you'll find them along weed edges, in the wood and near floating bogs. Beaver Bay on the south shore and Tagalder and Crappie bays on the east shore hold bass all season long.

Northerns are scattered throughout the lake, but you can target them by tossing big spinnerbaits and spoons in the same areas that hold largemouths.

Bluegills frequent the shallow bays in spring, where you can take them on fly rod lures or live bait. In summer, top spots include submerged bogs, deep weed edges and cribs wherever they are found. Crappies like bay mouths and bulrushes in spring and sub-

Charlie France launches at Gerlach's Landing on Nelson Lake, while daughter-in-law Kathi puts a life vest on granddaughter Adrian prior to setting out for a walleye and bluegill outing. Photo courtesy Charlie France

merged bogs, cribs and woody cover in summer. Live minnows work well, but you can take them on small feather jigs and plastics as well.

Nelson is also a popular ice fishing lake. Fast action for walleyes prompts local anglers to venture out when the lake first freezes over. For some, bagging a buck on the first weekend of rifle seasons means a Thanksgiving weekend outing for walleyes. Walleyes hit well in the evening on small suckers fished on tip-ups. Set up near stumps and run a line of tip-ups out to deeper water. Don't be surprised to pick up a big northern or largemouth in winter as well.

Ultralight tackle and tiny jigs tipped with waxworms produce good catches of bluegills in winter. To find active panfish, look for a group bucket-sitters intently watching their jig rods, but don't crowd them -- there is plenty of room.

Gerlach's Landing is now known as Dick and Lynne's Place. To reach the launch there, take Highway 63 north from Hayward to Nelson Lake Road. You'll pass Minnow Jim's Bait & Tackle on Nelson Lake Road. Stop for some minnows and a fishing report. Jim's phone number is (715) 634-4352. To reach Etlinger's Landing on the east shore, take Pfeifer Road north off Highway 63, then go west on Tagalder Road (gravel) for three miles to Etlinger's Landing, where there's a concrete ramp and ample parking.

Nelson Lake Landing and RV Park, off Highway 27 near the dam at the west end, features a black-topped ramp, plenty of parking, camping and a full-service resort, telephone (715) 634-4175.

For bait and tackle in Hayward, try Pastika's Sporting Goods, 217 Dakota Avenue, Hayward, WI 54843, telephone (715) 634-4466. For information on other area services, contact the Hayward Lakes Resort Association, P.O. Box 1055, Hayward, WI 54843, telephone (800) 826-FISH.

Oconto River And Machickanee Flowage

Oconto Falls to Oconto, Oconto County

Oconto River and Machickanee Flowage

The Oconto is a river of many moods. In its upper reaches, it is as fine a trout stream as flows through the hills and woodlands of northeastern Wisconsin, with long, dark runs shaded by alders and good insect hatches all season long. Then, about where it hops back and forth across the Oconto County line and turns east toward Lake Michigan, the Oconto turns into a sweetheart of a smallmouth stream, with deep holes and lots of boulders to provide cover for bronzebacks. Below Oconto Falls, the river changes character again, slowing and widening into Machickanee Flowage, where warm water species provide fishing action. The final stretch from the Stiles Dam downstream holds a little bit of everything, including a good run of rainbows up from the lake.

Let's focus on the Lower Oconto, beginning at Oconto Falls. There is a boat launch at the city park just above the dam where you can put in and motor upstream to fish most of the river up to Highway 32, or you can launch a small boat or canoe at the bridge and run downstream.

Smallmouths are the major species here, and you can catch them on small spinners and crankbaits. Try along the riprapped shoreline west of the park, over the hump just off the landing and in deep water near the dam. The extensive weedbeds that line much of the shoreline here hold some nice largemouths and northerns. Weedless spoons, topwater baits and spinnerbaits will take both species. Don't be surprised if you raise a musky, either, because some are present here, although their numbers are low. Panfishermen do well on crappies and bluegills off the weedbeds.

Back in 1981, the DNR drew down the Machickanee Flowage and used rotenone to remove carp from Oconto Falls downstream to Stiles. The flowage was then refilled and stocked with trout, bass, walleyes, and bluegills. The trout were intended to provide only a short-lived fishery. The walleyes did not do well for some reason, according to DNR fish manager Ross Langhurst, but bass and bluegills thrived and aquatic vegetation came back strong in the absence of carp. Enough northerns apparently came over the dam to repopulate the flowage as well. In the mid-1980s, a rejuvenated Machickanee Flowage provided fantastic fishing for bass, pike and panfish. This hot action has tapered off somewhat, but the flowage is still worth fishing, as many anglers have discovered.

A DNR survey of Machickanee's fish population in 1988 showed excellent growth rates for largemouths, northerns and perch. Bluegills and crappies were abundant but their growth rates were about average, and no outstanding individuals turned up. There are few, if any, walleyes, and smallmouth numbers are also low, but habitat for both species is quite limited. Ross Langhurst says the 463-acre flowage should be managed for largemouths, pike and panfish. In the past few years, pike numbers have declined somewhat, apparently due to an increase in the ice-fishing harvest and possibly to loss of spawning habitat.

You'll find all species easier to catch in late spring before the extensive weedbeds develop. Spoons, jigs and Reapers and spinnerbaits will take spring northerns, while plastics should do the job for early bass. Now that carp are no longer a problem here, weeds get rather heavy in midsummer and the weeds are where you should look for largemouths and pike at that time. A jig and pig, spinnerbaits, weedless spoons with pork trailers and other lures made to work in the heavy stuff should produce well. Try jigging with plastics in the old river channel above the dam for bass and work the deep weed edges for both species.

You can have fun with bedding bluegills in the shallows in May, but later in the year the larger ones will hang out in the river channel. You'll find perch near bottom here also, and crappies should suspend in the deeper water above the dam. Live bait will take all three species, but if you can find a school of crappies, you'll have more fun with small swimming jigs. There is a good boat landing with restrooms and plenty of parking above the dam off Highway 141.

The large pool below the dam collects a variety of species that migrate upstream in spring and fall, so you never know quite what you'll catch. In spring, nice walleyes, northerns and rainbows are taken here and in the river below the dam, while in fall chinooks and occasional browns and cohos add to the smorgasbord. You can either fish from shore or launch a cartopper or canoe just below the dam on either bank. If you wade, watch your footing, as this spot can be treacherous during high water.

Mike Mladenik with a largemouth bass taken from the Machickanee Flowage. Bass do well here in the fertile water and heavy weeds. Photo courtesy Mike Mladenik

My favorite stretch begins here and runs downstream almost to Oconto. Stiles Road follows the river closely for several miles. There is a new public access on North River Road a mile or so south of the Highway J bridge. You can float this stretch from Stiles down to Oconto, or jump from one point to another and wade.

You'll find smallmouths and a few walleyes in the holes and along brushy banks in the upstream portions and some good-sized northerns in the lower stretch right in town. Fisheries biologist Brian Belonger also reports a few lake sturgeon and large muskies are showing up now and then. Two boat launches at the mouth and one at Holtwood Park just above the Highway 41 bridge provide access to the lower river, but Suzy's Rapids, about a mile upstream from Oconto, prevents boat traffic from continuing upstream.

The Oconto is one of several Lake Michigan tributaries to receive large plantings of rainbow trout every year since the mid-1980s. The DNR currently stocks both Skamania and Chambers Creek rainbows, which migrate to Lake Michigan as smolts and return several years later to spawn, providing a fishery that lasts nearly nine months. All stocked rainbows are fin-clipped, and DNR biologists appreciate reports of any clipped fish you might catch to help them evaluate the success of their stocking efforts.

Most anglers fish for rainbows with spawn or hardware, but you can also take them on flies or yarn. Good numbers of rainbows often pile up below Suzy's Rapids and again at the dam. I like to wait for a warm rain, then drift chartreuse yarn balls on a fly rod in the deeper runs, behind boulders and along bank cover. This is precision fishing, somewhat akin to exploratory surgery, because you're prospecting for fish you can rarely see, hoping to detect a strike or delicate pickup on a graphite rod before a fish realizes it's been fooled by a phony egg. Once you hook a rainbow in this shallow water, it will put on an aerial display and often tear off downriver, leaving you to stumble along behind through rock and riffle as best you can. Four- to eight-pounders are common, but some run to 15 pounds or better.

The DNR also stocks browns at the mouth and chinooks at a park north of the mouth each year. Fall runs of these species provide the same opportunity as rainbows, and they're just as much fun to catch. Pink salmon show up in odd-numbered years, and each fall anglers take a few splake that have strayed here from plants elsewhere.

In addition to yarn, you may want to try bright streamers or other attractor patterns. You'll need an 8 1/2- to 10-foot fly rod for this type of fishing, equipped with a multiplier reel with a good drag. A fighting butt extension on the rod will give you more leverage to battle a big trout or salmon. Monofilament line provides better control for fishing yarn or

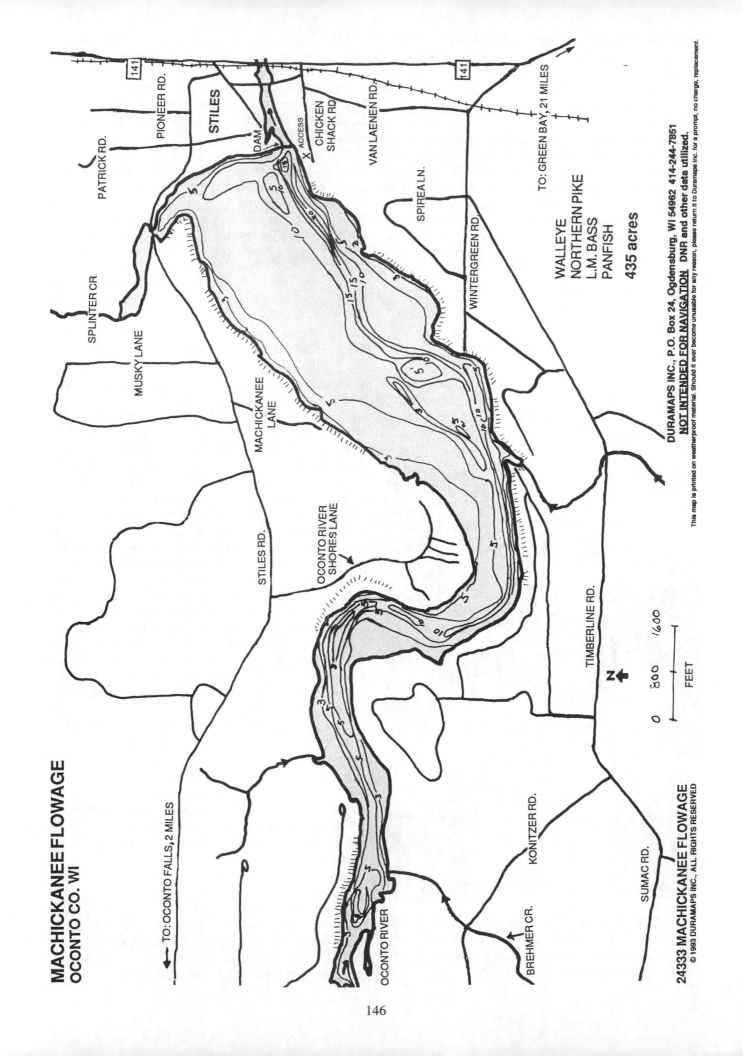

MACHICKANEE FLOWAGE
OCONTO CO. WI

STILES

PIONEER RD.
PATRICK RD.

DAM
ACCESS
X
CHICKEN SHACK RD.
VAN LAENEN RD.

141
141

TO: GREEN BAY, 21 MILES

SPIREA LN.
WINTERGREEN RD.

WALLEYE
NORTHERN PIKE
L.M. BASS
PANFISH

435 acres

SPLINTER CR.
MUSKY LANE
MACHICKANEE LANE
STILES RD.

OCONTO RIVER SHORES LANE

TIMBERLINE RD.

N

0 800 1600
FEET

KONITZER RD.
BREHMER CR.
OCONTO RIVER
SUMAC RD.

TO: OCONTO FALLS, 2 MILES

DURAMAPS INC., P.O. Box 24, Ogdensburg, WI 54962 414-244-7851
NOT INTENDED FOR NAVIGATION   DNR and other data utilized.

This map is printed on weatherproof material. Should it ever become unusable for any reason, please return it to Duramaps Inc. for a prompt, no charge, replacement.

24333 MACHICKANEE FLOWAGE
© 1993 DURAMAPS INC., ALL RIGHTS RESERVED

spawn, but to fish flies you'll want a sink-tip weight-forward line matched to your rod and a short, stout leader.

Polarized glasses will help you spot fish holding in the current or on the redds. Look for dished-out spots in the gravel bottom below a riffle or at the head of a pool. If you can see fish resting or spawning, you can sometimes take them by drifting your yarn, spawn or fly repeatedly in front of their noses. If you see a pair, try to take the male first, as he will be replaced by another, while once a female is taken off a redd, the males lose all interest.

This is strictly a put-and-take fishery, since the eggs do not survive, so you should have no qualms about catching spawning fish. Salmon die after spawning, but it's still a good idea to release the fish you don't need so others will have a chance to catch them. Releasing browns and rainbows gives them a chance to return to the lake and put on another year's growth before they migrate upstream again.

For bait and tackle from April through October, try Hi-Way Bait & Sport, 220 Main Street, Oconto, WI 54153, telephone (414) 834-3439. Hi-Way Bait & Sport has another shop with a more complete line of tackle on 2857 Sot Road, Abrams, WI 54101, telephone (414) 826-7887.

For a county recreation map and information on restaurants, lodging and other area facilities, contact the Oconto County Forestry and Parks Department, 300 Washington Street, Oconto, WI 54153, telephone (414) 834-6820.WI 54101, telephone (414) 826-7887.

Okauchee Lake

Okauchee, Waukesha County

Okauchee Lake

Located in the heart of Waukesha County's Lake District, Okauchee Lake seems much larger than its 1,200 acres. Five islands and a series of long, narrow bays help break up its shape and add to the abundant structure that makes this one of the most interesting lakes in southeastern Wisconsin. If it weren't for its heavily developed shoreline, you'd swear you were on a lake somewhere on the Canadian Shield. Even the names of some of Okauchee's features -- Breezy Point, Ice House Bay, Stumpy Bay and Crazy Man's Island -- suggest that this "civilized" lake would be right at home way up north.

The Oconomowoc River flows through Okauchee Lake, with an inlet on the lake's northeast arm, and an outlet to Lower Okauchee Lake at the end of the southwest arm. The lake bottom, composed mostly of sand and gravel with some areas of silt and muck, is heavily convoluted, with more natural structure than most lakes three times its size. A map and a sensitive locator are essential if you hope to learn the lake's weedy bays, sand and rock bars, deep weedlines and gravel points. Motor around the lake with your loca-

tor on and you'll see that depths change rapidly every few yards. The deepest hole is over 100 feet.

Weed growth is heavy, with extensive beds of coontail and cabbage. The deep weedline occurs at 15 to 20 feet, which is also where the main dropoff begins. A thermocline develops in summer in the central basin and northwest arm, and gamefish and forage species often suspend over deep water, seeking comfortable temperatures and adequate oxygen. Good populations of gamefish and panfish make Okauchee one of the area's best fishing lakes for most warmwater species.

Largemouth bass are Okauchee's primary gamefish, and it's no wonder, because there is good bass habitat everywhere you look. In spring, concentrate on the shallow bays: Stumpy Bay and Wittiger's Bay on the northwest arm, the inlet on the northeast arm, Ice House Bay on the southeast arm, and Bay 5, which is the lake's entire southwest arm, which all have good submergent weeds that hold bass. As its name suggests, Stumpy Bay is studded with stumps that also provide good bass cover. Lower Okauchee Lake, just downstream from the outlet, and Tierney Lake, accessible through a channel along the west shore of Ice House Bay, are also good shallow spots to try for early-season bass. All these areas are just made for such baits as a Slo-Poke jig with a Texas-rigged plastic worm or a jig-and-pig in your favorite color. Fish such offerings slow and easy early in the season.

Later in the season, bass hang out along the deep weed edges, especially where there are deep water slots that poke up into weedbeds. Look for these slots, or inside turns, at the mouth of the inlet bay and also at the mouth of Stumpy Bay south of Crazy Man's Island. Cast or troll deep-diving crankbaits here, or work dark-colored Texas-rigged plastics right to the weed edge.

Walleye numbers are low, despite heavy stocking since the late 1970s. Anglers are catching fewer walleyes than they did just a few years ago, and DNR fish manager Randy Schumacher says he may discontinue stocking them. The key to finding walleyes consistently here is to locate the small but numerous rock and gravel bars. There's a good rock bar off the broad point directly across the northwest arm from

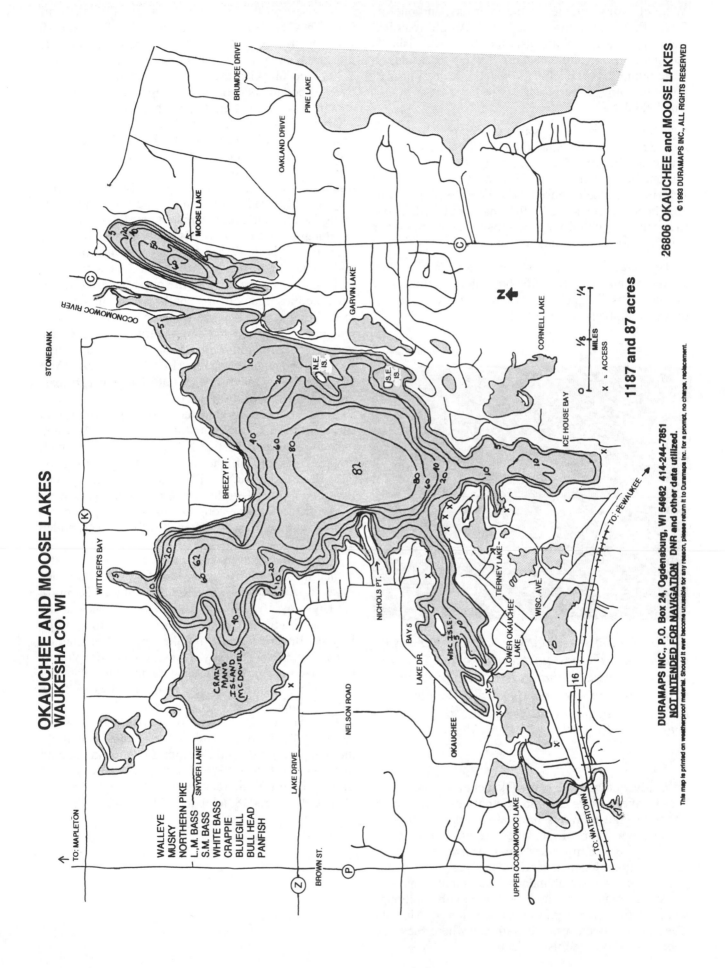

OKAUCHEE AND MOOSE LAKES
WAUKESHA CO. WI

WALLEYE
MUSKY
NORTHERN PIKE
L.M. BASS
S.M. BASS
WHITE BASS
CRAPPIE
BLUEGILL
BULL HEAD
PANFISH

26806 OKAUCHEE and MOOSE LAKES

1187 and 87 acres

DURAMAPS INC., P.O. Box 24, Ogdensburg, WI 54962 414-244-7851
NOT INTENDED FOR NAVIGATION DNR and other data utilized.

This map is printed on weatherproof material. Should it ever become unusable for any reason, please return it to Duramaps Inc. for a prompt, no charge, replacement.

Wittiger's Bay, another in the inlet bay, and one off Silver Point at the mouth of Bay 5. An old road bed running between Northeast and Southeast islands along the eastern shore also holds walleyes, as does a large hump known as the "Volcano," located just off Nichols Point, directly across the lake from Southeast Island.

While it's not great, walleye fishing is best early and late in the day, since there is often a lot of boat traffic at other times. Try heavy jigs that get down to bottom quickly in 20 to 25 feet of water. A local favorite is a blue or purple "Okauchee Killer," available in area bait shops. Trolling back and forth across the rock bars with diving crankbaits sometimes takes trophy-class walleyes late in the evening.

The shallower areas of these same rocky bars, gravel points and dropoffs hold good numbers of smallmouths. Tempt them with live bait, small jigs or diving crankbaits on light tackle.

DNR biologist Randy Schumacher says Okauchee is the best northern pike lake in southeastern Wisconsin, thanks to abundant spawning habitat in upriver marshes. The biggest pike hold just outside weedlines where they feed on schools of cisco. Photo by Dan Small

Randy Schumacher says Okauchee is one of the best northern pike lakes in southeastern Wisconsin, although pike numbers have also slipped a little in the last few years. Extensive marshes upstream on the Bark River provide stable spawning habitat, ensuring good hatches nearly every year. As a result, pike of all sizes are abundant. They inhabit many of the same areas frequented by largemouths, although some of the largest pike are taken just outside the weedlines in open water in summer where they suspend to feed on schools of cisco.

Muskies, on the other hand, have really taken off here. They've been stocked in Okauchee for about 10 years, hybrids at first, then half hybrids and half true muskies, as many as 2,000 a year in all. Now, about 1,200 true muskies are stocked each fall. Muskies over 20 pounds began showing up in the late 1980s, and anglers are catching legal fish in good numbers.

Muskies are new to Okauchee, so it's hard to pattern the big ones. Good spots to try are the shallower rock bars and outside weed edges. You can also bet some suspend in deep water where panfish and ciscoes hang out. Since trolling is legal here, a good way to find muskies might be to drag big crankbaits along the contours, rock bars and weed edges.

Bluegills and crappies dominate the panfish take here. Bluegills don't run big, but they are plentiful and it's not hard to catch a mess of seven- to eight-inch 'gills any time of year. In spring, try tiny jigs or even ice flies in any of the shallow bays. In summer, drift over deep water with slip bobbers for suspended bluegills. Ice House Bay and Stumpy Bay produce good catches of 'gills through the ice. Use ultralight jig rods, one-pound test line (Berkley's Trilene Cold Weather line is ideal) and minute fish-eye and teardrop jigs tipped with waxies or mousies.

You can take good catches of big crappies in spring in the flats at the mouth of the inlet bay and over the sand bar west of Breezy Point. In summer, crappies suspend off the deep weed edge along the west shore from Nichols Point north to Stumpy Bay. Swimming jigs in bright or natural colors work well. Go with the lightest you can manage. Slip bobbers and swimming jigs are often deadly for suspended crappies.

Of several access points, the best is the state-owned landing on the west side of Lower Okauchee Lake. Take Hewitt's Point Road (Highway R) north off Highway 16 to Town Road T which ends at the landing. There is a good winter access to Stumpy Bay on Bauer's Lane off Lake Drive. Here, as on other Waukesha County lakes, condo developers have razed the last of the boat rentals and on-water bait shops, so bring all the gear you'll need for a day's fishing.

Dick Smith's bait shop, in The Barn at I-94 and Highway 83, carries a wide assortment of minnows, including rosy reds and medium golden shiners, both of which produce well on Okauchee. Address: Dick Smith's Live Bait & Tackle, 2420 Milwaukee Street, Delafield, WI 53018, telephone (414) 646-2218.

Lake Onalaska

Mississippi River at Onalaska, La Crosse County

Lake Onalaska

Located just north of La Crosse and west of Onalaska in La Crosse County, Lake Onalaska lies in a wide valley bounded by the towering bluffs of the Mississippi River. Formed by the Dresbach Dam and located at the confluence of the Black and Mississippi rivers, Lake Onalaska's 7,700 acres cover a maze of sloughs, islands, stump fields, channels and bays, offering what was once Mississippi River backwater fishing at its finest. Water quality has declined over the last 20 years, however, slowly eroding the quality of the fishery as well. But a $1.8 million dredging project, 20 years in the making and now the flagship of a larger Environmental Management Plan for the entire Upper Mississippi, has helped slow the lake's decline around and restore some of the greatness that was lost.

Panfish are the big attraction here, but the Mississippi is a rich and diverse fishery with a total of some 130 different fish species, and you're likely to catch just about anything from bluegills, crappies and perch, to bass, northerns, walleyes, catfish, sheepshead, white bass and sturgeon. The main problem is

that Lake Onalaska is very shallow and sedimentation has intensified in recent years, contributing to lower oxygen levels and a decline in some of the invertebrates fish depend on for food. The dredging project, completed in 1989, has created new habitat for fish, waterfowl and other species that use this diverse ecosystem.

A joint project of the U.S. Fish and Wildlife Service and the U.S. Army Corps of Engineers, which manage the lake as part of Mississippi River Pool 7, and a host of other agencies, the dredged area totals about 70 acres and creates two deep channels in a wishbone pattern between Rosebud Island and the Wisconsin shore just north of the La Crosse airport on French Island. Before it was dredged, that area was two to four feet deep, low in oxygen, and choked with vegetation. It sometimes froze from top to bottom in winter. Now the channels run from 10 to 40 feet deep, with many holes, humps and banks.

Some of the sand and gravel dredged from the channels was used to build three new islands west of Rosebud Island. The islands are horseshoe-shaped, with rock riprap and a deep trench on the upstream side, and a sandy beach inside the horseshoe on the downstream side.

Ron Benjamin, Mississippi River fish biologist with the DNR, reports that fish changed their habits dramatically after the dredging was completed. "There's a good panfishery now where none existed before," he says. "And there are even walleyes in the dredge cuts." In summer, trollers take northerns along weed edges and walleyes right in the dredge cuts and in front of the new islands. In winter, ice fishermen are taking good catches of walleyes, bluegills and crappies from the cuts.

"This project has essentially created a brand new fishery on the east side of the lake," says Marc Schultz, La Crosse County Extension Resource Agent. "On most lakes, the locals have an advantage over outsiders coming in for the first time, but the dredging has put everyone on an equal footing. Anyone with a good depthfinder and a little basic fishing knowledge ought to be able to catch fish here."

Schultz, who lives on the lake and fishes it regularly, serves as a consultant to the Lake Onalaska Protection and Rehabilitation District. The lake district publishes a waterproof map, available at local sport shops, that shows all the lake's features, including landings, water depths and the dredge cuts and islands.

The lake's recovery suffered a setback during the drought years of 1988 and '89, when weedbeds died back and bass and panfish hatches failed. Areas that formerly held bass and panfish were devoid of fish for several years, but weeds are coming back and so are the fish. Ron Benjamin reports good hatches of both largemouth and smallmouth bass in the early 1990s. Both species have good grow rates, and the 14-inch size limit will help them recover quickly.

Crappies seem to have responded to post-drought changes faster than bluegills, says Benjamin, and Onalaska anglers are enjoying the best crappie fishing seen here in 20 years. In the winter of 1993, ice fishermen took limits of crappies up to 19 inches, with many fish over two pounds. The largest reported weighed just under three pounds. Ice anglers found some huge bluegills as well, but they were very selective.

While the channels and islands make fishing a portion of Lake Onalaska a whole new ball game, the affected area amounts to about one percent of the entire lake. Traditional hotspots should still continue to produce good catches. Fishing for major species is legal all year long, but the seasons dictate where you should fish on Lake Onalaska, as conditions vary tremendously and fish move accordingly on this big lake. Unstable water levels, caused by opening and closing of the dams, as well as by seasonal fluctuations, can shut down fish activity. During periods of stable water in midwinter and midsummer, most species tend to bite better.

In spring, the lake's north and east shorelines produce largemouth bass and bluegills. A favorite spot is the area inside the Brice Prairie Dike, which runs along the lake's east shore just out from the Upper Brice Prairie Boat Landing. Surface baits, weedless lures and shallow-running crankbaits work well for bass, while fly rodding is a great way to take big bluegills on the beds. Bass bugs fished on heavier fly tackle will take largemouths in the same areas.

In spring, crappies congregate in the "chutes" that lead to the main river channel along the lake's west side. They can be tough to locate, but look for them suspended in deep water. Jigs and minnows work well here, especially around fallen trees and other natural structure.

Anglers work the tailrace waters of the Dresbach dam below Lake Onalaska for white bass, walleyes and smallmouths. The dam creates Onalaska's 7,700 acres of fishing opportunities. Photo by Dan Small

LAKE ONALASKA

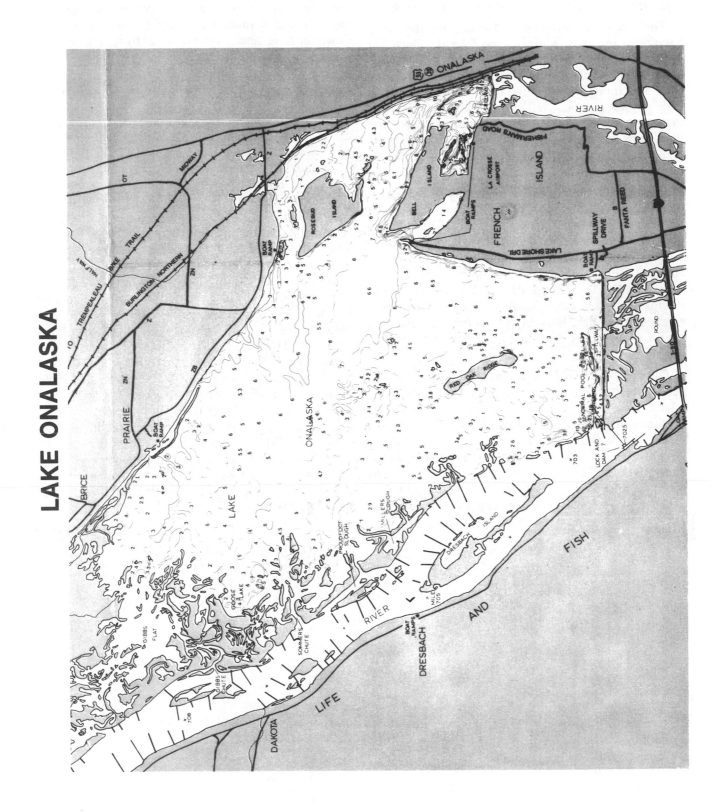

Perch, too, are hard to find, because they move around so much, but any channels or "chutes" with a current flow should hold them. When you find them, they often run to a pound or more. A jig and minnow is the traditional perch bait, but worms also work.

The extensive stump fields, found primarily along the north and west sides of the lake, produce big northerns as well as bass in early spring. Pike begin using weedbeds for ambush cover once they form in May and June. Spinnerbaits, topwater lures, spoons and live bait produce well. Northerns have been hard to catch in recent years, thanks to a bumper shad crop that keeps them fat and happy, but Benjamin expects pike fishing to pick up. Anglers take a few pike over 20 pounds every year.

In summer, most species traditionally moved to the center of the lake or to the edges of weedbeds. Drifting over the midlake region with live bait is a popular way to catch bluegills. The deepest midlake spots are only five to seven feet deep, so slip bobbers and Bait Rigs spinner rigs, or plain hooks and small flies baited with a chunk of crawler, waxies or red worms should work well. Weedbeds produce good catches of panfish, bass and northerns, especially in years when weeds are scarce and fish are concentrated.

Once the lake freezes, ice fishermen flock to the east shore between Brice Prairie Dike and Rosebud Island, where they take good catches of panfish, northerns and even bass. Tiny ice jigs tipped with waxies work well for the panfish, while heavy jigging spoons, such as the Jig-A-Whopper series, produce pike and bass. Live minnows on tip-ups also take pike and bass here. Try the weedlines and edges of the new channels. When oxygen levels in the shallows drop in late winter, look for fish in the deep channels themselves.

Regardless of when you fish it, Lake Onalaska provides plenty of visual excitement, according to Marc Schultz: "There's a lot going on out here," he says. "You can watch barges and trains move up and down the river, and it's not unusual to see cormorants and eagles. People who come for the first time are usually impressed."

Schultz also stresses that there is so much good habitat that the fish aren't always where you think they're going to be. Other fishermen and bait dealers can put you onto fish, but it's a good idea to plan a several-day trip, rather than a one-day lark. And hiring a guide is usually a good investment.

Excellent public boat ramps make access easy for fishermen. Highway Z, off Highway 53, will take you to Mosey's Landing, opposite the northern tip of Rosebud Island, while Highways ZB or ZN, both off Highway Z, lead to the Upper Brice Prairie ramp. There are also several ramps on French Island.

Bait shops include Monsoor's Sport Shop, 517 Copeland Avenue, La Crosse, WI 54603, telephone (608) 784-0482; Schaffer's Boat Livery, W7221 North Shore Lane, Onalaska, WI 54650, telephone (608) 781-3100; Mac's Sport Shop, 111 Irvin Street, Onalaska, WI 54650, telephone (608) 783-3349; and Sias Isles Boat Livery, 107 1st Avenue South, Onalaska, WI 54650, telephone (608) 783-5623.

Restaurants and lodging abound in the area. For a list, along with information on other area highlights, contact: La Crosse Area Chamber of Commerce, 712 Main Street, La Crosse, WI 54601, telephone (608) 784-4880; or La Crosse Area Convention and Visitor Bureau, P.O. Box 1895, La Crosse, WI 54602, telephone (608) 782-2366.

Palmer And Tenderfoot Lakes

Michigan Border, Northern Vilas County

"Just dress for bluebill hunting and you'll be fine," George Langley told me when I called him in Eagle River to plan a fall musky segment for *Outdoor Wisconsin*. Langley is one of these rabid musky chasers who quits fishing each year only when his boat can no longer break through the shore ice at the landing. Our trip was set for early October, but I had been fooled by early snowstorms before, and I intended to be ready for anything.

Palmer and Tenderfoot lakes

Langley and his clients had boated at least one musky over 20 pounds in each of the 10 days before our outing. We would either ride that success wave or break the string with our camera jinx as we had done in the past. For this adventure, George chose Palmer and Tenderfoot lakes, located on the Michigan border between Land O' Lakes and Presque Isle, which is to say about as far away from the rest of Wisconsin as you can possibly get.

On top of making sure we had clean audio bites, engineer Gary Sharbuno also handled the camera-boat skipper duties, a job he enjoys and one that I think takes him back to his Coast Guard days.

Videographer Marshall Savick tried to convince himself he'd be warm enough in his insulated parka and Gore-Tex wind pants.

The only public launch on either lake is an unimproved sand-beach landing deep enough for big boats, located on the northeast corner of Palmer Lake off Palmer Lake Road. There is plenty of roadside ditch parking, if you don't mind a little hike to the water. To get there, we took Highway 45 north to the Michigan line, then drove west forever on Highway B. Tenderfoot's shoreline is in private ownership. The only way you and I can reach it is to motor across Palmer to the Ontonagon River and follow this winding channel a mile or so to Tenderfoot.

Water levels were up that year, so Langley told Gary to stay right on our tail and we ran the river at full throttle. I have a great photo of our boat up on plane in this narrow, northwoods river, with Gary at the helm and Marshall hugging his tripod. When we got to Tenderfoot, George told Gary he had done a good job because stumps and rocks would have stopped him cold had he veered out of the channel. Because of low water levels the last couple years, Langley tells me you have to motor through at an idle now, which provides a good opportunity to break out the thermos and enjoy the beavers, eagles and other wildlife you'll almost certainly see against a backdrop of spruce and tamaracks.

Tenderfoot covers only 437 acres and has a maximum depth of 33 feet. Plenty of rock and rubble areas line the shore and provide excellent structure throughout the lake. Both muskies and walleyes concentrate on this structure, much of which is well defined by the bulrushes that grow on top of the bars. The DNR does not stock Tenderfoot, since there is no public access on the lake. Rumor has it, though, that a former state official who spent his summers on Tenderfoot saw to it that plenty of walleyes and muskies were planted there. Both species certainly come downriver from Palmer, where the DNR does stock 30,000 walleyes and 1,200 muskies every other year.

Tenderfoot's rock bars yield plenty of walleyes, many of them in the four- to six-pound range. The rubble shoreline produces nice smallmouths at times, and the deeper breaks hold walleyes and muskies in the summer. Tenderfoot also gives up some tremendous crappies, and anglers aren't the only ones who catch them. Langley reports catching a number of muskies with a telltale flat bulge in their stomach that was almost certainly a crappie.

"One of the ironies of catch and release is that we don't really know what the muskies are eating," Langley says. "I've done well here for years on a black and white Eddie jerk bait, thinking I was imitating a sucker, but now I'm convinced they take it for a small crappie."

Since Tenderfoot is a border lake, the musky season here opens the first Saturday in May, instead of three weeks later as it does elsewhere in northern Wisconsin. Langley has a few clients who like to fly fish for muskies, and they often hit Tenderfoot in early May. Using nine- or ten-foot salmon rods with sinking or sink-tip lines, they cast big streamers that imitate suckers. A shock tippet of Mason Hardline, a monofilament used by commercial tuna fishermen, prevents bite-offs.

TV engineer Gary Sharbuno steers the Outdoor Wisconsin camera boat down the Ontonagon River between Palmer and Tenderfoot lakes. George Langley told Gary to keep it on plane and to stay right on his boat's tail to avoid hitting submerged rocks and logs. Gary did. Photo by Dan Small

"You cast, let your fly sink, then strip line to retrieve it," Langley explains. "It's a lot like tarpon fishing, and it doesn't take a huge musky to give you a real battle on a fly rod."

But back to our October outing. Langley has found muskies often hold near the dividing line between soft and hard bottom types because that's where the baitfish go when the weeds die back. He reads this edge on his locator, then drifts along it or zig-zags back and forth across it with his trolling motor, while casting small jerk baits and diving crankbaits. We tried this for a couple hours with no luck, so we headed back to Palmer. Did Gary seem more nervous on the return trip, or was it my imagination?

Palmer is the larger but shallower of the two lakes, with an area of 635 acres and a maximum depth of 13 feet. It is very fertile and weedy, so fish grow well here, although natural reproduction is limited. Regular stocking takes care of that. Muskies and walleyes are scattered throughout the lake, especially in the extensive mud-flat weedbeds. Early in the season, walleye anglers do well on minnows along the gravel shoreline south of the landing. Later, jigs tipped with leeches or crawlers produce along the deeper weed edges, and floating Rapalas sometimes take good walleyes over cabbage beds at night. Panfish action can also be good here for crappies and bluegills.

There are a couple midlake rock bars with bulrushes on top, similar to those on Tenderfoot. When we came back out onto Palmer, we began a drift just north of one of these bars, letting the north wind push us along. An abandoned duck blind in the bulrushes seemed to be silently telling us we were practicing the wrong sport, although we weren't seeing any more bluebills than muskies.

Finally, over a thick cabbage bed near the west shore, a decent musky followed the Believer I had stolen from Pat Shields, but turned at the boat and disappeared. Moments later, something grabbed one of the big suckers we were dragging on our other lines and took off.

"Bingo, Baby!" George said. I grabbed the rod, while George cleared the rest of the lines, and we called the camera boat into action. While we waited for this fish to make a good run, George and I babbled on about how it was about time *Outdoor Wisconsin* caught a big musky on camera. I was psyched, and when the fish made its move, I struck once, twice, then reeled in a shredded sucker. The hook had simply missed the fish, as sometimes happens. We ended the segment on an upbeat note, since the suspense had certainly been exciting, but I sure felt dumb!

George still ribs me about the fact that our camera always seems to break his string of luck, and I still rib him about the fact that I have yet to catch a trophy fish with him in the boat. To book a trip with Langley, or one of 20 licensed Vilas County guides, contact: Eagle Sports, 702 Wall Street, P.O. Box 367, Eagle River, WI 54521, telephone (715) 479-8804. Eagle Sports also carries the most complete line of tackle and bait of any shop in the area.

For information on the many resorts and other services of interest in the county, contact: Vilas County Advertising Department, P.O. Box 369, Eagle River, WI 54521, telephone (715) 479-3648.

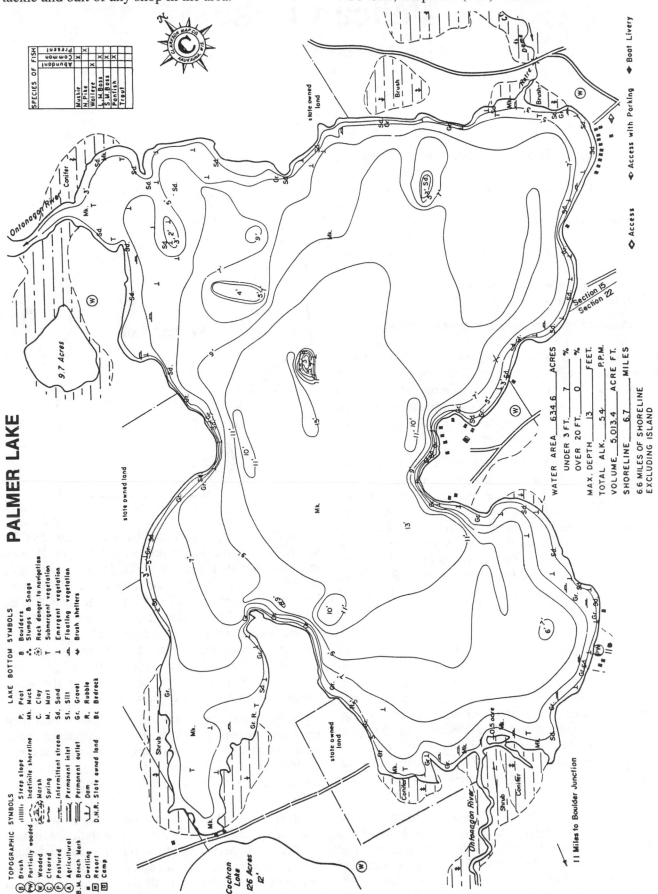

PALMER LAKE

SPECIES OF FISH	Abundant	Common	Present
Muskie			X
N. Pike			X
Walleye		X	
L.M. Bass			X
S.M. Bass			X
Panfish		X	
Trout			

WATER AREA	634.6	ACRES	
UNDER 3 FT.	7	%	
OVER 20 FT.	0	%	
MAX. DEPTH	13	FEET.	
TOTAL ALK.	54	P.P.M.	
VOLUME	5,013.4	ACRE FT.	
SHORELINE	6.7	MILES	

6.6 MILES OF SHORELINE EXCLUDING ISLAND

TOPOGRAPHIC SYMBOLS
- Brush
- Partially wooded
- Wooded
- Cleared
- Pastured
- Agricultural
- B.M. Bench Mark
- Dwelling
- Resort
- Camp
- Steep slope
- Indefinite shoreline
- Marsh
- Spring
- Intermittent stream
- Permanent inlet
- Permanent outlet
- Dam
- D.N.R. State owned land

LAKE BOTTOM SYMBOLS
- B Boulders
- Stumps & Snags
- Rock danger to navigation
- T Submergent vegetation
- Emergent vegetation
- Floating vegetation
- Brush shelters

- P. Peat
- Mk. Muck
- C. Clay
- M. Marl
- Sd. Sand
- St. Silt
- Gr. Gravel
- R. Rubble
- Bc Bedrock

9.7 Acres

Cochran Lake 126 Acres 12'

0.05 acre

11 Miles to Boulder Junction

Pelican Lake

Village of Pelican Lake, Oneida County

You know Pelican Lake. You drive past it every summer on your way north on Highway 45, and every time you do, you tell yourself: "Some day I gotta stop and fish here." Then you keep right on driving, perhaps because you have commitments farther north or because something tells you this lake can't be all that good if you can see it right from the main highway. The locals don't mind, but you're missing out on some good fishing, not only in summer, but all year long.

Pelican Lake covers 3,585 acres and has a maximum depth of 39 feet. Several large points and bays give it 13 miles of shoreline, most of which is developed with summer homes and resorts. Pelican's water is fairly clear, but a summer algae bloom murks it up a bit. The bottom is primarily sand and muck, with extensive areas of gravel and scattered rubble along some shorelines.

A look at the map will tell you there is abundant structure here in the form of gravel bars, underwater points and sharp dropoffs. Pelican is quite fertile, and extensive cabbage beds cover much of the lake's shallow, western end. Muskies, walleyes and northerns are the dominant fish species, and they grow to respectable size. Some nice bass and panfish are also present. According to DNR fish manager Ron Theis, muskies are the only species stocked here. Other fish populations are sustained through natural reproduction.

The DNR plants 2,500 musky fingerlings every other year. They grow well and provide fishing as good as in many lakes that get a lot more pressure. Some run to 30 pounds or better, and there are plenty of 20-pounders. Roger Bremer, who operates Bremer's Bait in town, reports that 1992 was the best year for muskies he's seen here. Bremer says a 52 1/2-inch, 37-pounder came out of Pelican in 1992. Anglers released numerous fish over 46 inches, including a heavy 52-incher.

The cabbage beds at the western end of the lake draw the most attention from musky anglers, but the beds are so large that muskies here are scattered and tough to pinpoint. Try bucktails or surface baits and plan to do a lot of casting to cover all the water.

Pelican Lake

Steve Worrall, who guided here for years, says the key to finding muskies more consistently on Pelican is to fish the rock structure. The large bar north of Antigo Island is the most obvious piece of structure here, but the entire southeast shoreline near Antigo Island and the Musky Bay shoreline on the west side of Mekanac Point also have good rock. Worrall does well on muskies with surface baits from opening day through the fall. When the weeds get thick, he likes to work a jig-and-creature combo along the weed edges and in pockets of open water.

Pelican produces some big pike, many of which are taken by musky anglers. To concentrate on them, work the cabbage beds with spinnerbaits and spoons, or drift large sucker minnows along the weed edges. Ice fishermen traditionally do well on pike using dead smelt or live minnows on tip-ups.

Most of the fishing pressure here falls on walleyes. Ron Theis told me a walleye population estimate conducted in the spring of 1990 confirmed that natural reproduction sustains a good population. Pelican's walleyes grow chunky on all the forage available to them, and some nice ones are taken all season long. The 15-inch size limit is in effect here and the daily bag will vary depending on Indian spearing quotas.

Early in spring, you'll find walleyes along the gravel shorelines on the east shore and around Indian Point on the south shore, where they may still be hanging out after spawning. Jigs and minnows will take them here and along dropoffs. Once the weeds are up, though, most of the larger walleyes head for cover there. On the north shore, the flats between Chicago Point and Crescent Island hold walleyes. A long weedline at the 10-foot depth runs north and south across the entire lake west of Crescent Island. Fish this edge with jigs tipped with leeches or plastic tails. Worrall also does well on weed-oriented walleyes in the shallow bays, where floating Rapalas and similar baits will take them.

Pelican's panfish provide good action all season long. Bluegills run big here, and the best time to get them is when they spawn in late May. Look for their saucer-shaped beds in the shallow bays and try live bait, fly-rod spiders and poppers, or tiny ice jigs on slip bobbers. I can't wait to give Mick Thill's balsa Mini Stealth floats a try for bedding 'gills. American panfishermen are just beginning to discover his light tackle techniques that have proven deadly in count-less European fishing tournaments. Thill's floats are not available everywhere, but you can get them at Dorn Hardware in Madison.

Crappies run big here, and anglers take good catches through the ice in late winter and over the cabbage beds in summer. Thill's floats should prove effective on these light biters as well. Most are taken on minnows, but small swimming jigs, such as the Slo-Poke Mini and Swimmin' Fool should produce.

Most panfishermen here seek the roving schools of perch, but their numbers have declined somewhat in recent years. Try small minnows and jigs along the deeper edges of rock bars and deep weedlines.

White bass are overlooked by most anglers, but they run big and can provide some fast action if you locate a feeding school. Look for surface commotion over open water and cast small crankbaits, spinnerbaits or Mepps spinners right into the boil.

There is a good boat landing on the east shore right in the village of Pelican Lake, but parking there is limited. On the south shore, a state-owned ramp with adequate parking is located off Highway G. Another ramp on the west shore off Highway Q on Root House Road also has plenty of parking. Two popular ice-fishing access points are located on the north shore, both off Highway Q. One is on Chicago

Pelican Lake is the birthplace of the Suick Muskie Thriller, when Frank Suick caught a legal musky for 30 consecutive days on the bait that later bore his name. The lake remains a top producer. Photo by Dan Small

Point in the Pelican River outlet bay and the other is on Sabinois Point, the other large point on the north shore. These are drive-on accesses, as parking is not provided on shore,

For bait, tackle and guide service, try Bremer's Bait, 750 Cato Street, Pelican Lake, WI 54463, telephone (715) 487-5806. For information on lodging, resorts and other area facilities, contact: Pelican Lake Chamber of Commerce, P.O. Box 45, Pelican Lake, WI 54463, telephone (715) 487-5222.try Bremer's Bait, 750 Cato Street, Pelican Lake, WI 54463, telephone (715) 487-5806.

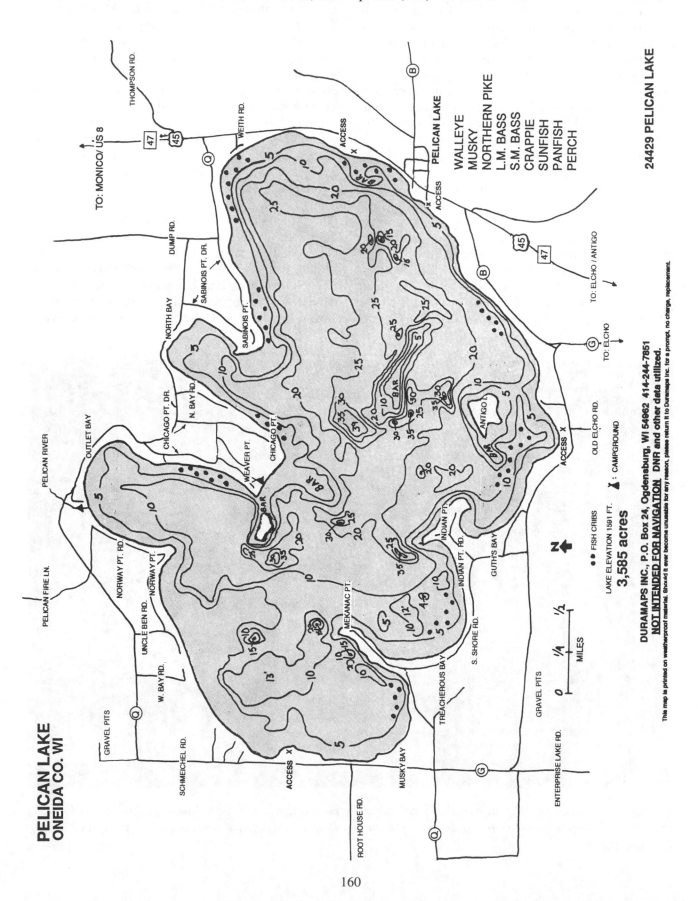

PELICAN LAKE
ONEIDA CO. WI

PELICAN LAKE

WALLEYE
MUSKY
NORTHERN PIKE
L.M. BASS
S.M. BASS
CRAPPIE
SUNFISH
PANFISH
PERCH

24429 PELICAN LAKE

DURAMAPS INC., P.O. Box 24, Ogdensburg, WI 54962 414-244-7851
NOT INTENDED FOR NAVIGATION   DNR and other data utilized.

LAKE ELEVATION 1591 FT.
3,585 acres

●● FISH CRIBS   ⚓ : CAMPGROUND

This map is printed on weatherproof material. Should it ever become unusable for any reason, please return it to Duramaps Inc. for a prompt, no charge, replacement.

Lake Pepin

Bay City, Pierce County, south to Pepin, Pepin County

The folks who live along Wisconsin's West Coast know what a treasure they have in the Mississippi River. The Mississippi offers a variety of fish species and fishing situations you won't find duplicated anywhere else in one watershed. The word has been leaking out to the rest of us, and slowly but surely Wisconsin anglers are heading west to sample this fishing smorgasbord.

A series of 27 locks and dams built by the U.S. Army Corps of Engineers between Minneapolis and St. Louis break the Upper Mississippi into a chain of "pools," each one numbered corresponding to the dam that created it. Lock and Dam #4 at Alma, Wisconsin, creates Pool 4, which extends some 44 river miles north to just above Redwing, Minnesota. Like every stretch of the upper river, Pool 4 lets you choose among several major types of fishing situations: dam tailrace, wing dam and main channel, and backwater and slough. But unique to Pool 4, and making up most of its length, is Lake Pepin, which reaches from Bay City south to Pepin.

Unlike Lake Onalaska and other extensive back-waters created by the locks and dams, Lake Pepin is a natural lake, with depths to 20 feet or more. Rock and cobblestones line much of the shore. Weedbeds are scarce, since most backwater areas on the lake itself have been converted to docks and marinas. This 30-mile basin covers some 28,000 acres and holds tremendous numbers of walleyes, saugers, white bass and other species. Together with the short stretches of river to the north and south, Lake Pepin offers a four-season fishery that can produce year-round action if you're willing to change your tactics and locale according to the time of year and the species you are seeking.

Take walleyes, for example. No one knows Pepin's walleyes better than tournament pro and tackle designer Keith Kavajecz. Kavajecz has fished Pepin for years with an intensity that few anglers could match. It is here that he and his partner, Gary Parsons, perfected many of the techniques that have made them one of the top teams among pro walleye anglers.

To take walleyes regularly here, Kavajecz follows their seasonal movements. Just after ice-out in early April, most of Pepin's walleyes move upstream and congregate just below Dam #3 about four miles upstream from Redwing. Vertical jigging with jigs and minnows will take them along the flats near the main channel break if water levels are not too high. High water in April finds walleyes out of the main current in back eddies and flooded timber. The back channels between Bay City and Redwing are another good spot in spring.

Walleye action in Lake Pepin itself really gets underway in late April, as spawned-out walleyes slip back downstream. The shallow flats at the head of the lake produce good catches now. Walleyes hold in the seven-foot holes that dot the flats, where Kavajecz likes to troll noisy crankbaits, like a Rattl'n Rap, on a long line. Jigging the river channel here also yields nice walleyes in May.

Once they reach the lake, walleyes scatter over a wide area and often suspend to feed on the abundant schools of gizzard shad. Kavajecz's strategy now is to use his locator to find fish and pinpoint their depth, then choose the combination of line, bait and trolling speed that will put a crankbait right in front of their noses. To figure out exactly how deep different crankbaits will run, refer to Mike McClelland's guidebook, Crankbaits, which charts the exact trolling depths for 200 crankbaits. Then clip planing boards, such as Wille Side-Liners, directly to your line and you can troll a number of baits at staggered depths and distances from your boat.

Kavajecz likes Shad Raps, Wally Divers, and Hot 'N Tots in small sizes that match the three- to four-inch shad the walleyes feed on. He recommends trolling flats such as those off Maiden Rock, Deer Island north of Pepin, and the Pepin Marina on the Wisconsin shore, those north and south of Central Point, a mile or so north of Lake City on the Minnesota side, and those near the east end of the lake.

In September, he likes to cast Jig-A-Whopper Walleye Hawger Spoons or bounce 1/16-ounce jigs with a half crawler or small fathead minnow along the rocky shoreline off Point-No-Point, just north of Frontenac on the Minnesota side. By October, many walleyes have moved back upstream to the dam where he takes some nice fish vertical jigging with spoons. He caught an 11 1/2-pounder that way a couple years back, and knows of one taken in October 1989 that topped 14 pounds.

As a rule, Kavajecz says, the deeper water yields more saugers, while the shallower depths produce the most walleyes. Saugers seem to outnumber walleyes in spring in the river, while in the lake during the warmer months, walleyes outnumber saugers.

Pepin's white bass (locals call them "stripers") are abundant and can run up to 2 1/2 pounds in a good year. With all that water to cover in summer, Kavajecz shares this tip: watch for flocks of gulls diving to feed on minnows driven to the surface by schools of white bass. When you find them, any small silver or white spinner, jig or crankbait will catch them. Walleye anglers also take plenty of incidental white bass in the river in September.

Northerns run big here, up to 25 pounds, but they are not abundant and very few anglers bother to fish for them. Most are taken by trollers after walleyes. Inlet mouths anywhere on the lake, weedy back channels or the extensive weedbeds downstream from Pepin and off Central Point hold good fish in summer, where soaking a sucker or trolling with flashy spoons will take them. Ice fishermen also take some big pike in the back channels, using tip-ups and dead smelt on quick-strike rigs.

Spinnerbaits will take largemouths from under piers and other man-made cover wherever you find it,

Fishermen on Lake Pepin and elsewhere on the Mississippi River share the main channel with barge traffic. Photo by Dan Small

as well as in the stump-lined back channels. These channels also produce good catches of crappies, both in summer and winter.

Contaminants from the Twin Cities have left high PCB levels in Lake Pepin in the past, but water quality has improved considerably. The latest DNR health advisory at the time of this writing (October 1992) lists walleye, sauger and small white bass in the lowest health risk category, but warns against eating white bass over 13 inches. Warnings on catfish vary, depending on size, so check the current advisory. Remember, too, that different regulations apply in Minnesota-Wisconsin boundary waters, so check the current rules booklet.

There is an excellent public landing near the Highway 63 bridge on the south bank of the Wisconsin Channel, although parking spaces fill quickly during the spring walleye run. Use this ramp to fish the back channels and the river from Redwing to Lock and Dam #3. Another fine ramp with an adjacent campground is located at the west end of Lake Pepin on Highway EE south of Highway 35 in Bay City Village Park. On the east end of the lake, use the landings at Stockholm, Deer Island, or the Pepin landing on Prairie Road south of Highway 35 in the Town of Pepin.

Aside from several small motels and bed-and-breakfast facilities, services are limited on the Wisconsin side of the river. There are plenty of services and several good boat landings on the Minnesota side. For bait, tackle, guide service and fishing information, contact: Four Seasons Sport Shop, 213 Hill Street, Redwing, MN 55066, telephone (612) 388-4334; or Digger's Bait Shop (summer only), 1702 N. Lakeshore Drive, Lake City, MN 55041, telephone (612) 345-4478.

For information on food, lodging and other services, contact: Lake City Chamber of Commerce, 212 S. Washington St., P.O. Box 150-FW, Lake City, MN 55041. For an excellent 70-page guide to boating on the Mississippi, write: Minnesota DNR, P.O. Box 46, St. Paul, MN 55155-4040.

Petenwell Flowage

Wisconsin River, Adams and Juneau Counties

Petenwell Flowage

Petenwell Flowage is one big body of water that, despite its size and a fishery that gets better by the year, just does not get the respect it deserves from Wisconsin's angling community. "Petenwell still hasn't lived down the bad reputation it gained when industrial pollutants made its fish unpalatable," says DNR fish manager Jack Zimmermann. "Twenty years ago, you wouldn't want a Petenwell walleye in your kitchen, but today the bad taste and smell are gone and Petenwell's walleyes are almost on a par with those from some northern lakes."

The upper of two flowages on the Wisconsin River that straddle the Adams-Juneau county line, Petenwell's water quality has always been poorer than Castle Rock's, probably because contaminants carried by the river tend to settle out in the large Petenwell basin before the water reaches the lower reservoir. The river is much cleaner today, and Zimmermann sees the upcoming federal relicensing of the Wisconsin River Power Company dams here and on Castle Rock, scheduled for 1998, as an opportunity to improve even further the fishery and general water quality of both reservoirs. In preparation for the relicensing review, the DNR's bureaus of Fish Management and Water Resources are currently working with the power company, several paper companies and representatives of the public on a comprehensive management plan for the flowages.

"The plan will assess the current resources of both flowages, catalog the problems and propose measures to correct them," Zimmermann says. Among other concerns, the new plan will address water levels, fish stocking quotas, new landings and improved public access.

Petenwell covers some 23,000 acres. Among Wisconsin's inland lakes, only Winnebago and Pepin are larger. The flowage's maximum depth at normal pool level is 45 feet in the former river channel, but there are vast areas of shallower water on what was once the old river flood plain. The dark brown water is usually quite turbid, due to wave action and a very high population of buffalo and carp.

Rough fish control remains a chronic, unsolved problem. According to Jack Zimmermann, Petenwell's carp are too high in contaminants to be sold as food and state waste-disposal sites won't even take them because of hazardous-waste restrictions, so they're allowed to remain in the lake. Despite their abundance, though, gamefish and panfish populations have done well.

The bottom varies greatly, from a shifting, sandy river channel to muck, gravel and rock. Petenwell has more submerged stumps than Castle Rock, and your locator may even pick up some unusual structure in the form of old roadbeds and home and barn foundations, for much of the flooded prairie was once farmland. Many of the old farms were located in what is now Strongs Prairie Flats, a broad, shallow area north of the east dike at the southeast corner of the flowage. The biggest stump fields are off Juneau County Wilderness Park, halfway up the west shore, and in the north end of the flowage.

Muskies are the only fish stocked in Petenwell today. DNR crews, assisted by a Wisconsin Rapids-based Musky Alliance affiliate, Muskies Today, have stocked some 100,000 musky fingerlings in Petenwell since the early 1980s, and this program will continue at the rate of 2,000 fish per year. Hybrids were stocked at first, but now only true muskies are stocked. Zimmermann doesn't know yet if the muskies are reproducing, but many have reached legal size and are being caught by anglers. In fact, the folks at J R's Baits say anglers have caught more muskies than northerns in the past several years.

Most muskies are taken by fishermen seeking northern pike or walleyes, but to concentrate on muskies, work the shallow bars at the north end of the flowage and any of the stump fields. Bucktails with fluorescent blades and bright dressing will be more visible in this murky water, and topwater baits should produce in the shallows.

The season is open year-round on all gamefish except muskies, but walleyes draw the greatest number of anglers here. Walleyes make a spring spawning run upriver to the Nekoosa Dam in March and April and another feeding run in the fall. Fishing is good just below the dam and at several points along the river all the way to the main flowage basin. A jig and minnow or river rig and floating jighead baited with a minnow are among the favorite set-ups.

After the spawning run, work the deeper holes at the north end of the flowage in the Sand Banks, Yellow Banks and Devil's Elbow regions, and off creek mouths wherever you find them. Trolling shallow-running crankbaits in the Strongs Prairie Flats can be productive before the water warms up in summer. The many breaks and shifting bars of the southern part of the main basin hold plenty of walleyes in the summer. Use a map to troll along breaklines with deep-running crankbaits, but keep an eye on your locator. If you find fish, backtrolling with bait rigs and leeches or drifting with the same bait on a slip bobber should catch them.

According to Jack Zimmermann, you'd have been hard pressed to find a smallmouth in Petenwell a dozen years ago, but today they are fairly abundant. Most bass are taken from the bars and eddies in the river below the Nekoosa Dam. In the main flowage basin, try the riprap along the dikes.

Habitat for northerns, largemouths and bluegills is limited, since weed growth is minimal. The sloughs and backwaters at the north end, especially Skibba and Brown's Creek sloughs on the west side and Ten Mile Creek on the east side, offer the best fishing for all three species in spring. Work up into the shallowest back bays you can find for early pike. Later in summer, the big bluegills are tough to locate, although a few locals manage to bring in a bucket of 10- to 11-inchers now and then.

Crappies are scattered here, as on Castle Rock, but in late spring you'll find them below the Nekoosa Dam and in marshy areas at the flowage's north end, as well as in some of the creek mouths. They also gather in the sloughs at the north end of Strongs Prairie Flats. If you can find an old barn foundation, you may hit an early-season crappie bonanza.

Like other Wisconsin River impoundments, the Petenwell Flowage is best-known for its walleye fishing. However, everything from sturgeon to white bass to muskies to rough fish inhabit these waters. Photo by Dan Small

Jack Zimmermann echoes reports from fish managers across the state who have told of another phenomenon they attribute to improved water quality over the past decade: a tremendous increase in the channel catfish population. Petenwell's cats are reproducing well and provide an exciting fishery in the deeper, slower side holes below the Nekoosa Dam. Cats from three to five pounds are common, although some up to 10 pounds have been caught. If you think big walleyes are fun to catch in a river, you haven't tangled with a 10-pound catfish on light tackle! I have taken cats on live minnows, but you'll catch more on crawlers or stinkbaits fished right on bottom in slack water.

And what Wisconsin lake would be complete without a white bass contingent? Petenwell has its share of the silver stripers, despite a large summer die-off a couple years ago that appeared to affect white bass only. Most of the harvest occurs in May below the Nekoosa Dam, but if summer action slows for other species, you might cruise the bays of the main basin looking for surface-feeding schools.

PETENWELL FLOWAGE

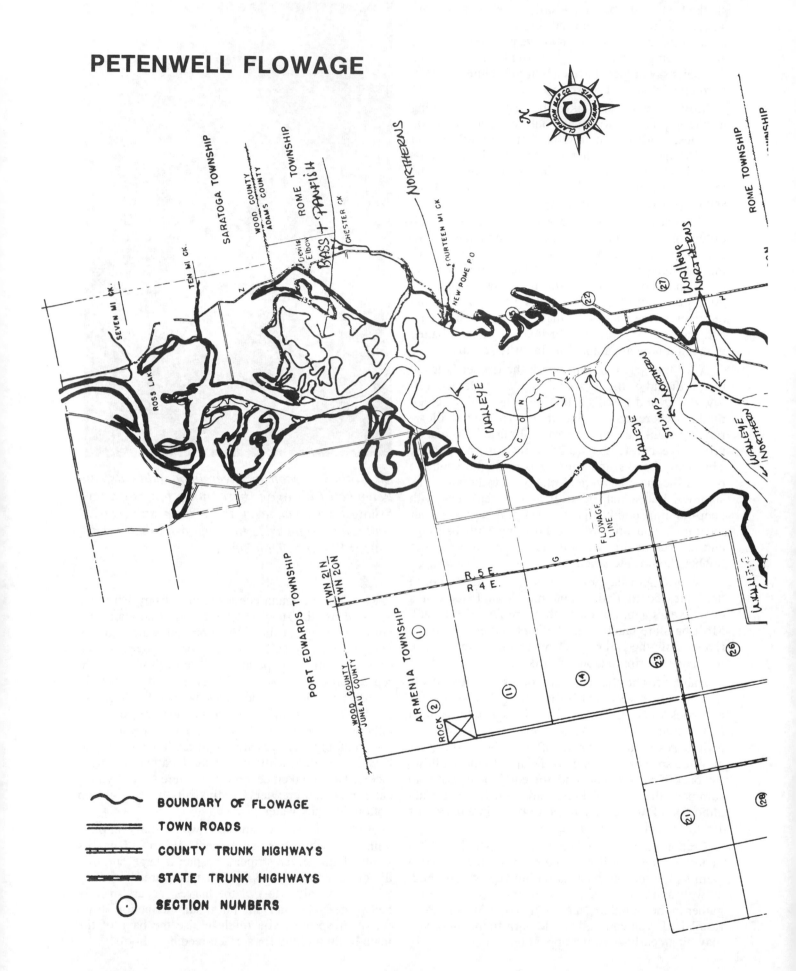

BOUNDARY OF FLOWAGE

TOWN ROADS

COUNTY TRUNK HIGHWAYS

STATE TRUNK HIGHWAYS

SECTION NUMBERS

There are numerous public landings off Highway Z on the east shore. The best, from south to north, are at Strongs Prairie Flats, Brown Deer Road, Adams County Park (where there are also a campground, picnic area and beach), Apache Lane, and Devil's Elbow.

On the west shore, to fish below the Nekoosa Dam, launch at the landing on the river at Sheila Lane south of Nekoosa. To fish the main flowage basin, launch at Wilderness Park. Follow the signs posted on Highway G.

Rose's Groceries and J R's Baits, near Devil's Elbow, has bait, tackle, a restaurant, boat and motor rental, and a campground. Address: 108 Highway Z, Nekoosa, WI 54457, telephone (715) 886-3530. Barnum Bay Marina is located five miles south of Devil's Elbow off Highway Z at 1735 Archer Lane, Nekoosa, WI 54457, telephone (800) 832-5122.

For information on resorts, campgrounds, restaurants and other services on the west shore, contact: Juneau County Visitors Bureau, P.O. Box 282, Mauston, WI 53948, telephone (608) 847-7838. For the same information on the east shore and guide service, contact: Adams County Chamber of Commerce, P.O. Box 301, Friendship, WI 53934, telephone (608) 339-6997.

For an excellent free map of Petenwell with all landings and services marked, contact: Wisconsin River Power Company, P.O. Box 50, Wisconsin Rapids, WI 54494, telephone (715) 422-3722. Another map showing both flowages and listing area services is available from: Castle Rock-Petenwell Lakes Association, Mauston, WI 54984, telephone (608) 847-5359.

Pewaukee Lake

Pewaukee, Waukesha County

Mention muskies to most city-bound anglers and they immediately think of remote lakes way up north somewhere where they'd love to spend a week or even just a few days in pursuit of Wisconsin's state fish. But the pace and demands of urban life often relegate such thoughts to dreamland, and the musky trip up north gets put off for another season. But what if there were a lake close enough, say, to Milwaukee so a guy with a taste for musky action could drop his boat in the water a couple evenings a week after work and have a reasonable chance of catching a legal musky?

Is 20 miles close enough? That's 20 freeway miles from downtown, and that's all the farther you'll have to drive to reach Pewaukee Lake. The one thing you won't find on Pewaukee is solitude, but the lake's convenient location and fantastic fishing more than make up for its lack of privacy. Pewaukee gets some of the heaviest use of any lake in the state, but year after year it provides great fishing opportunities for muskies, bass, walleyes and panfish.

The largest lake in Waukesha County, 2,500-acre Pewaukee Lake lies just west of the village of Pewaukee, a short hop off I-94. Pewaukee Lake is about five miles long and a mile across, and its shoreline is heavily developed. Vegetation is abundant, especially in the shallow east basin, formed by a dam on the Pewaukee River in the Village of Pewaukee. The lake bottom runs from sand to muck, silt and gravel in places. Rocky Point separates the east basin from the deeper west basin and provides good bottom structure that holds all species of gamefish and panfish. The bottom drops off gradually at the west basin's west end and along Rocky Point, and more sharply along the north and south shorelines. The lake's deepest spot is a 45-foot hole in the center of the west basin.

Several musky and bass fishing tournaments are held here each year, and the Milwaukee Chapter of Muskies, Inc. and other sportsmen's groups have helped instill a spirit of catch and release among Pewaukee Lake regulars. As a result, despite the heavy pressure, an angler stands as good a chance of boating a 20-pound musky, 15-pound northern or five-pound largemouth here as just about anywhere.

Pewaukee Lake

The DNR has stocked muskies in Pewaukee for years. True muskies stocked in the late 1960s produced a flurry of trophy fish, the largest of which was a 48-pound 9-ounce female caught by Joe Ehrhardt in 1977. In the 1970s, only hybrids were stocked; then in the 1980s, crews stocked about half true and half hybrid muskies. Hybrids are more easily caught than true muskies, and they rarely reach trophy size. Since 1990, only true muskies have been stocked. According to DNR fish manager Randy Schumacher, anglers have been catching true muskies in the 40- to 45-inch class since the late 1980s.

Most musky anglers concentrate on the west basin, casting bucktails and diving crankbaits among the weedbeds, along Rocky Point and around Cottage Island near the lake's west end. Large plastic lures such as Creatures and Reapers also produce along the deep weedline off the south shore due east of Cottage Island. Motor trolling is legal here and on all Waukesha County lakes, and trolling is an effective way to take the larger pike and muskies that hang out along the break outside the deep weedline in at least 15 feet of water, where boat traffic won't bother them and they are out of reach of shallow-running baits.

Don Wiedenhoeft of Milwaukee has made a science of trolling for Pewaukee's muskies, taking over 50 legal muskies and big pike in each of several years. Don uses two set-ups. Half his rods are rigged with heavy mono line. These he fishes on downriggers to put deep-diving crankbaits at a precise depth. His favorite crankbaits are Bagleys in sizes normally used for bass: Bang-O-Lures, DB3's and Small Frys. His other rods have roller guides and reels that can handle wire line. On these, he trolls large Spoonplugs. Using a locator to spot fish and stay with a given depth, Wiedenhoeft trolls parallel to the bottom contour between 17 and 25 feet deep, depending on where the fish are.

My son Jon and I joined Don a couple years back to do a segment for *Outdoor Wisconsin*. Our goal was to tape Jon catching his first legal musky -- a tough assignment, but one Don figured he could handle. Don had everything under control but the weather, though. An all-morning rain forced our camera crew to hole up at Musky Bill's, while Don, Jon and I donned rainsuits and fished in vain. At lunch time, we sent the crew home and of course the weather cleared, so we went back to fishing. In the next three hours, with our camera safe in Milwaukee, we boated three legal muskies, and Jon caught two of them, both on Spoonplugs. I have photos to prove it, but no videotape. So it goes with an outdoor show!

Creel census clerks report checking an occasional smallmouth over six pounds in recent years, but their numbers are few and the rocky shorelines they prefer are limited. Largemouths are far more abundant here, and you'll find them wherever there are weeds. Taylor's Bay, across from Rocky Point, is a favorite spot, but the 10- to 12-foot depths off Rocky Point, and most of the western basin's shoreline also produce well. Early in the season and in years when weed growth is less profuse, the east basin produces good bass fishing. Plastic worms, shallow-running crankbaits and weedless spoons all take bass around piers and in the weedy bays. Try a jig-and-pig combination in the deeper pockets between weedbeds and diving crankbaits along the Rocky Point shoreline.

Pewaukee's walleyes have come on strong in recent years after serious stocking began in 1981. DNR crews have planted about 100,000 fingerling walleyes in most years since then. Try jigs and minnows, crawlers or leeches around Rocky Point, along Waukesha Beach on the southwest shore and on both sides of the rock pile and sandbar on the north side of Cottage Island. The bigger the minnow, the bigger the walleye you're likely to catch. The area around Cottage Island also produces good catches of big walleyes through the ice in the evening.

Pewaukee holds a good variety of panfish, and Schumacher reports their size is increasing, thanks in part to predation by muskies and walleyes on smaller

panfish. For white bass and perch, try the deeper water around Rocky Point. Crappie anglers do well around Chester Island, just east of Rocky Point and off Waukesha Beach. The west basin's north shore produces good bluegills, but the biggest 'gills suspend in the middle of the west basin in midsummer. To catch them, drift over deep water with slip bobbers and tiny Bait Rigs spinner rigs baited with waxies, mousies, spikes or plastic tails. Another good slip bobber lure for suspended panfish is a tiny ice jig, like those made by Wisconsin Tackle, or a Bait Rigs Slo-Poke Mini.

Jon Small, son of Fish Wisconsin author Dan Small, watches as his first legal musky is admired by Don Wiedenhoeft. Photo by Dan Small

Perch are abundant but small. Most perch fishing is done through the ice in the deeper parts of the west basin. The area all around Rocky Point is another popular ice fishing spot for panfish and walleyes.

There are a number of boat launches, bait shops and boat rentals on Pewaukee Lake, including several right in town. The largest launch is the multi-ramp facility at Naga-Waukee County Park at the lake's west end. Smokey's Bait Shop has two locations in town. The main store is at 129 Park Avenue, Pewaukee, WI 53072, telephone (414) 691-0360.

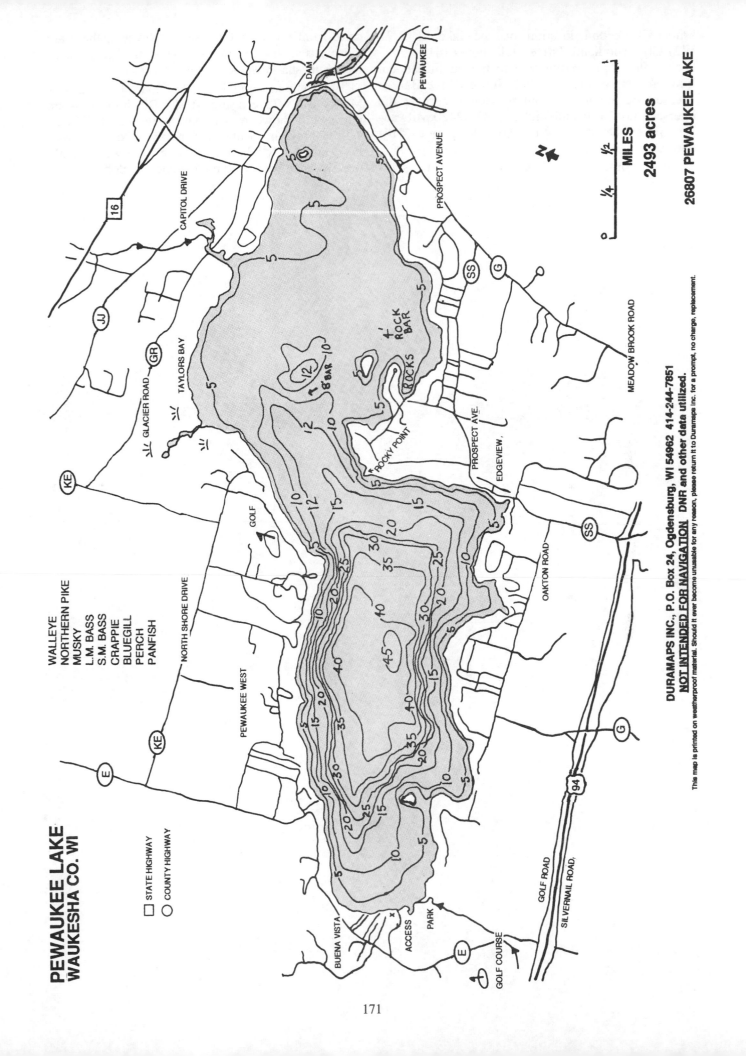

PEWAUKEE LAKE
WAUKESHA CO. WI

□ STATE HIGHWAY
○ COUNTY HIGHWAY

WALLEYE
NORTHERN PIKE
MUSKY
L.M. BASS
S.M. BASS
CRAPPIE
BLUEGILL
PERCH
PANFISH

2493 acres

MILES

26807 PEWAUKEE LAKE

DURAMAPS INC., P.O. Box 24, Ogdensburg, WI 54962 414-244-7851
NOT INTENDED FOR NAVIGATION   DNR and other data utilized.

This map is printed on weatherproof material. Should it ever become unusable for any reason, please return it to Duramaps Inc. for a prompt, no charge, replacement.

Smokey's second location on the lake, at N27 W27250 Woodland Drive, telephone (414) 691-9659, offers fee parking next to the public launch. You can also get bait at Dick Smith's Live Bait & Tackle (located in the smiling yellow barn at the intersection of I-94 and Highway 83), 2420 Milwaukee Street, Delafield, WI 53018, telephone (414) 646-2218.

Most people who fish Pewaukee are just a short drive from home, but for out-of-towners, there are numerous motels, restaurants and other services in the Waukesha-Pewaukee area.

Two long-standing Pewaukee Lake landmarks -- Musky Bill's Tavern and Musky Bill himself -- are now history, however. Bill passed away several years ago. His tavern, located just north of Naga-Waukee Park, hung on for three more years, but was recently torn down and replaced by a condo development.

Pike Lake

Hartford, Washington County

Every time I run into Rich Bierwirth, we end up talking fishing. Rich is a security officer at the technical college where our television station is located, so our paths cross fairly often. Each winter for several years, Rich has told me stories of great catches of perch from Pike Lake near Hartford. Although I've lived less than a half-hour from Pike Lake for years, I had never fished there. I always figured I'd try it sometime soon, since it was so close, but "sometime soon" never came. I kept heading north to fish lakes I was more familiar with.

When Rich offered to take me there a couple winters back, I decided it was about time I tried it, so on a late February morning, videographer Marshall Savick, engineer Nels Harvey and I met Rich on the ice. Rich had been fishing since sun-up and had a respectable pile of perch on the ice when we arrived about eight o'clock. He was set up off Eagle Point along a sharp break in about 40 feet of water.

"The perch are about six feet off bottom, and they just started to bite a little while ago," he said when we arrived. "I've got two rods ready to go for you. When they're in a feeding mood, two are all you can handle."

While the crew got set up, Rich handed me a Mendota Rig and a container of mayfly nymphs, or "wigglers." He showed me how he covers the hook point of a teardrop jig with a wiggler, leaving the tail free to move. To take this light lure down to where the perch are in a hurry, he uses pencil sinkers made of foot-long sections of braising rod. He flattens and drills a hole in each end, then attaches a snap swivel to each hole. He then ties the line from the rod to one swivel and a 10-inch leader to the other. The short leader keeps the jig from hanging up as the sinker takes it down. With a Mendota Rig, once you have determined how deep you want to fish, you can hook the line around a wire loop on the large, flat reel and quickly get your bait down to the same depth time after time.

We each fished two holes drilled close together so we could keep an eye on our rods. A Mendota Rig has a built-in stand that holds the rod propped over the hole. The heavy sinker keeps the rod bent slightly, so all you have to do is push down on the rod now and then to jig the bait, then wait for a bite. When a perch picks up the bait, the rod tip rises, and you're in business.

Rich's locator tracked the schools of perch as they moved beneath us, and we caught another dozen or so before the sporadic hits signaled the end of the morning bite. When the action slowed, I asked Rich how he likes to prepare perch.

"I fillet and skin them, then soak them in cold water with a pinch of salt," he said. "Then I beat an egg and melt a little butter in a skillet -- be careful to keep the heat low so you don't burn the butter. Then I dip the fillets in the egg, roll them in bread crumbs and pan-fry them in the butter until they're browned on both sides. I've tried all sorts of recipes, and this one leaves them light and makes them taste great."

Rich's recipe had our mouths watering for a fresh fish fry. We had all we needed for a segment, so I escorted Marshall and Nels back to shore, then hurried back out on the ice to catch the afternoon bite. That day showed me once again that the best fishing is often found close to home.

Pike Lake

Set in the glacial hills of the Kettle Moraine, Pike Lake covers some 450 acres just south of Highway 60 in Washington County. The western half of the lakeshore is in private ownership, while the eastern half fronts Pike Lake State Park, a delightful respite from city cares within a few miles of metro Milwaukee. Powder Hill rises abruptly along this east shore, and its oaks and sumacs provide a colorful backdrop for a fall outing.

Clear and spring-fed, Pike Lake's deepest spot is 45 feet off Eagle Point. Sharp dropoffs provide fish-holding structure along Eagle Point and the southeast shore, while much of the north end is a large, weedy flat. A bend of the Rubicon River flows through the marsh along this north shore. The bottom varies from sand and muck to extensive gravel in shoreline areas.

Years ago, walleyes were widely known as "wall-eyed pike," and that's where Pike Lake got its name. An anomaly among lakes in southeastern Wisconsin, Pike Lake supports a stable, self-sustaining walleye population. The DNR stocks other southern Wisconsin lakes with walleyes raised from eggs taken from Pike Lake fish each spring. On another *Outdoor Wisconsin* segment, I joined fish manager John Nelson and his crew as they took walleye spawn along the state park shoreline.

Hatchery superintendent Randy Link stripped spawn and milt from walleyes brought in from fyke nets set along the shore, then immediately released the spawned-out fish. Lake water is added to the spawn and milt mixture to ensure fertilization, then a clay substance is added to keep the eggs from sticking together and the eggs are transported to the Kettle Moraine Hatchery near Adell.

Far from depleting Pike Lake's abundant walleyes, this spawning operation actually adds to them, since a higher percentage of the fry are returned to Pike Lake than would likely survive from naturally spawned eggs. John Nelson says the walleye population here shows an excellent age and size distribution, with good numbers of larger fish.

In this clear lake, the best walleye action occurs early and late in the day. In spring, anglers do well trolling Rapalas in the evening off the sandbars along the east and west shores. Daytime action is best in the deep water off Eagle Point, where jigs and minnows produce. When there's a good chop, try drifting the bars with crawler rigs. When the mayfly hatch occurs in mid-June, walleyes move into the shallows to feed on the emerging flies. In winter, ice fishermen take walleyes on these same flats, as well as on the sand-bars and along the Eagle Point shoreline.

Northern pike are not abundant, but the lake yields some monsters, including a number of them between 20 and 30 pounds, and an incredible 35-pounder taken in 1980 by Mike Marinkovich of Milwaukee. Try the weedbeds along the north shore and in the southwest bay, or along the state park shoreline. Open-water anglers after pike troll large crankbaits,

while ice fishermen use large live minnows or dead smelt on tip-ups. Many of the biggest pike, including Marinkovich's fish, come through the ice.

For largemouths, try weedless artificials in the weedy flats and near piers and diving rafts. Work diving crankbaits and jigs along gravel shorelines and dropoffs for smallmouths. Wigglers will take perch and bluegills in spring and summer along the outside edges of weed pockets.

Dan Bierwirth shows the gear he uses for Pike Lake's deep water perch fishery Mendota rig, home-made pencil sinker, short leader, teardrop jig, wiggler, perch and a smile. Photo by Dan Small

There is no public launch on Pike Lake, but there are several private ramps where you can launch for a small fee. On the west shore, launch at Johnny's Landing, located at the dead end of High Road, or at Reef Point Resort on Lake Drive. Reef Point also sells live bait, rents boats and boat slips and offers cottages, a picnic area, volleyball court and swimming beach. Address: 3416 Lake Drive, Hartford, WI 53027, telephone (414) 673-7167. Dick Werner, who runs the bait shop there, can tell you how the fishing's been.

You can also camp, swim and hike the Ice Age Trail at Pike Lake State Park, but there is no boat launch there. For information and camping reservations, contact Pike Lake State Park, 3340 Kettle Moraine Road, Hartford, WI 53027, telephone (414) 644-5248.

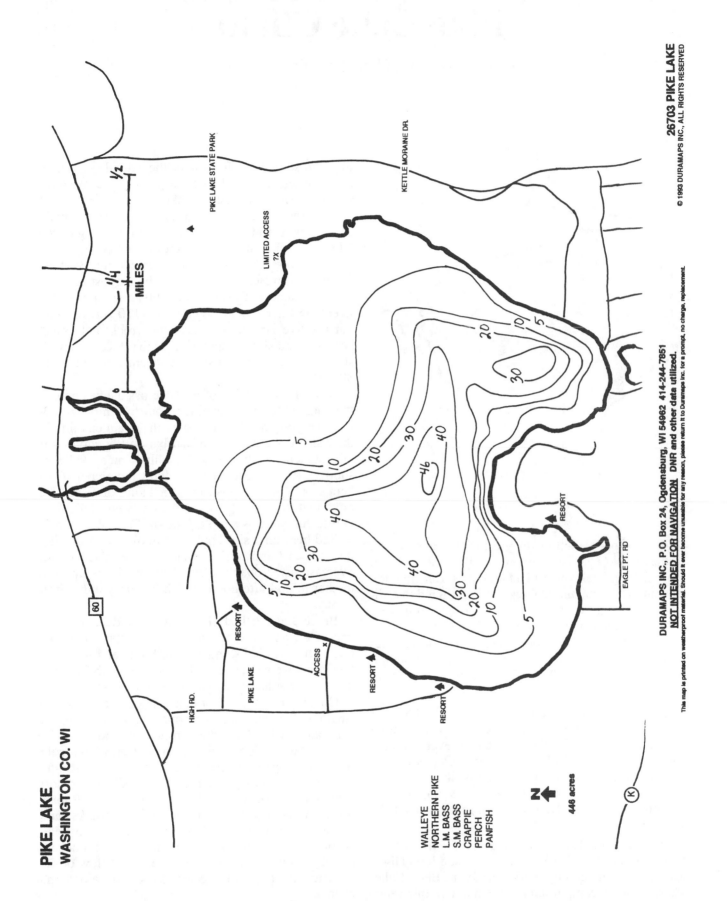

PIKE LAKE
WASHINGTON CO. WI

WALLEYE
NORTHERN PIKE
L.M. BASS
S.M. BASS
CRAPPIE
PERCH
PANFISH

446 acres

DURAMAPS INC., P.O. Box 24, Ogdensburg, WI 54962 414-244-7851
NOT INTENDED FOR NAVIGATION   DNR and other data utilized.
This map is printed on weatherproof material. Should it ever become unusable for any reason, please return it to Duramaps Inc. for a prompt, no charge, replacement.

Pike Lake Chain

5 Miles Southeast of Iron River, Bayfield County

A lot of people tell me they'd love to have my job so they could just fish all the time. The truth is, I did more fishing back when I had an honest full-time job teaching at Northland College up in Ashland. Northland is a friendly place, and this private, four-year college is dedicated to teaching courses in environmental studies and outdoor recreation, among other more traditional subjects. So it seemed only natural for me and colleague Bruce Goetz to offer a course in fishing one spring.

It was billed as an activity course in the Outdoor Education Department, and we called it simply "Angling." As part of the final exam, every student had to catch a fish. As I recall, everybody passed. We covered some basic theory and skills like knot-tying in class and taught students how to cast on the lawn in front of Wheeler Hall, but everybody agreed the best part was the field trips.

On one trip, Bruce and I led a caravan west on Highway 2 to Iron River, then turned south on Highway H to the county park on Twin Bear Lake. There's a nice campground there and a couple sand-

filled horseshoe pits in front of the caretaker's trailer. Son Jon and I played many a game there one year when Joe Hunt was the caretaker, but I digress.

The Twin Bear boat landing is one of the main access points to the Pike Lake Chain, a string of ten lakes as clear as my dad's Martinis that cover a total of just over 1,000 acres in west-central Bayfield County. Twin Bear and Hart are the biggest at about 260 acres apiece. Buskey Bay (100 acres), Lake Millicent (184 acres) and Eagle Lake (170 acres) round out the five largest. All have nice rock and gravel structure and similar depths of 50 to 60 feet. They all stratify in summer, so fish are concentrated in the top 30 feet or so.

Bruce led our string of boats across the bay and up the channel to Hart Lake, then out to a midlake bar that everyone who's ever fished the chain can find in their sleep. We parked on that bar and doggone it if our students didn't start catching nice walleyes shortly after we got set up. I don't remember if we kept score, but it seems to me the ladies outfished the guys that day, and their instructors were delighted. Our technique was simple enough: fathead minnows drifted beneath a slip bobber or hooked to a floating jighead, cast and retrieved slowly over the bar. An overcast sky probably coaxed the walleyes up onto the bar in mid-afternoon, which certainly didn't hurt us any.

Bruce and I fished Hart and Twin Bear, just the two of us, on one other occasion. That was the time one of us left his fishing license home and wouldn't you know we were checked by warden Bob Cleary. I don't think either of us will forget that lesson.

On that outing, we struck out on walleyes and smallmouths over the bars and deep weedbeds of Hart and Twin Bear, then trolled around Hart for awhile, but couldn't raise a musky either. A cold front had apparently put everything down. Trolling back to the landing after dark, I hooked and lost something big on a jointed fluorescent-orange Rapala just as we entered the channel. Two head shakes and it was off, so we motored slowly back to Twin Bear, accompanied by the hissing and popping of innocent mayflies drawn to the deadly blue-white glow of the electric bug traps that guard backyards along the channel.

Steve Heiting, editor of Wisconsin Outdoor Journal magazine, author of the book "Musky Mastery" and a guide on the Pike Lake Chain since the mid 1980s, with the "smaller" of two muskies he saw during an October day on the chain. Photo courtesy Steve Heiting

All that happened more than ten years ago. DNR fish manager Dennis Scholl tells me the biggest change since then is the size structure of the walleye population. The population is still as high as ever, with enough reproduction so no stocking is needed, but heavy fishing pressure over the years whittled down the average size of the walleye caught from 16 inches in the 1960s, to 14 inches in the '70s and 12 inches in the '80s. Like other small, clear lakes, the lakes of the Pike Chain are less productive than shallow, dark-water lakes, and the sport harvest can have a greater impact on them.

Managers hoped the 15-inch size limit would help bring the size of the average walleye caught back up, but it apparently didn't work. When the 15-inch limit was put in place several years ago, the population was essentially bi-modal, with lots of walleyes under 15 inches and a fair number of very big fish, but few in between. A survey done in the spring of 1991 showed tons of smaller walleyes and a substantial number over 26 inches, but virtually none between 15 and 26 inches. Those big fish must be doing something different to survive because those that make it through the four- to five-year-old window seem to hang in there and keep pumping out good hatches of offspring year after year.

As of this writing, it looks like the 15-inch limit will be lifted on the Pike Chain. Watch signs at the landings announcing this and perhaps other changes in the regulations as well. Steve Heiting, who guides on the chain, welcomes the change. "Last season, we boated about 110 walleyes on Memorial Day weekend, but only two were over 15 inches," he told me. "Removing the size limit will let people take home a few walleyes, and it should help the population structure as well, since there's plenty of spawning structure and an overabundance of young walleyes."

Evening hours or overcast days are best for walleyes on the chain because the lakes are so clear. Work the deeper edges of bars, humps and dropoffs in the morning and late afternoon, then move right on top of bars as night falls. Heiting does well on fathead minnows below a lighted slip bobber at night. In this clear water, he likes natural-colored baits: 1/16-ounce plain lead, white or subtle yellow jigs, for example. Flatline trolling in the shallows with minnow-imitation baits sometimes produces as well. Heiting says walleyes target the mayfly hatch in July, and some day I want to try fly fishing for them during the hatch. It would be a real kick to take one on a dry fly.

Muskies also reproduce naturally on the chain, although some are stocked annually to supplement natural recruitment. Anglers take a fair number of muskies between 20 and 30 pounds every year, and Heiting knows of at least two over 37 pounds caught in recent years. "One was caught the day after I released a 30-pounder, and I think it was the same fish that had followed my bait 20 minutes before I caught the 30," Heiting said. "I saw only two muskies that day, and the 'small' one was 30 pounds!"

Millicent and Buskey Bay produce good numbers of muskies, while Twin Bear yields fewer but larger fish. Heiting prefers natural colors for muskies, too. In summer, he likes DepthRaiders in a sucker or

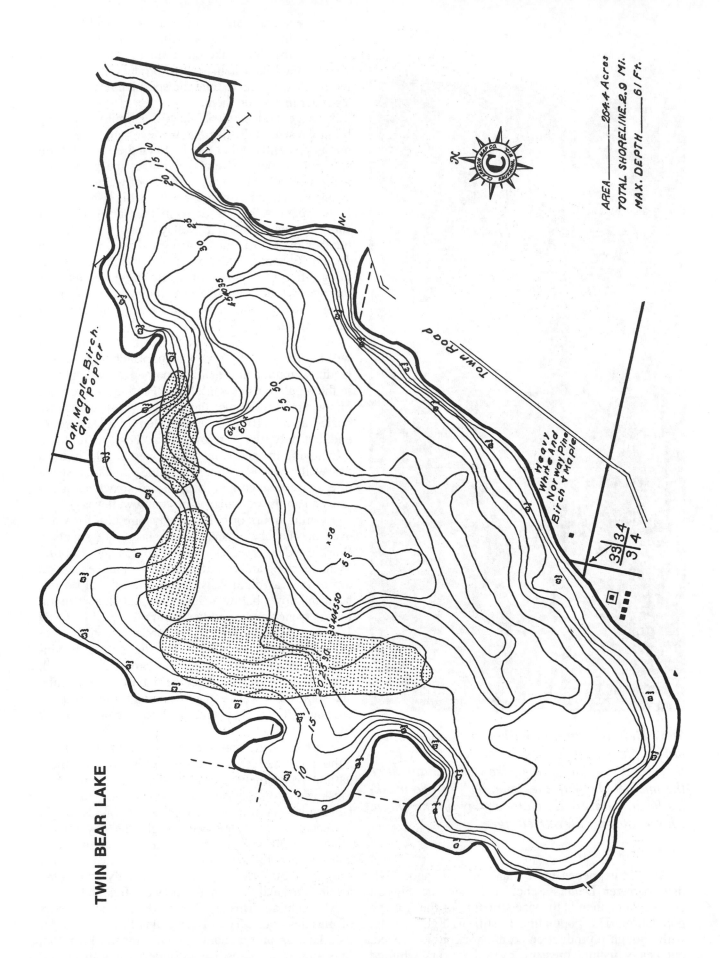

TWIN BEAR LAKE

Oak, Maple, Birch. and Poplar

Heavy White And Norway Pine Birch & Maple

Town Road

AREA _____ 264.4 Acres
TOTAL SHORELINE _ 2.9 Mi.
MAX. DEPTH _____ 61 Ft.

33 | 34
3 | 4

HART LAKE

SPECIES OF FISH	Present	Common	Abundant
Muskie	X		
N. Pike	X	X	
Walleye	X	X	
L. M. Bass	X	X	
S. M. Bass	X	X	
Panfish	X	X	
Trout			

"night shiner" pattern, a white bucktail with a nickel blade and a touch of red in the tail dressing, a nine-inch Grandma in a walleye pattern, or the new Burt jerk bait in the walleye pattern. In fall, he casts a sucker-colored Eddie or the sucker-colored DepthRaider. "Basically, I try to imitate the muskies' forage. Besides little walleyes, there are a lot of red-horse and white suckers in the chain," Heiting notes.

Smallmouths are holding their own through natural reproduction and Heiting has caught and released them up to five pounds. Any gravel or rubble shorelines will hold bass, especially early or late in the day. Small crankbaits seem to work best, but jigs and leeches or minnows also produce. Light line will help in this clear water.

You'll pick up an occasional northern when trolling or casting for muskies or working the bars for bass and walleyes. Muskellunge Lake and Flynn Lake, the shallowest and weediest of the chain, along with the bays of Buskey Bay and Eagle Lake, hold good numbers of fair-sized pike and some nice largemouths as well. Topwater baits, like a Moss Boss, as well as spinnerbaits and weedless spoons, should produce on either species.

Good catches of chunky panfish are common on the chain. Eagle Lake is known for its big crappies and perch. You'll find both species in shallow bays in spring, then suspended in deep water in summer. Pinhead minnows or swimming jigs tipped with tube tails dangled at their depth on a slip bobber will take both. Eagle and Twin Bear have good populations of bluegills now. In May and June, spawning 'gills pro-vide good action on all the lakes. In summer, you'll find them suspended off weedbeds in Eagle and near cribs in Twin Bear in 15-20 feet of water.

The Pike Lake Chain was once popular among local ice fishermen who caught some of the best walleyes of the year on tip-ups and shiners after dark. Ice fishing pressure has tapered off in years when the walleye bag limit has been reduced because of Chippewa spearfishing quotas. Some anglers still do well on perch and crappies through the ice.

Use the Twin Bear boat landing to fish the lower lakes: Twin Bear, Eagle, Flynn and Hart. To fish the upper lakes (Millicent and Buskey Bay), launch at The Hermitage Resort on Buskey Bay. The Hermitage has vacation cottages, rents boats, and carries tackle, bait, gas and supplies. Contact: The Hermitage, Route 2, Box 48, Iron River, WI 54847, telephone (715) 372-4580. Mr. T's Sport & Hardware on Highway 2 in Iron River carries a complete line of tackle, telephone (715) 372-4356. Heiting can be reached at PO Box 37, Iola, WI 54945, telephone (715) 445-4693.

For a brochure on the county campground at Twin Bear Lake, contact: Bayfield County Campgrounds, Route 2, Box 113B, Iron River, WI 54847, telephone (715) 372-8610. For more information on area services, contact: Iron River Chamber of Commerce, P.O. Box 64, Iron River, WI 54847, telephone (715) 372-8558, or Bayfield County Tourism & Recreation Dept., P.O. Box 832, Washburn, WI 54891, telephone (800) 472-6336.

Lake Poygan

Winneconne, Winnebago County

In a land thirsty for water and short on good fishing holes, a lake like Winnebago County's Lake Poygan would receive the attention it deserves. But east-central Wisconsin has more than its share of superlative waters -- Lake Winnebago, Green Lake and the Wolf River -- to name a few, so Poygan rarely draws notice among any but the local anglers who smile at the fact that their honey hole is Winnebago County's best-kept secret.

The largest of three lakes on the Lower Wolf-Upper Fox Chain, Poygan is part of the vast, nutrient-rich system that feeds Lake Winnebago. Along with lakes Winneconne and Butte Des Morts, Poygan offers quality fishing for the same species that helped build Winnebago's reputation. Poygan is the best of the three, with better vegetation and a more diverse fishery.

Poygan is shallow, with a maximum depth of about 10 feet. The water is fertile and quite turbid. Prevailing west winds keep the eastern half murky and laden with floating debris, making it hard to fish, while the western half is often much cleaner. Strong winds can put a severe chop on Poygan in a hurry, so watch for weather changes and head for shore if the wind picks up.

Structure here is quite subtle, and finding a break of just a foot or two can often put you onto fish. Sand and muck dominate the bottom substrate, although a few areas of rock, rubble and gravel break up the monotony and hold fish. A dredging project to deepen the Boom Cut channel, scheduled for completion in 1993, will create 5,000 feet of new riprap adjacent to five to eight feet of water, making excellent holding cover for smallmouths, walleyes and crappies. Submerged weedbeds are scattered throughout the lake, but there are vast areas of open water. Much of the shoreline is marshy with extensive bulrush and cattail growth.

Major inlets include the Wolf River and Rat River at the lake's northeast corner, and Pumpkinseed Creek, Willow Creek and the Pine River in the southwest corner. These provide a steady flow of oxygenated water and are spawning and feeding areas for many species of fish.

Lake Poygan

Walleyes are the prime gamefish targets of anglers on Poygan, followed by northern pike and bass. Perch and white bass attract the most interest among panfishermen, although there are good populations of bluegills and crappies as well. Muskies are present in fair numbers, but few people fish for them. There is no closed season for any major species except musky, which opens in May, and lake sturgeon, which may not be taken by hook and line at any time.

Good walleye hatches in 1990, '91 and '92 have helped boost the walleye population on all the lakes of the chain, according to DNR Oshkosh area fisheries supervisor Ron Bruch. Poygan also holds a good number of fish over six pounds, and there are still a few leviathans in the 10- to 13-pound range left from strong year classes in the late 1970s and early '80s.

Before the rotten ice has cleared the lake, the spring walleye run usually gets underway. Most Poygan walleyes run up the Wolf, contributing a major portion of that river's spring fishery. As they drift back to the lake in late April, fishing is quite productive in and around the mouth of the Wolf and the stump-infested Boom Bay Cutoff which leads to the Wolf River channel. Use Wolf River rigs and minnows where there is a current flow, and jigs or crankbaits elsewhere.

In summer, walleyes head for deeper water. Try bouncing swimming jigs down the dropoff along the east side of Old Indian Point, just east of Tustin on the north shore. Another good spot is the nine-foot hole midway between Old Indian Point and the south shore. With a west wind, you can drift through here with a slip bobber and leech or a crawler harness. You can also troll with bright, noisy crankbaits, such as Heddon Sonics, Rapala Rattl'n Raps, or Cordell Rattl' Spots. Other old favorite trolling baits include Sparkle Tails, Floating Rapalas and Bagleys.

More anglers may pursue walleyes, but northerns are the real headliners on Poygan. DNR surveys show Poygan has a tremendous pike population, including some up to 40 inches. Northerns spawn in the marshes adjacent to all the inlets in April and often hang out in these same spots until summer. Cast weedless spoons and large plastics along the edges of weedbeds off inlet mouths, or drift with big sucker minnows and bobbers.

By midsummer, most big pike have begun roaming open water where they feed on large schools of young perch and white bass. To find them, try trolling crankbaits in a criss-cross or figure-eight pattern. When you locate fish, mark the spot and cast with the same baits or flashy spoons. The cane beds a mile or so offshore south of Alder Creek and the Wolf River also hold pike in summer, as do the subtle midlake dropoffs and holes that you can only find by watching your locator carefully.

The shallow bays and creek mouths provide good largemouth action in spring and summer, as do the many channels dredged by shoreline residents to improve boat access. Be sure to try Boom Bay and the narrow channel at Old Indian Point. Weedless plastics, topwater baits and spinnerbaits should produce. You might pick up a smallmouth or two in the channel at the mouth of the Wolf River or along the dropoff east of Old Indian Point. Try crayfish-imitating crankbaits, Slo-Pokes or Jigs.

Perch, crappies and bluegills kick off Poygan's panfish parade with good early spring action near the major inlet mouths and in the many private boat-slip channels. Small minnows or swimming jigs tipped with plastic tails will take them. Later in summer, look for wandering schools of perch in deeper water.

Bruch says crappies are Poygan's most under-utilized species. Trollers after walleyes often take big crappies by accident, but few anglers target them. For those who do, crappie action is good in May and June

Tournament pro Daryl Christensen reaches for a nice Lake Poygan crappie. Photo by Dan Small

along the south shore west of the narrows to Winneconne and between Pony Creek and Tustin in the lake's northwest corner. Artificials like the Blue Fox Foxee, Bait Rigs Slo-Poke Mini, or Blakemore Road Runner will take crappies on the beds or when they school up after spawning.

You'll find bluegills in the bays once weeds develop, and most areas are shallow enough to make fly rodding with rubber spiders, nymphs and poppers productive and fun. Of all the panfish, though, none are more exciting than white bass. They gather in large schools around points, dropoffs and other structure, where they often roil the surface as they feed on baitfish. On a calm day, you can spot these schools from far off. Approach them quietly and cast small spinnerbaits or crankbaits into the fray and hang on.

Poygan is also a popular ice fishing lake, but the lake freezes late and currents keep the ice treacherous in places. Deep holes off the southwest shore and in the middle of the lake produce all species through the ice. Tip-ups baited with minnows and smelt should take walleyes and northerns. Ron Bruch reports that ice fishermen harvested more than 5,000 pike over five pounds in the winter of 1993 alone. Pike running 10 to 15 pounds are common.

Ultralight jig rods and jigs like the Swimmin' Fool, Rembrandt or Slo-Poke Mini should produce good catches of crappies and perch. When they get fussy, scale down to one-pound test line and tiny teardrops baited with a small strip of plastic.

Reduced weedbeds and increased predator activity has scattered bluegills schools in recent winters, making them tough to find.

Ten public and private landings provide good access. There is a public landing and wayside campground off Highway B midway along the south shore, a Town of Poy Sippi landing a mile south of Pony Creek on the west shore, and a county-run landing with two paved ramps and plenty of parking on Richter Lane off Highway MM at the north side of the narrows to Lake Winneconne. The old public landing at Pony Creek off Highway H near Tustin has been converted to a county park shore fishing site, with a wheelchair-accessible walkway and shore-fishing stations that produce good crappie action. Kiesow's Landing is a new private campground and boat launch facility on the Rat River north of Boom Bay, telephone (414) 836-2590.

Captain's Cove, just off Highway B at the lake's southwest end, has bait, a bar and grill, a boat ramp with a 100-foot pier, and drive-on access in winter. Owner Butch Nelson reports excellent pike action through the ice just offshore from his landing. Address: 9598 Welsch Road, Winneconne, WI 54986, telephone (414) 582-4757.

Wolf River Resorts, located eight miles east of Captain's Cove on Lake Winneconne and accessible by water from Poygan, is a resort-marina complex with four resorts, a bait and tackle shop, and boat and motor rentals. Address: 17 N. 1st Street, Winneconne, WI 54986, telephone (414) 582-4555.

Plum Lake

Village of Sayner, Vilas County

In 1924, Carl Eliason spent his spare time tinkering in the shop behind his general store in Sayner. Taking a pair of skis, some old bicycle parts, an outboard motor, part of a Ford Model "T" radiator and a cleated track, he slapped them all together on a toboggan and changed northwoods winters forever. You can see Eliason's original prototype machine and a half-dozen more, each one unique in its design, on display at the Vilas County Historical Museum in Sayner, where a state historical marker commemorates the birthplace of the snowmobile.

The museum is a great place to spend a rainy afternoon on a family vacation, but old snowmobiles are only one reason to visit the Sayner area of central Vilas County. The other reason is good fishing and lots of it in a handful of lakes that surround this tiny community. Highway 155, one of the shortest state highways, runs from St. Germain on Highway 70 north about six miles and ends at Sayner on the south shore of Plum Lake.

Plum Lake is fertile, clear and deep, with excellent water quality and good populations of walleyes, muskies and panfish. An abundant supply of forage species, which include suckers and ciscoes, helps gamefish grow fast and makes them tough to catch at times. Plum Lake covers 1,055 acres and has a maximum depth of 57 feet. It has inlets from Aurora Lake on its northwest shore and Star Lake on its northeast shore, and an outlet to Big St. Germain Lake on its southwest shore. The lake bottom is about evenly divided among sand, gravel and silt, with some excellent rubble in shoreline areas. A summer thermocline develops here at about 27 feet.

Plum is long and narrow, with two large bays off the east end. The northeast bay (Starlite Bay) and the main basin are deep, with abundant bars and sunken islands that come up to within five or 10 feet of the surface. Structure in the western half of the main basin is limited to steep shoreline dropoffs. The southeast bay (East End Bay) and extreme western end of Plum Lake, along with adjoining 53-acre West Plum Lake, are shallow and weedy. A six-foot culvert, navigable by small boats, connects Plum and West Plum.

Plum Lake

According to DNR fish manager Harland Carlson, walleyes were stocked for a few years in the late 1980s to supplement natural reproduction, but stocking has since been discontinued. A 1991 survey showed a low population density, but both males and females were larger than average. Muskies are stocked in alternate years and appear to be doing well. Other management activities include the placement of 23 fish cribs in 1985 and 1986 by the Sayner-Star Lake Chamber of Commerce. These are located along the northwest shore, on midlake bars at the east end, and along the northeast shore of Starlite Bay.

Walleye action is good in spring and fall, especially over the shallower bars and gravel points. In summer, walleyes are tough to come by, but try working the steeper dropoffs and sunken structure with leeches and slip bobbers, staying in close contact with the bottom. Forward motor trolling is not permitted here, but you might catch some bigger walleyes by drifting adjacent to deep structure with large minnows on slip bobbers. Look for suspended schools of ciscoes on your graph and fish at that depth. Ice fishing can also be very productive for big walleyes. Anglers take a few pushing 10 pounds through the ice each winter.

Plum Lake regularly ranks among the top half-dozen Vilas County lakes for the number and size of muskies produced. Alan Long, who runs Long's Taxidermy in Sayner, and his brother Brian guide musky anglers on Plum. The majority of legal muskies taken here are released to fight again, according to Long.

In spring, Long fishes small bucktails, crankbaits and jerk baits over the shallower bars, humps and cabbage beds. In summer, he has his best luck after dark when big fish come into the shallows to feed. For the best fall action, Long likes to work deep dropoffs with crankbaits, although many anglers do well on suckers.

Like big walleyes, muskies often suspend here to feed on ciscoes, and row trolling is an effective way to take them. Long now uses a 15-foot fiberglass boat built in a mold made from a lapstrake boat his grandfather fished with. Double-ended and set up for rowing, these boats glide easily through the water. With little effort, a rower can match the speeds of a five-horsepower motor. A row troller uses a locator to follow structure contours or stay with baitfish schools and drags crankbaits like a Grandma or Cisco Kid, and even topwater baits, like a Globe. Most active muskies, even when suspended, are within 12 feet of the surface, Long says, so downriggers are unnecessary.

The late Bob Ellis row trolled on Plum Lake in a nine-foot Shell Lake rowboat for over 40 years and kept a record of every musky he caught. Long says Ellis took upwards of 1,000 legal muskies in that time, many of them over 20 pounds. Ellis released most of those muskies.

Row trolling requires more patience than most anglers have today, says Long. "You might go two weeks without a strike, but then in a day you might take a musky and two or three big walleyes."

Plum Lake's panfish are an untapped resource, according to Long, who sees large schools of big crappies over cabbage beds when he is musky fishing. He suggests working the weedbeds of East End Bay in spring or summer. The few anglers who do try for them come in with 13- to 14-inch crappies regularly, Long says, and some run to 17 inches. There are also some nice bluegills here, but few people bother with them. Long says to try around the fish cribs for 'gills and crappies alike. Ice fishermen after walleyes take an occasional jumbo perch, but they are scattered.

Anglers have been catching more bass, both largemouths and smallmouths, in recent years, Long says. Try the gravel bars for smallies and the shallow bays for largemouths. Northern pike in the 20- to 30-inch range are also common and easy to catch, says Long.

You'll take them by accident when after walleyes, muskies or largemouths, but work the end of East End Bay or West Plum to catch them on purpose.

There is a wayside landing on Highway N on West Plum that is fine for small boats able to navigate the culvert to get into Plum. Another landing next to the public fishing pier in town on the south shore has a fair ramp, but parking is limited. There is also a state landing on Razorback Road, across the lake from the Sayner landing with a good ramp and lots of parking.

Guide Tony Rizzo outwitted this nice Plum Lake musky during a rainstorm. Photo courtesy Tony Rizzo

You can get bait and tackle at "W" Sport Shop, 2 miles west of Sayner on Highway N, telephone (715) 542-3800, or at Pat's Bait Bucket, located at the public pier in Sayner, telephone (715) 542-3349. For guide service, contact Alan or Brian at Long's Taxidermy, Sayner, WI 54560, telephone (715) 542-3728.

There is an 18-unit state campground on the lake just west of Sayner off Highway N. For information on resorts and other area services, contact: Sayner-Star Lake Chamber of Commerce, P.O. Box 191, Sayner, WI 54560, telephone (715) 542-3789.

PLUM LAKE

AREA_____ 1112.7 Acres
TOTAL SHORELINE___ 15.4 Miles
MAX. DEPTH_____ 48 FEET

LAKE BOTTOM SYMBOLS

PULPY PEAT	P
MUCK	K
CLAY	C
SAND	S
RUBBLE	R
EMERGENT VEGET.	⊥
FIBROUS PEAT	F
DETRITUS	D
MARL	M
GRAVEL	G
BEDROCK	Br.
SUBMERGENT VEGET.	T

TOPOGRAPHIC SYMBOLS

BRUSH REFUGE	⊕
SAPLING TANGLE	⊔⊔
SPAWNING BOX	▭
MINNOW SPAWNER	✳
WEED BED	⊕
ROCKY SHOAL	
DWELLING	■
ABANDONED DWELLING	□
RESORT	◉
STEEP SLOPE	≡ ≡ ≡
SPRING	
INTERMITTENT INLET	
BRUSH	
WOODED	Ⓦ
PASTURED	Ⓟ
CULTIVATED	Ⓒ
ENCROACH. SHORE	
PERMANENT INLET	
PERMANENT OUTLET	
MARSH	
PARTIALLY WOODED	PW
CLEARED	Ⓒ
BENCH MARK	B.M.

Lake Puckaway

Marquette, Green Lake County

Lake Puckaway

My good friend Charlie Thomas has taken more trophy bucks with gun and bow than anyone else I know. But as great a deer hunter as he may be, Charlie can't catch a walleye to save his life. Go ahead and ask him -- he'll admit it. Thinking we might each benefit from the other's expertise, Charlie promised to teach me all he knows about hunting monster whitetails if in turn I'd show him how to catch walleyes. "Piece of cake," I thought. So one sunny Saturday in April a few years ago found us heading south out of Montello with a bucket of minnows and Charlie's boat in tow on our way to the Fox River and Lake Puckaway.

Puckaway is a 5,500-acre flowage on the Upper Fox in western Green Lake County. It's about as shallow a lake as you'll find anywhere, with an average depth of only 5 or 6 feet. Historically, Puckaway had a good and diverse fishery, but then the carp population exploded and the lake's extensive beds of wild celery, coontail and other weeds were wiped out by the bottom-rooting bugle bass. The DNR began a carp control project there in 1979, and according to

area fish manager Jim Congdon, all that work is really paying off.

Carp numbers are down, water quality has improved markedly and the weeds are coming back very nicely. The Lake Puckaway Protection and Rehabilitation District and the Lake Puckaway Improvement Association, working with the DNR, have replanted celery beds all over the lake, and other vegetation has returned in force as well. There is some algae bloom in summer, but so far not enough to cause a problem. Commercial fishermen still removed nearly 200 tons of carp in 1992, as that program continues.

"The fishing on Puckaway now is excellent, and it gets better every year," says Congdon. Congdon cites abundant populations of walleyes, northerns, largemouth bass and panfish, including perch, crappies, bluegills and white bass. In addition, flathead and channel catfish are common enough to warrant fishing for them.

DNR fisheries crews stocked 5 million walleye fry, 5 million northern pike fry, and 50,000 largemouth bass fingerlings annually for several years. Walleye stocking will continue to sustain that fishery, according to Congdon. State walleye allocations for Puckaway have been cut back to a half million fry, but the first of several "walleye wagons" funded by a new conservation group, Walleyes For Tomorrow, will be in operation on Puckaway by the time this second edition is published. The "walleye wagons" have helped produce millions of fry for the Madison Chain, and Congdon has big hopes for the same kind of success on east-central Wisconsin lakes.

Northern pike and bass stockings have been eliminated because those species should sustain themselves now through natural reproduction. Since the late 1980s, the Portage Musky Club has stocked several hundred hybrid muskies annually. Anglers are starting to catch legal fish, and muskies may eventually provide a bonus trophy fishery.

The gamefish season never closes for all species but muskies on Puckaway and the Fox River, and walleyes are the primary target. The statewide 15-inch size limit on walleyes applies on Puckaway and the Fox River downstream to Highway 23 in Princeton. Ice fishermen do well on walleyes, taking many fish over seven pounds. In one fisheree last winter, a 32-incher beat out a bunch of 28-inchers for first place.

The best action occurs soon after ice-out when walleyes move up into the Fox River to spawn. Several miles of river, from the mouth upstream to the Grand River Lock and Dam, provide excellent fishing if you time it right. Jigs and minnows are the ticket, but crankbaits and river rigs with floating jig-heads also produce.

After spawning, the walleyes return to the lake and scatter, some roaming the open water areas and others homing in on the growing number of weed-beds. Find forage (primarily shiners and young pan-fish) and you'll find walleyes. Long-line trolling is effective, but most crankbaits run too deep for Puck-away. Try floating Rapalas, Bagley Bang-O-Lure No. 5s, Heddon Super Sonics or Shadling Shallows, and use a heavier line to get them to run even shallower. To avoid spooking fish, run trolling lines off to the side with skis or planer boards, like Wille's Sideliner. Drifting the open lake with live bait on slip bobbers or spinner rigs will also produce. On overcast days, try weedless spoons with a pork rind trailer right in the weedbeds.

Puckaway's pike are short but fat, and 10- to 15-pounders are common. You'll probably pick up as many northerns as walleyes by trolling the open water, but to concentrate on pike work the extensive weedbeds along the marshy west end of the lake and on the north shore across from Marquette at the east end. Big, noisy spinnerbaits, jigs and reapers, and flashy weedless spoons, like a Johnson Silver Minnow with a pork trailer, will draw hits. Ice fishermen take some very nice pike off Good Old Days Resort on the north shore. The resort also rents boats and cottages in summer, operates a bait and tackle shop and maintains a boat ramp. To get there, take Highway C east out of Montello and watch for signs. Address: Route 2, Montello, WI 53949, telephone (414) 295-6358.

Weedless plastics and topwater baits will produce well on largemouths now that heavy weed cover has returned. Try the bays in the lake's northwest corner and just west of the Fox River outlet, especially just as the lake begins to warm in spring.

For perch and bluegills, concentrate on weedbeds. Look for schools of crappies off the mouths of bays and near bulrushes. Live bait produces the best catches of perch and bluegills, but tiny swimming jigs and plastic tails will outfish live bait for crappies. Large schools of white bass roam the open lake, but the best white bass fishing occurs in spring and fall when they run up the river.

With all those species to try for, Charlie and I were optimistic that April day, even if the sun shone brightly in a sky too blue to make most walleyes want to eat. We turned left off Highway 22 at the big wooden DNR sign that points the way to the Grand

River Locks. The locks are actually on the Fox River a short ways upstream from the mouth of the Grand and a couple miles above Lake Puckaway. The dam stops the upstream movement of fish, so it's a popular spot for boat and shore anglers alike.

Joining a couple dozen boats working the main channel near the mouth of the river, we drifted with jigs and minnows to no avail. Then we dropped our jigs right into eddies swirling with foam near the brushy north bank, but still got no takers. We even motored out into the lake and tried the shallow bulrushes for bass, but apparently the cold front had put everything down. Finally, we switched to ultralight tackle and 1/16-ounce marabou jigs.

Charlie Thomas with two big carp caught by Fish Wisconsin author Dan Small on a marabou jig and light tackle. The pair did their part for Puckaway's carp removal program. Photo by Dan Small

I worked that little jig in the deeper pockets along the north bank of the river, swimming it along at mid-depth in hopes of taking a suspended crappie or two, when suddenly the jig stopped and I was into a submarine. "Big walleye!" I announced to Charlie, who grabbed the net expectantly. Ten minutes later we still hadn't seen the fish. By then I figured I had

189

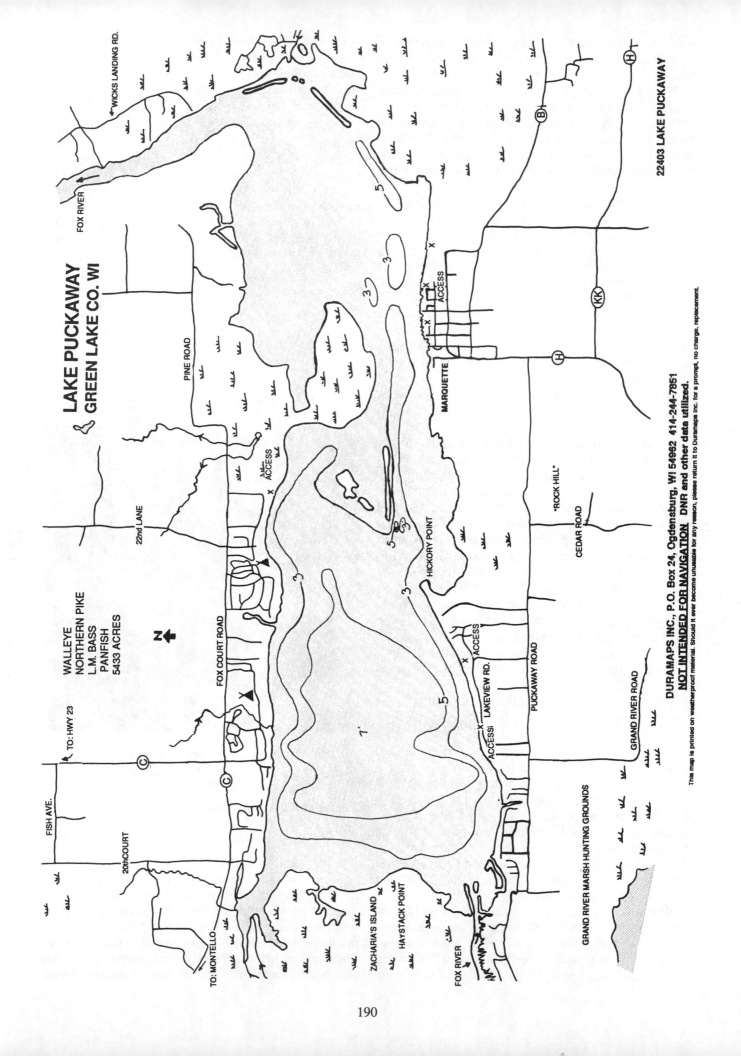

LAKE PUCKAWAY
GREEN LAKE CO. WI

WALLEYE
NORTHERN PIKE
L.M. BASS
PANFISH
5433 ACRES

TO: HWY 23

FISH AVE.

20thCOURT

22nd LANE

PINE ROAD

FOX RIVER

WICKS LANDING RD.

FOX COURT ROAD

TO: MONTELLO

ZACHARIA'S ISLAND

HAYSTACK POINT

ACCESS

HICKORY POINT

MARQUETTE

ACCESS

ACCESS

LAKEVIEW RD.

ACCESS

PUCKAWAY ROAD

GRAND RIVER ROAD

"ROCK HILL"

CEDAR ROAD

FOX RIVER

GRAND RIVER MARSH HUNTING GROUNDS

22403 LAKE PUCKAWAY

DURAMAPS INC., P.O. Box 24, Ogdensburg, WI 54962 414-244-7851
NOT INTENDED FOR NAVIGATION   DNR and other data utilized.

This map is printed on weatherproof material. Should it ever become unusable for any reason, please return it to Duramaps Inc. for a prompt, no charge, replacement.

190

hooked a catfish, which was OK, even though we had come for walleyes. The fish finally tired and Charlie slipped the net under 12 pounds of shining carp!

That sucker had taken an unbaited feather jig, and yes, folks, it was hooked in the mouth. Just a fluke, we figured, until I caught another one the same way a short while later. Guys in nearby boats were yukking it up, but we did our part for Puckaway's carp removal program and slipped those babies into the livewell. That was all we caught that day. I think Charlie finally broke his walleye jinx, but I'm still waiting for my first Boone & Crockett whitetail.

Aside from the landings at the Grand River Locks and Good Old Days, there are four with concrete ramps and parking in Marquette. The best of these, located on Charlevoix Street, has a wheelchair-accessible pier alongside the ramp. Strahota's Marine, 273 Lyon Street, Marquette, WI 53947, telephone (414) 394-3406, provides on-water service and also carries bait and tackle and rents cottages. Another public ramp is located right next to Strahota's.

For a complete listing of area services, including guides, resorts, campgrounds and more, get a copy of the Green Lake County Guide from: Fox River Publishing Co., Inc. P.O. Box 54, Princeton, WI 54968, telephone (414) 787-4808.

Red Cedar Lake

Northeastern Barron County

When the Superior lobe of the great continental ice sheet ground its way south and west during the most recent ice age, it took the last big bite out of what was once a mountain range with peaks of 20,000 feet and left a rolling plateau known as the Blue Hills in a delightful chunk of real estate now shared by northern Rusk and Barron counties. Red Cedar Lake lies on the edge of the glacial outwash plain, tucked up against this plateau in the northeast corner of Barron County.

Red Cedar Lake

Red Cedar is out of Hayward's musky zone, and even the panfish factories of Big Lake Chetac just to the north at Birchwood, and the Chetek Chain of Lakes, some 30 miles south at Chetek, get a lot more press and draw more vacationers. But the folks in the quiet lakeside towns of Angus and Mikana don't mind, because they're sitting on some of the best smallmouth and walleye water in this part of the state.

The Governor's Fishing Opener, held here in 1992, helped spread the word about Red Cedar's fishery. An invitational event started over 25 years ago by then-governor Warren Knowles and sponsored by Wisconsin Indian Head Country, the Governor's Opener attracts a couple hundred guests from the outdoor media and fishing tackle industry each year. Former Governor Knowles was there last year, as always, and so was Governor Thompson. We all got to sample Red Cedar's fishing and Barron County's hospitality at Tagalong and The Island of Happy Days resorts.

We arrived on Friday afternoon to enjoy summerlike temperatures in the mid-80s, but a cold front blew in overnight. On opening day, blustery winds and temperatures in the mid-30s kept us in the lee of islands and points, but the stalwart anglers among us managed to catch (and release) four smallmouths, 51 largemouths, 48 walleyes, 10 northerns and hundreds of panfish.

Less than 20 miles from Rice Lake via Highway 48, Red Cedar Lake covers some 1,800 acres, has 16 miles of shoreline, and plunges to depths of over 50 feet. Red Cedar is the middle and largest of three lakes on the Red Cedar River. Just upstream and north of the Highway 48 bridge over the Washburn County line lies Balsam Lake, while to the south is Hemlock Lake. The smaller lakes cover about 300 acres each, and navigable channels connect them with Red Cedar Lake.

Balsam Lake and the northern two-thirds of Red Cedar have similar structure. Both are deep, with steep shoreline dropoffs and extensive areas of gravel and boulders. Balsam is essentially one deep basin, while on Red Cedar, rock and gravel bars rise abruptly from deep water to top out at 10 to 20 feet everywhere. The southern third of Red Cedar and all of Hemlock Lake are shallow and weedy. As you might expect, the fishery changes from north to south. Walleyes and smallmouths dominate in the deeper sections, while largemouth bass, northern pike and panfish are predominant in the shallower southern basins.

According to DNR fish manager Rick Cornelius, Red Cedar Lake is not normally stocked because the major species all reproduce successfully there. Red Cedar did receive a one-shot stocking of 90,000 walleyes in 1992, though, thanks to an available surplus of fingerlings. All age classes of walleyes are present, and the 15-inch size limit applies here, since growth is adequate.

Walleye fishing is best in May and June, but tapers off quickly in mid-June and becomes tough in the summer months, due to an abundance of forage. Early in the season, work the shoreline gravel areas at the north end near the Red Cedar River inlet and near the Pigeon Creek and Sucker Creek inlets on the east shore. The many shoals in the northern third of the lake and the shallow bars surrounding the mid-lake islands also hold walleyes in spring. Most anglers go with a jig and minnow early in the season, bouncing this combo down the gravel slopes. Casting with Countdown Rapalas will also produce here.

Wisconsin Pharmacal Company supplied Governor's Opener attendees with their new biodegradable Baitmate Ultimate Baits, so I tried them out while fishing with writer Larry Van Veghel and guide Dave Lewis. I took several decent walleyes on chartreuse three-inch grubs fished on a quarter-ounce jig along gravel shorelines.

When walleye action slows in midsummer, try slip bobbers and leeches over the deeper shoals early in the morning or in the evening. Ice fishermen also do well on walleyes in December, using tip-ups and minnows over the shallower bars.

Smallmouths are abundant and for some reason underfished, but that could change as more anglers pay attention to the mercury contamination advisories here and on other lakes which warn against eating larger walleyes. The bass are clean, if you want to take some to eat, and if you're into catch and release, they're a lot more fun to catch than walleyes any day.

The entire north end of Red Cedar Lake and Balsam Lake have good smallmouth habitat. Concentrate on the gravel and rubble shorelines and on the shallower bars and shoals in Red Cedar. You'll take some smallies while walleye fishing with jigs and minnows, but more will come on jigs tipped with leeches or dark-colored pork strips, rubber crayfish and the like. Small crankbaits, like Rebel's "R" and crawfish series will also take bass. Cast these into shallow water near rocks, boulders and sunken logs and bump them along bottom on the retrieve. Larry Van Veghel caught a couple nice smallmouths on jigs on the same structure that produced walleyes for me.

Over deep-water bars, try inflated nightcrawlers or leeches on floating jig heads with enough weight to take them down to bottom. Cast this rig into deep water and work it slowly up onto the bar. If the wind is right, drifting over bars with a crawler harness or spinner rig can also be effective.

Perch are not as abundant here as on many lakes, but they run big. When you can find a school, you'll take perch in the nine- to 12-inch class. Writer Gene Cooper hauled in a perch weighing 1.16 pounds during the Governor's Opener. Ice fishermen have the most consistent luck on perch with jigs and minnows or teardrops and wax worms in 25 to 30 feet of water, primarily in the north half of Red Cedar.

Outdoor writer Larry Van Veghel with a nice smallmouth from Red Cedar Lake during the 1992 Governor's Opener. Photo by Dan Small

Work the bays and channel to Hemlock Lake at the south end of Red Cedar for largemouths and northerns. At the Governor's Opener, Wisconsin Pharmacal president John Wundrock and vice-president Chuck Nevsimal battled stiff winds here to boat some nice largemouths using their twin-tail Ultimate Baits on spinnerbaits. The Pigeon Creek inlet is another spot worth trying. Weedless spoons and topwater baits will take both species, while jig-and-pig combos or plastics rigged weedless will consistently take bass.

The Red Cedar River is one of the state's top smallmouth streams, in case you'd like to vary your

RED CEDAR LAKE

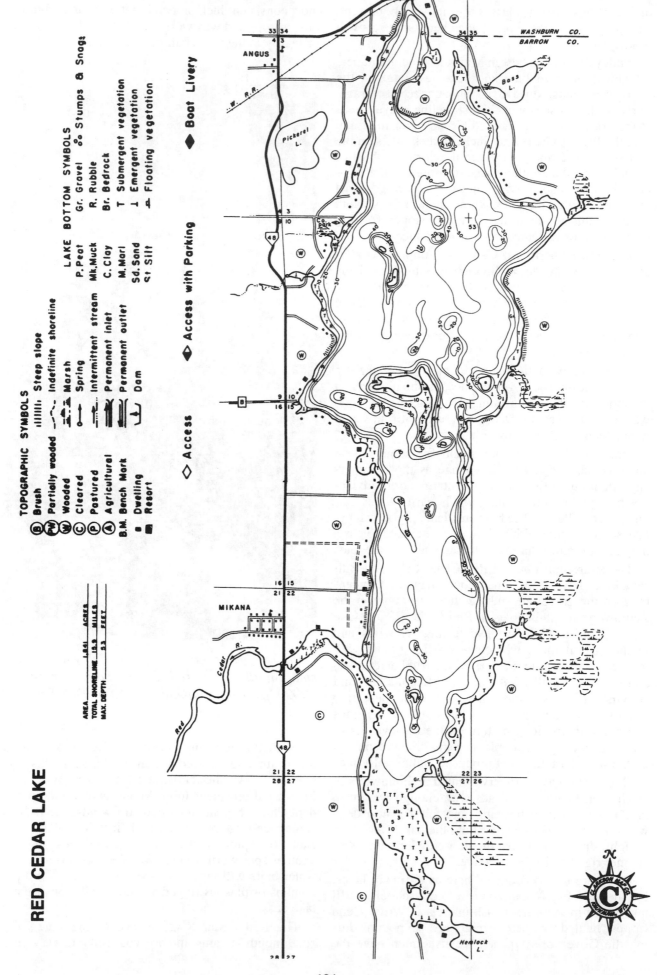

TOPOGRAPHIC SYMBOLS

- ⓑ Brush
- ⓟⱳ Partially wooded
- ⓦ Wooded
- ⓒ Cleared
- ⓟ Pastured
- Ⓐ Agricultural
- B.M. Bench Mark
- ■ Dwelling
- ■ Resort

- ||||||| Steep slope
- Indefinite shoreline
- Marsh
- Spring
- Intermittent stream
- Permanent inlet
- Permanent outlet
- Dam

LAKE BOTTOM SYMBOLS

- Gr. Gravel
- R. Rubble
- Br. Bedrock
- ⅏ Stumps & Snags
- P. Peat
- Mk. Muck
- C. Clay
- M. Marl
- Sd. Sand
- St. Silt
- T Submergent vegetation
- ⊥ Emergent vegetation
- ⚘ Floating vegetation

- ◇ Access
- ◈ Access with Parking
- ◆ Boat Livery

AREA   1841   ACRES
TOTAL SHORELINE   18.9   MILES
MAX. DEPTH   53   FEET

ANGUS

MIKANA

Pickerel L.

Bass L.

Hemlock L.

Red Cedar R.

WASHBURN CO.
BARRON CO.

194

fishing with a float trip. From the lake outlet downstream to Rice Lake, the river is fairly slow and the fishing not so hot, but from Rice Lake all the way to the Chippewa River at Menomonie, faster current and better instream cover provide excellent habitat for smallmouths and walleyes as well. There are public landings and picnic areas that provide access every few miles along the river in Barron and Dunn counties. Both spinning and fly rod tactics will take fish.

The best boat landing on Red Cedar Lake is located along the northwest shore on 29th Avenue at a county park that also features a campground, picnic area and swimming beach. There is a smaller landing with less parking at the end of Highway V on the west shore. You can reach both of these ramps off Highway 48 between Angus and Mikana. There is a landing suitable for small boats on the east shore at Pigeon Creek, and one on the east side of Balsam Lake. Both can be reached off Highway 48 between Angus and Birchwood.

Barb's General Store, located in the Mikana Mini-Mall on Highway 48, carries bait, tackle and groceries and is open seven days a week. Address: 120 Lake Street, Mikana, WI 54857, telephone (715) 234-3119.

The classy Tagalong Resort, where we stayed for the Governor's Opener, features a golf course patterned after the Famous St. Andrew's course in Scotland, an RV park, restaurant, boat launch and rental, gift shop and even an air strip. Address: P.O. Box 68, Birchwood, WI 54817, telephone (800) 657-4843. For information on other area resorts and services, contact: Rice Lake Area Chamber of Commerce, 37 S. Main Street, Rice Lake, WI 54868, telephone (715) 234-2126; or Birchwood Area Lakes Association, P.O. Box 9, Birchwood, WI 54817, telephone (800) 236-2252.

Rock Lake

Lake Mills, Jefferson County

Next time you find yourself truckin' along the "I" between commitments in Milwaukee and Madison, take a break at the Lake Mills exit and motor on south through town on Highway 89 (Main Street) until you come to Sandy Beach Road. Park at the Chicago & Northwestern depot and walk out on the old railroad grade. You'd wait a long time for a train today -- the track's gone for scrap iron and most of the ties are anchoring terraced flower beds in the 'burbs a half-hour east.

You're standing on the Glacial Drumlin State Trail. If you like, you can hike it east 50 miles or so to where it meets up with the Ice Age Trail near Wales, then turn north and follow that trail to Green Bay or south and eventually you'll end up on the St. Croix River -- it's a thousand-mile hike one-way end-to-end.

No time for a thousand-mile hike today? OK, then turn west and walk a couple hundred yards along the grade and out onto the old trestle. Keep going until you're over water, then stop and look north. Rock Lake. Pretty, isn't it? Now turn around and look south. Still Rock Lake, but they call this part Marsh Lake. Good name, huh? Look at all those weeds. Ought to be full of bass and bluegills, maybe some northerns, too. Yes, it is, and Rock Lake's main basin has more of the same, plus walleyes, smallmouths, crappies...

Sound good? The DNR plans to build a public fishing pier attached to the trestle so you can walk right out from here and fish. Maybe next time you stop off on your way home from Mad-Town, you'll have your rod along and you can unwind and wind in a couple bass.

Although it's just a spit and a holler from the busy interstate, Rock Lake is one of southeast Wisconsin's best fishing lakes. Aptly named, this 1,140-acre lake is studded with rocky structure, the kind of stuff walleyes and walleye anglers love. Its clear water dives to 60 feet in places, but there are several nice bars and shoals that rise to within 10 or 15 feet of the surface, good dropoffs lined with coontail and pond-weed, and a shallow, bulrush-and-lily-pad-lined west shoreline that just shouts: "Bass! Bass! Bass!"

Rock Lake

Up until a couple years ago, Rock Lake boasted a well-balanced fishery, with self-sustaining populations of walleyes, smallmouths and panfish. Bass and panfish are still doing great, but walleyes are not, according to DNR fish manager Don Bush. There are still good numbers of older walleyes, but there has been virtually no natural reproduction here in recent years. DNR crews stocked 50,000 fingerlings in 1990 and again in 1991 and 167,000 fry in 1992, but these little guys have disappeared. Bush plans to initiate a study in 1994 to try to find out what happened to the lake's walleyes.

There were enough older walleyes to provide good fishing in the early '90s. Anglers took fish up to eight pounds in the summer of '92, and fair numbers of fish in the 20- to 24-inch class were caught through the ice in 1993. Trolling is legal here and is a popular way of taking walleyes. Two midlake bars are top walleye producers. Fremont Bar, located right in the middle of the lake, tops out at about 12 feet, but most of this structure is 25 feet deep. This bar drops off on the west side into the lake's deepest hole. Center Bar is a sprawling structure due west of the mill pond channel in town. Troll over these spots with a crawler harness or drift with jigs and live bait.

Three underwater points well out from the west shore attract walleyes in summer. Use a locator to find them and fish the 12- to 15-foot depths along the deep weed edges. Trolling the contour with deep-diving crankbaits should pull good fish out of the weeds. Night fishing is often productive on the shallow sand flats on the east shore and extending out from the trestle on the south shore. Cast with floating Rapalas or Slo-Pokes tipped with plastic shad tails. Consider releasing the walleyes you catch, since there are no young fish coming up to replace the current supply of adults.

As the walleyes declined, smallmouths have really taken off, and today Rock Lake is one of the top bronzeback lakes in southern Wisconsin. The best smallmouth spots are the shallower gravel points that extend out several hundred yards offshore and the two midlake bars described above, although it is possible to wade out from shore at the county park on the north end and catch smallmouths.

Diving crankbaits that imitate crayfish are the ticket for smallmouths. Everybody makes them: Rapala, Bomber, Rebel -- take your pick. During cold fronts, when you want to slow down your presentation, switch to black marabou jigs, Foxee jigs or any one of the swimming jigs and plastic tail combos in dark colors: brown, orange, black -- crayfish imitations, again. Ultimate Baits in crawfish patterns ought to work well on bass here, too.

Rock Lake's incredibly varied structure lets you pick your species and then choose a spot to try for that fish, spreading anglers out all over the lake. If the shoals and gravel bars don't do it for you, head for the shallow west shoreline or Marsh Lake and try for largemouths, pike or panfish. "Big Bobber" (Bob Willey), who runs Big Bobber Bait and Tackle on the lake's northeast side, reports some largemouth anglers caught and released better than 30 bass a day in 1992, including a fair number of five- and six-pounders.

Try a shallow crankbait, like Rapala's Shallow Shad Rap, just over the weed tops, or work a jig-and-pig or Texas-rigged worm right in the weeds for largemouths. In the evening, surface baits should draw jolting strikes. These same areas will produce northerns. Big, noisy spinnerbaits, weedless spoons or the tried-and-true Dardevle sweetened with a strip of pork rind are tough to beat.

Don't be too surprised to tangle with a musky here. Rock Lake received some hybrids in the 1980s, and anglers are catching (and releasing) them up to 45 inches. Try the deeper weed edges and rock bars. You can troll diving crankbaits, but it's more fun to toss plastics or those same crankbaits. Ask Big Bobber where most of the action is.

Rock Lake yields some nice crappie action in addition to being a good smallmouth and walleye lake. Photo by Dan Small

Rock Lake's crappies run big. You'll find them spawning on the midlake shoals in late May and suspended off dropoffs later in the summer. Tiny swimming jigs tipped with Gitzits will take them, but use very light line in this clear water. White, pink and yellow are good colors.

Bluegills here are also heavyweights. Big Bobber has seen them up to 13 inches. Work the shallow west shore or Marsh Lake with fly rod poppers and spiders or ice fishing jigs tipped with waxies or mousies in May and June. Later, when the lake stratifies, you'll find them suspended 8 to 15 feet down over deep water, where they feed on zooplankton. You'll take all you can handle drifting with slip bobbers and Bait Rigs panfish spinner rigs tipped with live bait or tiny plastic tails.

The Lake Mills Conservation Club has put over 75 fish cribs in the lake, most of them north of the trestle on the east side in 12 to 15 feet of water. They hold bluegills and crappies all year, but don't be surprised to pick up a bass there as well.

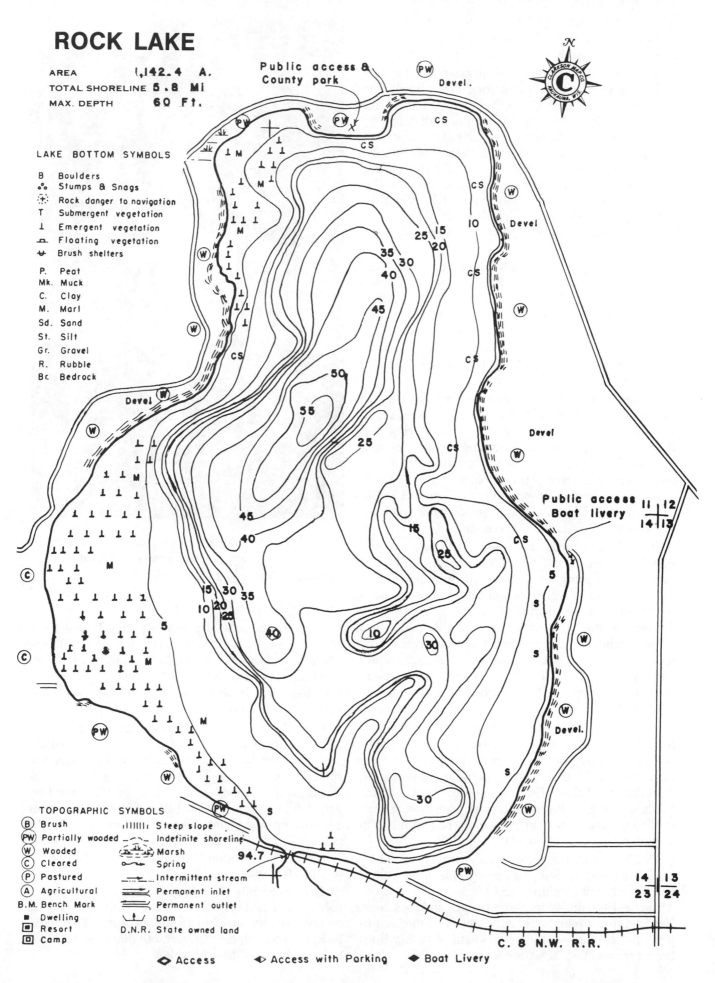

ROCK LAKE

AREA 1,142.4 A.
TOTAL SHORELINE 5.8 MI
MAX. DEPTH 60 Ft.

LAKE BOTTOM SYMBOLS

B   Boulders
∘₀   Stumps & Snags
⊕   Rock danger to navigation
T   Submergent vegetation
⊥   Emergent vegetation
⊐   Floating vegetation
⊌   Brush shelters

P.   Peat
Mk.   Muck
C.   Clay
M.   Marl
Sd.   Sand
St.   Silt
Gr.   Gravel
R.   Rubble
Br.   Bedrock

Public access &
County park

Devel.

CS

TOPOGRAPHIC SYMBOLS

Ⓑ Brush ||||||| Steep slope
ⓅⓌ Partially wooded   Indefinite shoreline
Ⓦ Wooded   Marsh
Ⓒ Cleared   Spring
Ⓟ Pastured   Intermittent stream
Ⓐ Agricultural   Permanent inlet
B.M. Bench Mark   Permanent outlet
▪ Dwelling   Dam
▣ Resort   D.N.R. State owned land
▣ Camp

Public access
Boat livery

Devel.

94.7

C. & N.W. R.R.

◇ Access   ◈ Access with Parking   ◆ Boat Livery

There is a concrete ramp and large parking lot at the county park at the north end of the lake on Highway B. In town on Willow Road, the paved, city-owned ramp on the channel that leads to the east shore will handle boats up to 16 feet long. You'll pass under two bridges to reach the lake, one with a four-foot clearance. There's another municipal ramp at the end of Sandy Beach road near the trestle. You'll pay a small fee to launch here, but the other two ramps are free.

There's a city-run boat rental and bait shop on Sandy Beach Road from May to October. Big Bobber Bait & Tackle, located a few blocks off the lake's northeast side, is the nearest year-round bait shop; address: W7809 Highway V, Lake Mills, WI 53551, telephone (414) 648-2081. Lake Mills Locker, N6797 Highway A, Lake Mills, WI, telephone (414) 648-5514, also sells bait and will process your fish.

Bob Hein's Sportsman Saloon, 129 N. Main Street, Lake Mills, WI 53551, telephone (414) 648-5061, is where it's at for pre-fishing information or post-fishing refreshments. Accommodations are limited, but you can get a brochure listing cabin rentals and Bob Hein's annotated lake map from: Lake Mills Area Chamber of Commerce, P.O. Box 125, 106 E. Lake Street, Lake Mills, WI 53551, telephone (414) 648-3585.

Shawano Lake

City of Shawano, Shawano County

Let's say you're on the planning team for a crappie fishing tournament circuit -- now don't laugh, they're commonplace down in Dixie. And let's say you want to hold a tournament up north someplace, to give the gang a change of scenery from the usual circuit lakes like Eufala in Alabama, Oconee in Georgia or Lake of the Ozarks in Missouri. Someplace way, way up north, say in Wisconsin, maybe. Just what kind of lake would you be looking for?

Well, for starters, it would have to be jammed with crappies, good-sized ones. And it would have to be pretty big, so competitors wouldn't be casting into each other's boats, with enough varied structure and cover and such that would attract crappies yet make anglers have to hunt for 'em a little. Someplace like Shawano Lake.

No kidding. Since 1990, Shawano Lake has been the site of the only Zebco/U.S. Crappie Association tournament held in Wisconsin. At a tad over 6,000 acres, Shawano is the smallest lake chosen for the tour. It is also the northernmost lake, and its date -- late April -- the last event in the tournament circuit. OK, so maybe tournaments and fishing lotteries don't excite you. But you can bet on one thing: if the boys from Georgia come up to a Wisconsin lake for one of their big-time crappie shindigs, then folks who like to eat crappies instead of using 'em as gambling chips sure ought to take a long, hard look at said lake when planning a panfish outing.

Located in a basin between the city of Shawano on the west and the village of Cecil on the east, Shawano Lake is a popular summer vacation spot with numerous resorts, campgrounds and family recreation opportunities on the lake and nearby, including canoeing, kayaking and rafting on the Wolf, Red and Oconto rivers. A navigable outlet, Shawano Creek, flows along the north edge of town to Wolf River Pond, a 300-acre impoundment on the Wolf River.

The lake's deepest hole is 40 feet, but most of it is much shallower. Vegetation becomes extensive in summer, especially in the shallow western half. Good structure in the form of sunken islands and dropoffs exists roughly in the middle of the lake's eastern third. There are also numerous subtle depressions left from sand-dredging operations years ago that hold fish.

Shawano Lake is probably best known for its great numbers of northern pike. Pike grow slowly here, and small ones are so numerous that the lake had a 25-fish daily limit for many years. The bag limit was reduced to the state-standard five pike a few years ago, and anglers are now taking good catches of bigger fish. A few dandies up to 20 pounds or so are taken every year.

Catching pike is no problem, but working your way through the hammerhandles to a decent fish might be. Some anglers do well on larger pike by speed-trolling deep-diving crankbaits outside deep weed edges. This makes good sense because mature northerns seek the cooler temperatures deep water often provides.

I taped a fishing segment for *Outdoor Wisconsin* on Shawano Lake in the fall of 1992 with crappie tournament director Tim Tumanic. We worked the bars and dropoffs on the east end and north shore for several hours, trying for walleyes, but they wouldn't cooperate on that dead-calm Indian Summer afternoon. We were marking suspended fish that wouldn't hit our leadhead jigs, so I switched to a floating jig-head and small fathead minnow, weighted down with one small split shot. I jigged it vertically, hoping those marks were crappies, or anything that might help us salvage a slow segment, when something grabbed the bait and nearly ripped the ultralight rod from my hand.

When you're doing a TV show, one fish can make the difference between a bust and a bonanza, so I played it gingerly and eventually landed a modest northern with the camera rolling. Both Tim and videographer Marshall Savick were relieved. I don't think I've ever been so happy to see a northern. That's the first fish I've felt like kissing in a long time.

Big-time crappie tournaments and abundant pike aside, Shawano's most impressive asset is probably its largemouth bass fishery. The 14-inch size limit has really boosted the number of bass in the 11- to 14-inch range, and there are plenty of larger fish as well. DNR fish manager Ross Langhurst suggests the northwest corner west of the county park and the southwest corner near the airport, as well as the outlet, as good spots to try when the season opens in May. Later, any weedbed will hold bass, although the larger fish are likely to hang out along the same deep weed edges and holes in the middle of weedbeds as northerns do.

Walleyes pulled off the largest year-class ever in 1991, thanks to efforts to enhance the major spawning reef off Schumacher's Island. The DNR trucked hundreds of tons of rock out onto the ice beginning in the winter of 1989, and Langhurst is pleased with the project's success.

"Shawano's walleyes grow fast," says Langhurst. "These fish will reach 15 inches by late 1993 and 1994, and they'll have a tremendous impact on the fishery for years to come."

Walleye action is good in May and again from October through December. Early in the season before weed growth is heavy, try the shallow reefs at the east end that top out at 10 or 12 feet. Jigs and minnows and other traditional fare produce well. Trolling at night with diving crankbaits and crawler harnesses along dropoffs and deep weedlines is the way to take walleyes in the summer. Tip-ups baited with shiners take them through first ice.

Bluegills spawn literally all along the lakeshore, and the best fishing comes when the big bull 'gills are on the beds. Later, look for them in deep water off weedlines where they suspend to feed on zooplankton. Drifting with tiny jigs or Bait Rigs spinner rigs tipped with plastic grub tails and waxworms ought to do the trick.

Shawano's crappies are abundant and they run big, 12 inches and bigger if you find the right school. If I were fishing for fun or money, I'd try the extensive bulrushes along both the north and south shores. Shortly after ice-out, try a couple hundred yards off

the rushes, and as the water warms and spawning nears, move right into the reeds. Minnows are the most popular bait, but if you know how to swim a tiny marabou jig, Slo-Poke Mini or Road Runner, you'll catch all you can handle without the mess of live bait.

Perch fishing can be good in late fall when everybody else is hunting. The jumbos move around, but if you can locate a school you'll do well with live bait. Try dropoffs outside remaining deep weedbeds at the east end.

If it's too windy to fish the main lake, you can duck into 75-acre Washington Lake via the channel on the north shore or work the outlet to Wolf River Pond at the east end of the lake. Both have good bass, pike and panfish habitat. Survey nets in Washington Lake turned up some huge largemouths a few years ago. The DNR stocks muskies in Wolf River Pond, and some are caught there, in the outlet channel and in Shawano Lake every year.

Jerry Honeyager landed this northern pike on a jig pole from Shawano Lake. Shawano is one of the top northern pike lakes in Wisconsin, though it is known more for numbers than size. Photo by Dan Small

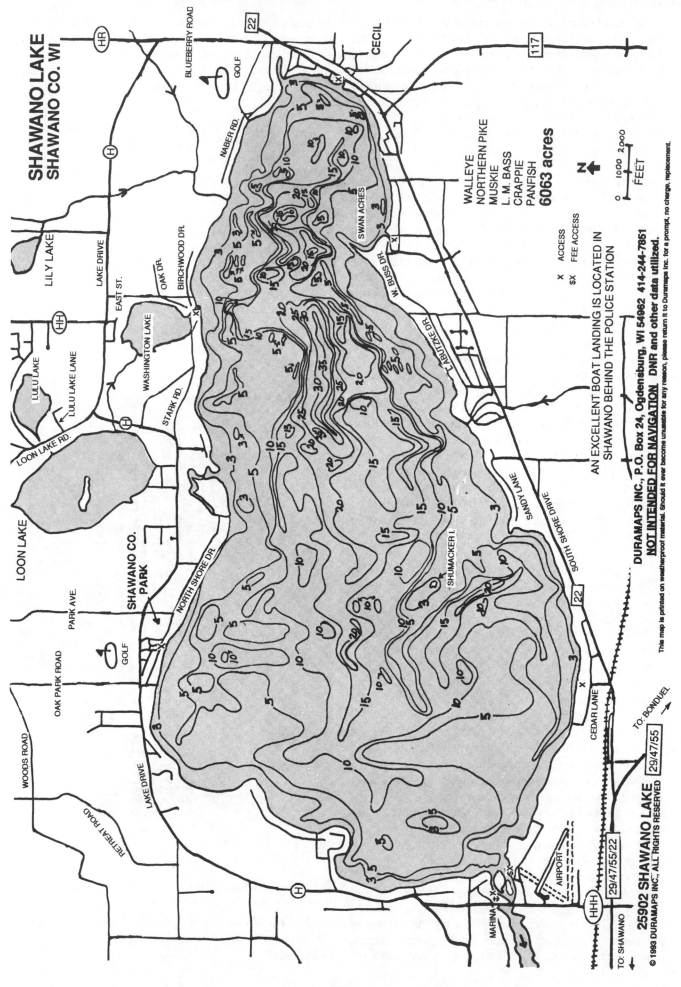

SHAWANO LAKE
SHAWANO CO. WI

WALLEYE
NORTHERN PIKE
MUSKIE
L. M. BASS
CRAPPIE
PANFISH
6063 acres

X ACCESS
$X FEE ACCESS

AN EXCELLENT BOAT LANDING IS LOCATED IN SHAWANO BEHIND THE POLICE STATION

DURAMAPS INC., P.O. Box 24, Ogdensburg, WI 54962 414-244-7851
NOT INTENDED FOR NAVIGATION DNR and other data utilized.

This map is printed on weatherproof material. Should it ever become unusable for any reason, please return it to Duramaps Inc. for a prompt, no charge, replacement.

25902 SHAWANO LAKE
© 1983 DURAMAPS INC., ALL RIGHTS RESERVED

202

Shawano Lake is fished heavily by vacationers in the warm months, but according to Ross Langhurst, 60 to 70 percent of the harvest is taken through the ice! Judging from the number of ice shanties on many Wisconsin lakes all winter long, this phenomenon is probably not unique to Shawano Lake. It would be very interesting to see some statewide data on the open-water take compared with the hard-water harvest.

Jerry Olsen, owner of Bamboo Bar on the lake's southwest shore, says fishing for perch and walleyes is hot early in the winter, but slows as the ice thickens. In late winter, ice anglers take suspended crappies in 12 to 15 feet of water. Minnows on jig rods or light tip-up rigs produce for all three species. Olsen plows seven miles of roads on the lake once the ice is safe for automobile travel.

Undaunted by our fall TV outing, we returned in the winter of 1993 to ice fish with Dave Hull and Don Trester. Trester operates Don's Sport Shop in Cecil, and Hull spends every spare minute hunting, fishing or trapping on area lakes and streams. We lucked into another dead-calm day, but this time the mercury was well below zero when we drove out onto the ice from Bamboo Bar early in the morning. Hull and Trester said our best bet was bluegills, so we tried several locations on the western half of the lake. Our best luck came in sparse weeds west of Schumacher's Island and off the west shore, where we took a mess of decent 'gills. It sure helps to have a couple guys along who know the water. Without them, I'd probably still be drilling holes out there.

Bamboo Bar also has a fee launch, boat rental, and lunch menu, as well as winter and summer events (including a nine-hole golf outing and a volleyball tournament on the ice in March). Address: W1984 Cedar Lane, Shawano, WI 54166, telephone (715) 524-0470.

Clockwise from the west end, there are boat landings at the outlet off Highway HHH in town, at the county park off Highway H, at the Washington Lake outlet off Washington Lake Road, off Highway 22 in the village of Cecil near the Pickerel Creek inlet, and at the foot of Swan Acre Drive on the southeast shore.

For bait and tackle, try Don's Sport Shop, 101 E. Green Bay Street, Bonduel, WI 54107, telephone (715) 758-2388; or Bahr's Baits, 204 Airport Road, Shawano, telephone (715) 526-3610. S&S Marina, also on Airport Road, is a full-service marina and boat rental; telephone (715) 524-3388. For on-water service, try American Marina, W2443 Weber Point Road, telephone (715) 526-4300. For information on lodging, campgrounds, events and additional services, contact: Shawano Area Chamber of Commerce, P.O. Box 38, Shawano, WI 54166, telephone (800) 235-8528, or (715) 524-2139.

Shell Lake

City of Shell Lake, Washburn County

Shell Lake

When I was a youngster, more years ago now than I care to recall, one of the highlights of a fishing trip with Dad was a stop for some pre- or post-fishing refreshments. This was long before the fast-food chains invaded nearly every town in America, spreading like a plastic cancer and running one little burger joint after another out of business. My favorite was a place that served root beer in thick glass mugs -- "shoopers" Dad called them -- that were kept in the freezer until you placed your order, so that on a hot summer day a heavy frost grew on them, then sloughed off and clung to your chin as you guzzled your drink.

Ever since those days, I have gone out of my way to find and patronize those little snack bars and hot dog stands that dare to assert their uniqueness in the face of the franchised intruders. Sam Hick's Drive-In on the north side of Spooner is one of those places. Sam Hick's is nothing but a tiny kitchen with an order window and a pick-up window in a rustic facade, and the homemade food tastes as genuine as the place looks. A place like that takes me back to a

simpler time when a burger and a root beer gave me all the confidence I needed for a day of fishing. Fortified with a Sam Hicks burrito and a frozen yogurt, you'll be ready to take on the toughest lake the North Country can dish out.

A few miles south on Highway 63, just about when you finish that cone and wish you had ordered a jumbo, you'll come to just such a lake. Shell Lake is as unusual as Sam Hick's. At 2,580 acres, it's the largest landlocked lake in the state. A seepage lake, its water level fluctuates with the water table. Shell Lake is clear and moderately deep, with a 36-foot hole in the middle of the north basin, but it does not stratify in summer. Oxygen is adequate all the way to the bottom and summer algae blooms are mild.

The shoreline is ringed with private homes and cottages, the last of the resorts having been split up and sold in recent years. The north basin lacks natural structure outside of a rock and gravel shoreline, but there are several hundred fish cribs located about 100 yards offshore all around the basin. A gravel bar off the east side of Morley's Point on the north shore provides good spawning habitat for smallmouths and walleyes.

Rolf's Point on the east and a state-owned island on the west separate the two basins. Walleyes and smallmouths also spawn on the gravel and rubble bars along the shoreline here. Two rock bars split the smaller south basin into two bays. The east bay is a smaller version of the main basin, and the shallower west bay has the only significant vegetation on the entire lake, since wave action and a hard-bottomed shoreline prevent weeds from taking root elsewhere in the lake.

Gamefish dominate the lake and keep panfish numbers low. The major species here are walleyes, muskies and smallmouths. The DNR stocks 2,500 musky fingerlings every other year, but walleyes and bass reproduce well and none are stocked.

Fish manager Larry Damman reports large numbers of smaller walleyes, with more in the 18- to 21-inch range showing up every year. The only shadow on Shell Lake's walleye scene is cast by mercury contamination. The latest health guide recommends reduced consumption of walleyes over 15 inches, so there is no size limit on walleyes here. (For details, pick up a copy of the "Health Guide for People Who Eat Fish From Wisconsin Waters" at any DNR office.) Still, there's nothing wrong with releasing the walleyes you catch.

Walleye action can be good early in the season in the south basin's shallow west bay. Slip bobbers and live bait will take fish along the developing weed edges, while jigs and minnows are effective along the gravel bars and dropoff north of the island. Later, concentrate on the fish cribs in the north basin. Troll crankbaits in an "S" pattern between and over the cribs or backtroll with jigs and leeches.

Unlike in most walleye lakes, the fishing gets better here as summer wears on. Walleyes hug bottom now where fast-sloping shoreline sand and gravel meet the muck of the midlake flats in 30 feet of water. Drifting with spinner rigs and live bait will take fish. At slow drift speeds, the new Finesse rig with an in-line Panther Martin blade by Ray's Custom Tackle is deadly on deep water walleyes. Try along the sharpest dropoffs on the southwest shore near the airport and on the west side of Morley's Point.

Muskies produced outstanding action in the early '90s. Forty-inch fish are typical, and Shell holds some fish in the 40- to 50-pound class. Trolling or casting near fish cribs with deep-diving crankbaits may take a musky now and then, but you'll probably have more follows than strikes. To trigger strikes in these circumstances, pump your rod when trolling, and when casting, keep your rod tip in the water until your bait is beneath the boat, then rip it toward the surface to simulate an escaping baitfish and hang on. Some anglers do well on big muskies at night. Use noisy surface baits just about anywhere along the shoreline, especially east of Morley's Point and in the south basin. There are deep weedbeds west of Morley's Point and east of Rolf's Point that are also worth trying.

The 14-inch size limit has proven a boon to Shell Lake's excellent smallmouth fishery. Larry Damman reports that smallmouth numbers have increased and the average fish is larger than just a few years ago. He sees several fish over 20 inches every year. Look for smallies anywhere there is gravel or rubble, and try crankbaits and jigs tipped with leeches or plastics. Dark colors are traditionally the best, but don't be afraid to try white or yellow. Shell Lake lies in the southern bass zone, but consider releasing any larger bass you take along the rocky shorelines in late May and June, as they will soon be spawning.

Perch are the most abundant panfish. Look for them along weedbeds and around fish cribs. The cribs will produce some crappie action, as will the

Catch and release fishing has made a difference for Shell Lake's musky fishery, just as it has made improvements throughout Wisconsin. Photo by Dan Small

SHELL LAKE

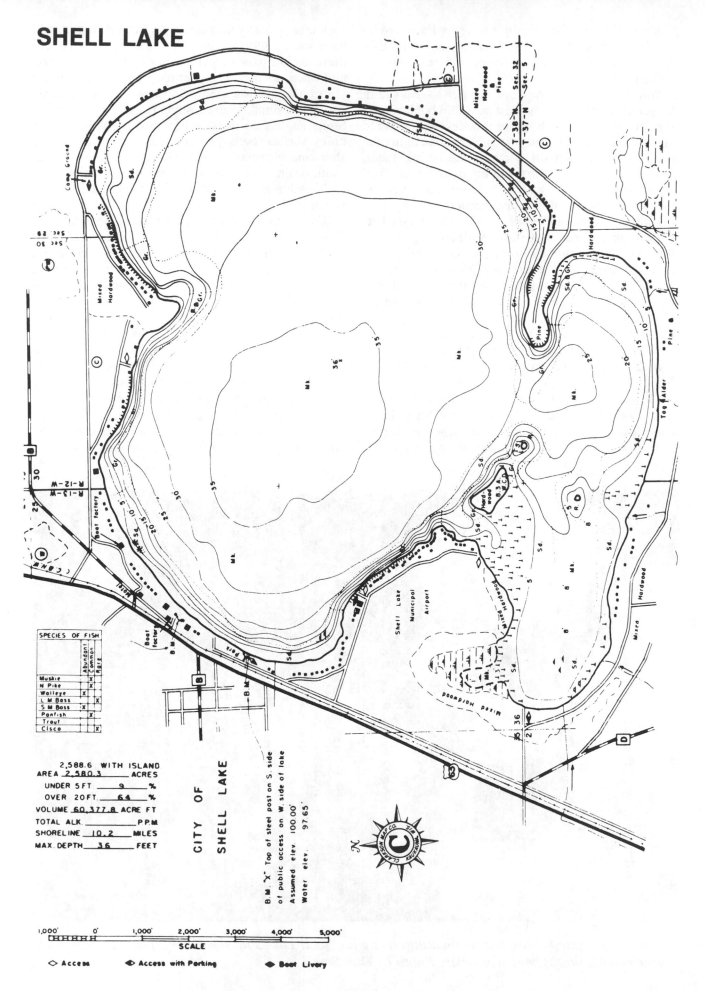

SPECIES OF FISH	Abundant	Common	Rare
Muskie		X	
N Pike		X	
Walleye	X		
L M Bass			X
S M Bass		X	
Panfish		X	
Trout			
Cisco			X

2,588.6 WITH ISLAND
AREA __2,580.3__ ACRES
UNDER 5FT __9__ %
OVER 20FT __64__ %
VOLUME __60,377.8__ ACRE FT
TOTAL ALK. _____ P.P.M
SHORELINE __10.2__ MILES
MAX. DEPTH __36__ FEET

CITY OF SHELL LAKE

B.M. "X" Top of steel post on S. side
of public access on W. side of lake
Assumed elev. 100.00'
Water elev.   97.65'

1,000'	0'	1,000'	2,000'	3,000'	4,000'	5,000'
SCALE

◇ Access   ◆ Access with Parking   ◆ Boat Livery

south basin early in the year. The south basin's weedy west bay also produces some bluegills in summer.

There is a fair population of northerns over 30 inches, especially in the south basin, but low water levels in recent years have prevented them from spawning successfully, so there are no smaller fish to speak of. Some good fish in the 20-pound class show up every year. Ice fishermen take some pike on tip-ups, and trollers catch an occasional hefty northern on musky baits.

There is a blacktopped boat ramp at the city park along the west shore, slated for improvement in 1993 or '94, and another good one a little south of there on Aster Avenue. Several other ramps around the lake may be too shallow during low water periods.

Shell Lake Campground, near the city park public launch, offers paddleboat and camper rentals. Telephone: (715) 468-7846. The Red Barn Campground, located along the north shore on Highway B, offers full-hookup camping and a variety of recreational activities. Memorial Day-Labor Day telephone (715) 468-2575; off-season telephone (507) 645-9089. You can rent a pontoon boat at the Tip Town Steak House on the southwest shore, telephone (715)468-7768. There are no tackle shops in the immediate area, but bait is available at several gas stations and other small outlets. The nearest full-service bait and tackle shops are five miles north in Spooner: End-Of-The-Line, Inc., 720 River Street, Spooner, WI 54801, telephone (715) 635-8128; or Spooner Sports at the corner of Highways 63 and 70 in Spooner, telephone (715) 635-6500.

For more information on area services, contact: Washburn County Tourism Association, Rt. 1, Box 327, Sarona, WI 54870, telephone (800) 367-3306 or (715) 635-3976; or Shell Lake Chamber of Commerce, P.O. Box 121, Shell Lake, WI 54871, telephone (715) 468-2256.

Upper St. Croix River

Douglas, Burnett and Polk Counties

Upper St. Croix River

Larry Dahlberg taught me a game he likes to play with a fly fishing partner and the St. Croix River's abundant smallmouths. He calls it "One Fish, Two Fish," and it's based on the premise that a struggling bass often attracts another that either tries to steal whatever bass No. 1 has hold of or else scarfs up the half-digested crayfish and other tidbits regurgitated by the first bass as it tries to shake the hook.

The game goes like this: When one angler hooks a bass ("one fish") and plays it in the current, his partner quickly casts near the hooked fish, hoping to draw a strike from a second bass. If he does hook one ("two fish"), angler No. 1 quickly lands and releases his fish and casts near the second fish, hoping to hook a third ("three fish") before the second fish is landed. If he succeeds, angler No. 2 lands and releases his fish and casts his fly near fish No. 3, and so on. In a good stretch of water, you can sometimes run a dozen fish before breaking the string. The Upper St. Croix has lots of water this good.

I taped an *Outdoor Wisconsin* segment on the St. Croix north of Grantsburg with Dahlberg back in

1985. Most people venture out in canoes on this stretch, but Larry, who grew up fishing and guiding on the river, knows every log and boulder, so audio engineer Mike Behlen and videographer Marshall Savick launched our 16-foot Lund and followed me and Larry in his boat up the winding channel. We motored upstream a mile or so, then let the current carry us as we worked behind logs and boulders, along cutbanks and in riffles with eight-weight fly rods and a deadly fly pattern Larry himself designed, the now-famous Dahlberg Fur-Strip Diver.

Tied with a deer hair head trimmed to look like a bullet wearing a collar, and a rabbit fur body and tail, the Diver floats like a cork when at rest, then dives and swims a foot or so beneath the surface when you strip line to retrieve it in short jerks. Smallmouths (and largemouths, pike and even muskies) come unglued in an effort to eat this fly, which has become a legend in less than a decade.

I wish I could say we caught bass until our arms ached, but even Dahlberg and his Diver couldn't overcome the effects of the cold front that often seems to follow us around when we tape fishing segments. We did cast until our arms ached, however, and took several small bass, including a "one fish, two fish," but the string ended there. Larry rigged a larger Diver with a short wire leader in an effort to seduce a pike or river musky, but had no takers. After eight hours on the water, I had learned a couple new fly rod tricks, Marshall put a segment in the can, and Mike was happy to get the camera boat back on the trailer without dinging the prop. Not a bad day, considering all the things that can go wrong when you mix a shallow, rocky river, two motor boats, a cold drizzle in August, an exhausted camera crew and two fly fishing nuts who had to be reminded now and then that we were doing a TV show, not just having fun.

One of the first rivers preserved as a National Scenic Riverway, the St. Croix more than lives up to that honor. From its headwaters near Solon Springs in Douglas County at the outlet of Upper St. Croix Lake, the St. Croix flows south, then west through St. Croix Flowage near Gordon, then southwest through Burnett County and Governor Knowles State Park to define the state line with Minnesota, and on down to the Mississippi at Prescott. From the Gordon Dam to the dam at St. Croix Falls, the upper river flows for 100 miles unfettered by dams or development. It is common to see bald eagles and ospreys fishing its waters and the usual contingent of northwoods wildlife making a living on its banks.

At the end of the last ice age, runoff from Glacial Lake Duluth, Superior's precursor, swelled the St. Croix to many times its present size and carved the wide, deep valley through which it now flows. Later, it was a major travel route for Indians, trappers and voyageurs during the Fur Trade, and later still it carried its share of the northern pinery to the mills during the brief logging heyday.

The entire river is normally canoeable in spring, but portions of the upper river are too fast to float and fish. From the CCC bridge on the St. Croix Trail in northern Burnett County, downstream to Nelson's Landing about 10 miles north of Grantsburg, several excellent one-day float trips are possible. Smallmouth bass are more common than walleyes in the upper reaches, but both are present in catchable numbers, while you're likely to encounter anything from these two species to northerns, muskies, largemouths, catfish and sturgeon as you move downstream.

DNR fish manager Larry Damman says the river's smallmouths have responded well to the 14-inch size limit. Their numbers have increased and they run bigger than they did a few years ago. He's concerned about the sturgeon population, though. His crews boom-shocked the river in 1991 and found few small sturgeon, so he is recommending the sturgeon season be closed on the St. Croix. Damman is also concerned about a recent Minnesota DNR decision to allow the Mille Lacs Chippewas to fish the river commercially. Since both states share the river, any commercial harvest by Minnesota tribes will have an impact on sport fishing for Wisconsin anglers.

Much of the river is shallow enough to fly fish for bass and pike. You'll be well-equipped with a nine-foot rod or longer, a floating bug-taper or rocket-taper line, short leaders and an assortment of flies from the Dahlberg Diver to fur leeches, Zonkers, Wooly Buggers, bass poppers and the like. Work them close to cover, casting across the current and down as you float along.

Most anglers rely on light spinning tackle for bass and walleyes, and baitcasting or heavy spinning gear for pike, muskies and catfish. Floating Rapalas, small spinnerbaits and Mepps spinners all work well in this

Fish Wisconsin author Dan Small and fly-fishing ace Larry Dahlberg fish for smallmouths on the St. Croix River. Says Dan, "Notice who has the better form here." Photo by Dan Small

dark water. Live bait is a hassle in the boulder runs and riffles, but can be productive in slow, deep stretches.

DNR fish manager Rick Cornelius makes several float trips each year for bass and walleyes, but admits that he has the most fun in June and July catching big redhorse suckers on worms. If you want to turn a youngster on to river fishing, I can't think of a better way than to put the kid, a light-action spinning rod and a bucket of worms in a canoe on a short stretch of the St. Croix, say between the St. Croix Trail and Highway 35 at Riverside. Pull up on a sand bar near a deep bend hole and be prepared to bait up and unhook redhorse all afternoon. You can keep some to smoke, if you like, but there's no harm in just catching them and tossing them back. Then, come evening, you can switch to a floating Rapala and station your protege below a riffle where he or she can tangle with a jumping smallmouth or two, while you work the slower water behind a sand bar for breakfast walleyes.

The stretch below Riverside produces an occasional musky and plenty of northerns, along with bass and walleyes. Work the edges of grass beds and deep, shaded holes for pike and muskies. Shallow crankbaits, like a Believer, spinnerbaits and bucktails, or topwater baits, like Mudpuppies and Hawg Wobblers, will all draw strikes from the Esox clan.

Since water levels can vary considerably depending on the season and amount of rainfall, the best way to pick a stretch to float is to contact the National Scenic Riverway Headquarters, P.O. Box 708, St. Croix Falls, WI 54024, telephone (715) 483-3284. They will supply you with maps, information on campgrounds, canoe rentals and everything else you'll need to know before you go.

Several small towns -- Solon Springs, Gordon, Riverside, Danbury and Grantsburg -- offer services along the river. For one guidebook covering resorts, campgrounds, motels, restaurants, canoe rentals, family recreational activities and other services in all these communities and surrounding areas, contact: Wisconsin Indian Head Country, P.O. Box 628, Chetek, WI 54728, telephone 1-800-472-6654 (in Wisconsin), or 1-800-826-6966 (outside Wisconsin).

Big St. Germain Lake

St. Germain, Vilas County

Big St. Germain Lake

The first time I fished Big St. Germain Lake, a three-day late-September storm did its best to blow us off the water. The guys I was with had planned this fall musky outing for months, so we weren't about to let a little nasty weather stop us from fishing. We pulled on rainsuits over deer hunting clothes to take the biting edge off the wind and did a lot of fast drifting over bars, then worked the weed edges on the one shoreline the wind wasn't pounding. We even tried the calmer waters of Lake Content, which connects to Big Saint via a navigable channel, but got no takers.

The morning after the front blew through, frost on the dock and boat carpets greeted us as we took one last futile shot at salvaging the trip. Of our four boats, I think one guy boated a sub-legal musky to foil the skunk. As we loaded our gear for the long drive back to Milwaukee, we tried not to notice the wind was dropping and the lake beginning to settle down. We heard the locals really kicked Esox butt on Monday afternoon, but those are the breaks.

A big soupbowl of a lake like Big Saint can kick

up like that, but those who know her take their lumps and come back for more because this is one heck of a fishery. Muskies and walleyes get most of the attention here, but the lake also offers good crappie and perch action, with enough northerns and bass tossed in to make things interesting.

Private resorts and campgrounds ring this popular vacation lake that covers 1,600 acres just north of Highway 70 in southern Vilas County. Lost, Plum and Mud creeks enter the lake on the north shore, while the St. Germain River drains it on the southwest shore, passing through shallow, weedy Fawn Lake. Big Saint's stained, fertile water supports good weed growth in bays and shoreline areas and an algae bloom in summer.

Most of Big Saint's main basin is deep and devoid of structure, but there are a couple key offshore areas that hold fish. Just west of midlake, there is a small, narrow island with a north-south orientation. This island is the top of a long, narrow bar with coontail patches and sharp dropoffs to deep water. The lake's deepest hole plunges to 35 feet off the northeast end of this bar. To the west, another smaller hump rises to within 10 feet of the surface. Both these structures hold walleyes, perch and muskies. There are several other good bars off the north and south shores, while cabbage and coontail provide cover on the east and west shores.

According to DNR fisheries biologist Harland Carlson, Big St. Germain has a stable walleye population with good size distribution and strong year classes in recent years. He is planning to conduct a walleye population estimate in the spring of 1994, but reports that Great Lakes Indian Fish and Wildlife Commission biologists found loads of fingerlings during a shocking run in the fall of 1991. Those walleyes are now entering the fishery and should provide good sport for the next few years. Although natural reproduction is normally good, some fingerling walleyes are stocked here to supplement the population. The DNR also stocks 2,500 muskies every other year, but no management effort is directed toward other species.

For spring walleyes, Minocqua-area fishing guide Greg Bohn suggests to try the inlet mouths or the island bar, both good spawning areas, and the large bar off the Lost Creek inlet. Work with lightweight jigs and minnows or floating crankbaits. In summer, you'll find walleyes on all the offshore bars. Drift the deep edges with live bait rigs during daylight hours and work the tops of the bars with floating crankbaits or slip bobbers and leeches in the evening.

Cold fronts chase walleyes into weeds here, where you can sometimes finesse them with slip bobbers and leeches. The larger cabbage beds along the east shore and in the outlet bay often hold greater numbers of walleyes, but the bigger fish tend to stay in smaller weed patches near deep water. In fall, try jigging sharp dropoffs wherever you find them.

Minocqua-area guide Greg Bohn releases a 27-inch, eight-pound walleye back to the waters of Big St. Germaine Lake.

Muskies run big here and they grow faster than on other area lakes because Big Saint has a good cisco population. Muskies home in on emerging weedbeds in spring, where they feed on perch, walleyes and other forage. Fish the inlets with small bucktails and shallow-running crankbaits, or try twitching a large, live chub or small sucker.

In summer, you'll find muskies in weedbeds, on offshore bars and along sharp dropoffs. Work the dropoffs with large jigs and plastics or try to locate suspended fish feeding on ciscoes, then jig for them. In the weeds, throw big bucktails or, on calm days, surface baits. Some of the biggest muskies taken here come off the offshore bars in the evening and at night.

For fall muskies, try diving crankbaits over the deeper bars and along dropoffs. The rock bar just off the public landing is a good fall spot, as are the offshore humps along the south shore.

You'll find largemouths and northerns in Big Saint's abundant weedbeds and in Fawn Lake and Lake Content as well. Try Texas-rigged plastic worms for bass and weedless spoons and spinnerbaits for both species. Look for smallmouths on the bars off the north shore and the island and near the brush shelters that line the north shore on both sides of Plum Creek.

Lake Content is a prime spawning area for crappies, Bohn says, and anglers take good catches here on minnows and artificials in May and June. You'll also take crappies, along with some nice bluegills in the inlet areas and shallow bays. In summer and fall, try jigging the brush shelters for crappies. Perch anglers do well on live bait along deep weed edges and off the island.

Big Saint Germain yields walleyes and panfish through the ice as well. Try the offshore bars for walleyes and bay mouths for panfish.

The public landing on the northeast shore has a good concrete ramp, turnaround and plenty of parking. To reach it, take Big St. Germain Drive west off Highway 155.

You can book a guide and get all the bait and tackle you'll need at Eagle Sports, 702 Wall Street in Eagle River, telephone (715) 479-8804. For information on the many area resorts and other services, contact the Vilas County Advertising Department, Vilas County Courthouse, P.O. Box 369, Eagle River, WI 54521, telephone (715) 479-3649.

Greg Bohn's Strictly Walleye Headquarters carries bait and tackle and books 12 guides for St. Germain, Woodruff, Minocqua and Boulder Junction area lakes. Address: 8600 Highway 51 North, Minocqua, WI 54548, telephone: (715) 356-9229.

Star Lake

Village of Star Lake, Vilas County

One mid-June day a few years back, Tony Rizzo was fishing with a friend who prided himself on being an accomplished musky fisherman. When his partner rigged up a large jerk bait, Rizzo suggested muskies might want something smaller this early in the season. But the guy insisted on a big bait for big fish, so Tony shrugged and went to work with his choice of lures for early season -- a small spinnerbait.

An hour later, Rizzo had tallied 12 follows and boated and released 4 muskies, 2 of them legals, while his friend with the jerk bait was still looking for his first follow. Mr. Jerk Bait humbly switched to a lure like the one Rizzo was using, and both anglers spent the rest of the afternoon fighting muskies. One lure doesn't often outperform another 12-zip, but that one incident shows just how critical bait size and presentation can be at times when fishing for muskies.

Tony Rizzo has spent more than 20 years guiding anglers to muskies in northern Wisconsin and has written five books on musky fishing. He gladly obliged when I asked him to share just a pinch of his musky expertise. Here, then, in a nutshell, is the Rizzo system for muskies.

"Early in the season, when water temperatures warm into the 55- to 62-degree range, muskies are moving slowly and their metabolism is slow, too," he explains. "They're feeding on small fish, so you want to give them small, slow-moving baits. Small spinnerbaits are ideal because the blade and pulsating skirt give them a lot of flashy action, even at very slow retrieve speeds."

Rizzo designed a small spinnerbait with a plastic skirt, called the Rizzo Wiz, that does just that. He fishes this bait early in the morning and on overcast days, working it slowly over the new cabbage beds in five to 10 feet of water. During midday, or on bright, sunny days, he moves to deeper water where he throws small crankbaits that will dive down to 10 or 15 feet. His favorites include many bass baits, some of them perennial picks: jointed Pikie Minnows, Rapalas, Heddon Vamp Spooks, Bill Norman lures, and others that will dive deep and wiggle.

"Summer is actually the easiest time to catch muskies," Rizzo says, "because all types and sizes of lures will take them now." In summer, he likes to throw bucktails, jerk baits, crankbaits and topwater lures, depending on where the fish are and how they respond to his offerings.

Other anglers have caught suspended muskies in midsummer, but Rizzo pioneered a deep-water casting system for them using diving crankbaits and sinking jerk baits. Exploring what he calls "the last frontier" of musky fishing, Rizzo spent countless hours locating trophy fish suspended near or adjacent to bottom structure in very deep water, then set about catching them. These fish are sometimes feeding on suspended baitfish, but more often than not they're simply hanging out at the depth where the water temperature is at or close to 65 degrees. That's the temperature at which their metabolic rate peaks. It's all detailed in one of his books, *The Summer Musky*.

In fall, when water temperatures begin to drop and musky metabolism slows back down, Rizzo works deep structure and weed edges with diving crankbaits, including his own Rizzo Diver, which goes deep and has good action at slow speeds. He and his clients have also done well on a new bait he developed, called Muskie Magic, which looks like a jerk bait but dives with less effort than most jerk baits, so he calls it a "pull" bait. It hit the market for the first time in 1990.

It seems nearly every musky guide in Vilas County has his own line of baits, but none can match Rizzo's local success record. Rizzo products accounted for more muskies registered in the season-long Vilas County Musky Marathon than any other brand of lure from 1987 through 1990. In 1989, Rizzo lures took an even 300 muskies in the competition, while Mepps came in a respectable but distant second with 193. The Musky Marathon folks dropped the lure listing after 1990, but insiders know Rizzo baits are still at the top.

Don't call Rizzo on the phone with a lake map in hand and ask him to reveal where he has caught big muskies, but if you hire him to take you fishing for a day you'll learn more about muskies than you ever thought there was to know. What's his favorite musky lake? I doubt he'll tell you that either, but his home base is Silver Muskie Resort on Star Lake, if that's any help.

Star Lake's 1,200 acres are divided almost equally into two large basins separated by a long peninsula called Rocky Point. The lake's deepest hole, some 67 feet, is in the middle of the deeper south basin. Vegetation is sparse, except in several bays in the shallower north basin. The bottom is mostly sand, with a scattering of muck, gravel and rubble. Star Lake stratifies in summer, and most species suspend over deep structure once this occurs.

There is an abundance of good natural structure in the form of humps and bars in both basins. In addition, the Sayner-Star Lake Chamber of Commerce placed 20 cribs in the lake in the mid-1980s. Most are in three locations: along the west shore across from Rocky Point, on a bar midway up the south basin's east shore and along another bar on the south shore.

The DNR stocks musky fingerlings here in alternate years, but stopped stocking walleyes several years ago because there is good natural reproduction. A 1986 population survey estimated the walleye population at 3.9 heavy-bodied adults per acre, which is very good for area lakes. When I talked with DNR fish manager Harland Carlson in February 1993, he was planning another survey here for just after ice-out. Perch, bluegills and crappies are also present in good numbers, and there are northerns and both species of bass as well.

In spring, work the shallower gravel and sand bars for walleyes, especially in the north basin. Later,

Guide Tony Rizzo and a guide client with a good musky taken on a Rizzo Tail from Star Lake, site of Tony's Silver Musky Resort. Photo courtesy Tony Rizzo

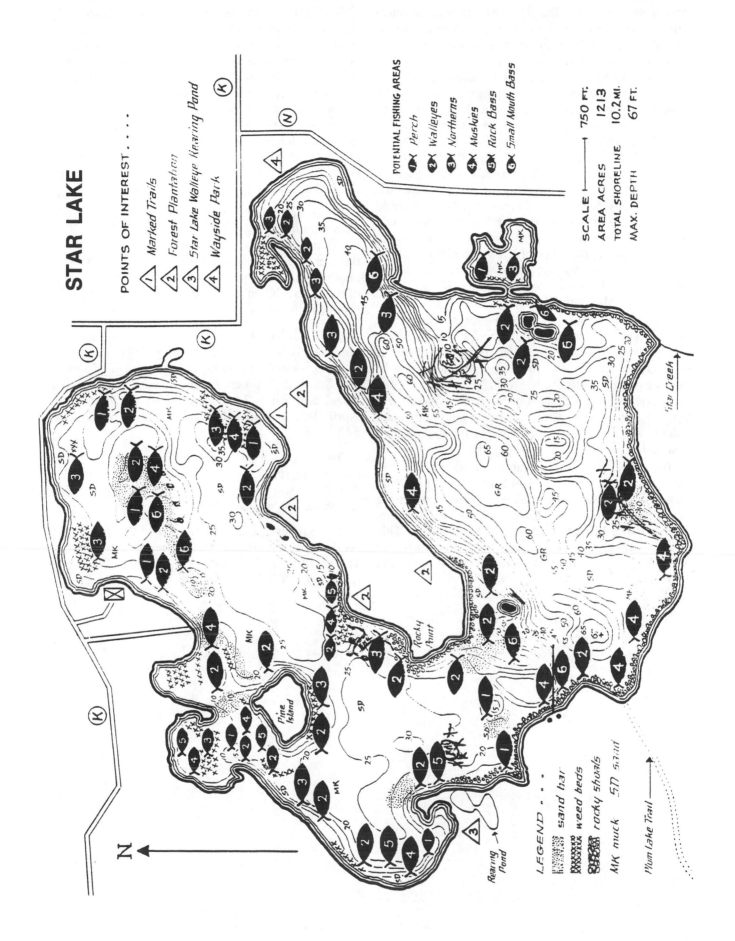

STAR LAKE

POINTS OF INTEREST . . . . .

△1 Marked Trails
△2 Forest Plantation
△3 Star Lake Walleye Rearing Pond
△4 Wayside Park

POTENTIAL FISHING AREAS

1 Perch
2 Walleyes
3 Northerns
4 Muskies
5 Rock Bass
6 Small Mouth Bass

SCALE ⊢——⊣ 750 FT.
AREA ACRES 1213
TOTAL SHORELINE 10.2 MI.
MAX. DEPTH 67 FT.

LEGEND . . . .

sand bar
weed beds
rocky shoals

MK muck   SD sand

Rearing Pond

Mom Lake Trail

Star Creek

Pine Island

Rocky Point

N

deeper structure and the fish cribs should produce. The outside weed edges in the north basin are worth trying in the heat of summer, and don't neglect suspended fish at this time as well. When walleyes are shallow, go with swimming jigs or bait rigs and minnows, and when they're deep, try jigging spoons, like a Mepps Syclops, tipped with a chunk of minnow, or a slip bobber and leech. You may be able to reach suspended fish by row trolling with deep-diving crankbaits or drifting a big chub on a slip bobber.

For muskies, follow Tony Rizzo's seasonal advice outlined above. The rocky south shoreline and the sand bars and weedbeds of the north basin all hold muskies. If you decide to hunt for suspended fish, stick with baits that look like ciscoes, keep them deep, and don't give up easily. If you can find ciscoes spawning on rocky shoals in November, you should be able to fool a musky or two with a Rizzo Diver, Grandma or Magnum Cisco Kid.

Smallmouths and largemouths are nowhere near as abundant as walleyes, but they're worth fishing for. For bronzebacks, work the rocky shorelines of the south basin, around fish cribs and near islands. Small diving crankbaits -- Storm Wee Warts, Rebel "R" Series, or No. 5 Shad Raps -- are tough to beat. If you do run into smallies in June, put them back quickly because removing an aggressive male from a nest endangers the fry he was guarding.

You may find a few largemouths in shallow, weedy bays, but odds are you'll take more pike than bass in such spots. Go armed with sturdy baitcasting gear and try baits like the Mepps Timber Doodle, tipped with a Mister Twister Split Double Tail. This combo is absolutely weedless and virtually snagproof when dragged through any cover, even fish cribs and brush piles.

You're likely to find perch in two sorts of spots: very deep rocky structure or weed edges. Live bait on light tackle should net you enough for a fish fry. For crappies, try the mouths of bays and the fish cribs, and for bluegills, work the shallow bays. Both crappies and bluegills will also suspend over deep water in midsummer. The tight schools you mark in deep water will probably be ciscoes, while the loosely grouped schools closer to the surface are most likely crappies and big 'gills. Drop a small spinner rig tipped with waxworms down among 'em and you'll find out soon enough.

There are several public landings on Star Lake. Two are off Highway K: on the west shore off Rearing Pond Road, and at a state forest campground on the peninsula on Statehouse Road. A third is at another state campground off Highway N just south of Highway K on the east shore. The two campgrounds have 60 sites between them.

For local bait and tackle, try Star Lake Store, on Highway K in Star Lake, telephone (715) 542-3464 or Fredrickson's Minnow Stand, a local institution and Star Lake's oldest business, operated by sisters Hazel and Edith Fredrickson and featured in the April 1993 issue of *Field & Stream*, telephone (715) 542-3788.

To book a guided trip with Tony Rizzo or for a copy of his lure catalog, you can reach him at Silver Muskie Resort, P.O. Box 154, Star Lake, WI 54561, telephone (715) 542-3420.

The Sayner-Star Lake Chamber of Commerce will send you a free brochure listing area resorts and services. Address: P.O. Box 191, Sayner, WI 54560, telephone (715) 542-3789.

Sturgeon Bay And Larson's Reef

Sturgeon Bay, Door County

Remember your first-grade teacher, Mrs. Davis, and how she taught you we all carry a map of Wisconsin in our right hand? Hold your hand out in front of you, class, and look at your palm. Good. Now put your fingers together like a mitten. That's it, now stick your thumb out a little bit -- not too far. That's Door County, and the space between your thumb and fingers is Green Bay. OK, now wiggle your thumb and find your knuckle. See that little crease? That's Sturgeon Bay.

The Sturgeon Bay ship canal actually cuts Door County in half at the knuckle, making the northern part an island, but everybody calls it a peninsula and there's no point in arguing about that. Most people agree on one thing, though: Sturgeon Bay is one of the top fisheries in the state. About 10 years ago, when I lived on Lake Superior's Chequamegon Bay, Dave Otto and the boys at Mac's Sport Shop in Sturgeon Bay challenged me and the northwoods gang to a little friendly contest to see which of the two bays could produce the biggest fish of each species. The results of this annual competition were published in the old *Wisconsin Sportsman* magazine.

As I recall, it was a close race the first year, but Sturgeon Bay won in all but two categories the next. Problem was, the folks up on Chequamegon Bay like to eat fish so much that some of the big ones never got registered. The year a 10-pound 2-ounce Sturgeon Bay walleye beat our best fish by six ounces, some guy from Ashland filleted an 11-pounder without bothering to enter it in the contest! The contest sort of petered out after that, but Dave had made his point: Sturgeon Bay produced hefty fish back then, and it still does today.

Sturgeon Bay's strongest suit is its variety. In the spring, there are trout; in the summer, northerns and smallmouths; in the fall, salmon and trout again; and all year, perch and walleyes the likes of which you've never seen. Then, come freeze-up, Sturgeon Bay offers some fantastic ice fishing for northerns, perch and trout. You can fish the bay itself or venture out into Lake Michigan or Green Bay, depending on the season and wind direction. Some fisheries virtually shut down at certain times of the year, but there is always something worth fishing for in the crease of the thumb.

Sturgeon Bay and Larson's Reef

Walleyes reproduce naturally now in Sturgeon Bay and Green Bay, so the DNR curtailed the massive stocking program that revitalized this fishery. Dunlap Reef, where the bay narrows near downtown Sturgeon Bay, produces some big walleyes right after ice-out. Walleyes spawn along the rocky shoreline of Quarry Point and Potawatomi State Park, and fishing is good here well into May for pre- and post-spawners. Slow trolling, bumping a jig and minnow on bottom, or still fishing with slip bobbers will take fish.

In summer, Sawyer Harbor, inside Sherwood Point at the southern lip of Sturgeon Bay, holds some nice walleyes. Fish the weedbeds here with floating Rapalas and Mepps spinners until the weeds become too thick, then switch to weedless baits, like a Texas-rigged Slo-Poke and plastic worm. Trolling the shoreline at night near the Sherwood Point Light produces some very big fish.

Larson's Reef, a huge series of offshore humps and ridges that run from Sherwood Point southwest to Snake Island, is the biggest chunk of walleye structure on Green Bay. A good locator is essential

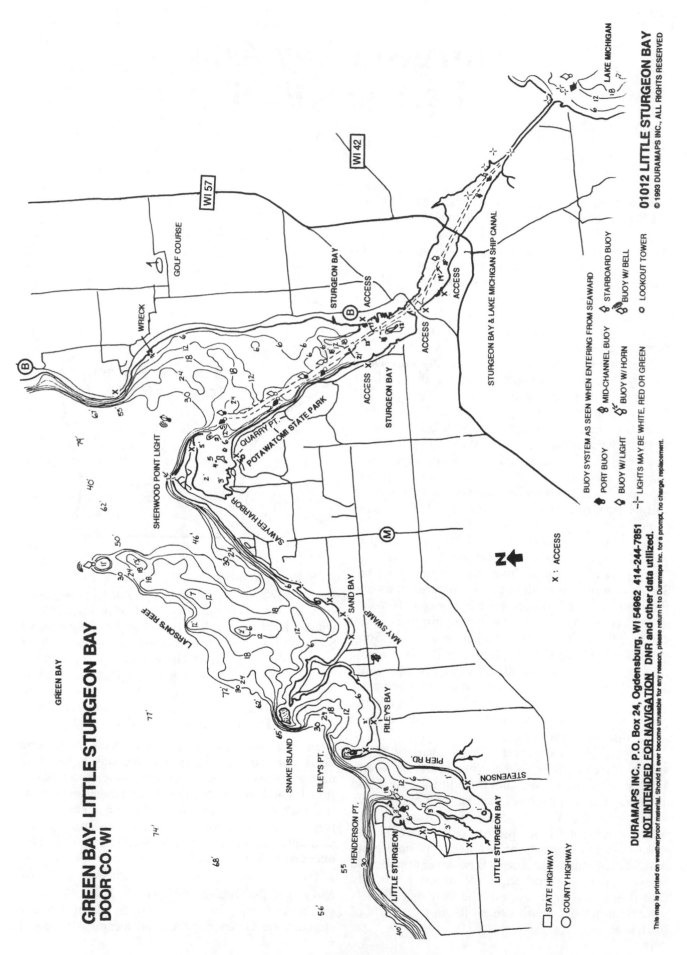

GREEN BAY- LITTLE STURGEON BAY
DOOR CO. WI

GREEN BAY

WI 57

WI 42

LAKE MICHIGAN

GOLF COURSE

WRECK

STURGEON BAY

ACCESS

SHERWOOD POINT LIGHT

QUARRY PT.

POTAWATOMI STATE PARK

SAWYER HARBOR

STURGEON BAY

ACCESS

ACCESS

ACCESS

Sturgeon Bay & Lake Michigan Ship Canal

LOOKOUT TOWER

LARSON'S REEF

SAND BAY

MAY SWAMP

RILEY'S BAY

SNAKE ISLAND

RILEY'S PT.

HENDERSON PT.

PIER RD.

STEVENSON

LITTLE STURGEON

LITTLE STURGEON BAY

X : ACCESS

BUOY SYSTEM AS SEEN WHEN ENTERING FROM SEAWARD

- ▮ PORT BUOY
- ◈ MID-CHANNEL BUOY
- ◈ STARBOARD BUOY
- ◇ BUOY W/ LIGHT
- ◈ BUOY W/ HORN
- ◈ BUOY W/ BELL
- ○ LOOKOUT TOWER

-∤- LIGHTS MAY BE WHITE, RED OR GREEN

DURAMAPS INC., P.O. Box 24, Ogdensburg, WI 54962 414-244-7851
NOT INTENDED FOR NAVIGATION DNR and other data utilized.

This map is printed on weatherproof material. Should it ever become unusable for any reason, please return it to Duramaps Inc. for a prompt, no charge, replacement.

01012 LITTLE STURGEON BAY

- ☐ STATE HIGHWAY
- ○ COUNTY HIGHWAY

here to stay in touch with structure. Troll over the shallower humps with shallow-running crankbaits. The Door County shoreline east of Larson's Reef also produces good walleyes from summer well into fall.

Spring perch fishing is often good along the north shore of Sturgeon Bay near the bridge and the ship-building docks. Sawyer Harbor's open water areas also produce perch in spring. The old stone quarry docks on the north side of the bay mouth are a great spot to catch summer perch without launching a boat. Larson's Reef yields some real jumbos in summer, but you'll have to move with the schools and may have trouble locating them in the first place.

Sturgeon Bay and the rocky shoals around Snake Island offer some of the best smallmouth fishing anywhere in Green Bay. Work Sawyer Harbor and The Flats from the old stone quarry to Sunset Park in late May and June, then try the dropoffs near the old quarry docks in summer and fall. The cut between Snake Island and the mainland also produces nice catches of bass in summer. Crankbaits, live bait and dark jigs all work well.

You'll find Sturgeon Bay's northerns wherever there are weedbeds: Sawyer Harbor, The Flats, Dunlap Reef and the mouth of Big Creek are all good spots to try. Try casting large spinnerbaits and in-line spinners or ripping the weeds with swimming jigs and plastics like Creatures and Reapers. Trolling is legal but may spook fish in shallow areas. The piers and moored Great Lakes boats in the shipyards also provide cover that some of the bay's biggest pike use to ambush baitfish. Don't be surprised to connect with a big walleye here as well.

The DNR would like to implement a trophy management plan for northerns throughout Green Bay, including Sturgeon Bay, that would call for a 32-inch minimum size and a reduced bag limit. Public sentiment has so far opposed the lower bag limit, but fish manager Terry Lychwick has hope that a compromise can be reached. "We'd like to smooth out the ups and downs in pike populations," Lychwick says. "Right now, when we have large year classes of pike, anglers gang up on them and harvest them off before they can reach trophy proportions."

The same areas that hold pike are the spots to try for muskies. True muskies, stocked in the bay on and off from the late '70s to the mid-'80s, show up often enough to make life interesting for pike fishermen.

Trollers take some nice brown trout, along with rainbows and an occasional laker just after ice-out on The Flats and off Potawatomi State Park. Jointed crankbaits in bright colors, like Rapalas, Rebels and the like should produce. Use light line and skis or troll flatlines well behind the boat to avoid spooking fish in the clear, shallow water.

In fall, mixed catches of trout and salmon are the rule for trollers working the ship canal and mainland shoreline areas on the Lake Michigan side and Green Bay side alike. Run heavier line in fall because you're as likely to tangle with a 25-pound king as a five-pound brown. Strawberry Creek is the main chinook spawning tributary for all of Door County, and the DNR takes eggs for its chinook stocking program here.

Ice fishing is popular and productive throughout the area. Larson's Reef yields good perch and walleyes, but watch for pressure ridges and rough ice. The Flats and Dunlap Reef produce walleyes, pike and perch, while the shallow mouth of Big Creek is worth trying for trout.

Four public boat ramps provide access to the bay; one at Potawatomi State Park on the south side, one at the old stone quarry on the north side, one at Sunset Park in town on the north side and one off Madison Avenue at the bridge on the south side. The stone quarry site is slated for improvement, with additional ramps and more access for shore-bound anglers.

Mac's Sport Shop, 33 South Madison Avenue, Sturgeon Bay, WI 54235, telephone (414) 743-3350, carries everything you'll need to fish the bay and then some. For information on the area's many resorts, restaurants, seasonal attractions and guide service, contact: Sturgeon Bay Information Center, P.O. Box 212, Sturgeon Bay, WI 54235, telephone (414) 743-3924. For information on all of Door County, contact: Door County Chamber of Commerce, P.O. Box 346, Sturgeon Bay, WI 54235, telephone (414) 743-4456 or (800) 527-3529. For a 24-hour recorded fishing and recreation report, call (414) 743-7046.

Smallmouth bass yield exciting action on Sturgeon Bay throughout the summer months. Photo courtesy Tom Newbauer

Three Lakes Chain
(Burnt Rollways Reservoir)

Town of Three Lakes, Oneida County

You get some interesting geography lessons from chamber of commerce brochures. Here's a tidbit from the Three Lakes brochure: "Due to a geological formation of headlands in the area of Big Lake, it is possible to leave Three Lakes by canoe, travel completely around the world by water, and return to within a few short miles of the point of embarkation."

If you ever start your summer vacation in Three Lakes and find yourself on a river in Finland, now you'll at least know how you got there, even if you can't find your way back.

They must have named the town of Three Lakes before the dam was built because the Three Lakes Chain consists of 17 or 20 lakes, depending on how you make your count. Technically speaking, the lakes make up Burnt Rollways Reservoir, formed by a Wisconsin Valley Improvement Company dam on the Eagle River at the outlet of Long Lake near the Oneida-Vilas county line. This is the same Eagle River that flows through the Eagle River Chain of Lakes a few miles to the north.

Three Lakes Chain

Because you can put a boat in the water at The Thoroughfare between Whitefish and Big lakes at the upper end of the Three Lakes Chain and motor all the way to Watersmeet Lake at the lower end of the Eagle River Chain, some folks simply call the entire string of 28 (or 31) lakes the Eagle River Chain. They consider the Oneida County portion the Upper Chain and the Vilas County portion the Lower Chain.

It is understandable that folks from Eagle River want to consider all the lakes part of "their" chain, and it's also understandable that folks from Three Lakes don't want "their" lakes to be confused with those a few miles up the road and in a different county. And it's also understandable that everybody up in that part of the state wants everyone else to know that "their" lakes are part of the world's longest chain of interconnected freshwater lakes.

Anyway, there's a bunch of lakes up north that are all hooked together, see, and depending on which brochure you pick up in which town, some of them are part of one chain or another or they're all part of one chain. So, welcome to the Three Lakes Chain of 17 or 20 lakes on the Eagle River, or the Upper Eagle River Chain of Lakes, or Burnt Rollways (Local historian Walt Goldsworthy tells three versions of the story behind that name involving a fire that destroyed the logs stacked there one winter back in the logging days at the turn of the century.) Reservoir, whichever you prefer. The important thing to remember is they're all full of fish and there are more than three of them.

The water on the Three Lakes Chain ranges from crystal clear on Spirit Lake to dark stained on most of the rest. Medicine and Big Stone are the deepest, but the balance of the lakes are shallow, with depths of less than 30 feet. There is an abundance of midlake rock structure, especially on Long, Planting Ground and Big Stone lakes, that does not appear on any lake map, so you can have a field day exploring new territory with your locator and a box of jigs. All the lakes are blessed with deep coontail weed flats that draw fish like, well, like deep weed flats.

These lakes do not receive the summer boating or fishing pressure of the more popular Eagle River Chain (Lower Chain), but they have a lot to offer anglers, such as world-class crappies, good perch and walleye, and some nice northerns. They are also some of the better musky lakes you'll find anywhere in the country. Several, especially Medicine and Big Stone, have cisco populations, which means they are capable of producing big muskies and walleyes. Muskies are stocked in the larger lakes at the rate of one fingerling per acre every-other year, and some bluegills taken from other lakes in the area are also put in. Natural reproduction sustains walleyes and all other species here.

Planting Ground and Long are super summer musky lakes, according to Eagle River guide George Langley. For some reason, their muskies go wild for surface baits in June, July and August. These are the last two lakes on the chain, so you can quickly move to the other if the action slows on one. I've taped several segments for *Outdoor Wisconsin* on the chain, the most recent in the summer of 1992 with guide "Ranger Rick" Krueger. Rick boated a 35-inch musky on a bucktail on Planting Ground, then I took a 34-incher on a topwater bait on Little Fork. Those are not huge muskies, but it was the first time we've boated two legals in one TV segment.

The next evening, writers Dave Hansen, Bill Wiese and I skipped out early after a Wisconsin Outdoor Communicators Association barbecue and hit the chain again for some evening fishing. As I recall, one of us boated a short musky -- Wiese, I think. Then we rejoined a cluster of WOCA members carousing at Trees for Tomorrow and stayed up half the night telling lies and singing songs from the '60s.

Thus cleansed, Bill Wiese and I chose to fish the chain the next morning for the annual WOCA catch and release musky tournament. Wiese tossed bucktails while I worked Dahlberg Divers on my fly rod. We never saw a musky, but a three-pound smallmouth gave me a thrill when it pounded that big chartreuse fly on the same Little Fork drift that produced my musky with Rick Krueger.

It seems every time I fish the Three Lakes Chain in fall, it snows. George Langley and I raised a big brute of a musky in a fierce October snowstorm, but couldn't get it to strike. Then a couple years later, I spent several days in November taping segments for *Outdoor Wisconsin*. The first day, I tried for muskies with guide John Turk. My intrepid crew consisted of videographer John McKay, engineer Gary Sharbuno and camera-boat pilot Charlie Thomas. We launched on Big Stone Lake and worked our way through Deer and Dog lakes to Big Lake, stopping to fish submerged structure we never would have found without Turk. The day started off bright and cold, but as soon as we got on the water, one snow squall after another pelted us until we thought it couldn't get any worse.

The muskies would not cooperate, so John suggested we hit a couple bays where he knew we'd find crappies. Those crappies saved the day. We caught a mess of big ones on chartreuse Slo-Poke jigs and on little blue-feathered jigs made locally by a friend of

John's, both tipped with fatheads. Charlie couldn't resist fishing himself. When the camera shows a crappie from the angler's point of view, you know that's one Charlie caught. Intermittent squalls interrupted our taping all day long, but when some serious black clouds appeared to the northeast, we decided to pack it in.

Fish Wisconsin author Dan Small and "Ranger" Rick Krueger with twin muskies taken from the Three Lakes Chain during a taping for Outdoor Wisconsin. Photo by Dan Small

It couldn't happen two days in a row, we thought, as we met Steve Markotic, our guide for another shot at muskies the following morning. Fortified by a lumberjack's breakfast at LBJ's, we picked up sack lunches at Cindy's Cafe and headed for the lower end of the chain. We launched on Town Line Lake and motored through a channel to Planting Ground Lake, where we hit several points and offshore bars, but again had no luck on muskies.

When it started snowing sideways, Steve suggested we try for walleyes. We had a couple hits drifting over shallow bars with jigs and minnows, but the walleyes were biting lightly and we were too numb to hook any. We finally came around a point out of the howling wind along a lee shore, where Steve knew of a couple brush piles that held fish.

BIG LAKE

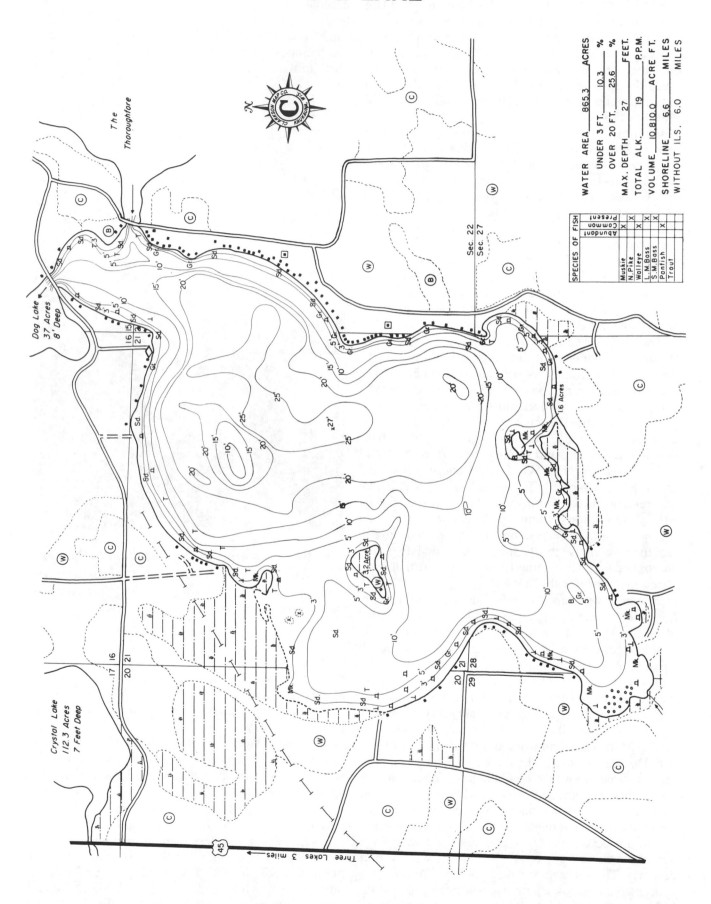

SPECIES OF FISH	Abundant	Common	Present
Muskie		X	
N. Pike		X	
Walleye		X	
L.M. Bass		X	
S.M. Bass		X	
Panfish		X	
Trout			

WATER AREA   865.3   ACRES
  UNDER 3 FT.   10.3   %
  OVER 20 FT.   25.6   %
MAX. DEPTH   27   FEET.
TOTAL ALK.   19   P.P.M.
VOLUME   10,810.0   ACRE FT.
SHORELINE   6.6   MILES
WITHOUT ILS.   6.0   MILES

Dog Lake
37 Acres
8' Deep

Crystal Lake
112.3 Acres
7 Feet Deep

The Thoroughfare

Sec. 22
Sec. 27

1.6 Acres

3.2 Acre Sd

Three Lakes 3 miles

LONG LAKE

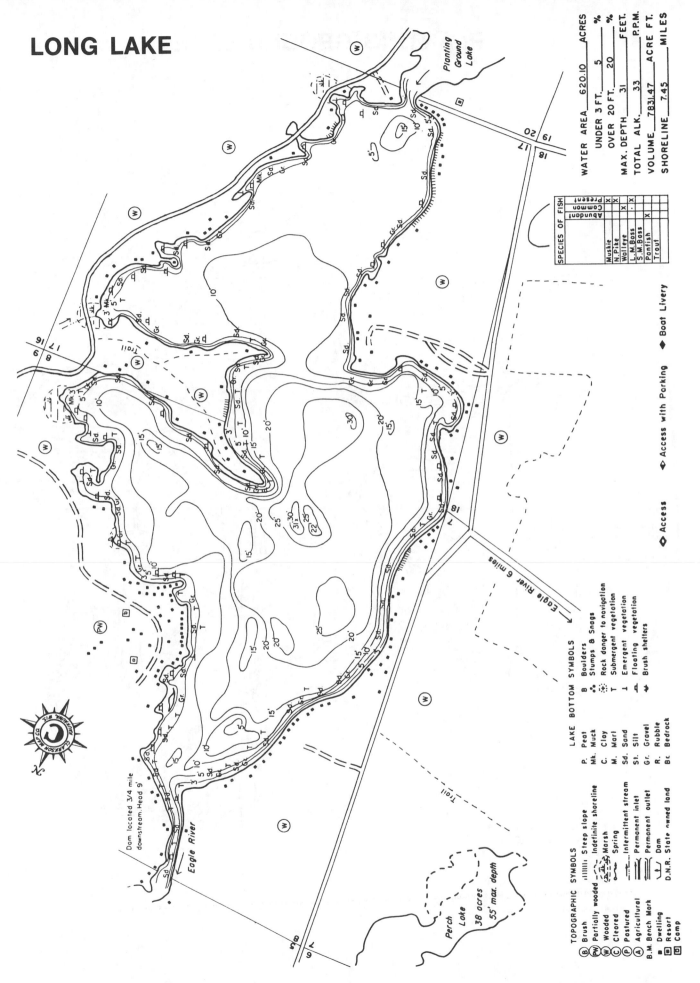

PLANTING GROUND LAKE

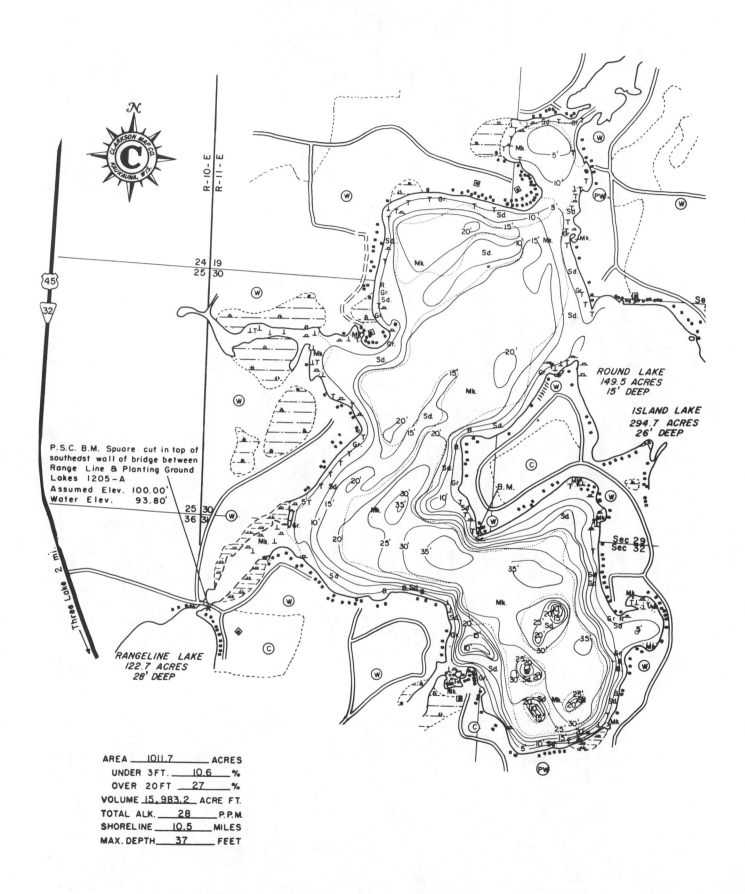

P.S.C. B.M. Square cut in top of
southeast wall of bridge between
Range Line & Planting Ground
Lakes 1205-A
Assumed Elev. 100.00'
Water Elev. 93.80'

ROUND LAKE
149.5 ACRES
15' DEEP

ISLAND LAKE
294.7 ACRES
26' DEEP

RANGELINE LAKE
122.7 ACRES
28' DEEP

Three Lake 2 mi.

AREA	1011.7	ACRES
UNDER 3FT.	10.6	%
OVER 20FT	27	%
VOLUME	15,983.2	ACRE FT.
TOTAL ALK.	28	P.P.M.
SHORELINE	10.5	MILES
MAX. DEPTH	37	FEET

SPIRIT LAKE

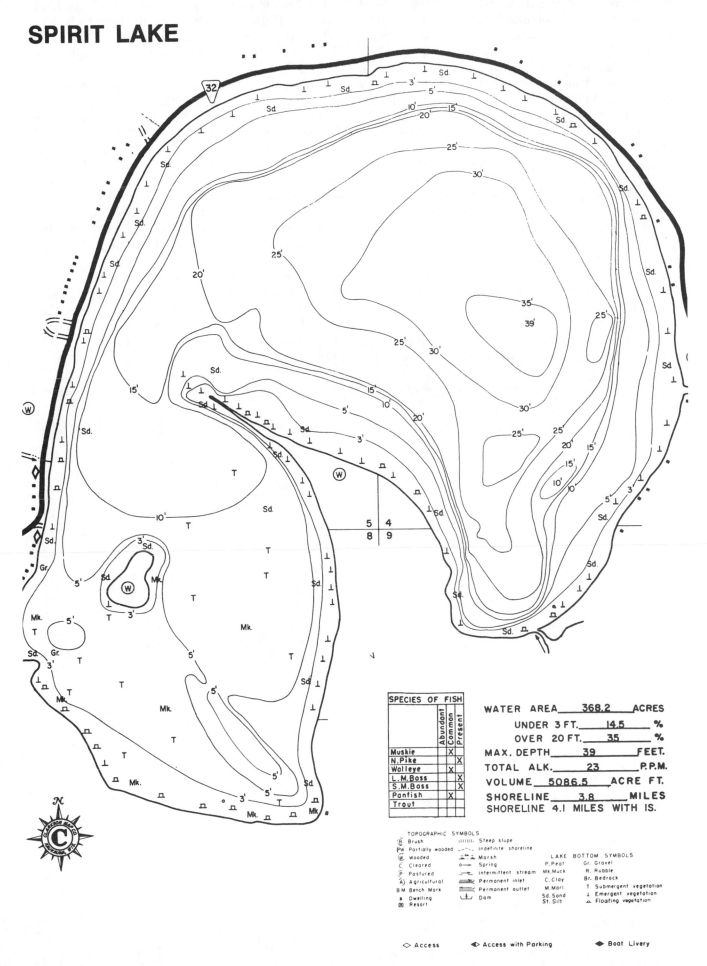

SPECIES OF FISH	Abundant	Common	Present
Muskie		X	
N. Pike			X
Walleye		X	
L.M. Bass			X
S.M. Bass			X
Panfish	X		
Trout			

WATER AREA _____368.2_____ ACRES

UNDER 3 FT. _____14.5_____ %

OVER 20 FT. _____35_____ %

MAX. DEPTH _____39_____ FEET.

TOTAL ALK. _____23_____ P.P.M.

VOLUME _____5086.5_____ ACRE FT.

SHORELINE _____3.8_____ MILES

SHORELINE 4.1 MILES WITH IS.

TOPOGRAPHIC SYMBOLS

B Brush
PW Partially wooded
W Wooded
C Cleared
P Pastured
A Agricultural
BM Bench Mark
▪ Dwelling
▣ Resort

‖‖‖‖ Steep slope
—·—·— Indefinite shoreline
Marsh
o→ Spring
Intermittent stream
Permanent inlet
Permanent outlet
Dam

LAKE BOTTOM SYMBOLS

P. Peat   Gr. Gravel
Mk. Muck   R. Rubble
C. Clay   Br. Bedrock
M. Marl   T Submergent vegetation
Sd. Sand   ⊥ Emergent vegetation
St. Silt   Floating vegetation

◇ Access   ◈ Access with Parking   ◆ Boat Livery

Again, several short strikes left us wondering what the gods who are supposed to shine on TV productions were up to. The camera boat was laying back, letting us fish, when I finally hooked a walleye. I hollered to Charlie, but by the time he got the boat into position, the fish had shaken free. We knew they were there, but unfortunately I can't prove it on TV.

The snowstorm we battled on the way back to the landing made the one the day before look like light flurries. I have a photo of Charlie and the crew grinning madly as they approached the landing at the end of the day. You can barely see them through the snow. The fish fry at Hobart's Eagle's Nest south of town more than made up for a bummer day on the water.

I swear I'm going back there on a mild, spring day and have at those crappies and walleyes again. Turk claims he gets crappies pushing two pounds regularly, and the walleye I lost was no slouch. I think a Planting Ground-Long Lake musky-walleye-crappie outing in late May sounds like a darn good idea.

There are good public landings off North Big Lake Loop Road on Big Lake, off Highway 32 at Three Lakes Marine on the southwest shore of Big Stone Lake, off Highway X on the north side of Medicine Lake, off Timbershore Drive at the south end of Town Line Lake, and at the dam on the Eagle River below Long Lake.

For bait and tackle in Three Lakes, try Jerry's, telephone (715) 546-3414. For local guide service, contact: Steve Markotic, P.O. Box 56, Three Lakes, WI 54562, telephone (715) 546-2312; John Turk, P.O. Box 345, Three Lakes, WI 54562, telephone (715) 546-3025; or Rick Krueger, 696 Meta Lake Road, Eagle River, WI 54521, telephone (715) 479-6251. The nearest full-service sporting goods store, which is also headquarters for booking 20 area guides, is Eagle Sports, 702 Wall Street, P.O. Box 367, Eagle River, WI 54521, telephone (715) 479-8804.

For a brochure on area resorts and other services, and detailed maps of all lakes on the chain, contact: Three Lakes Information Bureau, P.O. Box 268, Three Lakes, WI 54562, telephone (800) 972-6103. 367, Eagle River, WI 54521, telephone (715) 479-8804.

Lake Tomahawk

Between Minocqua and Village of Lake Tomahawk, Oneida County

There was not much breeze to bring relief on a steamy midsummer afternoon back in 1956, as Ray Kennedy and two clients began casting bucktails over yet another of the countless bars on Lake Tomahawk. They were after muskies, but a long, hot day of pounding the water had not produced so much as a follow. In those days, there were no electric trolling motors, so to keep showing his clients new water, a guide had to spend most of his time on the oars. As Kennedy recalls, it was about 4:30 when he suddenly saw a good musky swirl on the surface in pursuit of another fish.

At Kennedy's instruction, both clients cast toward the swirl, but one cast was way off the mark and the other landed in the middle of the widening ring, just behind the fish. Kennedy spotted the musky moving off just under the surface and tossed his bucktail out in front of it. The fish smashed it and the fight was on.

"I was so excited that I have no idea how long I fought that fish," Kennedy says. He does recall one image clearly: that of the huge musky rubbing its

snout on the bottom in an effort to rid itself of the hook. The hook held, though, and Kennedy eventually landed the fish. You can see it for yourself on the wall at Bosacki's in downtown Minocqua. That musky weighed 50 pounds and was the heaviest of eight fish over 40 pounds Kennedy has caught in a lifetime of fishing Lake Tomahawk. To his knowledge, it's the biggest anyone has taken there.

"Lake Tom," as some affectionately call it, is a large and enigmatic body of water located southeast of Minocqua and west of the village of Lake Tomahawk in northern Oneida County. The largest lake on the famed Minocqua Chain, Tomahawk covers 3,400 acres and plunges to depths of 80 feet in places. Its clear, fertile waters support a variety of forage species, including large populations of ciscoes and shiners, that in turn provide abundant food for gamefish.

The lake bottom rises and falls dramatically, creating the kind of deep structure walleye and musky fishermen dream about: gravel and rubble points, steep shoreline dropoffs, and midlake humps that jut up abruptly out of the depths to top out at 10 to 20 feet. You can see shallow bars and breaks in the clear water, but a good locator is essential to follow the deep structure. A summer thermocline restricts most fish species to the upper 25 feet of water, concentrating them around the humps and dropoffs.

Tomahawk is a tough lake to fish, but one well worth the effort, because it produces big muskies and walleyes, along with consistent smallmouth action. There are also good numbers of panfish, but they are sometimes hard to locate. This is not the kind of lake where you'd want to take a boatful of kids who expect to catch a mess of perch or bluegills. Tomahawk is big enough to get unfriendly in a hurry when the wind kicks up, but there are many bays and several connecting lakes you can duck into and keep fishing if the main lake basin is too rough. Forward motor trolling is not allowed.

Some musky spawning occurs in marshy areas and in the Tomahawk Thoroughfare at the northwest end of the lake, but DNR fish manager Ron Theis reports that 2,500 musky fingerlings are stocked here in alternate years to supplement natural reproduction. The lake's muskies are hit hard by major tournaments held practically every weekend throughout the sea-

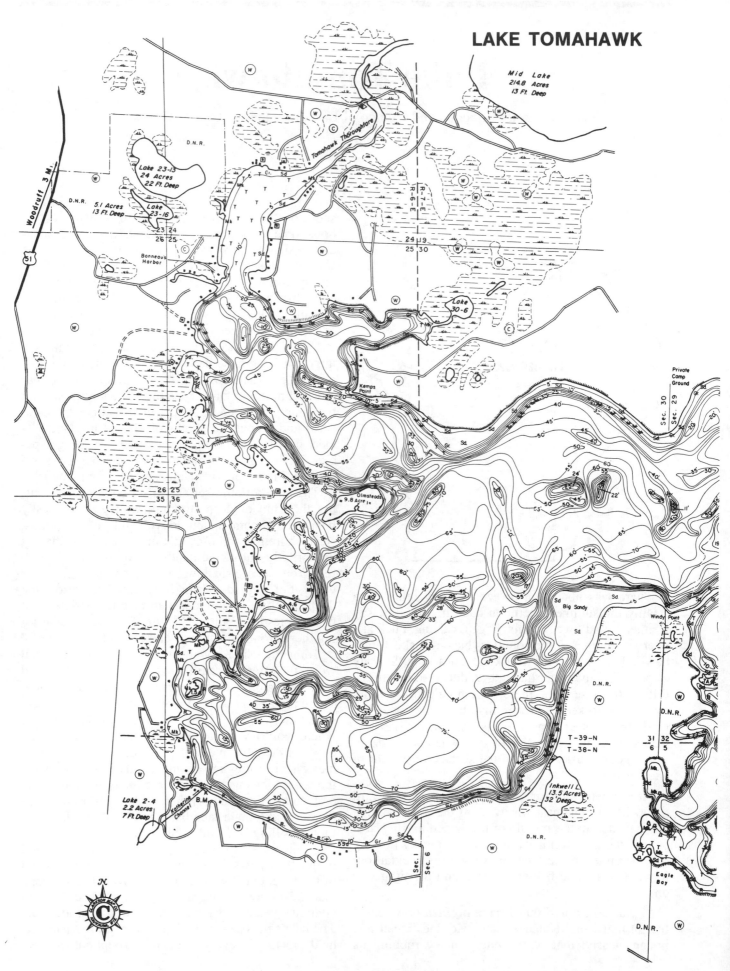

LAKE TOMAHAWK

TOPOGRAPHIC SYMBOLS

B	Brush	⦀⦀⦀⦀ Steep slope
PW	Partially wooded	⸺ Indefinite shoreline
W	Wooded	Marsh
C	Cleared	Spring
P	Pastured	Intermittent stream
A	Agricultural	Permanent inlet
B.M.	Bench Mark	Permanent outlet
▪	Dwelling	Dam
▣	Resort	D.N.R. State owned land
⊡	Camp	

LAKE BOTTOM SYMBOLS

P.	Peat	B	Boulders	
Mk.	Muck		Stumps & Snags	
C.	Clay		Rock danger to navigation	
M.	Marl		Submergent vegetation	
Sd.	Sand		Emergent vegetation	
St.	Silt		Floating vegetation	
Gr.	Gravel		Brush shelters	
R.	Rubble			
Bc.	Bedrock			

◆ Access　◆ Access with Parking　◆ Boat Livery

SPECIES OF FISH	Abundant	Common	Present
Muskie		X	
N. Pike		X	
Walleye	X		
L.M.Bass		X	
S.M.Bass			X
Panfish		X	
Trout			
Cisco			X

WATER AREA	3,392	ACRES
UNDER 3 FT.	4	%
OVER 20 FT.	70	%
MAX. DEPTH	84	FEET.
TOTAL ALK.	47	P.P.M.
VOLUME	111,958	ACRE FT.
SHORELINE	30.20	MILES
WITHOUT ISL.	27.33	MILES

son, with 200 or more boats working every conceivable bit of musky habitat for two or three days at time. Even though the tournaments stress catch and release, Kennedy contends they have an impact and says the lake's muskies don't come as easily as they used to.

Kennedy's advice for successful musky fishing here is straightforward: "Being out there and working your rear end off is the way to catch them," he says. Kennedy likes to work the edges of the many shallow bars and breaks, where larger fish hang out. He throws bucktails 75 percent of the time, and likes deep-running baits like the Mepps Lusox, although he also fishes jerk baits all year as well. Unlike many guides, Kennedy uses big baits and suckers right from opening day on. He argues that a big fish will take a big bait as readily as it will a small one.

In the summer months, musky fishing on the bars and reefs is better early and late in the day, says Kennedy. It is a safe bet that some big muskies suspend in summer to feed on schools of ciscoes, but it would take a sensitive locator capable of differentiating between large and small fish to find them. Deep-diving crankbaits might work under those conditions. In November, big muskies follow spawning ciscoes into the shallows, but food is so plentiful then that it is hard to interest them in artificials.

Lake Tomahawk produces big walleyes all season, from opening day right into the winter, with a number of fish in the 10- to 12-pound range, but Kennedy says the average size of those harvested has declined somewhat in the past ten years or so. There is little or no successful reproduction, so the DNR stocks around 100,000 fingerlings every-other year. A DNR walleye population estimate conducted in 1992 showed walleyes were more abundant than four years earlier, thanks, in part, to the 15-inch size limit. Bag limits have been reduced because of the Chippewa treaty-fishing quotas, but the walleyes are definitely worth a go.

In spring, you'll find walleyes along the shallow gravel shorelines and edges of weedbeds. Kennedy does well on spring walleyes using leeches and small minnows. Crankbaits like Shad Raps and any of those that rattle are also effective. The summer thermocline forces most walleyes to hang out on top of the deeper shoals and bars, where drifting or backtrolling with jigs and leeches or crawlers often accounts for some nice fish. When he marks suspended fish working schools of ciscoes in open water, Kennedy likes to drift through them with a jig and minnow or just a plain marabou jig.

Natural reproduction has sustained an excellent smallmouth fishery for years. Most are on the small side, but there are enough three- to four-pounders to make fishing for them interesting. Kennedy waits until late July or August, when smallies are active on the surface over bars in 15 to 20 feet of water to fish

for them. Look for them chasing lake shiners on top the way white bass do and toss a floating crankbait or small spinner, like a No. 0 Mepps, into the fray.

If you work closer to weedbeds, you'll also take perch on smallmouth baits. You can usually scrape up enough perch or bluegills for a shore lunch by dangling live bait along weedbed edges, but few anglers concentrate on either species. Perch have increased in size in recent years.

You won't catch many crappies here by accident, Kennedy warns, but serious crappie fisherman can usually come up with some. Try small minnows over shallow bars or in the mouths of bays. You might also look for suspended crappies in open water in summer. Ron Theis reports crappies provide fair to good action through the ice near the outlet and along the village of Lake Tomahawk shoreline.

A pair of nice smallmouth bass fell to the presentation of Chris Newbauer while fishing Lake Tomahawk. Photo courtesy Tom Newbauer

Three good public landings serve the lake: one at the Tomahawk Thoroughfare on Thoroughfare Road just south of Minocqua, another on the north shore at a state forest campground on Tomahawk Landing Road off Highway 47, and a third in the village of Lake Tomahawk at the east end of the lake. There is also a public campground in the village just south of the landing.

For bait and tackle, try BJ's Sportshop, 917 Highway 51 N., Minocqua, WI 54548, telephone (715) 356-3900. In summer, for bait, tackle and boat rentals, contact: Bosacki's Boat House, P.O. Box 1193, Minocqua, WI 54548, telephone (715) 356-5292. To book a guided fishing trip with Ray Kennedy, contact him at P.O. Box 64, Minocqua, WI 54548, telephone (715) 356-5734. Other area guides include: Russ Smith (maker of Smity Baits), P.O. Box 462, Minocqua, WI, 54548, telephone (715) 356-5565; and Terry Strutz, P.O. Box 1024, Woodruff, WI 54568, telephone (715) 356-7489.

For information on area resorts, restaurants, additional guide service and the many area attractions, contact: Greater Minocqua Chamber of Commerce, P.O. Box 1006, Minocqua, WI 54548, telephone (800) 44-NORTH, or call their 24-hour activities hotline, (800) 33-NORTH. You can also contact the Lake Tomahawk Information Bureau, Lake Tomahawk, WI 54539, telephone (715) 277-2602.

Turtle-Flambeau Flowage

Southwest of Mercer, Iron County

Turtle-Flambeau Flowage

John Olson and Jeff Wilson make climbing a 100-foot white pine look as easy as a stroll to the mailbox. And when they get to the top, they calmly saw it off and nail down a wood-and-wire-mesh platform the size of your dining-room table. It's all part of the winter wildlife management work of the DNR's Mercer office. Why? To provide nests for ospreys when they return to the North Country in spring.

The *Outdoor Wisconsin* crew and I joined Olson and Wilson one midwinter day a few years ago as they put up one of these nest platforms on the Turtle-Flambeau Flowage. We hiked a half-mile across the frozen lake to an island that had a suitable tree, set up our camera on the ice and taped the whole process from start to finish. Olson now works out of Park Falls as the DNR's treaty wildlife manager, but wildlife technician Wilson still keeps an eye on the flowage's osprey, loons and eagles, three species that find the fishing here good enough to call this place home during the open-water months.

The Turtle-Flambeau is one of the biggest and wildest pieces of flooded real estate in Wisconsin,

and you own it. That's right. In 1990, using Stewardship Fund money, the state bought it from the Chippewa-Flambeau Improvement Company for nine million bucks in a land deal similar to the one that acquired the Chippewa Flowage a few years earlier, assuring its preservation for wildlife habitat and recreation.

One strategically placed hydro dam built in 1926 backed up the Flambeau, Turtle and Manitowish rivers and connected nine natural lake basins to create this 14,000-acre flowage, with over 200 miles of shoreline and 150 islands. Big Island divides the two parts of the flowage: Turtle Flowage lies to the north and west, while Flambeau Flowage lies to the east and south. Navigable narrows connect these basins and the other former lakes, forming one large reservoir with depths of up to 55 feet. Much of the flowage is shallower than 10 feet. The water is stained brown and relatively fertile.

Vegetation is scarce and deep structure is limited, so fish use the river channels and stump fields extensively. The bottom varies from sand and gravel to rubble, boulders and bedrock. A summer thermocline develops at 10 or 15 feet in some of the deeper basins, but temperatures are uniform throughout most of the flowage. Because of the dark water and shallow structure, fishing can be quite productive right among the stumps, even in summer. These same stumps can make navigation hazardous: boaters who run a big motor wide open here are asking for trouble.

The DNR has stocked musky fingerlings here annually for years and the population is doing well. Currently, 2,500 muskies are stocked in the main flowage basins, along with an additional 1,500 in Trude Lake. When available, 2,500 more have been planted each year for the past several years. "This is trophy musky water," says fish manager Dennis Scholl. "Some fish in the 30-pound class turn up every year." The 40-inch size limit has helped boost the average size of muskies caught, but most anglers release them anyway.

Muskies are scattered throughout this large flowage. In spring, look for them in the inlet bays and in the shallower stump fields. On the Turtle Flowage, the Four Mile Creek inlet is worth trying, as is the shallow, weedy area on either side of the Trude Lake outlet. Any of the marshy shoreline areas will also produce. In the middle of the flowage, try the islands off Schenebeck's Point and in Baraboo Lake for muskies. There are some dropoffs and bars here that hold fish. Most anglers use dark bucktails, with jerk baits and shallow-running crankbaits running far behind in popularity.

Scholl reports that comprehensive gamefish populations estimate were conducted on the flowage in 1989 and 1992, followed by a creel census through the following winter seasons. The adult walleye population declined slightly in that period, but Scholl says the decline was insignificant. Most walleyes measure between 12 and 17 inches, but a few range to 29 inches. The 15-inch size limit applies on Trude Lake, but elsewhere on the flowage any walleye is legal.

Walleyes are not stocked here. Outstanding natural reproduction and slow growth rates are responsible for the abundance of smaller walleyes, according to Scholl. "The big ones are there," he says, "but small ones far outnumber them, so anglers shouldn't come here expecting to catch a trophy walleye."

Walleyes hit well in May, then slow down in summer and pick up again in September. In May, work the inlets and shallow bays. There is a refuge for 1,000 feet below the falls at the north end of the Turtle Flowage, but below here and in the Manitowish River channel on the Flambeau side, spring action can be fast and furious on jigs and minnows or floating crankbaits. Stick to the deeper channel and stay close to bottom. Trude Lake provides good walleye fishing after the run has ended in the river channels. Work the 10-foot breakline along the north shore or the humps on the southwest side of the lake.

The best summer walleye action occurs in the many stump fields and log jams, especially on overcast days. Much of this good woody cover is rotting away, but where you can find vertical wood, you'll find walleyes. Use a stiff rod and strong line to jig with crawlers and leeches between the logs. Drifting with a minnow along the old Turtle River channel in Bastine Lake above the dam and southeast of the dam along the shallow Beaver Flats can be productive in summer. Backtrolling with bait rigs and leeches should also produce well here. Ice fishing for walleyes is both popular and productive on the bars near Schenebeck's Point and on Beaver Flats.

After several years of good natural reproduction, smallmouth numbers are up and the average fish is bigger, too. Rocky shoreline areas offer fair smallmouth fishing, but few anglers try for them. Northerns here run small and are not worth fishing for. Fall

Guide Bud Wahl unhooks a nice walleye from the Turtle-Flambeau Flowage. Photo courtesy David Ford Hansen

perch fishing can be quite good, but you'll have to go deep to find them. Most are taken in the original lake basins in 20 to 30 feet of water. The cribs installed in Bastine Lake a few years ago ought to hold perch most of the year.

The flowage is also known for its large crappies. The most productive spots seem to be Blair Lake and the bars north of Schenebeck's Point, and fall is the best time to get them. You should be able to find crappies off the marshy shorelines in spring and summer as well, but you may have to hunt some to locate them.

There is a good public ramp on the Turtle Flowage at the county park on Highway FF just below the falls. On the Flambeau Flowage, the best landing is located on the north side at the end of Fisherman's Landing Road off Popkos Circle Road. The ramp here is made of a plastic honeycombed material called "Geoweb" that is buried in the sand and pro- vides stability for the fill material and traction for vehicles. The town of Springstead ramp, at the base of Schenebeck's Point on Flowage Road off Highway 182, is slated for replacement in 1993 with the aid of Dingell-Johnson funds. On Trude Lake, there is a new landing on the south shore on Chippewa Road. Several sand-beach landings provide access for smaller boats.

Bait, tackle and guide bookings are available at Angler's Choice, 3164 Highway 51, Mercer, WI 54547, telephone (715) 476-2526. Camping is per- mitted on some islands and at the county park at the north end of Turtle Flowage. For information on resorts and other area facilities, contact: Mercer Chamber of Commerce, P.O. Box 368, Mercer, WI 54547, telephone (715) 476-2389, or Turtle-Flam- beau Flowage Association, Route 2, Butternut, WI 54514, telephone (715) 476-2506.

North And South Twin Lakes

Phelps, Vilas County

North and South Twin Lakes

If you wanted to design a trophy musky lake, the first thing you might do is dig out an irregular basin, leaving a mix of gravel bars, shallow bays and rock ledges that drop suddenly out of sight into deep holes. Line one shore with bulrushes, scatter cabbage beds in all the bays, and put an osprey nest on a big island surrounded by a deep trench and broad, shallow bars, the kind where heart-stopping mama muskies like to roll on the surface at dusk.

Then just for fun, pinch your lake at the waist to make one long basin and a smaller one sheltered from strong north and west winds, with just enough depth at the narrows for a musky boat that will plane at full throttle to clear the sand. Give that smaller lake a deep shelf that follows one shore, a long bar that juts out from the narrows, and lots more cabbage and bulrushes. Fill both basins with water, sprinkle liberally with some prime musky forage: perch, walleyes, suckers and ciscoes; then add a vigorous, self-sustaining population of muskies and watch those puppies grow!

Now take the whole caboodle way, way up north

and drop it into the prettiest bunch of hills and woods you can find. Here and there along the shore, set down a small resort, a dockside tavern or two where a worn-out musky hunter can renew his flagging spirits for another go at it, and a village that caters to such craziness.

Sound too good to be true? Well, wake up, pal, and meet North Twin Lake, 2,800 acres of musky heaven right here on earth in northern Vilas County. North Twin and its smaller sister, 640-acre South Twin, are among Wisconsin's finest natural musky lakes. The village is Phelps, the structure is even more exciting than I've described it, and yes, a pair of ospreys nest on the island every year. To get there, take Highway 45 north out of Eagle River, then hang a right on Highway 17. Highway 17 follows the south shore of both South and North Twin, but you won't see the lakes until you get to Phelps.

These lakes attract many thousands of musky anglers and several tournaments each season, but they still produce more than their share of big fish. Twenty-pounders are fairly common, and several over 30 pounds are usually taken each year. Pay your dues to these lakes and perhaps you'll join the ranks of those who tell tales of red-finned giants that followed a bait to the boat or cruised by in tantalizing slow motion just out of reach.

The DNR stocks muskies every-other year to supplement natural reproduction. "We used to stock it every year," says fish manager Harland Carlson, "but we backed off because of the high density of smaller fish. There are a lot of 36-inchers sailing around in there, and we want to let 'em grow up."

While muskies are the major draw here, both lakes also produce big walleyes, perch and bass. I once took a three-pound smallmouth on a musky bait, and DNR survey nets have turned up several walleyes that, if caught by sport fishermen, would set a new state record.

North Twin is the kind of lake that makes musky fishing enjoyable, even for someone just getting into the sport, because the structure is so varied you're never bored. The rugged hills that surround the lake are echoed in the incredible bottom relief that will make you think your locator has gone mad. It will take some time to learn the many bars, reefs and sunken islands (Some aren't even on the lake map!), but the rewards can be worth the effort.

North Twin's musky action starts slowly in late spring, builds all summer, and peaks in fall when the fish pork up for winter. You'll need a variety of baits to fish the different depths and types of structure. Shorelines, shallow bars and submerged weedbeds call for bucktails, surface baits or shallow crankbaits. I fish North Twin every fall with a gang of musky nuts who do well with white, black or yellow bucktails, perch-scale Believers, silver Cranes and Grandmas, and black or yellow surface baits.

Deeper structure calls for diving crankbaits, such as Bagleys, Cisco Kids and DepthRaiders, and other baits that will reach suspended fish. Wildlife artist Scott Zoellick showed me how to fish North Twin's deep humps with Bagleys and the weirdest-looking blue spinnerbait with a half-pound white plastic grub tail. I stopped laughing when Zoellick hooked a fish that broke his rod and line and made off with his ugly bait. On that four-day trip, eight of us caught eleven muskies, nine of them legals, and we lost that many more to broken lines, net-paralysis and just plain dumb mistakes. We quit counting follows after day one, but they must have numbered in the dozens.

Zoellick has fished North Twin since high school, sometimes driving up from Milwaukee late at night with a friend to fish for walleyes until dawn, then spending the entire next day chasing muskies. Scott figures the real trophies here -- and he swears there are fish that will top 50 pounds -- have seen every conventional musky lure and presentation at least once, so he watches what other anglers are doing and then does the opposite. If boats are pounding the weed edges from deep water, Scott works them from the shore side. Where most people throw bucktails or Hawg Wobblers, he digs out goofy plastic depth charges and nameless old wooden baits that limp along the surface and draw strikes while other lures draw follows.

Top musky spots along North Twin's south shore include the Hospital Bar, just out from the Northwoods Hospital in Phelps, and west of there, the Holiday Bar, a broad flat bar that runs out in front of Holiday Lodge before plummeting into deep water. I was fishing this area with Bob VanderVenter, inventor of the Bobbie Bait, a couple years back when he raised a musky he thought might go 40 pounds. That fish made a pass at Bob's Bobbie, the second or third in as many days, but she refused to hit it.

Continuing west, a long bar covered with bulrushes runs far out into the lake. The lake's deepest point is off the tip of this bar, but the extensive cabbage beds in the notch on its north side and all along its south side hold muskies. Fishing along these bulrushes one September afternoon, I raised one fool

musky on seven consecutive casts with a yellow Mudpuppy. Later that evening, I caught and released a 38-incher in the same area on the same bait.

Between this bar and the island lies a shallow bar known as the Rock Pile. This structure, marked with a white float to warn boaters, comes up to a depth of just a foot or two in the center, but it runs about six to ten feet deep elsewhere. In the evening, muskies often roll here and on the larger bar northwest of the island. It was on the Rock Pile one September evening that I landed my first musky on a fly rod. Fishermen in other boats had been gawking at me all weekend, but when that fish jumped with my Dahlberg Diver in its mouth, three boatfuls of guys cheered. Dan Olson netted the fish for me, then snapped a couple photos before I put it back. I think he got as big a kick out of the whole thing as I did.

Rick Koschnik shows off a 30-pound musky from North Twin Lake. The Vilas County lake has some of the best musky structure of any lake. Photo by Dan Small

On the north shore, a broad, flat bar juts out into the lake across from the Phelps landing. A tall white flagpole on the north shore marks this bar. Muskies sometimes move up onto this shelf, but bigger fish

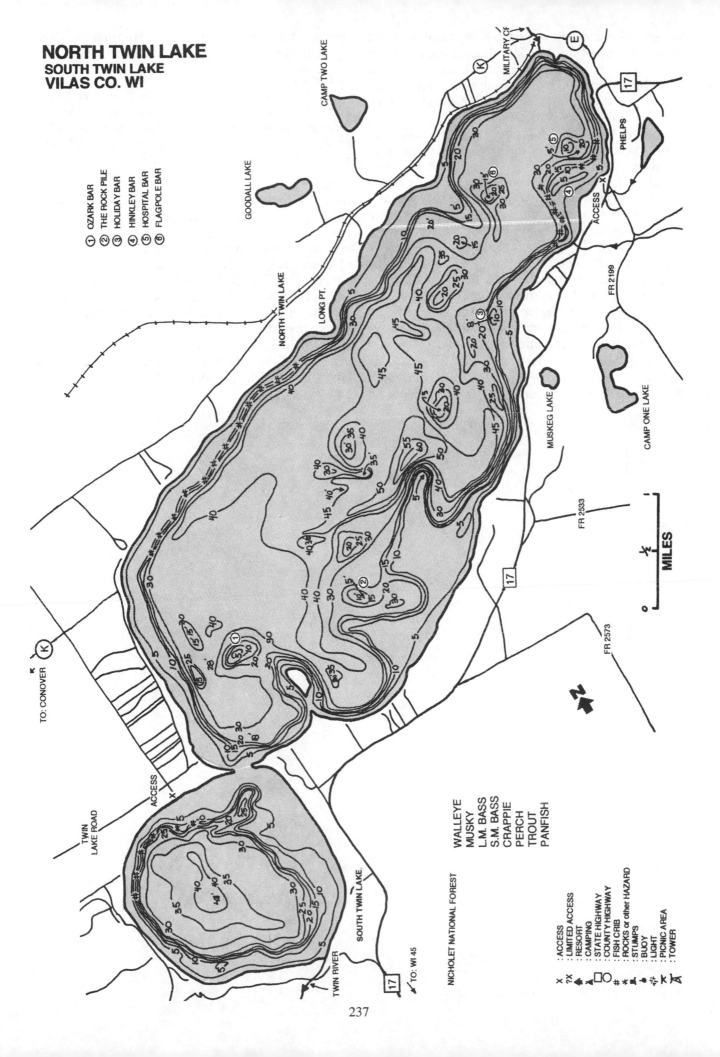

NORTH TWIN LAKE
SOUTH TWIN LAKE
VILAS CO. WI

① OZARK BAR
② THE ROCK PILE
③ HOLIDAY BAR
④ HINKLEY BAR
⑤ HOSPITAL BAR
⑥ FLAGPOLE BAR

NORTH TWIN LAKE

LONG PT.

GOODALL LAKE

CAMP TWO LAKE

MILITARY CR

PHELPS

MUSKEG LAKE

CAMP ONE LAKE

FR 2199

FR 2533

FR 2573

TO: CONOVER

TWIN LAKE ROAD

ACCESS

TWIN RIVER

SOUTH TWIN LAKE

TO: WI 45

MILES

N

WALLEYE
MUSKY
L.M. BASS
S.M. BASS
CRAPPIE
PERCH
TROUT
PANFISH

NICHOLET NATIONAL FOREST

X : ACCESS
?X : LIMITED ACCESS
▲ : RESORT
⌂ : CAMPING
□○ : STATE HIGHWAY
: COUNTY HIGHWAY
* : FISH CRIB
▲ : ROCKS or other HAZARD
♦ : STUMPS
✤ : BUOY
⚓ : LIGHT
⅄ : PICNIC AREA
⅄ : TOWER

suspend near the series of deep humps both east and west of the tip of this bar, just about in the middle of this end of the lake. Scott Zoellick and I watched Tom Bailey of Green Bay land and release a 40-incher here the day after Scott had released a similar fish he estimated went 20 pounds.

For muskies on South Twin, work the long bulrush-covered bar south of the narrows, the east shore between the dam and the narrows, and the deep weedline that parallels the north shore. Diving crankbaits can be especially effective on this last stretch.

A 1991 survey showed walleye density at about two or three adults per acre. Good spring walleye spots on North Twin include the north shore west of the old factory dock pilings and the humps off the flagpole. Later in summer, work the dropoffs along the bulrushes on the south shore, the deeper portions of the Island Bar or the deep cabbage beds in South Twin. Feed 'em minnows early, leeches later, or scented tails and swimming jigs anytime.

You'll find perch most anywhere there is rock structure, including the deeper edges of all the musky bars. Small jigs and minnows should produce in spring, while crawlers and plastic grubs on the same jigs will take a mess of perch in summer.

There are two public landings off Highway K, one on the northwest end of North Twin, the other on the north shore of South Twin. Another landing serves the east end of North Twin, just as you enter Phelps on Highway 17. To reach this one, turn left just before the Mobil Station and follow the signs.

Eagle Sports, 702 Wall Street, P.O. Box 367, Eagle River, WI, 54521, telephone (715) 479-8804, is headquarters for bait, tackle and guides for North and South Twin, as well as other area lakes. For information on resorts in the area, contact: Phelps Chamber of Commerce, P.O. Box 78, Phelps, WI 54554, telephone (715) 545-3800. Holiday Lodge Resort on North Twin is a traditional musky hunters' hangout, and the Friday night fish fry is a real winner when you've been on the water all day. Owner Jerry Sobiek knows the lakes as well as anyone, and he has more than a few fish on the wall to prove it. Address: 2618 Highway 17, Phelps, WI 54554, telephone (715) 545-2515.

Lake Winnebago

Winnebago, Calumet and Fond Du Lac Counties

Covering 137,700 acres, Lake Winnebago is by far Wisconsin's largest inland lake. The cities of Appleton, Neenah, Menasha, Oshkosh and Fond du Lac, along with many smaller communities, line its shores, but once you're out on this sprawling lake, civilization seems far away. Winnebago is relatively shallow -- 21 feet deep at its deepest -- and its water is often murky, but this fertile lake probably holds more walleyes than any other lake in the state. Saugers, perch, white bass, crappies, northerns, smallmouths and an occasional musky complete the sportfishing picture, and a large lake sturgeon population offers a unique spear fishery that draws thousands of participants each winter.

The Fox River enters Lake Winnebago at Oshkosh and exits between Neenah and Menasha on its way to Green Bay. Many smaller tributaries also feed the lake. The bottom is mostly muck and sand, but there are extensive rock reefs and gravel bars along the west shore. The shallow bays along the west shore contain most of Winnebago's sparse vegetation. A heavy algae bloom in late summer often makes fishing difficult, but there is adequate oxygen the year around to support a large and varied fish population.

A lake as broad and shallow as Winnebago can get rough in a hurry if the wind picks up. A 16-foot deep-V boat is as small a rig as you should consider if you venture far from any landing. While taping an *Outdoor Wisconsin* segment with tournament pro Keith Kavajecz a couple years ago, we kept one eye on a thunderstorm to our north while we desperately tried to roll enough tape for a show. When the lightning got too close for comfort, Keith and I ran for the landing and watched our young camera boat pilot Nate Kalkofen pick his way neatly through the waves to spare our camera and crew from too brutal a beating.

Fishing season never closes on Winnebago and motor trolling is legal, yet the lake's sheer size intimidates many anglers and often makes locating fish frustrating. The biggest mistake most people make is trying to fish too large an area. To do well here, it helps to have a game plan. Know what you're after and concentrate on one portion of the lake until you

connect. Progressively, you will decipher Winnebago's code and learn where to consistently take its most popular species.

The drought years hurt walleye reproduction on the Wolf River where most of Winnebago's walleyes spawn, but excellent hatches in the past several years have produced an abundant crop of walleyes that now range from 15 to 18 inches. DNR area fisheries supervisor Ron Bruch expects these fish to feed heavily on trout perch and shiners along the rocky reefs on the lake's west shore, bringing back the traditional reef fishery that practically dried up over the past few years. There is still a good population of older walleyes that hang out in deep water and along shallow shorelines.

Winnebago's walleyes were tough to catch for several years, thanks to an abundant gizzard shad population that provided easy meals and kept them fat and happy. According to Ron Bruch, shad numbers have dropped dramatically, so walleyes should be hungry and easier to catch now.

Lake Winnebago

Open-water walleye fishing begins in earnest when the walleyes drift back to the lake from their spawning run up the Fox and Wolf rivers. On the rocky west shore, troll diving crankbaits back and forth across the numerous reefs there. Look for places where the rock comes up out of 10 to 15 feet of water and try to drag bottom with perch-imitation baits. Even with a map, you'll need a good locator to find and stay on these reefs, as they are often isolated by many acres of unproductive water.

Along the east shore, structure is almost non-existent, but trolling can produce walleyes here as well. The trick is to cover enough water until you start marking or catching fish, then toss out a marker buoy and work that school until it moves on. If you run into sheepshead, the same area should hold walleye and sauger. The northeast shoreline between Calumet County Park Harbor and High Cliff State Park is a major sauger spawning area and good catches of saugers running up to five pounds are taken here.

Pro anglers fishing the many walleye tournaments of the last decade popularized several newer techniques that have begun to produce good catches of larger walleyes. Some, like Gary Roach and Randy Amenrud, work jigs and leeches on slip-bobbers over rock piles and reefs to coax strikes from walleyes that ignore fast-moving crankbaits. This trick works especially well when waves are pounding the reefs, making it difficult to stay in touch with the bottom with conventional methods.

Mike McClelland, the all-time top money-winner among walleye pros, theorizes that there are at least two distinct walleye populations in Winnebago -- those that inhabit the deepwater reefs and mud flats, and those that remain in very shallow water all year. McClelland takes big walleyes from rocky shorelines and shallow gravel bars with ultralight tackle, tiny jigs and leeches. McClelland fishes this rig much the same way a bass angler would fish a Texas-rigged plastic worm -- hopping it slowly along the bottom. Most of Mike's hotspots aren't even on the lake maps. He finds them by watching for rocks on shore and by keeping an eye on his locator as he moves from spot to spot. Heavy moss growth makes this presentation unproductive in summer, even though the fish are still in the shallows.

Several other pros, most notably Gary Parsons and Bob Zimmerman, have found a mother lode of big walleyes in the deep water mud flat areas. When I fished with Zimmerman and marina operator Doug Wendt to tape an *Outdoor Wisconsin* segment in June a couple years ago, Zimmerman had already caught and released over 300 walleyes topping three pounds that year. Big walleyes lie right on the mud bottom when inactive and suspend when feeding on schools of young perch and white bass. Zimmerman trolls deep-diving crankbaits, some on bottom-dragging wire line and some suspended off trolling skis. The

wire-line rigs kick up a cloud of mud and trigger strikes from inactive fish, while the suspended lures catch feeding walleyes.

Most smallmouths, northerns and muskies taken are caught by accident, but a few anglers fish for them on purpose. The reefs south of Neenah are good for smallmouths. Try any of the bays near Oshkosh or in the Point Comfort area along the west shore for pike. Mike McClelland and I caught several pike in the eight- to 10-pound class there while walleye fishing with jigs and crankbaits, and McClelland once tussled with and lost a big musky that grabbed a sheepshead he had hooked.

Mike McClelland, all-time money winner in walleye tournaments, lands a nice walleye from Lake Winnebago. The fish fell for Mike's favorite technique in Winnebago -- ultralight line, a tiny jig and leech, fished near a rocky shoreline. Photo by Dan Small

In summer, most anglers turn to panfish. Live bait, such as crawlers and helgrammites, will take good catches of perch running 12 to 14 inches along the deeper edges of reefs, but you may have to move around to locate a school. White bass, on the other hand, often feed near the surface where they can be seen slashing at baitfish. Approach an active school quietly and you can have a ball catching fish after fish on light tackle. A small floating crankbait or Mepps spinner will do the trick. The southern end of the lake and the mouths of bays along the west shore produce some nice catches of crappies on small minnows, jigs and spinners.

Winnebago is also a popular ice fishing lake. Schools of walleyes and saugers move along the east shore in winter. Try for them near shore just after ice-up and in deeper water in midwinter.

Each February, thousands of shanties form temporary villages as spear fishermen sit patiently beside chainsawed holes the size of a refrigerator, hoping they will beat the odds and luck into a sturgeon. When the water is clear, spearing success runs higher, but for most spearbearers, it's a long, cold, uneventful wait. Fully equipped spearing shanties are available for rent all around the lake.

We have taped two sturgeon spearing segments for *Outdoor Wisconsin*. The first time, a blizzard overtook us out on the ice, so Mike Wendt plowed snow all the way back and we spent the day at Wendt's Tavern eating homemade chili. Next time out, Larry Bandy and I joined Jim Gantner of the Brewers for an exciting afternoon of watching the lake bottom through a coffin-sized hole in the ice. We struck out and ended the segment with Gantner grinning imp-ishly from his shanty and telling us to "have a nice walk back to shore," while we walked 10 yards to the van you couldn't see on your screen.

There are excellent launch sites every few miles around the lake. Two of the largest are located in Fond du Lac, one at Lakeside Park off Oregon Street and the other off Litscher Memorial Drive. On the west shore, the private ramp at Wendt's Bar and Marina on Highway 45 at County Line Road and the public launch at Black Wolf Point County Park provide access to some of the better walleye reefs. On the northwest shore, there are several good ramps in Oshkosh, Neenah and Menasha, and on the northeast shore, a large ramp and marina complex at High Cliff State Park. A few miles farther south, the launch at Calumet County Park has a protected harbor and a new handicapped-accessible pier.

Services of all sorts are available in the cities adjacent to the lake, and there are numerous bait shops around the lakeshore. For boat gas or motor service, try Wendt's Marine on the west shore, telephone (414) 688-2601. For a complete list of area services and seasonal events, contact: Fond du Lac Convention and Visitors Bureau, 19 W. Scott Street, Fond du Lac, WI 54935, telephone (800) 937-9123.

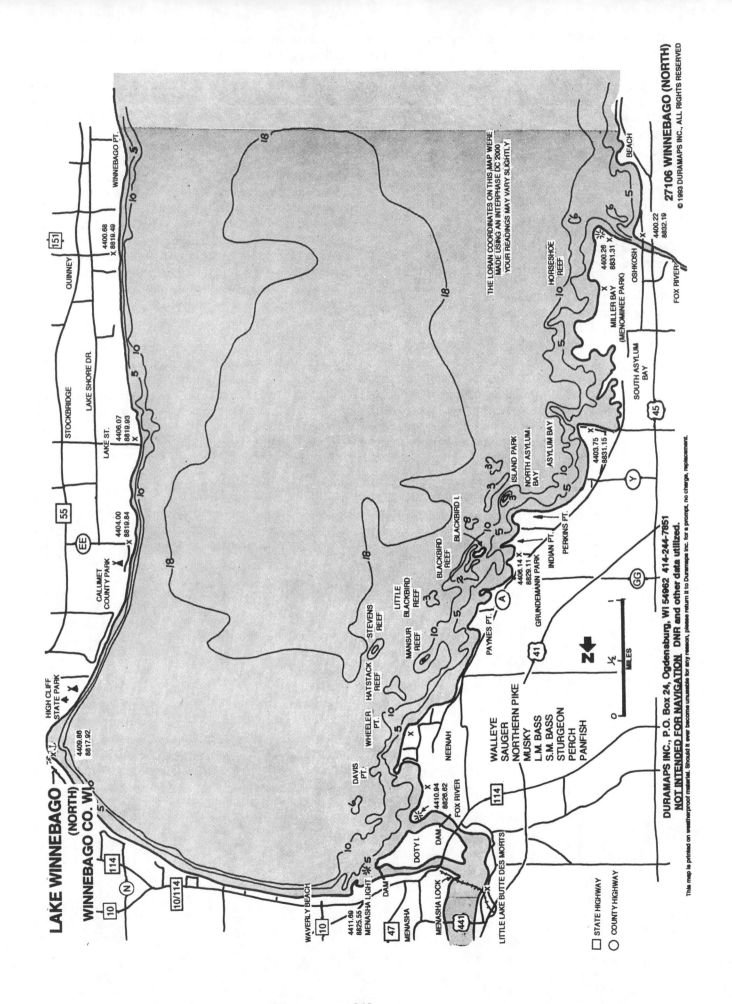

LAKE WINNEBAGO
(NORTH)
WINNEBAGO CO. WI

27106 WINNEBAGO (NORTH)
© 1993 DURAMAPS INC., ALL RIGHTS RESERVED

THE LORAN COORDINATES ON THIS MAP WERE
MADE USING AN INTERPHASE DC 2000
YOUR READINGS MAY VARY SLIGHTLY

DURAMAPS INC., P.O. Box 24, Ogdensburg, WI 54962 414-244-7851
NOT INTENDED FOR NAVIGATION DNR and other data utilized.

This map is printed on weatherproof material. Should it ever become unusable for any reason, please return it to Duramaps Inc. for a prompt, no charge, replacement.

☐ STATE HIGHWAY
◯ COUNTY HIGHWAY

WALLEYE
SAUGER
NORTHERN PIKE
MUSKY
L.M. BASS
S.M. BASS
STURGEON
PERCH
PANFISH

242

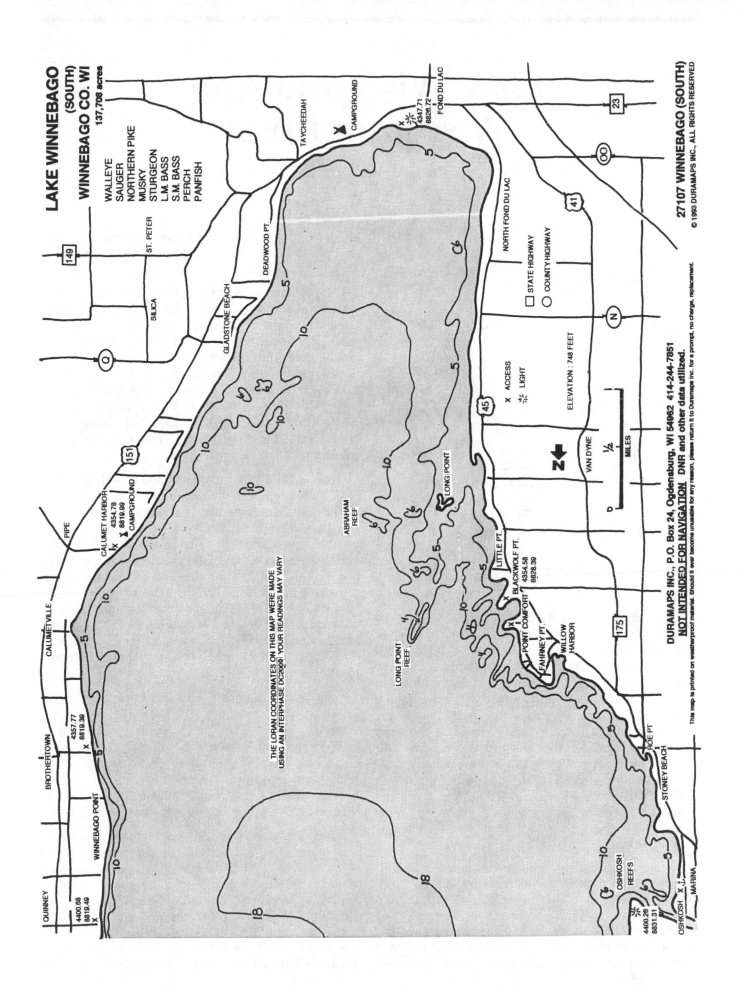

LAKE WINNEBAGO
(SOUTH)
WINNEBAGO CO. WI
137,708 acres

WALLEYE
SAUGER
NORTHERN PIKE
MUSKY
STURGEON
L.M. BASS
S.M. BASS
PERCH
PANFISH

27107 WINNEBAGO (SOUTH)

DURAMAPS INC., P.O. Box 24, Ogdensburg, WI 54962 414-244-7851
NOT INTENDED FOR NAVIGATION DNR and other data utilized.

This map is printed on weatherproof material. Should it ever become unusable for any reason, please return it to Duramaps Inc. for a prompt, no charge, replacement.

THE LORAN COORDINATES ON THIS MAP WERE MADE
USING AN INTERPHASE DC2000! YOUR READINGS MAY VARY

STATE HIGHWAY
COUNTY HIGHWAY

ELEVATION : 748 FEET

X ACCESS
LIGHT

MILES
½

N

QUINNEY
BROTHERTOWN
WINNEBAGO POINT
CALUMETVILLE
PIPE
CALUMET HARBOR
CAMPGROUND
ST. PETER
SILICA
GLADSTONE BEACH
DEADWOOD PT.
TAYCHEEDAH
CAMPGROUND
FOND DU LAC
NORTH FOND DU LAC
VAN DYNE
ROE PT
STONEY BEACH
MARINA
OSHKOSH X I.
OSHKOSH REEFS
WILLOW HARBOR
FAHRNEY PT.
POINT COMFORT
BLACKWOLF PT.
LITTLE PT.
LONG POINT
LONG POINT REEF
ABRAHAM REEF

4400.68
8819.49
4357.77
8819.39
4354.78
8819.99
4347.71
8828.72
4354.58
8828.39
4400.26
8831.31

149
151
Q
N
23
8
41
45
175

243

Lake Wisconsin And Wisconsin River

Wisconsin Dells Dam to Prairie du Sac Dam, Sauk and Columbia Counties

Lake Wisconsin

On the Wisconsin River one chilly April day a couple years ago, Scott Hill and I caught and released a bunch of walleyes ranging from three to almost 10 pounds. While most anglers were plumbing the deep holes just below the Dells Dam, we launched his boat at River's Edge Resort and worked our way carefully downstream. It's easy to lose a lower unit on the rocks here, but Hill knows the river like I know my driveway. Working the slow, shallow water, we picked up those walleyes and a three-pound smallmouth on the Slo-Poke jig Hill designed. Tipped with plastic tails, the Slo-Poke crawled through brush and over rocks without snagging, letting us make a slow presentation that drew strikes from both feeding and resting fish.

I taped an *Outdoor Wisconsin* segment with Hill several miles farther downstream on another April outing two years earlier. That day we caught and released four walleyes in the seven- to nine-pound class and a sauger that had to be pushing the state record. All were females and all came from a current break below a point, where they were resting in brush and logs prior to completing their spawning run. We took those fish on jigs and plastic grub tails while wading the shallows.

On yet another April *Outdoor Wisconsin* shoot, Tom Newbauer and I joined the late Hal Walker on Lake Wisconsin for an early-season bass fishing segment. We launched in Okee Bay and motored out around Pine Bluff, then into Sticky Bay and up into the Harmony Grove boat channels, dredged out by developers to give every home access to the waterfront. This early in the year, the main body of the lake still runs cold, but back bays and shallow side channels like these warm up more quickly, and that's where you'll find bass.

Tom and Hal fished the piers and shoreline structure, while I followed them with our crew in the camera boat, maneuvering close enough so we could get the shots we needed, yet trying to stay out of their way so they could fish. The bass had been hitting over the weekend, but cloud cover kept the weather cool on this Monday morning and Tom and Hal had to work hard for fish. They caught enough to show how it's done, and Hal talked about the early days of TV outdoor shows when everything was shot on film and narrated afterward in a studio, rather than produced on tape in the field as most programs are done today.

The Wisconsin Power and Light Company dam at Prairie du Sac created this 9,000-acre flowage on the Wisconsin River. The stretch below the Merrimac railroad bridge is known as Southern Lake Wisconsin, while Lake Wisconsin proper runs from that bridge upstream to the I-90/94 bridge, but the entire flowage from the Prairie du Sac Dam upstream to the Wisconsin Dells Dam can be considered one fishery.

Lake Wisconsin's fertile water is stained brown and often murky, especially in summer when an algae bloom develops. The deepest spots are just above the Prairie du Sac Dam and in the river channel below Merrimac, where depths of 30 to 40 feet are found. Above Merrimac, the lake is quite shallow with vast areas under 15 feet. Vegetation is very sparse except in some bays and in spring-fed Whalen's Grade Bay where Highway V crosses the easternmost lobe of the lake. The lake bottom is mainly sand and muck but there are areas of rock and gravel.

Natural structure consists of steep shoreline dropoffs, several reefs and underwater points, shallow stump fields and the river channel breaks. To supplement this, the DNR has placed over 300 fish cribs at 17 sites around the lake, paid for with Dingell-Johnson funds. Made of wooden pallets and weighted with concrete blocks, the cribs are readily visible on sonar units and all are marked on a map available from the DNR or the Lake Wisconsin Chamber of Commerce.

Scott Hill, designer of the Slo-Poke jig, eases a 10-pound walleye back into the Wisconsin River. Photo by Dan Small

Gizzard shad, shiners and minnows make up most of the forage base. The fishery is extremely diverse, ranging from walleyes and saugers to bass, crappies, bluegills, white bass, pike, muskies, catfish and sturgeon.

According to DNR fish manager Tim Larson, walleyes and saugers are abundant and fast-growing here. Natural reproduction is excellent, so no stocking is required. Not all walleyes run up the river in April to spawn. Some remain in the lake and spawn along rocky shorelines. You can take them there in April and May on jigs and minnows. Later in spring and summer, trolling crankbaits is productive, especially along dropoffs and in the river channel.

By using side planers, you can troll a variety of crankbaits at different depths all at once. Put the shallowest-running baits, like Ripplin' Red Fins and floating Rapalas on your inshore boards, and put a deeper-running bait on each successive board until you have covered the entire range of depths. Mike McClelland's book, *Crankbaits*, includes comprehensive charts showing the depths reached by over 200 crankbaits now on the market. Line diameter and trolling speed will affect a crankbait's depth, so you may want to use Wille's new Bait Data device to determine exactly how deep your baits are running.

Anglers take walleyes all year, but the highest catch rate occurs in November, when shoreline fishing with shallow crankbaits or minnows produces best.

Largemouths attract more attention here every year, and there are plenty of them in the shallow bays and stump fields. Tim Larson reports the 14-inch size limit has boosted the number of smaller bass and improved fishing considerably.

Hybrid muskies have been stocked here at the rate of about 2,000 per year since the late 1970s, but few people try for them. The bars off most of the bay mouths in Southern Lake Wisconsin should hold muskies, as should the stump fields in both halves of the lake. Try dark bucktails, spinnerbaits and shallow crankbaits. You'll also take northerns in the same areas and on the same baits. Northerns are legal all year, but musky season opens the first Saturday in May, so be sure you can distinguish between a big northern and a small hybrid musky before you keep either.

White bass run upriver when the lilacs bloom, according to Larson. Their numbers are down somewhat in recent years, but anglers still take good catches on small spinnerbaits, spinners and crankbaits near the power-plant discharge upstream from the I-bridge in May, where they come to spawn and feed on shad. In summer, trollers take them on walleye baits in the open lake.

Crappies run 10 to 14 inches here and are very abundant. The cribs concentrate them, but you can also find them in the Harmony Grove channels, in Moon Valley Bay on the west shore of Southern Lake Wisconsin, and on both sides of the causeway at Whalen's Grade. Little swimming jigs, spinners and minnows are all productive.

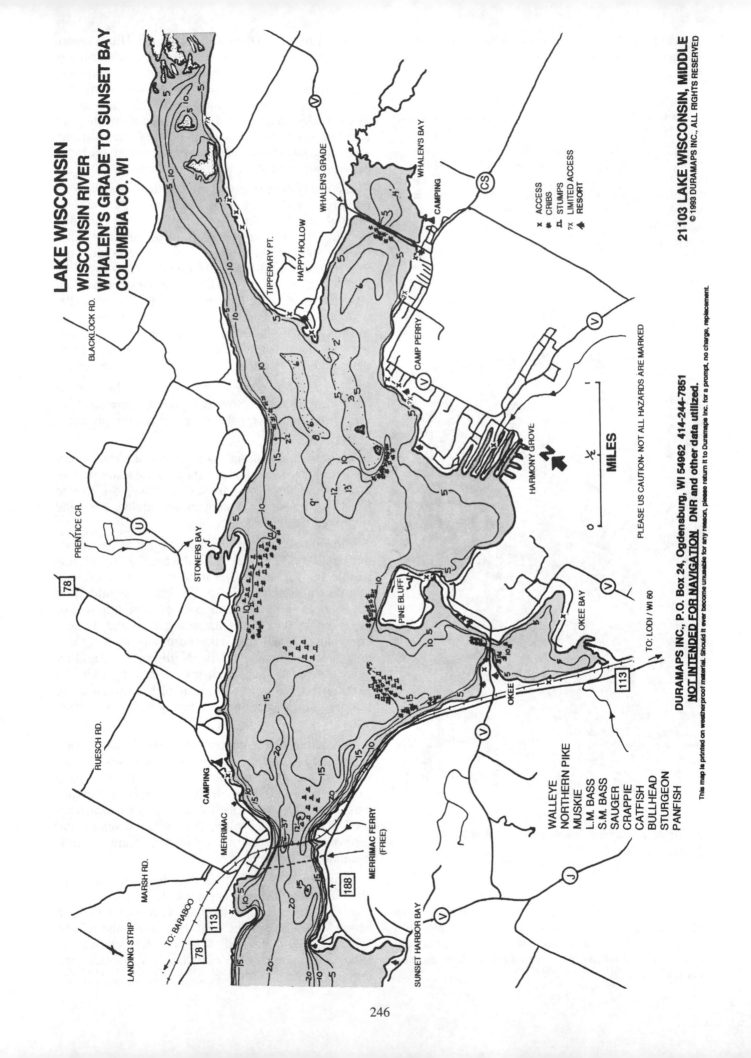

LAKE WISCONSIN
WISCONSIN RIVER
WHALEN'S GRADE TO SUNSET BAY
COLUMBIA CO. WI

MILES

PLEASE US CAUTION- NOT ALL HAZARDS ARE MARKED

ACCESS
CRIBS
STUMPS
LIMITED ACCESS
RESORT

21103 LAKE WISCONSIN, MIDDLE
© 1993 DURAMAPS INC., ALL RIGHTS RESERVED

WALLEYE
NORTHERN PIKE
MUSKIE
L.M. BASS
S.M. BASS
SAUGER
CRAPPIE
CATFISH
BULLHEAD
STURGEON
PANFISH

DURAMAPS INC., P.O. Box 24, Ogdensburg, WI 54962 414-244-7851
NOT INTENDED FOR NAVIGATION. DNR and other data utilized.

This map is printed on weatherproof material. Should it ever become unusable for any reason, please return it to Duramaps Inc. for a prompt, no charge, replacement.

246

Whalen's Grade, or simply "The Grade," is a hotspot for spawning bluegills in May. Okee Bay also once held good numbers of bluegills, but there are fewer there now than in past years because of a complex chain of events. Commercial fishing for carp has ceased, due to a depressed market for rough fish, and the abundant carp have rooted up much of the vegetation in the bay. With less vegetation, bluegills don't concentrate here the way they used to. Ice fishing for bluegills is quite productive at The Grade and at Harmony Grove.

Lake Wisconsin is one of the few lakes in the U.S. with a good sturgeon population, but Larson says the annual harvest has declined and angling pressure may be hurting them. He plans to initiate a study in the fall of 1993 to try to get a handle on sturgeon reproduction.

West of the Merrimac bridge, there are public landings on the west bank off Highway 78 at a Sauk County park and at Moon Valley Bay, and one on the east bank off Highway 188 on Harmon Road. On Lake Wisconsin proper, there are landings on the east bank at Okee Bay, Whalen's Grade and two off Tipperary Road. Most of these landings have been improved in recent years, and others are slated for improvement soon. Some have wheelchair-accessible piers. There are other, smaller town landings on both shores.

There are several bait shops on the lake. The most central is Bear's Bait & Tackle, W11579 Highway V, Okee, WI 53555, telephone (608) 592-4806. For bait, tackle, food, lodging and boat launch upriver, contact: River's Edge Resort, S1196 Highway A, Wisconsin Dells, WI 53965, telephone (608) 254-7707.

For a map and brochure on area services and a copy of the DNR's fish crib map, contact: Lake Wisconsin Chamber of Commerce, P.O. Box 262, Lodi, WI 53555, telephone (608) 592-4880.

LAKE WISCONSIN
WISCONSIN RIVER
SUNSET BAY TO PRAIRIE DU SAC
COLUMBIA CO. WI

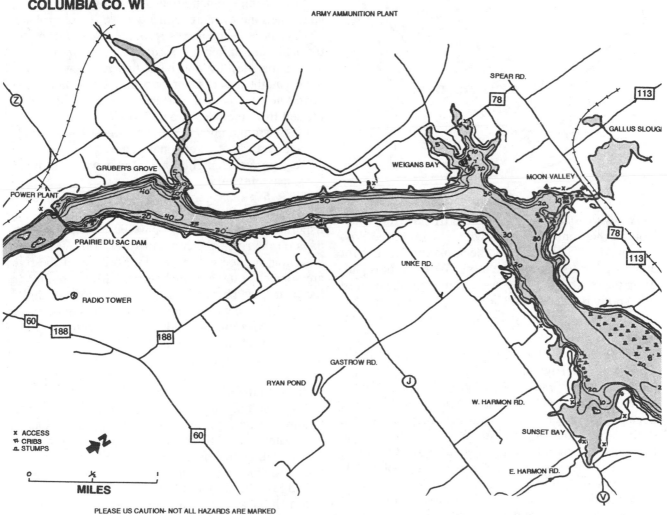

Lower Wisconsin River

Prairie du Sac, Sauk County, to Prairie du Chien, Crawford County

Lower Wisconsin River

A few years ago, I joined some friends from Madison on their annual float down a stretch of the Wisconsin River. This gang had been making the trip for at least 10 years and maybe more. We took turns paddling the two canoes that carried our freight, but most everybody rode one of those fat truck-tire inner tubes that have put places like the Apple River on the summer recreation map.

We tied most of the tubes together, "launched" our fleet below the Highway 23 bridge at Spring Green in the shadow of Frank Lloyd Wright's Spring Green Restaurant, and wallowed downstream a few miles. Breaking for lunch on an island sand bar, we watched flotillas of canoes drift by. We explored a couple side channels, but mainly went with the flow. One thing that struck me was the number and variety of people who, in their own way, were doing the same thing: an angler tending bank poles in a deep bend hole, families picnicking on sand bars near the Spring Green Bridge, and the unending parade of canoes -- "tin maggots," as one acquaintance calls them.

Multiple-use recreation is in full bloom on the Lower Wisconsin River. Rampant, some would argue, even abusive at times. One small, noisy bunch of day trippers might not constitute abuse, but 20 or 30 such groups on one stretch of river on the same day certainly make it tough to do anything else but join the party. DNR boat counters have logged as many as 450 canoes per hour passing the Mazomanie landing. That's probably too many, but maybe our lone fleet of donuts was one too many for the catfisherman who remembered a quieter time.

I didn't think much about it that day, but in retrospect the kind of recreation I was enjoying probably altered more of the river's resources than did the traditional "consumptive" forms of recreation, represented that day by one bank fisherman who might have caught a catfish or two that we would never have known was there and that would not have been missed from the overall population. I'm not trying to confess wrongdoings here, nor paint a bleak picture of river use, but recreational patterns on the Lower Wisconsin are changing, as anyone who has fished there can tell you.

DNR fish manager Gene Van Dyck says one-trip casual users are slowly replacing the traditional local fisherman who might in the past have spent dozens of days on the river and come to know it in ways those who float it once will never do. Portions of the river are subject to intense use at times. Most notable are the boat jams below the Prairie du Sac Dam during the spring walleye run and the constant canoe traffic between Mazomanie and Spring Green on warm summer weekends. The Lower Wisconsin is not a river you can expect to fish in solitude, but at times and in certain places, it offers fishing opportunities well worth the effort required to enjoy them.

"At best, only about 10 percent of the river is fish-holding water," Gene Van Dyck explains. During low-water years, that percentage drops somewhat, concentrating the fish, but also the fishermen. "It's tough to find a spot that somebody hasn't already fished just ahead of you," says Van Dyck. His advice is to fish on weekdays and to expect that you'll have plenty of competition on popular stretches.

Catfish, both flatheads and channel cats, make up the traditional fishery and they are still tops in terms of fish harvested, followed by smallmouths and walleyes. In terms of overall fishing pressure, though, more people probably fish for walleyes than any other species and most of that pressure occurs below the Prairie du Sac Dam in spring. Van Dyck says the makeup of the river's angling fraternity is gradually shifting away from locals after catfish to out-of-towners after bass and walleyes.

Rumors of commercial overharvest of catfish in the Mississippi near the mouth of the Wisconsin River have triggered several population studies since the 1960s, the most recent one a massive joint venture involving DNR management and research biologists who radio tagged cats and tracked their movements, monitored fishing pressure, and concluded the fishery is in good shape, with good growth rates and a low exploitation rate of perhaps 10 percent.

To catch cats, choose any deep hole and soak a crawler, stinkbait or live minnow on bottom. You'll catch more channel cats using a slip-sinker rig that keeps your bait down, yet does not alert fish. The bigger flatheads are most often taken on setlines or sturdy bank poles baited with large live minnows -- suckers, carp or even bullheads. These rigs are governed by special regulations and require permits that can be obtained at DNR or county clerk offices in counties along the river.

Smallmouths are found wherever there is good habitat for them: rocky shorelines, instream cover, rapids, and so on. They grow fast and fish under 14 inches are abundant, but anglers quickly crop them off once they reach legal size. Van Dyck says many serious anglers are releasing larger fish now. As a rule, bass will be scattered rather than schooled like walleyes. There is good rock structure between Sauk City and Mazomanie, and again along the Richland County shore. Some stretches are wadeable, but be sure to wear a life vest or use a float tube. Small crankbaits, Mepps spinners, spinnerbaits and jigs will take smallies on light spinning tackle, and fly fishermen can have fun in the evening with poppers, bass bugs and flies like the Dahlberg Diver.

Everybody wants to catch walleyes, it seems, and so everybody goes where they think all the walleyes go in spring -- up the river to the Prairie du Sac Dam. Van Dyck says there are good numbers of walleyes in the 17- to 20-inch range below the Prairie du Sac Dam all year long. He reports many anglers are also releasing legal walleyes to improve the fishery. A DNR team is still working on an intensive walleye population investigation to assess their current status and determine just what pressure anglers are putting on the resource.

There are plenty of saugers and some hybrid saugeyes in the river as well. As of this writing, there is no minimum size limit on saugers, but there has been talk of changing that, so check the current regulations booklet before you keep any fish under 15 inches that looks like a walleye or sauger. For law

enforcement purposes, a white tip on the lower lobe of its tail means a fish is a walleye, otherwise it's considered a sauger.

Since the river is open to year-round fishing, there is always someone at the dam, but most of the activity there occurs in March and April when the walleye spawning run is on. Boats jockey for position and anglers dunk jigs and minnows here, as they do below every other big river dam this time of year. Most have hopes of taking a trophy or two, but more realistically, says Van Dyck, they should expect to come away with a few scrawny saugers and maybe a legal walleye.

Scott Hill prepares to unhook a smallmouth bass caught from the Wisconsin River on a Slo-Poke jig. Photo by Dan Small

A better tactic might be to work the riffles and slower side-currents well downstream of the dam. The big mamas do run to the dam, but the males spend far more time there, while females lounge about in shallow water near brush and other cover for days before and after spawning. I can't prove it first-hand here, but I've seen it myself below the Dells Dam (the next one upstream), and there's no reason to believe the walleyes here should act any differently.

In summer, jigs or river rigs in the deeper downstream holes will take walleyes. Fish near the mouths of tributaries, especially after a thunderstorm in the hills. According to *Wisconsin Outdoor Journal* field editor Wendell Smith, of Muscoda, white bass have come on strong in recent years. You'll find them in the same areas frequented by walleyes -- deeper water between bars -- where small spinners and crankbaits will take them.

The backwater sloughs found all along the river are a whole different fishery that would require another chapter to cover adequately. Suffice it to say that in years following a high-water spring, fishing can be super for largemouths, northerns and bluegills. There are motor restrictions in some areas, so inquire locally before you go. There are also a few muskies in the lower river, although most are taken incidentally by walleye and bass anglers.

The Lower Wisconsin is a small-boat river. Smart boaters go with old, flat-bottomed 14-footers powered by 10- to 25-horse kickers. Channels change all the time, and water levels fluctuate, so it is wise to call ahead and plan a short trip rather than a week-long foray. Night boating is out of the question because of all the mid-river snags that can skewer you without warning.

Boat landings, many of them at public hunting grounds, are located about every seven miles along this 91-mile stretch, most of them on or near main highways or at bridge crossings. On the upper end, for bait, tackle and guide service contact: Ace Hardware, 500 Water Street, Sauk City, WI 53583, telephone (608) 643-2433. For information on lodging, canoe rentals, campgrounds and other services, contact: Sauk Prairie Chamber of Commerce, P.O. Box 7, Sauk City, WI 53583, telephone (608) 643-4168.

On the lower stretch, for bait and tackle, try: Ike's Sporting Goods, 802 N. Wisconsin Avenue, Muscoda, WI 53573, telephone (608) 739-3616; Dan's Bait Shop, 133 N. Wisconsin Avenue, Muscoda, WI 53573, telephone (608) 739-3864; or Quent's Bait & Tackle, 101 W. LeGrand, Boscobel, WI 53805, telephone (608) 375-5540. For lodging information, contact the Prairie du Chien Tourism Council, P.O. Box 326, Prairie du Chien, WI 53821, telephone (800) 732-1673; or UW-Extension Resource Office, P.O. Box 31, Lancaster, WI 53813, telephone (608) 723-2125.

Lake Wissota

Chippewa Falls, Chippewa County

A few years back, a DNR fisheries crew conducting a routine electroshocking survey on Lake Wissota rolled over a fish that stunned even these guys who sometimes see more big fish in one work day than most of us hope to see in a lifetime of angling. The fish was a musky of awesome proportions. It shook off the effects of the shocker and swam away before they could corral it, but they got a good enough look to estimate its length at six feet and its weight at over 80 pounds.

That's a good 10 pounds heavier than the world record. The DNR crew members were not the only ones stunned by this find. "Sturgeon!" insisted some disbelievers. "An overestimate!" said others. Still, that year and the next, musky hunters from all over the country found their way to Wissota to heave big baits and hope for a miracle. No one reported seeing a fish that big again, so the excitement died down.

Then a couple years later, an angler trolling for walleyes near where the big musky was seen hooked something huge. He got it close enough to the boat to see that it was a musky with its jaws clamped around a three-pound walleye that had taken his bait. The musky let go, then later made a pass at a 42-inch northern the angler hooked. The bug-eyed angler estimated the musky's length at 6-1/2 feet.

Were the angler and the fisheries crew hallucinating? DNR fish manager Joe Kurz doesn't think so. He wasn't present for either sighting himself, but he knows Wissota's potential for producing monster muskies is real and he for one believes Wissota might indeed hold a world-record musky.

A flowage on the Chippewa River just northeast of Chippewa Falls, Lake Wissota itself covers some 5,800 acres. Several miles of river upstream from the lake to the dam at Jim Falls give the entire flowage from dam to dam a total of 6,300 acres. Joe Kurz describes Wissota as "a big bathtub that needs some lumps in it to make it more fishable." With depths to 40 feet and miles of very subtle deep-water structure, Wissota can be tough to fish without a good locator and map.

Two smaller flowages join the lake: Little Lake Wissota, or Paint Creek Flowage, at the south end, and Yellow River Flowage on the northeast side. These flowages and their connecting channels are navigable, as is the Chippewa River upstream of Wissota. These areas have more weed cover, a varied bottom contour, and a well-defined river channel that provide better habitat for forage species like young perch and bluegills, thus they hold higher concentrations of Wissota's primary gamefish -- walleyes, northerns and muskies -- than the lake's main basin. Warmer water in spring can make early-season fishing here productive well before the main lake turns on, and ice fishermen take good catches of pike and walleyes in all three areas.

Much of the good habitat that was present in Wissota's early years has washed away with time. In an effort to improve that situation, the Chippewa Rod and Gun Club has placed over 400 cribs in the three flowages since the early 1980s. The cribs are especially attractive to crappies and smallmouths, but other species use them as well since they concentrate baitfish. Cribs are located along the west shore above the Highway S bridge, along the north shore just east of the Highway S bridge, along the west shore north of the dam, and at the mouths and along the shorelines of the two smaller flowages.

Wissota is not stocked, but recent surveys show healthy populations of muskies, northern pike and walleyes. Walleyes, especially, are reproducing well, and Kurz says there are good numbers of two- to three-year-old fish.

Willie Wiese with his first legal musky -- 43 inches and 17-1/2 pounds -- from Lake Wissota in October 1992. While catch and release is recommended to promote the future of musky fishing, there's nothing wrong with taking home your first keeper. Photo by Dan Small

Most of Wissota's walleyes spawn below the Jim Falls Dam, although some use the Yellow River and Paint Creek. During the post-spawn dispersal period, though, many walleyes move right through Lake Wissota, over the Lake Wissota Dam, and into the Chippewa River Flowage below. A spring 1990 survey conducted below the Lake Wissota Dam turned up more walleyes that had been tagged above the dam than below it. A fair number of northerns and muskies also migrate downstream in spring. The dam is scheduled for relicensing in the year 2000, so Kurz plans to start working with Northern States Power Company in 1995 to try to reduce these fish losses.

When the season opens in May, walleyes have already finished spawning, but they are still fairly concentrated in the river below the Jim Falls dam. Kurz says extensive weedbeds in the upstream portion of the bulge in the river about halfway between the lake and Jim Falls holds lots of walleyes in spring, fall and winter. Slo-Poke jigs rigged weedless with a chartreuse or smoke plastic shad, worm or grub tail should produce well in these flats.

When the walleyes move downstream into Wissota for the summer, this stretch is good for muskies and northerns. Bucktails and weedless spoons tipped with pork trailers should take both species, while noisy surface baits are always a good bet for river muskies in the evening.

All three species relate to the weedy offshore bars and humps scattered along the shoreline in Wissota itself. The best way to fish these spots is to troll parallel to the contours at different depths until you locate fish, then toss out a marker buoy and drift with a jig or slip bobber and live bait. If you mark occasional lone fish in deep water, try Spoonplugging with wire line or downrigger trolling with big diving Bagleys. If you connect, it will most likely be a musky or pike, but Joe Kurz says there's a good possibility for taking spawned-out female walleyes in excess of 10 pounds in deep water.

Wissota's early-season crappie fishing is outstanding. Shortly after ice-out, you'll find them near cribs, brush and downed trees in the two smaller flowages where fathead minnows or lightweight jigs with plastic tails in white or yellow will take them. In summer, they roam the main lake but are tough to find. Bluegills are also easy to catch on floating fly-rod lures or live bait in May and early June when they're on the spawning beds. Later, look for them off weedlines in the smaller flowages and on bars in Wissota.

Wissota also has a good population of bass, although few anglers try for them. Smallmouths relate to gravel points, riprapped shorelines and rock bars on Wissota and brush, logs and other cover in the river and smaller flowages. Try floating crankbaits in the shallow areas and feather jigs tipped with leeches or pork crayfish bumped down rocky points in deeper water. The shallow, weedy bays of Little Lake Wissota and Yellow River Flowage hold some whopper largemouths. Try weedless baits, plastics and surface lures such as buzzbaits and spinnerbaits.

Lake Wissota State Park, on the northeast shore, has a good public boat ramp and a permanent fishing pier accessible to the handicapped, with several fish cribs just offshore. The park has three campgrounds, making it a good choice for a family fishing and camping trip. For reservations and more information,

LAKE WISSOTA

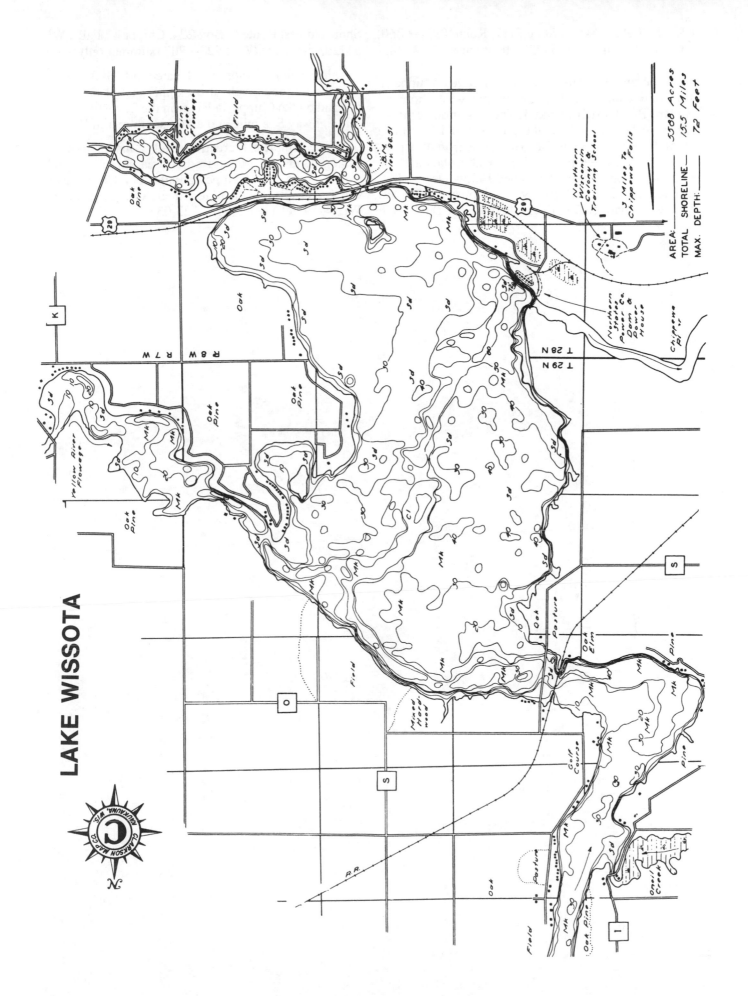

AREA: 5308 Acres
TOTAL SHORELINE: 15.5 Miles
MAX. DEPTH: 72 Feet

contact: Lake Wissota State Park, Route 8, Box 360, Chippewa Falls, WI 54729, telephone (715) 382-4574.

There are two ramps at the improved Chippewa Rod and Gun Club landing on the west shore on Redard Road, off Highway I. There is another public ramp on Highway X at the narrows to Little Lake Wissota. Wissota View Tavern, across from this public ramp, has a ramp as well as boat rentals and the only bait shop on the lake, called Below Decks. Tavern address: 17779 Highway X, Chippewa Falls, WI 54729, telephone: (715) 723-5356. Below Decks Bait Shop address: Route 6, Box 224, Chippewa Falls, WI 54729, telephone (715) 723-7207 (summer only).

Other public ramps are located off Highway S near the railroad trestle at the upper end of the flowage and on the Chippewa River in the Town of Anson off Highway S, a mile and a half south of Jim Falls.

For a complete recreation packet listing motels, campgrounds, resorts and other area attractions and events, contact the Chippewa Falls Area Chamber of Commerce, 811 N. Bridge Street, Chippewa Falls, WI 54729, telephone (715) 723-0331.

Lower Wolf River

Shiocton, Outagamie County, to Lake Poygan, Winnebago County

In its upper reaches, the wild Wolf River is one of Wisconsin's better trout streams. Deep, boulder-strewn runs, numerous shelves and rapids and long stretches of riffles hold good numbers of hefty trout that attract fly fishermen from faraway places. The Upper Wolf's superb whitewater also draws recreational boaters -- canoeists, kayakers and rafters -- who float the foam in spring.

Then at Shawano, the Wolf leaves the rugged hills behind and enters a broad, rolling plain punctuated by woodlots and dairy farms. Here, the river slows down, deepens and gradually warms up as it winds through Shawano, Outagamie and Waupaca counties. Gone are the browns and rainbows of its beginnings, replaced now by a host of warm water species: bass, northerns, walleyes, panfish and sturgeon.

You may catch all but the sturgeon, which swim upriver from the lakes below each April to spawn along the rocky shorelines from New London to Shiocton and are protected from hook-and-line anglers.

Lower Wolf River

From Shawano to Lake Poygan, the Wolf offers 75 miles of year-round fishing opportunities, but the spring spawning runs of walleyes and white bass on the lower half of this section attract the most attention. As soon as the ice breaks up in April, walleyes begin to move up the Wolf from Lakes Winnebago, Butte des Morts, Winneconne and Poygan. Walleye fishing is usually good upstream to the Shioc River and Spoehr's Marsh above Shiocton.

Most strains of walleyes spawn on rocky lake or river shorelines, but those in the Winnebago system spawn in flooded and flowing grassy areas in the bayous of the river bottoms. Walleye spawning success was poor during the drought years, but good year classes since 1990 have given the population a boost, according to DNR Oshkosh area fisheries supervisor Ron Bruch. Walleyes now provide good fishing in the river well into late spring and early summer. DNR fisheries crews and conservation clubs worked hard in the early 1990s to improve spawning areas by removing old dikes, brushing and mowing to facilitate water flow through some of the historic spawning areas. These efforts have literally recreated hundreds of acres of walleye spawning habitat. Many of these same areas have become no-entry zones in spring to prevent intentional or accidental harassment of spawning fish and incubating eggs.

Spawning takes place when water temperatures in the flooded marshes that border the river reach 45 degrees, but walleyes may be on the move for a week or more prior to spawning. As they swim upstream, walleyes hug bottom in the deeper holes by day and feed in nearby shallows and along sand bars at night. Fishing is best on warm, overcast days and nights, while a cold front usually puts the fish down for a day or two.

The time-honored Wolf River Rig is as good a way to take walleyes on the run as ever was invented. You can buy them at any tackle shop near the river or make your own: tie two droppers on a three-way swivel, one for a bell sinker and a longer one for a plain hook, floating jig, crankbait or what have you. Vary the weight of the sinker and length of droppers according to the water speed and depth. Bait hooks and jigs with a minnow and fish the rig near bottom in deep holes.

You may have to move several times before you locate a school of walleyes, but the action is usually fast when you find them. Most fish taken on the pre-spawn run are smaller males. You may luck into spawners in the shallows on a warm night, but most of the larger females are taken as they drift back downstream after spawning. Post-spawn walleyes ride higher in the current, where spinners and floating crankbaits will take them.

Night fishing from houseboats, rafts and piers turns the river into one floating party from Fremont to Shiocton. Tom Eisch and Glen Bunnell of Shiocton let me and our TV camera in on the fun one warm April evening. Fishing from a raft tied to a pier in downtown Shiocton, we took walleyes on minnows and Rapalas hung below us in the current. From the sound of the whooping and hollering up and down the river, I'd say we were not the only ones catching fish that night.

Crappies are the next species to move upriver, and you can take good catches along brushy banks and off creek mouths on small minnows or jigs and plastic tails. The bends just above Lake Poygan and Mill Bayou just above the Highway 10 bridge in Fremont are especially good for crappies.

For most Wolf River regulars, though, crappies are just a prelude to the real spring panfish action: the white bass run, which begins in late April and lasts through May. White bass move upriver in veritable hordes as far as New London. Located right in the middle of the best white bass stretch, Fremont calls itself the White Bass Capital of the World, and I don't hear any town clamoring to take away its title.

The walleye run is sedate compared to the frenzy of white bass fishing. The main channel, deep bends and creek mouths are good spots to try, and at the peak of the run you can almost walk across the river from boat to boat in many areas. White bass bite eagerly during the daytime, and you can catch them on nearly anything white, silver or yellow. Minnows on river rigs work fine, but why bother when they'll knock little Mepps, Road Runners, jigs and crankbaits silly?

Once the white bass run is over, things calm down on the Wolf. There are plenty of largemouths and smallmouths to be had, but fewer anglers go after them. The weedy backwaters and bays produce some nice largemouths in late May and June. Try Page's Slough just upriver from the mouth, Mill Bayou and Partridge Lake in Fremont, and Templeton Bayou near the Waupaca County Park at Gills Landing. You'll find smallmouths in the deeper bayous and in the main river wherever there are rocks.

Partridge Lake is shallow, but worth fishing for largemouths, northerns and bluegills. It becomes weed-choked in summer, but you can take some big bluegills on fly rods and rubber spiders when they're on the beds in late May and early June.

Glen Bunnell hefts a stringer of Wolf River walleyes taken at night during the spawning run from his river raft anchored near Shiocton. Photo by Dan Small

Walleyes and white bass also run upriver in fall. Look for them feeding on schools of minnows in bends and shallow backwaters. White bass drive schools of baitfish to the surface -- just watch for the commotion and you'll locate them easily. Spinners and small crankbaits produce well in September and October.

Ice fishing yields panfish and northerns near Fremont, but be wary of ice conditions and walk, don't drive because river currents can erode ice that still looks safe.

There are numerous boat landings from Lake Poygan upriver to Shiocton, including several in Fremont. Ma's Bait & Tackle, located on Highway 10 in Fremont, and open at 6 a.m. seven days a week, is headquarters for bait, tackle and information on fishing conditions. Telephone: (414) 446-2444. For a map of the river and listings of the many resorts, campgrounds, restaurants and other services available, contact: Fremont Area Chamber of Commerce, P.O. Box 114, Fremont, WI 54940, telephone (414) 446-3838.

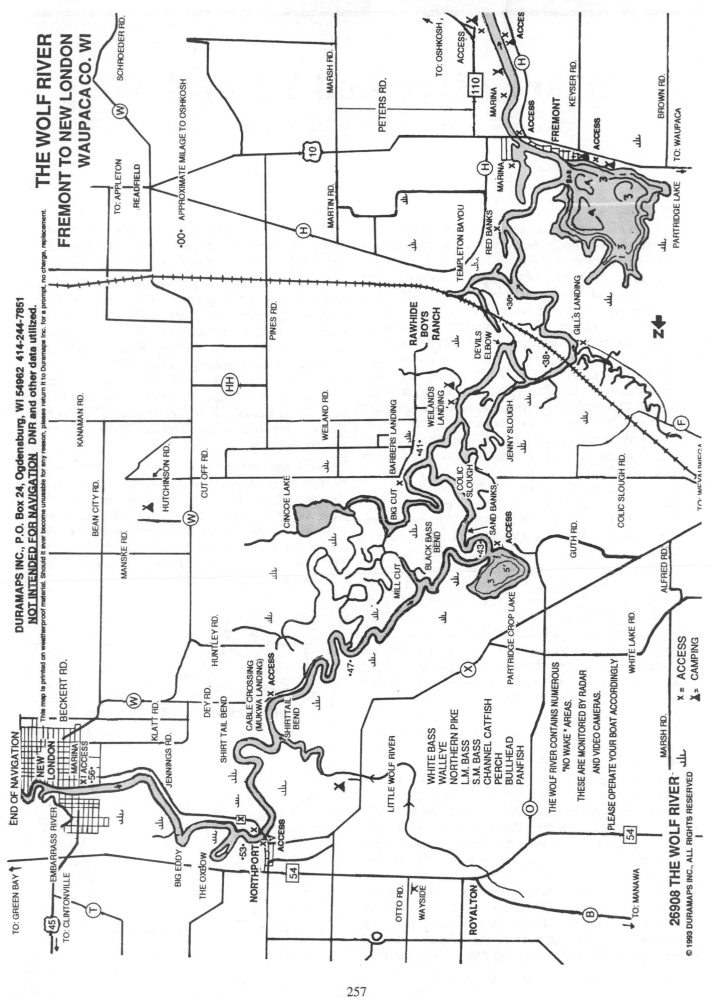

THE WOLF RIVER
FREMONT TO NEW LONDON
WAUPACA CO. WI

DURAMAPS INC., P.O. Box 24, Ogdensburg, WI 54962 414-244-7851
NOT INTENDED FOR NAVIGATION   DNR and other data utilized.

This map is printed on weatherproof material. Should it ever become unusable for any reason, please return it to Duramaps Inc. for a prompt, no charge, replacement.

END OF NAVIGATION

WHITE BASS
WALLEYE
NORTHERN PIKE
L.M. BASS
S.M. BASS
CHANNEL CATFISH
PERCH
BULLHEAD
PANFISH

THE WOLF RIVER CONTAINS NUMEROUS
"NO WAKE" AREAS.
THESE ARE MONITORED BY RADAR
AND VIDEO CAMERAS.
PLEASE OPERATE YOUR BOAT ACCORDINGLY

X = ACCESS
⚑ = CAMPING

26908 THE WOLF RIVER

Yellow River And Yellow Lake

Spooner Lake to St. Croix River, Washburn and Burnett Counties

It takes a careful observer to spot the few remaining traces of dams, sluiceways and sorting booms that today bear mute testimony to the Yellow River's role during the heyday of the logging era around the turn of the last century. In most cases, all that is left of these once-imposing structures is a rotted timber or two at a bridge crossing or a handful of weathered pilings that poke up among the rice beds in a shallow backwater. The last massive rafts of pine sawlogs that jammed the river from bank to bank have long since floated to the St. Croix and downriver mills, and the shouts of the drivers echo no more along her flood-swollen banks come ice-out, but the Yellow flows on as before, unperturbed by the historic events that changed the face of the northwoods through which she flows.

The Yellow River heads at the outlet dam of Spooner Lake and flows southwest through the city of Spooner and the Yellow River Flowage, then meanders through western Washburn County, crosses Burnett County from east to west, then turns abruptly north to join the St. Croix at Danbury. Along its route, it passes through several more lakes, the largest of which is 2,300-acre Yellow Lake in north-central Burnett County.

Along much of its route, the Yellow is wide, fairly shallow and sluggish, with lots of eelgrass and few gamefish. On several stretches, though, faster flow, deeper water and adequate instream cover provide excellent habitat for smallmouths, walleyes, northerns and muskies. These portions of the river will float a canoe or small boat and they are accessible at bridge crossings, so anglers need not waste time drifting through unproductive water.

The first good stretch begins just below the dam on the Yellow River Flowage in the city of Spooner. The DNR operates the world's largest musky hatchery on this site, and fingerlings left over when lake stocking quotas have been met are occasionally put into the river here, resulting in several miles of fine musky fishing.

Topwater baits work well near rock and log cover, while bucktails and live suckers produce more strikes in the deeper holes. Prime spots include the deep stretch below the Tozer Lake Road bridge and the pool below the old Hector logging dam at the next road crossing downstream. To float this stretch, put in off the roadbank at The Culverts, just south of Highway 70 about one and a half miles west of Spooner.

From Hector Dam down to County Line Road, the river has a moderate gradient, with numerous sandbars, rocky riffles and easy rapids. Smallmouths ranging from 10 to 16 inches are fairly abundant here on this half-day float. Floating Rapalas and small spinners will take bass right in the riffles and in side eddies below the rapids, especially early and late in the day. Work leeches and crawlers in the deeper holes along banks and below sandbars. Take out at County Line Road or the Highway 70 bridge a couple miles upstream.

Good smallmouth water continues for several more miles to Highway H. Below there, though, the Yellow widens, slows and fills with weeds. A few locals fish this stretch for northerns and largemouths, but for 20 miles or so the river wanders through county forestland, much of it bordered by swamp. You wouldn't want to get caught in here overnight without a couple gallons of bug dope.

258

About five miles west of Webster, the Yellow deepens and offers excellent walleye and musky fishing all the way to Yellow Lake. You can float from Keyser Bridge off Highway X down to Connors Bridge on Austin Lake Road in about three hours, and to the Highway 35 bridge landing in another two. Jigs tipped with crawlers and minnows will take walleyes in the deeper holes and below the few low-hazard rapids. Northerns and muskies will hit bucktails, topwater baits and big chubs and suckers.

Yellow Lake, Little Yellow Lake and Danbury Flowage all offer a balanced fishery that features muskies, northerns, walleyes and panfish. There are resorts on all three lakes and three public launch sites on Yellow Lake. Navigable channels allow access by boat to Little Yellow and the flowage.

Yellow Lake is a broad, shallow bowl with a maximum depth of 31 feet. Midlake structure is limited to several small bars on each side of the outlet at the west end, another subtle hump along the southwest shore, and a couple small rock bars that don't even appear on the maps. The entire lake is ringed with heavy weed growth out to a depth of 12 feet, which provides cover for gamefish, panfish and forage species alike.

DNR fisheries biologist Larry Damman reports that a 1992 spring survey showed a good walleye population of about 10,000 adults over 15 inches. They are tough to catch, though, because of abundant forage that keeps them from going hungry. Supplementary stocking of some 50,000 fingerlings per year bolsters the population. The St. Croix Chippewa tribe spears Yellow Lake, but the tribe also operates a walleye hatchery. Fingerlings from the tribe's hatchery are added to the state quota in good production years and used to help meet it when production is down.

Walleyes here run up the river in spring, then hang out on the bars and in cabbage and coontail weeds. Jigs and minnows work well early, then slip bobbers and leeches take fish once the weeds are up. Forward trolling is allowed, so some anglers ride around the lake's perimeter at the deep weed edge with small crankbaits in tow.

The DNR stocks 2,500 muskies every other year, instead of annually as it did until recently, to give them a chance to grow.

"Yellow Lake produces lots of muskies, including an amazing number of 45-inchers," Damman says. "A large forage base of ciscoes, redhorse and suckers keeps them well-fed."

In spring, look for muskies near the Yellow River inlet, wherever new weed growth appears and over the lake's few humps and bars. Work sucker-imitation baits and bucktails slowly to draw strikes from lethargic fish. Once the weeds are up, that's where the muskies will be. Try bucktails and shallow-running crankbaits over submerged weeds and deep-diving crankbaits along weed edges.

In fall, most musky hunters go with live suckers on quick-strike rigs, big bucktails or crankbaits. I haven't tried it here, but I can't believe deep jigging won't produce fish, especially if you can locate a school of ciscoes. The lake also cranks out lots of big northerns. Every year anglers take some over 40 inches, most of them on musky baits.

Damman says the largemouth fishery is also outstanding, with good numbers of fish over 20 inches. Numerous bass tournaments are held here each year. Panfish species also hold up well here and offer good action in spring in the bays and inlets and later on the humps and along weedlines.

When a nice musky is hooked, nobody breathes a sigh of relief until the fish is corralled with a net or release cradle. Photo by Dan Small

Yellow Lake produced the state record lake sturgeon back in 1979. According to Damman, the sturgeon population is stable and the harvest currently at a safe level. A few dedicated anglers fish for them during the brief fall season, but most fish caught are released. If you want to try for them, the river mouth is the place to go. Skewer a half-dollar's worth of night crawlers on a hook and let it soak on bottom. You might as well soak a sucker on another line for a musky or grandma northern.

There are three public landings on Yellow Lake, all with shallow but decent ramps and parking. On the east side, take Jeffires Road off Highway 35 to a gravel ramp, loading pier, picnic area and parking for six rigs. On the north side, take Lake Avenue off Highway U to a concrete ramp and parking lot. To reach the paved ramp and parking lot at the south side of the outlet to Little Yellow Lake, take Yellow Lake Road off Highway U.

For information on resorts, tackle shops and other facilities in Washburn County, contact the Washburn County Tourism Association, Route 1, Box 327, Sarona, WI 54870, telephone (800) 367-3306. For bait, tackle and guide service on Yellow Lake, contact Lyle Carlson at Shanty Bait Shop, 25597 Highway 35, Webster, WI 54893, telephone (715) 866-4135. For information on other services in the Yellow Lake area, contact the Webster Chamber of Commerce, P.O. Box 48, Webster, WI 54893, telephone (715) 866-4251.

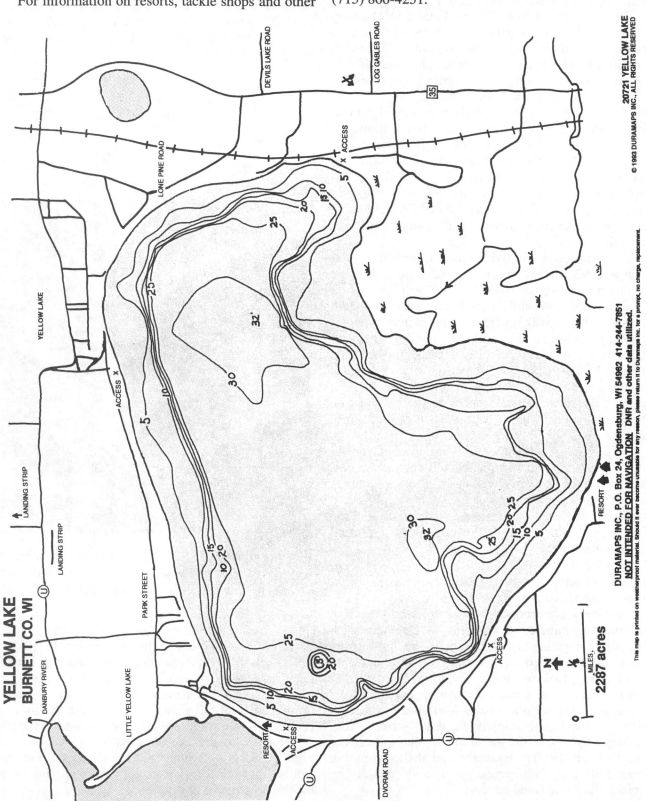

Wisconsin's Top Trout Waters

Trout fishing in Wisconsin has changed more in the past several years than it has in decades. First, the drought of 1988 dropped stream levels dramatically over much of the state, severely reducing trout numbers and practically eliminating natural reproduction that fall and the next in many streams. Emergency closures and catch and release regulations followed in 1989 and 1990 to allow trout populations to recover. Meanwhile, the DNR revamped the entire system of trout regulations to provide fish managers with more flexibility to manage vastly different stream types and provide anglers with a variety of fishing opportunities.

The DNR lifted emergency rules in 1991 on streams in southwestern Wisconsin, and in 1992 on northeastern Wisconsin streams, opening the entire state to the new five-category regulations outlined in the special trout pamphlet. Simply stated, you can catch and keep lots of smaller trout in category one, two or three waters and enjoy good action for medium-sized fish with a chance to harvest a few large trout in category four waters. If you want the chance to catch and release many trout or keep an occasional trophy, then category five waters are for you.

Trout fishing remains good in northwestern and southeastern Wisconsin, where the drought had less effect on streams. Streams in the southwestern counties have pretty well recovered and are, for the most part, back to normal. The situation in the northeast is mixed, however. Water levels are back to normal, but trout populations need several more years to recover. When the season reopened in the northeast in 1992, anglers found good numbers of larger trout -- those that survived the drought years -- but very few medium-sized fish.

According to DNR trout specialist Larry Claggett, poor reproduction during the drought years left a gap in the year class structure of streams in the northeast. Heavy fishing pressure early in the season knocked trout populations on some of these waters back to levels seen during the drought or lower because anglers took out most of the larger trout early in the season in many category one, two and three streams, and there were no younger fish to replace those removed. On category four and five streams, how-ever, which offered protection for larger fish, the two-year closure helped build up a very good fishery, with large numbers of big trout.

Claggett is projecting some fine tuning of trout regulations for the 1995 season. "We're looking for ways to protect larger fish," Claggett says. "We'll probably restructure the category system, and we may drop the whole-county approach to the early season now in effect in the southwest and instead apply it to specific streams scattered throughout the state."

Claggett also cites radio-telemetry studies on the Beaver and Oconto rivers that showed brown trout move far more than was believed, suggesting a more holistic approach to watershed management would give better protection to fish that migrate.

"We can protect a large brown trout in a category five stream," says Claggett. "But that same fish can easily move several miles upstream into a category one, two or three stream and be caught and legally kept."

DNR biologists are also working on a plan to raise trout for stocking from eggs taken from wild fish.

"The fact that wild trout have better growth and survival rates than domestic trout is well documented," says Claggett. "If we can get the eggs we need without reducing the wild brood stock, we'd like to raise and plant wild fish in areas where they'd have a chance to survive beyond the first two weeks in May. We'd then continue to plant domestic fish in put-and-take streams that get pounded early in the season and let the wild trout grow up to produce a high-quality fishery."

Trout inhabit nearly 10,000 miles of streams in Wisconsin, ranging from big, whitewater rivers to tiny brooks that meander for less than a mile through a northwoods bog. It would take several lifetimes to fish every mile, though I know a few guys who are making a valiant effort to do it in one. Here's an overview of some of the better trout streams around the state, along with just a few of the hundreds of trout lakes where you can expect to enjoy good fishing.

261

Pond, Beaver, Nymphia
And Overby Lakes

Bayfield County

These four tiny lakes in the Chequamegon National Forest in Bayfield County offer superb fishing for brook trout. Balsam Pond and Beaver Lake are open to fishing only in odd-numbered years, while Nymphia and Overby lakes are open only in even-numbered years. During closed years, these lakes are stocked with brook trout, which gives the fish a year to grow and acclimate themselves to their environment. Category two rules apply to these waters: the daily bag limit is five trout over seven inches.

Ranging in size from six to 20 acres, these lakes are deep and clear, with undeveloped bog shorelines. Here, you can enjoy fishing for brook trout measuring 13 inches or better in as wild a setting as any in Wisconsin. Your best bet is to launch a canoe and drift, while casting spinners or flies.

All four are located several miles north of Drummond. Take Delta-Drummond Road north from Highway 63, then Cisco Lake Road east to Overby Lake. Continue another mile or so to Nymphia Lake Road and turn right to reach that lake. Beaver Lake is accessible off Delta-Drummond Road in the Rainbow Lake Wilderness Area, and there is a walk-in access to Balsam Pond in the Flynn Lake Wilderness Area.

You can get tackle at Bear Country Sporting Goods on Highway 63 in Drummond, telephone (715) 739-6645. For more information on these lakes, contact DNR fisheries management in Brule, telephone (715) 372-4866. For camping information, contact the District Ranger's Office, Chequamegon National Forest, P.O. Box 578, Washburn, WI 54891, telephone (715) 373-2667.

Big Green River, Blue River, And
Castle Rock Creek

Grant County

Three of the best spring-fed trout streams in southwestern Wisconsin, Big Green River, Blue River and Castle Rock Creek, are located in northern Grant County, all a short distance from Fennimore. Like most spring creeks, these three maintain water temperatures in the upper 40s and low 50s through the winter months, and trout remain active even in cold weather. They are excellent fly-fishing streams, with good hatches of caddis and mayflies from March through June.

Sections of all three streams have been improved with riprap, wing deflectors and other instream structures. DNR fisheries crews stock plenty of browns annually, including extra brood fish when these are available. Since all three have significant no-kill areas, they provide some tremendous fishing opportunities. Browns over 20 inches in these areas are "recycled" three or four times each season.

"These and a few other top streams in the southwestern counties came through the drought years in great shape," says DNR fisheries biologist Gene Van Dyck. "They support more big trout than at any time since the mid-1940s, although we lost some recruitment potential during the drought. These streams provide lots of opportunity for a quality fishing experience, especially early in the season before the nettles and mosquitoes appear."

Big Green River flows from just west of Fennimore northwest to the Wisconsin River near Wauzeka. Several town road crossings provide access. From its headwaters downstream to Highway T, it is a category three stream, but from Highway T down to Highway 133, it is category five water, with artificials only and catch and release rules in effect.

The Big Green is a narrow stream, averaging only 10 to 15 feet in width, but it runs deep. Over much of its length, the river meanders through pastureland and occasionally brushes up against a forested ridge. Trout hold in bend holes and pools below rapids and along rocky banks.

To the east, the Blue River also flows north into the Wisconsin River. Fourteen miles of the Blue are classed as trout water. From its headwaters in Iowa County downstream to Bluff Road, and again from Snow Bottom Road downstream to Biba Road, it is category four water. Between Bluff Road and Snow Bottom Road, category five artificials-only, no-kill rules apply.

A tiny midge pattern fooled this brown trout. Photo by Dan Small

There are several road crossings where you can get on the Blue, but the five-mile stretch between Bowers Road and Shemak Road twists through a steep, secluded valley, where you can fish all day and never see another soul.

Castle Rock Creek, a tributary to the Blue River, differs from the first two streams. It is broad and very fertile, with a good deal of riprap and slow pools that alternate with shallow gravel runs. Castle Rock has just over six miles of good trout water, most of it in category four classification. On the stretch between Church Road and the first bridge crossing on Highway Q, though, as well as on all of a short tributary, the Doc Smith Branch, category five, artificials-only, no-kill rules apply. This is superb fly-fishing water, with open meadows on both banks, which means even I can fish here without hanging up my backcast every five minutes.

Castle Rock's milky, limestone-rich water supports an abundant insect population and its trout grow to hefty proportions. Some time after we taped an *Outdoor Wisconsin* segment there one May with John Beth and Mike Rock, Mike showed me photos of a 28-inch brown he had taken a week later. That cannibal brown grabbed a smaller trout that had taken his fly, then swam up and down the creek with the 10-incher crossways in its mouth, the way a dog would carry a bone. The big trout wouldn't let go, so Mike landed it, freed the smaller fish, then released them both.

Gene Van Dyck would like to see more no-kill trout water to give anglers more opportunity for high-quality fishing. "Only three percent of our trout stream mileage is currently no-kill water, but those stretches receive 40 percent of the fishing pressure," he says. "If a quarter of our streams were set aside as category five waters, they could handle three or four times the angling pressure they support now."

These streams survived the drought and have benefited from habitat improvement, but several problems remain, according to Van Dyck. "Our biggest problem now is the impact of livestock management practices on water quality," he says. "Agricultural leaders here recognize the problem and are working toward an acceptable solution."

Another obstacle is the increase in the number of herons in recent years. "Herons have established rookeries on all the major trout streams here and are keying in on stocked trout," says Van Dyck. "At the rate of a pound and a half of fish per heron per day, they're capable of drastically reducing the number of trout on any stretch they choose to fish."

In spite of herons and cows, these fine spring creeks still offer some great fishing opportunities. Lodging and other services are available in any of the towns along the Wisconsin River. Boscobel is the most centrally located town, if you plan to fish all three streams. For more information on these streams and other spring creeks in Grant and Iowa counties,

contact DNR Fisheries Management, Route 1, Box 10, Dodgeville, WI 53533, telephone (608) 935-3368.

Black Earth And Mt. Vernon Creeks

Dane County

It's a little hard to believe that great fishing for wild trout can be had so close to downtown Madison, but these two gems are just a half-hour's drive from the State Capitol. Trout held up well through the drought in these two Dane County streams, thanks to strong springs and deep holes that kept water levels adequate during the worst of times. Natural reproduction sustains good numbers of nine- to 12-inch brown trout in both streams, while rainbows are stocked annually in the lower reaches of Black Earth Creek. Both are category three streams, with a three-fish daily limit and nine-inch minimum size, although each stream has a category five stretch where brown trout must measure 20 inches and only one may be kept.

Black Earth Creek parallels Highway 14 between the villages of Cross Plains and Black Earth, where it meanders through agricultural land flanked by high cedar bluffs to the north and south. Often slightly turbid, Black Earth Creek has a gravel bed covered in places with sand or silt. Trout stamp proceeds have funded instream habitat improvement work to supplement the natural cover provided by deep holes and outside bends. Two tributaries, Garfoot and Vermont Creeks, also offer good fishing for browns and brookies.

Fisheries biologist Scot Stewart reports that the new regulations have improved the size distribution of trout here and that anglers are generally happy. Trout are spawning farther downstream each year, thanks to the habitat work. To evaluate the new regulations and habitat improvements, Stewart is concluding a two-year study consisting of spring population estimates and season-long creel censuses on the category five section, along with fall population estimates on both the category five and category three sections. Halfway through the study, Stewart was pleased with what he found. In five days in the fall of 1992, he measured 6,000 trout, including a fair number between 20 and 25 inches long.

Formed where two brook trout streams, Deer Creek and Frye Feeder, come together, Mt. Vernon Creek flows southeast through hilly farmland along Highway 92. Numerous springs keep it cold and clear even in the hottest weather. Bottom types vary from sand and gravel to clay in the lower stretches, where wading can be treacherous. Deep holes and woody debris provide cover. Scot Stewart reports good densities of legal browns in all sizes up to and over 20 inches, but clear water and trickier currents make them tougher to catch than those on Black Earth Creek.

Both streams are popular with fly-fishermen and both feature scuds and good caddis, mayfly and midge hatches. Mount Vernon's trout have a reputation for being very fussy eaters. Still, they can be taken on carefully presented small flies during hatches and on terrestrials all season long.

Like Black Earth, Mount Vernon is less crowded on weekdays. Fishing at night during the Hexagenia hatch in June is a good way to avoid running into other anglers at every bend. Easements and state-owned land along both streams make access easy along the highways that border them. For information on both streams, contact Verne Lunde at Lunde's Fly Fishing Chalet on Highway 92 south of Mount Horeb, telephone (608) 437-5465.

Bois Brule River

Douglas County

The Bois Brule is without a doubt Wisconsin's best-known trout stream. Five United States Presidents have fished the Brule, and Calvin Coolidge was so taken with the river that he moved the White House here for the summer of 1928. Unlike some rivers whose notoriety has outlived their good fishing, the Brule still offers some of the best -- and most varied -- trout fishing in the Midwest.

Located entirely in Douglas County, the Brule has a split personality. For 30 miles, the river meanders slowly through a cedar bog and several natural widespreads or lakes. But for its last 19 miles, it cuts through steep red clay banks in a headlong rush to Lake Superior

The 50,000-acre Brule River State Forest surrounds the river over its full length, protecting the watershed and offering camping and other recreational opportunities. Access to the river, however, is limited to several road crossings and state-owned access points, since most of the riverbank is under private ownership.

From Highway 2 downstream, the Brule is one of a dozen or so Lake Superior tributaries open to fishing from the Saturday nearest April 1 through November 15. On the Brule, fishing is prohibited from one-half hour after sunset to one-half hour before sunrise from opening day until the first Saturday in May and from October 1 through November 15.

New size and bag limits now in effect on all Lake Superior tributaries have been designed to reduce the harvest of wild steelhead and afford reasonable protection to other trout and salmon species. The daily limit is five trout or salmon in total, only two of which may be brown trout over 15 inches and only one of which may be a rainbow trout or steelhead. The new size limits are: brook trout, eight inches; brown trout, 10 inches; salmon, 12 inches, and rainbow trout, 26 inches. The 26-inch limit on steelhead allows every returning fish to spawn at least once.

Unlike the Lake Michigan salmonid fishery, which is almost 100 percent stocked, the trout and salmon in Lake Superior are nearly 100 percent self-sustaining through natural reproduction.

"We consider our tributaries to be fish hatcheries," says Dennis Pratt, western Lake Superior fisheries manager for the DNR. "If we overfish our brood stock, we will hurt the future of the resource. Spawning success varies from one tributary to another and from one year to the next. A lot of what happens to the anadromous fishery here depends on nature."

During the early season, steelhead are the main quarry. All steelhead spawning here occurs in spring, although some fish run upriver in fall and hold in deeper holes over the winter. The spring run of fresh fish begins shortly after ice-out and usually peaks in mid-April. Steelhead average four to six pounds, but some run larger. Spawn is the traditional bait, but many anglers have switched over to yarn or attractor fly patterns, especially since this is now essentially a no-kill fishery. Flashy spoons and diving plugs in bright orange and chartreuse are also effective.

The best early-season action occurs in the deep, slow stretch known as "The Meadows," which runs from the Highway 2 bridge downstream about eight miles to Coop Park. You can get on the river at the upstream end from Highway 2, at several fishermen's parking lots along Highway H, or at Park Road at the downstream end. Expect a crowd for both openers and for any weekend in April and May. On weekdays, though, you can have long stretches all to yourself.

After the May opener, steelheaders take some fish from the DNR Ranger Station upstream to the bridge at Winneboujou on Highway B, but most anglers in May and June are fly-fishermen seeking the native browns and brookies above Winneboujou. You can wade some stretches, but most fishing is done from canoes. There are two additional access points upstream: Fishermen's Landing on Highway P and Stone's Bridge on Highway S.

The river supports excellent caddis and mayfly hatches through July, including the legendary Hexagenia hatch, which occurs after dark beginning in late June.

Fall runs of browns, cohos, chinooks and steelhead begin in July and run through November. Water conditions affect the exact timing of these runs, so the peaks may vary from year to year. Browns tend to run earliest, followed by chinooks, steelhead, and cohos, but they all overlap to some degree. Spawn, yarn, flies and hardware will take all trout and salmon species.

This Brule River steelhead fell victim to a yarn fly. Photo by Dan Small

Other Lake Superior tributaries with good spring and fall fishing for trout and salmon include the Amnicon, Middle and Poplar rivers in Douglas County and the Flag, Cranberry, Siskiwit and Sioux rivers in Bayfield County. When conditions are not just right on the Brule, one of these streams often offers superlative fishing for the same species.

You can get tackle and fishing information in Brule at Brule Classics, telephone (715) 372-8153. There are two state forest campgrounds on the river. For maps and information on camping and other recreation, contact the Brule River State Forest, P.O. Box 125, Brule, WI 54820, telephone (715) 372-4866. For more fisheries information, contact the DNR, 1705 Tower Avenue, Superior, WI 54880, telephone (715) 392-7988.

Buffalo (Beef) River

Jackson and Trempealeau Counties

Depending on whom you ask or which map you have, this stream is known by either name. The North and South Forks of the Buffalo rise in northwestern Jackson County and flow east into Trempealeau County, where they meet in Osseo, then west along Highway 10 to Strum, and eventually southwest to the Mississippi at Alma. Except for a short stretch of category five water on the Buffalo between Highway O and Town Road, both forks and the main river downstream to Strum are category four streams. Together, they constitute 35 miles of some of the best trout fishing in western Wisconsin.

Wild brook and brown trout make up the bulk of the Buffalo's fishery, although some rainbows are present. To supplement wild fish, the DNR stocks some 10,000 brown trout in the Trempealeau County portions of the river each year. The resident trout population was hurt during the drought years, when stream flows dropped as much as 60 percent, drying up some spawning areas and putting undue stress on young fish. According to DNR fisheries biologist Jim Talley, the population should continue its slow recovery over the next several years.

Extensive stream improvement projects, including cattle fencing, streambank brush removal, riprap, instream devices and deflectors, have boosted the river's capacity to produce and hold trout. The DNR continues to purchase and lease land along the river to improve angler access. You can reach the river at numerous road crossings and several state access points along Highway 10 and Highway B in both counties. The Buffalo River Trail parallels the river downstream from Osseo, providing opportunities for non-motorized recreation and giving anglers a good way to get from one point on the stream to another on foot or by bicycle.

In places, the Buffalo is a narrow, brushy stream, typical of northwoods brook trout water, with a shifting sand bottom and a wetland border thick with alders. Elsewhere, it meanders through farmland. Insect hatches provide some fly-fishing opportunities, although an ultralight spinning rod and bait or small spinners are more popular combinations.

Visiting anglers can find lodging in Osseo. Contact the Osseo Commercial Club, P.O. Box 111, Osseo, WI 54758, telephone (715) 597-3121. For a county brochure and map showing campgrounds and other areas of interest, contact the Trempealeau County Clerk, 1720 Main Street, Whitehall, WI 54773, telephone (715) 538-2311.

Clam River

Burnett County

This fertile stream offers excellent fishing for browns and brookies in a wild, northwoods setting in southeastern Burnett County. Both the North and South Forks of the Clam flow through a state-owned public fishing area before they meet just south of Highway EE. To find them, take Burnett County Highway H south from Highway 70, or Washburn County Highway J west from Highway 63 between Baronett and Shell Lake.

Both forks feature riffles and pools over a gravel and rock bed, while downstream the Clam slows down and meanders through marsh over a sand and silt bottom. The best water lies upstream from Spencer Lake to the county line. DNR fisheries biologist

Larry Damman reports problems with beavers in some sections in recent years, but says fishing is still very good. Brookies and browns share the upper reaches, while browns dominate on the lower stretch. Trout grow fast here and some browns reach 20 inches or better.

The DNR stocks some browns in the lower river each year and brook trout in a small, shallow spring pond at the very headwaters, where fishing pressure is heavy early in the season.

Fly hatches provide good fishing throughout the season, and the mid-June Hexagenia hatch brings out big browns at night. For more information on the Clam, contact DNR fisheries management in Spooner, telephone (715) 635-4089. Bait, tackle, lodging and other services are available in Spooner. For information, contact the Spooner Area Chamber of Commerce, P.O. Box 406, Spooner, WI 54801, telephone (800) 367-3306.

West Fork Kickapoo River

Vernon County

A few years back, DNR fisheries manager Dave Vetrano developed a new artificial fish habitat system he dubbed "lunker structures." Made of rot-resistant oak planks, lunker structures are permanently wedged into banks to provide the kind of overhead cover that produces and holds large trout. Vetrano and his crews have used lunker structures to shore up sagging banks in coulee streams throughout southwestern Wisconsin, and the trout have responded well.

The West Fork of the Kickapoo River is a good example of a coulee stream whose trout fishing has taken a dramatic turn for the better thanks to lunker structures and to catch and release regulations. The West Fork is a typical large coulee stream, with a rock rubble bottom, deep holes and plenty of snags. For most of its length the West Fork is a warmwater stream, but its upper reaches and many of its tributaries run cold enough to support trout. On the 7-1/2-mile stretch from Highway 82 upstream to the village of Bloomingdale, catch and release and no-kill rules have helped boost both the size and numbers of trout.

With guidance from the DNR, the West Fork Sportsmen's Club has installed lunker structures that provide permanent cover for larger fish on this stretch. DNR crews stock browns and rainbows annually here, and abundant forage species help them grow fast. Since all fish caught are released, carry-over is excellent and the browns especially grow big.

Dave Vetrano reports that browns over 18 inches are common and one occasionally reaches 24 inches. Trout this big are minnow eaters, and lures such as large Mepps and Roostertail spinners or small Count-down Rapalas can be deadly. Cast upstream close to cover, in deep holes and at the tail-end of riffles, and keep a tight line as you retrieve downstream. Strikes often come as soon as a lure hits the water. Fly fishers will take trout on streamer patterns.

Several bed-and-breakfasts in the area cater to trout fishermen, and the West Fork Sportsmen's Club maintains a rental cabin and campground in the village of Avalanche for public use. Club president Roger Widner, Jr., who runs the general store in Avalanche, can supply information on the river and local services. Contact him at (608) 634-2303.

Kinnickinnic River

St. Croix and Pierce Counties

Known locally as the "Kinni," this river is one of the top brown trout streams in the state. From its headwaters in St. Croix County downstream to the lower dam in River Falls, the Kinni is a category two stream with a daily bag limit of five trout over seven inches. The Pierce County stretch, from River Falls downstream to the St. Croix River, is category five water with a slot-size limit protecting fish between 12 and 16 inches.

Thanks to fences that keep cattle out, the upper river meanders clean and clear over a rubble bottom through miles of farmland. Man-made habitat structures put in place by the DNR and members of the Kiap-TU-Wish Chapter of Trout Unlimited provide good cover. Natural reproduction sustains 5,000 to 12,000 trout per mile here, one of the highest population densities in the state. DNR easements and numerous road crossings provide adequate access to this stretch, but anglers should watch posted signs as some landowners do not allow trespassing to reach the river.

The lower river flows over a bed of fragmented limestone and gravel through a steep, wooded canyon. The wide valley makes this stretch popular among local fly-fishermen. Trout here are fewer, but larger. Public access on the lower river is limited to Glen Park below the dam in River Falls and the Highway F crossing at Kinnickinnic State Park two miles from the mouth. The intervening eight miles or so of river flow through private land and can be reached only by walking upstream or down from the two access points.

For tackle and more information on the Kinni, contact Four Seasons Sport Shop in River Falls, telephone (715) 435-2013.

Lower Genesee And
Lower Nashotah Lakes

Waukesha County

Just a short drive from Milwaukee, these two Waukesha County potholes offer urban anglers a chance to catch trout close to home. Both are stocked prior to opening day each spring with 6,000 browns and rainbows averaging nine or 10 inches long. Most of these fish are taken early in the season when the lakes are hardest hit by anglers, but both produce holdover browns that reach trophy size. Six-pounders are taken regularly, and 14-pounders have been reported. These are both category three waters, with a daily bag limit of three trout and a minimum size of nine inches.

Shore fishing is possible, but most anglers launch small boats. Live bait and spinners are quite productive, but fly-fishermen may have luck with streamers or other attractor patterns. Trout roam the open water at various depths, so fishing is likely to be good anywhere.

To reach Lower Genesee, take Highway 67 south from I-94 or north from Highway 18 to Genesee Lake Road, then head west to the landing, located at the north end of the lake.

Lower Nashotah is located north of I-94 just west of Delafield. To get there, use the landing on the channel between Upper and Lower Nemahbin Lakes, plainly visible from I-94. Take the Highway C exit north off I-94 to Delafield Road, then proceed west to the landing. Once you've launched, head northwest across Upper Nemahbin to the channel that leads to Lower Nashotah.

For information, bait and tackle, stop at Dick Smith's Live Bait and Tackle in The Barn at Highway 83 and I-94, telephone (414) 646-2218.

Plover River

Marathon County

The Plover River is a gem of a brook trout stream that rises near the Langlade-Marathon County line and flows southwest through eastern Marathon County. The Highway 153 crossing at Bevent marks the end of the trout water. Abundant springs keep the Plover cold and clear throughout the summer. Trout stamp funds have paid for boom cover, lunker structures and other habitat improvement work along the stream. The bottom varies from sand to gravel.

The upper third meanders through alders and other brush, making it tough to fish, while the lower stretch is broad and open enough to permit fly-fishing. Category four regulations apply to most of the stream, but a short stretch above Highway Z is managed as category five water, with a 14-inch minimum size limit on brook trout. Browns, rainbows and some brookies are stocked in the lower river annually.

Max Johnson says anglers took lots of big fish out of the Plover when it was reopened in 1992, but he expects fishing there to continue to improve over the next several years.

"We're getting back to a normal size distribution on the Plover," says Johnson. "The population should hold up well and we can expect an increase in the average size of trout here, since there were good hatches in 1990, '91 and '92."

Much of the upper river flows through state-owned land, with good access at well-marked parking lots. The lower river flows through private land, but there is plenty of access at bridge crossings. For information on the Plover, contact DNR fisheries management in Antigo, telephone: (715) 627-4317. Lodging and other services are available in nearby Wausau.

Prairie River

Langlade and Lincoln Counties

The Prairie River is another stream that was closed following the drought and open in 1991 to catch and release fishing only, followed by a general opening in 1992. From The Langlade County line near Parrish all the way to Merrill, Highway 17 parallels the Prairie's best trout water. The Prairie is fairly large, with lightly stained water and a rock rubble and gravel bottom. Several Trout Unlimited chapters have helped the DNR with habitat improvement projects here.

The Prairie holds a good mix of species and sizes, with brookies dominating the upper reaches, browns and brookies in the middle stretch and browns and rainbows in the lower third. The lower stretch is stocked annually, but natural reproduction sustains the upper river. Except for a short category five stretch between Hackbarth Drive and R & H Road, managed for trophy browns and brookies and open to fishing with artificials only, the Prairie is a category four stream.

Anglers sated their pent-up demand for big trout early in the 1992 season by taking some real trophies out of the Prairie, although the three-fish limit slowed the slaughter somewhat. Max Johnson says it will take several years to restore the large fish population, but three good year-classes of younger fish make him optimistic for the future.

Most of the river is broad and open enough to permit easy fly-fishing. About half the stream frontage is state owned, and there are numerous parking lots at access points along Highway 17. For more information, contact the DNR fisheries management staff in Antigo, telephone (715) 627-4317. You'll find lodging and other services in Merrill.

Wolf River

Langlade County

The largest trout stream in Wisconsin, the brawling Wolf River is also one of the best. The 24-mile stretch through Langlade County, from Pearson to the Menominee Indian Reservation, offers superlative fishing for big browns, while several tributaries harbor smaller browns and brookies. Closed during the drought years, the Wolf was open to catch and release fishing in 1991 and reopened for harvest in 1992.

DNR fisheries biologist Max Johnson, who fishes the Wolf regularly, told me that after fishing in Montana one recent summer, he couldn't wait to get back to the Wolf. This is one river that can produce a sustained trophy fishery if anglers release the big trout they catch and keep a couple smaller fish. Johnson saw fewer anglers on the Wolf in 1992 than he expected. Anglers who did fish the Wolf found its browns rather unsophisticated, Johnson reports, since most of them hadn't seen a lure for several years.

State-owned frontage provides good access along Highway 55 and at several bridge crossings. The Wolf runs high and deep in spring, so belted or neoprene waders and a wading staff are a must. There are excellent fly hatches all season long, although streamers and hardware will take trout when no flies are present. Most of the river is category four water with a three-fish bag limit, but six miles of catch and release, artificials-only water below Hollister offers the best chance to tangle with big fish.

On one of our most adventurous *Outdoor Wisconsin* segments, I joined Herb Buettner, *Wisconsin Outdoor Journal* columnist Galen Winter and several friends for a raft trip on this stretch of the Wolf. We floated several miles of river, stopping to fly-fish some of the better holes. Unfortunately, cold spring rains had raised the water level and made fishing tough. Galen lost a nice brown and Herb saved the day when he caught a respectable brookie in an eddy below one of the many rapids on this stretch. After bumping over countless rock ledges in one of Herb's rubber rafts, videographer Marshall Savick was happy to get his camera back on dry land.

For tackle and fishing information, contact Bob Talesek at the Wolf River Fly Shop just south of Langlade, telephone: (715) 882-5941. Local angler Wayne Anderson and nationally known fly fisherman Gary LaFontaine have produced an entertaining 90-minute audio tape called *Fly Fishing The Wolf River*. The tape comes with a map and hatch chart and describes all the fly hatches on the Wolf. You can order a copy from Wayne at N4324 Highland Drive, White Lake, WI 54491, telephone (715) 882-4111, or from Grey Cliff Publishing Company, P.O. Box 1273, Helena, MT 59624, telephone (800) 874-4171. Grey Cliff also publishes the *Pocket Guide To Fly Fishing* and *Pocket Guide To Emergency First Aid*, two handy guides printed on indestructible plastic that no trout fisherman should be without.

There are several lodges and campgrounds right along the river, and camping is also available in the nearby Nicolet National Forest. Herb Buettner's Wild Wolf Inn offers lodging, meals and raft rentals, and Herb can put you on some of the best fly-fishing on the river. Contact him at Wild Wolf Inn, N2580 Highway 55, White Lake, WI 54491, telephone (715) 882-8611. You can get information on additional lodging and other area services from the Lakewood Area Chamber of Commerce, P.O. Box 87, Lakewood, WI 54138, telephone (715) 276-6500.

Fish Wisconsin author Dan Small took this nice brown trout on an inchworm pattern. Wisconsin's trout streams are making a strong comeback after the drought years of 1988-89, and no-kill stretches now hold good numbers of larger trout. Photo by Dan Small

These and many more trout waters that provide good fishing are listed in the *Trout Fishing Guide* available at all license outlets. Be sure to check the guide carefully before you fish, as regulations change every few miles on some streams. The new rules are complex, but they're a vast improvement over the old system and they should ensure that Wisconsin's trout fishing opportunities will continue to be among the best anywhere

About The Author

Dan Small is a full-time free-lance writer and television producer. Since its premiere in 1984, he has been host/producer of *Outdoor Wisconsin*, the popular and award-winning weekly television program produced by WMVS-TV in Milwaukee and seen on more than 30 public television stations in 12 states. His writing has won awards sponsored by the Outdoor Writers Association of America, the Association of Great Lakes Outdoor Writers and the Council for Wisconsin Writers. He was named Conservation Communicator of the Year in 1986 by the Wisconsin Wildlife Federation. In 1990, he received the Gordon MacQuarrie Award for excellence in environmental communication from the Wisconsin Academy of Sciences, Arts and Letters.

He is a field editor for *Wisconsin Outdoor Journal* magazine and a regular contributor to *Wisconsin Sportsman* magazine. His articles on fishing and other outdoor activities have also appeared in numerous regional and national magazines. He serves as Outdoor Writer in Residence at Northland College in Ashland, Wisconsin, where he teaches courses in magazine writing and environmental journalism. He has fished and reported about fishing in literally every corner of Wisconsin, but his favorite haunts are the Bayfield County shores and tributaries of Gitchee Gumee.